D1598802

Forgotten Dead

Forgotten Dead

*Mob Violence against Mexicans in
the United States, 1848–1928*

WILLIAM D. CARRIGAN
AND
CLIVE WEBB

OXFORD
UNIVERSITY PRESS

OXFORD
UNIVERSITY PRESS

Oxford University Press is a department of the University of Oxford.
It furthers the University's objective of excellence in research, scholarship,
and education by publishing worldwide.

Oxford   New York
Auckland   Cape Town   Dar es Salaam   Hong Kong   Karachi
Kuala Lumpur   Madrid   Melbourne   Mexico City   Nairobi
New Delhi   Shanghai   Taipei   Toronto

With offices in
Argentina   Austria   Brazil   Chile   Czech Republic   France   Greece
Guatemala   Hungary   Italy   Japan   Poland   Portugal   Singapore
South Korea   Switzerland   Thailand   Turkey   Ukraine   Vietnam

Oxford is a registered trademark of Oxford University Press
in the UK and certain other countries.

Published in the United States of America by
Oxford University Press
198 Madison Avenue, New York, NY 10016

© Oxford University Press 2013

Library of Congress Cataloging-in-Publication Data
Carrigan, William D., 1970–
Forgotten dead : mob violence against Mexicans in the United States,
1848–1928 / William D. Carrigan and Clive Webb.
pages cm
Includes bibliographical references and index.
ISBN 978-0-19-532035-0 (acid-free paper)   1. Mexican Americans—Violence against—
History—19th century.   2. Mexican Americans—Violence against—History—20th century.
3. Mobs—United States—History—19th century.   4. Mobs—United States—History—
20th century.   5. Lynching—United States—History—19th century.   6. Lynching—United
States—History—20th century.   7. United States—Race relations—History—19th century.
8. United States—Race relations—History—20th century.   I. Webb, Clive, 1970–
II. Title.
E184.M5C3675 2013
305.868'7207309034—dc23
2012039424

For Emily
and
for Kathy

Contents

Acknowledgments

THIS BOOK STARTED out with the desire of two friends situated on other sides of the Atlantic to keep in touch by researching and writing an article together. Over the course of fifteen years that project turned into the book that you now hold in your hands. Given the long duration of the project, we have inevitably incurred many debts. It is a pleasure now to be able to thank the people who have in various important ways assisted us.

We have conducted research at institutions in the United States and Mexico and wish to thank the librarians and archivists, too numerous to list, who helped us locate materials. Several undergraduate and graduate students also provided important research assistance, including Thomas Bodall, Taryn Calamito, Jeffrey Flanagan, Cara Flodmand, Nancy Gonzalez, Nadja Janssen, Christopher Kosienski, Helen McLure, Willy Melendez, Samantha Sullivan, and Mark Walter. Leigh Botner and Denise Williams of Rowan University provided essential administrative support. Patricia Lozano Carrigan provided translations of some material. Mojdeh Hojjati served as an invaluable guide to us during our time in Mexico City. We would also like to thank Daniel Oliva for creating the map of the American Southwest and Laura Shelley for the indexing. Our editor at Oxford, Susan Ferber, has been nothing short of the paragon of the position.

Along the way, we have also received advice, encouragement, and information from many colleagues, some of whom read and commented insightfully on our work. Our thanks in this regard to Manfred Berg, Carlos Blanton, W. Fitzhugh Brundage, Stephanie Cole, Arnoldo De León, Neil Foley, Trinidad Gonzales, Benjamin Heber Johnson, Carlos Larralde, Christine Marin, Clare V. McKanna, the late Erik Monkkonen, F. Arturo Rosales, Douglas Monroy, Michael J. Pfeifer, Christopher Waldrep, the late David J. Weber, Simon Wendt, Elliot West, and Amy Louise Wood. While this book is undoubtedly better for their support, we accept entire responsibility for any errors of fact or interpretation.

We are also thankful to family and friends of all types for providing us with an important sense of perspective, including Julia, Sara, Wiley, Nika, Boo, and the late, great, Grover. Our most profound debts are to our nearest and dearest: Emily Blanck and Kathleen Kendall. This book is dedicated to them with love.

Note on Terms

THERE ARE NUMEROUS terms used in this book that require special attention and discussion. First among them is the term "lynching" itself. As historian Christopher Waldrep has convincingly demonstrated, the word lynching has no precise, stable definition and is politically charged. Historical actors, seeking to advance their own agenda, have contested the meaning of the word lynching during Reconstruction, during the Civil Rights Movement, and even, famously, during a Supreme Court confirmation hearing.[1] These struggles over definition have affected perceptions of extralegal violence over time. This book shies away from the term lynching at times because of this instability. For instance, it is not used in the book's title or at the head of the inventory that concludes it because we do not want the debate to distract from what this book is really about, the acts of mob violence committed against Mexicans in the United States. Some readers will no doubt think all of the cases enumerated are justifiably called lynchings. Others will believe that only a fraction of what we label acts of mob violence are "true" lynchings.

Yet, we do occasionally use the term lynching for several reasons. The word itself was used by both English and Spanish speakers ("linchamiento"). In such cases, we feel that it is appropriate to refer to mob members as lynchers and to describe their actions as lynching. Different mobs in different places at different times might all have referred to themselves as lynchers, but these mobs did not always define the word in the same way. The very potency of the word to shape contemporary and historical reaction to mob violence against Mexicans merits attention to the term at times. Imperatives of style have also played a role in employment of the more concise term lynching rather than cumbersome formulations. When we do so, we define lynching as the summary killing of one or more individuals by a self-appointed group without regard to established legal process. Although some contemporaries also deemed the need for widespread community sanction important, we do not think that the historical record allows us to judge this important element in many cases of anti-Mexican mob violence.

Terms akin to lynching, such as "vigilantism" and "mob violence," may also raise questions in the minds of some readers. Men and women in the late nineteenth and early twentieth centuries frequently used the term "vigilantism." Like "lynching," they often imbued it with specific political meanings. In general, vigilantes were thought to have been more organized and enduring than lynch mobs. The historical record suggests that no such rigid line exists, and this book does not draw a sharp distinction between lynching and vigilantism, both of which are collapsed under the term mob violence, which also might seem far from objectively neutral to some readers. We have chosen to use mob violence instead of such terms as crowd violence and collective extralegal violence because we find it both simple and appropriate for our subject. While we sympathize with those individuals and groups in the past who felt, for a variety of reasons, that their circumstances warranted the use of extralegal summary justice, we believe that such violence is a blow to due process and the legal institutions needed for a community's long-term safety. Fully conscious of our bias against extralegal violence, we have endeavored to be fair to all of the historical actors, who labored under very different stresses and historical conditions.

While neither was mutually exclusive of the other, there were two broad categories of mob violence. The first type includes mobs that targeted and killed particular individuals for specific crimes or actions, such as murder or inappropriate social behavior. The second involves the indiscriminate slaying of individuals based on group identity, such as being from Mexico. Although scholars have traditionally analyzed these two categories separately in cases of violence against persons of Mexican descent, this division does not always have value. Mobs were often animated by a particular crime, such as a murder (actual or alleged), but varied greatly in the care with which they went about investigating and punishing suspects. In some cases, mobs went to great lengths to ensure that they were executing the right person. In other cases, it is clear that mobs cared little about the connection of the person executed to the crime that prompted the mob action in the first place. In still other cases, it is impossible to tell how discriminating the mob was in its killing. For these reasons, we prefer not to make precise distinctions among incidents.[2]

Equally challenging is what word to use for the group of people we study. We use the word "Mexicans" in the book to refer both to persons born in Mexico but resident in the United States and persons of Mexican descent born in the United States. While the distinction between Mexican nationals and Mexican Americans is an important one, the sources often make it very difficult to distinguish the nationality of those referred to as "Mexican" victims of mob violence. When possible, we draw attention to the national status of these victims because it was certainly an important factor in the national and international reaction to Mexicans killed by mobs in the United States.

We do not use the term "Hispanic" or "Latino" because such terms were not commonly used at the time and it would therefore be anachronistic. Most, though certainly not all, nineteenth-century Westerners distinguished between Mexicans and South Americans. To conflate these groups would also imply a diversity among those lynched that did not exist. Most native Spanish-speaking victims of mob violence in the United States were of Mexican descent. Although Anglo mobs murdered men born in other Spanish-speaking nations, such as Spain, Chile, and Peru, these victims constituted a tiny fraction compared to Mexicans. Finally, the story of remembering and forgetting mob violence in the United States is connected to the Mexican government and Mexican American communities in the United States.

Although the surviving sources force us, on occasion, to use an unsatisfying general term such as Spanish speaker, we refer to populations as specifically as possible, referencing the country of origin for native Spanish speakers in the United States.[3]

While this study focuses on persons of Mexican descent, it also acknowledges the diversity within the Mexican community in the United States. Even though the vast majority of Spanish speakers in the Southwest Borderlands were descendants of Mexican nationals, there were and still are significant and important differences among them. When these are explored, these terms will be used to designate a person of Mexican descent resident in the correlating state: Tejano (Texas), Nuevomexicano (New Mexico), Californio (California), and Arizonense (Arizona).

One final point is the importance of comparative analysis in this study of the lynching of Mexicans. Comparison between the extralegal execution of Mexicans and parallel attacks against other ethnic and racial groups in the United States will be employed at times to bring the entire subject of mob violence into greater focus, revealing new dimensions in the history of lynching and opening new areas for study. Although comparisons of Mexican victims of mob violence will be made with the larger universe of those lynched, the primary focus of our comparisons will be with African American victims of mob violence. There are several reasons for this, but the most important reason is that historians have devoted far more attention to the study of African Americans murdered by mobs than they have other groups, such as Chinese immigrants, Native Americans, and even victims from the Anglo majority. Of the several studies made of black lynching victims in the American South, Stewart Tolnay's and E. M. Beck's *A Festival of Violence: An Analysis of Southern Lynchings, 1882–1930* contains the most systematic, comprehensive and reliable data.[4]

For most of the twentieth century, historians of lynching largely concentrated on black victims in the American South. The theoretical work and the quantitative analysis that emerged from this research were both very important, but this historiographical focus reinforced the belief that lynching was solely a tragedy of the African American people. By simply not investigating or analyzing the lynching of Mexicans, historians played their own role in the creation of the "forgotten dead." The rich work that scholars have done on mob violence against African Americans nonetheless provides an important point of comparison that helps us better understand mob violence against both Mexicans and African Americans.[5]

Forgotten Dead

Introduction

IN JANUARY 2000, the doors opened on a new exhibit of photographs at the Roth Horowitz Gallery in New York City. As visitors surveyed the show, they viewed the disquieting images of lynching victims. Many photographs captured dead corpses hanging from trees, bridges, and telephone poles. Some showed mutilated or burned bodies. A number of photographs included the crowds—filled with men, women, and children posing for the camera lens—that attended these killings. A few of the exhibit images were actually picture postcards sold as souvenirs by entrepreneurial photographers. For most visitors touring the exhibit, the images were shocking and disturbing, revealing a troubling chapter in American history. Widely acclaimed, the exhibit was later toured, and its photographs would be published in James Allen's *Without Sanctuary: Lynching Photography in America*.

The exhibit and the book, however, obscured as well as enlightened. Even for those visitors strong enough to gaze upon every image, one of the most important stories in the history of lynching in the United States was missing. The vast majority of images on display were quite rightly those of African Americans, the group that suffered more than any other at the hands of lynch mobs in the United States. Yet the exhibit failed to include any Mexican victims of lynching. Although there were numerous images of white, or Anglo, victims as well as photographs of a Jewish victim and an artifact related to a Chinese victim, none of the fifty-four images or items displayed in the exhibit (and the ninety-eight plates later published in *Without Sanctuary*) captured an image of a Mexican lynching victim.

From the California Gold Rush to the last recorded instance of a Mexican lynched in public in 1928, vigilantes hanged, burned, and shot thousands of persons of Mexican descent in the United States. The scale of mob violence against Mexicans is staggering, far exceeding the violence exacted on any other immigrant group and comparable, at least on a per capita basis, to the mob violence suffered by African Americans. Yet despite its importance and pervasiveness, mob violence against Mexicans has never been fully studied. More than almost all other victims of lynching, Mexican victims have been the "forgotten dead."

This book is, in part, an attempt to figure out who these men and women were. Where, when, by whom, and why were they lynched? What did their deaths mean? What was the scale and significance of mob violence against Mexicans? How did their fellow Mexicans respond to these killings and how did they attempt to protect themselves from similar acts of mob violence?

But this book is about more than the lynching victims. It is also about the deeper question hinted at in the title. Why were their deaths forgotten by so many? For those who did not forget, why didn't they, or why couldn't they, share their memories with others so that the lynched would not be so forgotten? In short, the book is about both the actual mob violence that claimed the lives of so many persons of Mexican descent in the United States and the reactions by Mexicans, whites, and blacks—at the time and over the past one hundred and fifty years—to that violence.

The study of Mexican victims of vigilantism presents some startling new perspectives on patterns of mob violence. The lynching of blacks and its significant place in American history is not undermined or lessened but instead revealed in a new way when compared to the lynching of Mexicans. The similarities and the differences between mob violence against these two minority groups illuminate larger questions of racial and ethnic conflict in American history.

To give just one example, the study of anti-Mexican mob violence sheds new light on the relative cultural distance between whites and blacks. Most studies of the lynching of African Americans in the late nineteenth and early twentieth centuries portray whites and blacks as alien from one another. Historian Joel Williamson famously wrote that the era of lynching in the American South coincided with "the crystallization of a separate and viable black culture."[1] Yet, when compared to Mexicans, the gulf between blacks and whites in the South seems less vast. Despite the violent brutality that characterized the American South, by the mid-nineteenth century both blacks and whites shared a common cultural connection in their language, religion, folkways, and food. By contrast, Mexicans spoke a different language and practiced a different religion than the vast majority of Anglo settlers in the West. This created a sense among whites that Mexicans were strange and alien, fueling suspicion and mistrust.

The contrasting legal cultures of the United States and Mexico were equally significant in distancing Anglos from Mexicans. Mexico, a country long under European colonial rule and subsequently under dictatorship, based its system of jurisprudence on the Napoleonic code. By contrast, the United States, the first colony in the New World to secure its independence, boasted a federal legal system immersed in notions of popular sovereignty and shaped by English common law traditions. Although whites often restricted access to the courts, African Americans had a long history of successfully utilizing the legal system to push for freedom, beginning with freedom suits during the American Revolution and continuing through Dred Scott and into the twentieth century with the great lawsuits of the Civil Rights Movement. Comparatively, Mexicans were at a much greater legal disadvantage than blacks. This was true especially for those Mexicans who were not citizens but mere residents with limited legal rights in the United States, but it was also the case for many of those Mexicans who became American citizens.

These comparisons help place the African American experience in context and suggest fertile lines for new research. Such comparisons do not detract from the heroism of African American activists, who were terribly disadvantaged in their struggle for equal rights, but it does help explain why different groups took different approaches to the problems besetting racial and ethnic minorities in the United States. For example, if a comparison with Mexicans reveals a relative advantage for African Americans with regard to the American judicial system, that same comparison demonstrates that Mexicans possessed different resources unavailable to blacks in the United States. Despite the advantages of the Northern states and Canada for enslaved runaways and postbellum black migrants, African Americans had no easily accessible refuge in the New World. Mexicans could, and did, flee across the border from Anglo oppression. While Mexico, with its widespread poverty and often neglectful government, was no Eden, it was "home" to Mexicans in the United States, not only for those born there but even to the many ethnic Mexicans born or naturalized in the United States. Perhaps more importantly, Mexicans in the United States could urge diplomats from their native country to intervene in cases of mob violence against Mexican nationals in the United States.

Mexican resistance to mob violence is one of the central stories of this book, and it is a narrative that sometimes parallels but often diverges from the experience of African American antilynching activists. The pages that follow highlight acts of heroic resistance by a number of individuals whose names are largely unknown. They include José T. Canales, the state representative whose protests led to a public investigation into the actions of the Texas Rangers, a group long regarded by Mexicans as an instrument of racial oppression and terror. For his efforts, Representative Canales was stalked and threatened with death. In dramatically publicizing mob violence against Mexicans, Canales served a role similar to that of African American activist Ida B. Wells in her crusade against the lynching of African Americans. Opponents threatened to kill both of them for their efforts to expose lynching and end mob violence. Yet, Canales possessed direct access to political power that was denied Wells, a significant difference that helps explain their tactical choices.

Even less well-known than Canales are diplomats such as Manuel Téllez, Ignacio Mariscal, Manuel de Zamacona, and especially Matías Romero, who tirelessly petitioned the State Department in Washington to protect the rights of Mexican nationals in the United States. Other activists include courageous journalists such as Carlos I. Velasco, Nicasio Idar, Francisco P. Ramírez, and Praxedis G. Guerrero, who editorialized against the brutal mistreatment of their people.

This study stretches over eight decades, beginning in 1848, the year that the United States won the US-Mexican War, secured the contested annexation of Texas, and forced Mexico to sign the Treaty of Guadalupe Hidalgo. This treaty transferred to the United States a half million acres of land in what is today the American Southwest. Under the terms of the treaty, the residents of this territory became US citizens, thus introducing into the United States a large number of persons of Mexican descent. Mob violence does not, of course, follow political turning points such as this one. There are examples of Americans who, prior to 1848, exacted mob justice against Mexicans in Texas or along the border. And the first confirmed case of mob violence against a Mexican after the signing of the Treaty of Guadalupe Hidalgo did not take place until 1849. Nevertheless, 1848 marked the American government's extension of citizenship rights to Mexicans in the expanded American West and is a logical starting date.

The end point is 1928, the year that a mob lynched Rafael Benavides in Farmington, New Mexico. Benavides's hanging was the last known case in which a mob publicly executed a Mexican in the United States. Although violence against Mexicans continued for decades after 1928, Benavides's death was the last of its kind and a turning point in the history of mob violence against Mexicans. Extralegal executions of Mexicans after 1928 have become shrouded in secrecy and were never carried out in public without fear of legal punishment. Benavides's murderers were known and continued to live in the community for some time afterward without fear of arrest. Subsequent murderers of Mexicans were not so bold and took greater precautions or faced legal action.

In 1999, an episode typical of this new, more mysterious type of violence took place in a remote part of New Mexico. A maintenance worker discovered the decomposing corpse of a man chained to an electric pole near Deming. A preliminary examination suggested that the man had been dead for one or two months and that he was not immediately executed but subjected to a slow, tortuous death.[2] The reasons for the killing are as elusive as his murderers. Was he killed by drug lords or as part of a hate crime? With such deaths, historians simply have too little information to place them in any kind of comparison with public lynchings that took place in the late nineteenth and early twentieth centuries. For these reasons, the book concludes the systematic study of anti-Mexican mob violence in 1928 and includes more recent materials primarily when it relates to the memory of that earlier violence.

Between 1848 and 1928, mobs killed an unknown number of Mexicans. Conservative estimates place the number in the thousands. This study is not, however, based upon a collection of estimates but instead utilizes a set of data compiling cases of actual individuals murdered by mobs. This inventory, incomplete to be sure, contains data on 547 victims and can be found in the appendix.

Some historians suggest foregoing the compiling of any systematic data out of concern for how such numbers will be perceived by a public that reifies statistics. Readers might conclude that this list of victims somehow equals the actual number of Mexicans killed by mobs in the United States, when in fact they are a fraction of the actual number of Mexicans lynched, a total that will never be known because it is impossible to recover the names and dates and places of all those killed by mobs.[3]

Despite the difficulties of parsing all of the cases of mob violence against Mexicans, we have persevered in compiling our list of Mexican victims for two reasons. First, such a list can be a stimulus to further research on the subject. The inventories compiled by the NAACP and other civil rights groups, flawed as they were, clearly galvanized sociological and historical research on African American lynching. Second, as long as the subject of anti-Mexican mob violence rests upon anecdotal evidence alone, without an actual count of victims, it will continue to be received skeptically by both scholars and the general public. Many people tend to disbelieve in

Table 0.1 Mob Violence against Persons of Mexican
Descent by State, 1848–1928

State	Victims of Mob Violence
Texas	232
California	143
New Mexico	87
Arizona	48
Colorado	25
Nevada	3
Louisiana	2
Nebraska	2
Oklahoma	2
Montana	1
Oregon	1
Wyoming	1
Total	547

great tragedies until forced to face overwhelming evidence to the contrary. Determining the precise number of people killed in the Holocaust, for example, is impossible, just as it is for Mexican victims of mob violence. Yet, in both cases, numbers matter.[4]

With hundreds of specific victims in our list, mob violence against Mexicans cannot be dismissed as a rare occurrence. This violence was, not surprisingly, concentrated heavily in those states bordering Mexico (see Table 0.1). As a consequence, this book largely focuses on the four southwestern states of Arizona, California, New Mexico, and Texas (see Figure 0.1).

The number of Mexicans executed by vigilantes compels us to reconsider the geography of mob violence as a whole. A standard lynching map of the United States depicts mob violence as being predominantly a phenomenon of the Deep South. By including data on mob violence against Mexicans, it can be seen as a much more common occurrence in the southwestern states than has been previously understood. This changed perspective will be even clearer when there are more studies of mob violence in the American West that detail vigilantism against the Chinese, Native Americans, and men and women of European descent.

In 1949, progressive journalist and bestselling author Carey McWilliams wrote in *North from Mexico*, his classic survey of Mexicans in the United States, that "vast research would be required to arrive at an estimate of the number of Mexican lynchings."[5] In researching this book, we have come to a fuller appreciation of the truth of this statement. We have seen only a few

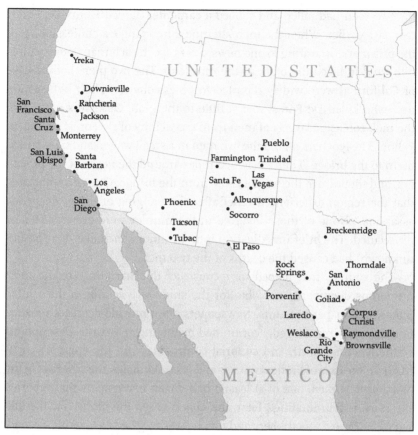

FIGURE O.1 The Southwestern United States, circa 1900, courtesy of the Department of Geography and the Environment, Rowan University, Glassboro, New Jersey.

mentions of Mexican lynchings in the traditional sources used by lynching scholars, such as the archival records of the National Association for the Advancement of Colored People (NAACP). Had we known then what we had embarked upon, we might have deemed the project unfeasible. Given the number of Mexicans killed by mobs in too many places, it is impossible to uncover every surviving document related to the lynching of Mexicans in the United States. Nevertheless, we have pored over a wide variety of sources to create the first systematic study of Mexican victims of mob violence. One narrative episode constructed from our research may help illustrate our methodological approach.

At two o'clock in the morning of May 3, 1877, a mob seized Francisco Arias and José Chamales from their jail cells and hanged them from the Upper San Lorenzo Bridge in Santa Cruz, California. The mob alleged that the two men had killed and robbed a carpenter named Henry De Forest two days earlier. When the mob attempted to wrangle a confession from the prisoners, according to one newspaper report, each man denied culpability and indicted the other as the murderer. The two men, both natives of California, were widely reported to be ex-convicts. Their obfuscation over who killed De Forest meant little to the mob. Observers noted that the mob consisted largely of men from the vicinity of De Forest's home in Felton. The lynchers placed the two men in a small wagon and transported them to the bridge. There, they tied ropes around the necks of the prisoners, and then drove the wagon away from the bridge. One account stated that the region experienced relief after the hanging of these "desperate assassins." None of those involved in the murder were ever indicted or prosecuted. The brief investigation into the affair concluded that "parties unknown" had caused the deaths of the two men.[6]

The sources that helped us reconstruct this narrative are the most numerous documents available for the study of lynching in the United States: newspaper accounts. Newspapers often provide detailed information on the crime allegedly committed by the mob's victims, descriptions of the lynching itself, and editorial commentary on the episode's aftermath. In the case of Francisco Arias and José Chamales, the coverage of the Sacramento Union, one of at least a half dozen newspapers that reported the story, is illuminating.[7] First, the Union stated the motive for the killing of De Forest was robbery and that he was targeted at random. Second, the paper noted that the mob broke open the jail yard door and forced the jailer and the deputy sheriff to turn over the keys to the cells holding Arias and Chamales. The two men were then taken from the jail, their hands and feet bound with hay ropes, and transported to the bridge where they were hanged. Third, the Sacramento Union concluded with an editorial endorsement of the affair: "we really do not see how such wretches could have been more satisfactorily disposed of than upon the gallows."[8]

Newspapers were not objective reporters, but they are critical for the reconstruction of mob violence in the nineteenth and early twentieth centuries.[9] Many small communities supported weekly newspapers, making it possible to recover local details on lynchings in remote locations. Even when the last copies of those smaller newspapers have disappeared, their reporting often survives because it was clipped and copied in larger urban newspapers.

Several Spanish-language press sources, such as Francisco P. Ramírez's El Clamor Público of Los Angeles, have also survived. Though

Spanish-language newspaper accounts do not exist for most cases of mob violence against Mexicans, taken collectively, these sources reveal much about Mexican reactions. Displaying the same wide range of attitudes as the Anglo press, these newspapers defended and at other times condemned lynching. They often provide differing interpretations of cases involving Mexicans and were far less sympathetic, in general, to contemporary defenses of mob violence.

Another invaluable category of sources is government documents: county level criminal court proceedings, prison records, death and birth certificates, the files of state agencies and police authorities, federal census records, diplomatic materials received and produced by the US State Department, and the correspondence of diplomats, governors, adjutants general, and other officials. Any particular case is unlikely to be recorded in very many, if any, of these sources, but the few instances where such documents can be tied to lynching victims are valuable.

Although nothing could be found on José Chamales in California's penitentiary records, the file for Francisco Arias tells us that he was born in 1832 in California when it was still part of Mexico. He stood nearly five feet nine inches tall. In 1859, when the prison at San Quentin admitted him for the first time, officials listed him as a laborer. Convicted of grand larceny, he also bore evidence of a difficult life. The prison records indicate that scars covered his body, including his ears, wrist, arms, and shoulders. His thumb was crooked from being broken at some point in his life. Nothing is known of his life after his release from San Quentin in 1860 until the time he reentered the prison on conviction of assault to do bodily harm on March 6, 1871. He served eighteen months of a twenty-four-month sentence and was released on November 20, 1872. He again disappears from the historical record until his fateful encounter with De Forest.[10]

Most of the time our searches for prison records turned up nothing because nineteenth-century penitentiary documents from the American West are so incomplete. We were fortunate to find Arias's prison record, but the most unusual source uncovered related to the lynching of Arias and Chamales was a photograph (see Figure 0.2). For years, there was very little attention given to the photographic record of lynching victims in general and virtually no analysis of images of Mexican victims of mob violence.[11]

As with most lynching photographs, "Hanged at the Water Street Bridge" was taken after the lynching. It was clearly shot during daylight

FIGURE 0.2 The Hanging at the Water Street Bridge, May 3, 1877, Santa Cruz, California, courtesy of Covello and Covello Photography, Santa Cruz, California.

hours, whereas Arias and Chamales were hanged at two o'clock in the morning, meaning that their corpses had been suspended for many hours when they were discovered. The men who committed the lynching are almost surely not pictured, having departed the scene. The suit-wearing men and the barefooted boys photographed were spectators. That they did not cut down the bodies but instead called upon and then posed for a photographer says much about the culture of lynching in Santa Cruz in 1877.[12]

Our use of photographs emphasizes the value of sources other than the traditional written record to reconstruct the stories of Mexican lynching victims. Oral testimony may be even more significant. Many Mexicans living in the nineteenth and early twentieth centuries could neither read nor write, preserving stories of mob violence not in written sources but rather through oral tradition and folklore. There is little doubt that Mexicans in the Santa Cruz region talked about the lynchings of Arias and Chamales and fashioned their own interpretation of that event's meaning. Indeed, the episode must have been particularly painful because newspapers reported that Arias still had relatives in the area. What was said at the time and later, however, has not been preserved. Still, whatever oral tradition did exist combined with the widely reproduced photograph to keep alive the memory of the lynching among Latinos in the United States. In 2002, the Latino poet Martin Espada published a poem inspired by the photograph of the lynched Arias and Chamales.[13]

Two Mexicanos Lynched in Santa Cruz, California, May 3, 1877

> *More than the moment*
> *when forty gringo vigilantes*
> *cheered the rope*
> *that snapped two Mexicanos*
> *into the grimacing sleep of broken necks,*
> *more than the floating corpses,*
> *trussed like cousins of the slaughterhouse,*
> *dangling in the bowed mute humility*
> *of the condemned*
> *more than the Virgin de Guadalupe*
> *who blesses the brownskinned*
> *and the crucified,*
> *or the guitar-plucking skeletons*
> *they will become*
> *on the Dia de los Muertos,*
> *remain the faces of the lynching party:*
> *faded as pennies from 1877, a few stunned*
> *in the blur of the execution,*
> *a high collar boy smirking, some peering*
> *from the shade of bowler hats, but all*
> *crowding into the photograph.*

We have not emphasized such contemporary references in our research, but we have sought out folktales and oral records of Mexicans from the late nineteenth and early twentieth centuries. Spanish-language ballads called *corridos* were very popular forms of conveying narratives and interpretations of Mexican American history in the Southwest, and we have relied upon these sources for inklings of Mexican attitudes toward the violence that was so prevalent in the Borderlands. In addition to *corridos*, we have also learned much from commonly repeated legends and myths. Finally, we have been fortunate to find that local historians conducted numerous oral interviews with Mexicans, especially in Texas, that allow us to recover, however imperfectly, an important dimension of mob violence in the United States.[14]

Studying lynching means contending with the scattered nature of the sources. Although the lynching of Arias and Chamales was relatively well documented, there are several significant categories of primary sources relied upon in this study for which there are no records in this particular case. For example, among the most important sources for this study are diplomatic records maintained by both the United States and Mexico. We have not exhausted these sources, to be sure, but the correspondence, investigative files, and newspaper clippings collected by US and Mexican diplomats were absolutely crucial to our research. Unlike materials Mexican diplomats kept and later deposited in the Archives of the Secretaría de Relaciones Exteriores in Mexico City, Mexican officials did not investigate the lynchings of Arias or Chamales because both men were identified in the earliest accounts of the lynching as having been born in the United States. Indeed, Chamales was said to have been born three hundred yards from where he was hanged. Yet, the fact that Arias and Chamales were not Mexican nationals means that they produced no diplomatic records for historians to consult.

At the opposite end of the spectrum from diplomatic records were the sources created by ordinary men and women in the Borderlands. Particularly during the Gold Rush era, thousands of miners wrote letters, made entries in diaries and journals, and found time later in life to compose their memoirs. While no such sources could be located for the Arias and Chamales case, such documents were essential to our research of mob violence in the 1850s and, upon occasion, very helpful in later years. These sources, especially memoirs, are irreplaceable documents revealing the inner thoughts of the men and women living amidst the violence of the American West in the nineteenth and early twentieth centuries.

Almost all studies of lynching in the United States have relied upon the files of several civil rights organizations, notably the records of the

NAACP, the lynching clipping files collected by sociologist Monroe Work at Tuskegee Institute, and the archival collections of the Association of Southern Women for the Prevention of Lynching. These sources proved much less complete and useful for studying Mexican lynching victims than they are for studying African American lynching victims (or even Anglo lynching victims in the American South). To begin with, the published summaries of the data collected by these organizations divided lynching victims into two racial categories, black and white. No allowance was made for the fact that the "white" category included Mexicans, Native Americans, Chinese, and a host of other ethnic minorities who were not considered fully "white" by the Anglo mobs that lynched them. For example, Tuskegee reported that mobs lynched thirty-six people in New Mexico between 1882 and 1968. Thirty-three of these victims were listed as "white" and the other three were listed as "black." Our investigation of these records indicates that nine of the thirty-three whites were Mexicans and that one was a Native American. The pattern of ethnic misidentification is prevalent throughout the data on the western states. We have partially overcome this difficulty by our direct inspection of the archival materials, but we were often forced to use surname, an imperfect instrument to be sure, to identify potential Mexican victims of mob violence. We then tracked down the individuals in other sources, such as newspapers, to find clues as to the ethnic identity of the victim.

Beyond the binary racial categorization, there is another serious problem with relying upon these inventories for data on Mexican lynching victims. They seriously undercount victims of western vigilantism in general and Mexican victims in particular. According to Tuskegee's archival records, the states of Texas, New Mexico, Arizona, and California played host to fifty lynchings involving Mexican victims during the same period that our research has turned up over two hundred Mexican lynching victims. Even more limiting is the fact that none of the major inventories of lynching victims begins earlier than 1882, and more Mexican victims of mob violence died prior to that date than after. Nonetheless, these inventories and collections were still helpful. Organizations like the NAACP did not intentionally refrain from collecting material on Mexican victims of mob violence, and they have preserved important materials in several instances.[15]

It is ultimately impossible to recover from the obscurity of history every Mexican murdered by vigilantes in the United States. While this study represents the most exhaustive treatment of the subject to date, some of the victims remain unknown.

The book begins with an exploration of causes and origins of mob violence suffered by Mexicans in the United States and ends with a discussion of the reasons for the post-1928 decline in Anglo tolerance for public executions of Mexicans. It is organized thematically, with the first half exploring characteristics and patterns evident in the history of anti-Mexican mob violence, and the second half turning to the history of Mexican resistance to lynching.

The book balances the social scientist's desire to generalize broad patterns from particular data with the historian's understanding of the powerful impact of time and place on people and events. Thus, the book cites evidence drawn from multiple eras and regions to buttress arguments while also dedicating sections to the variations that come from studying a region as diverse as the American West.

It begins by focusing on some of the most basic questions surrounding Mexican victims of lynch mobs. The first chapter aims to chart the scale, scope, and general characteristics of mob violence against Mexicans, explaining why so many persons of Mexican descent were killed by lynch mobs from 1848 to 1928. While Chapter One underscores the degree to which lynch mobs targeting Mexicans were often motivated by the same compulsions that drove vigilantes more broadly, the second chapter analyzes the lynching of Mexicans from a comparative perspective, highlighting those aspects of anti-Mexican violence that diverged from more general patterns, especially the patterns found in African American lynching.

The second half of this book is dedicated to the struggle against lynching by Mexicans and their allies. Chapter Three examines the reaction of Mexicans resident in the United States to lynching and vigilantism. Due to the proximity of the border, many Mexicans fled from such violence, returning to the shelter of their ancestral homes and kin networks to the south. Others chose not to flee but to protect themselves and their families by aligning with sympathetic Anglos and assimilating to American culture to a greater or lesser degree. Numerous Mexicans, however, responded in kind to the attacks and violence they suffered. Such men became "bandits" in the eyes of Anglos but folk heroes in the songs and oral tradition of the Mexican people. Finally, Mexican civic leaders from newspaper editors to politicians consistently voiced strident criticism of mob violence and vigilantism.

Despite the impressive resistance orchestrated by Mexicans in the United States, the most effective form of opposition to this violence in the United States came from Mexico City. Chapter Four explores diplomatic protest against the abuse of Mexican nationals living in the United States. Such protests waxed and waned according to the internal politics of Mexico. Furthermore, officials in Washington often ignored the pleas of Mexican diplomats. Yet, few opponents of lynching in the United States equaled in resources those Mexican diplomats who protested anti-Mexican mob violence. In the late nineteenth and early twentieth centuries Mexico City could claim real progress relative to opponents of African American lynching in the American South.

For all of their political power, those diplomats who sought to end abuse of Mexicans by mobs had very little control over how the media and popular histories would frame the memory of anti-Mexican violence. In the decades that followed the lynching of Rafael Benavides, historical memory of Mexican lynching largely faded from public consciousness.

Not everyone, of course, forgot that Mexicans were lynched in the United States. Even when confined to the margins, native Spanish speakers in the Southwest held onto their stories through a powerful oral and written tradition. As the Latino presence in the United States increased during the twentieth century, they were increasingly able to raise voices of protest in the mainstream culture. The Conclusion traces the reasons for the decline of lynching of Mexicans, the limited attention paid to this history in the mainstream culture, and how Mexicans in the United States, despite this neglect, preserved their memories of what took place in the late nineteenth and early twentieth centuries.

In the first decade of the twenty-first century, a new vigilante movement emerged in Arizona targeting Mexicans. In 2000, an organization known as Neighborhood Ranch Watch launched a campaign against Mexican migrants along the border between Sonora and Arizona. According to its leader, Roger Barnett, the ranchers had arrested thousands of illegal immigrants and said that a serious accident "with me or somebody else" was inevitable.[16] Throughout the decade, numerous Mexicans were found dead in the Arizona desert. Some had clearly been murdered, whether by Anglo vigilantes or by Mexican criminals was not clear. While the murderers of these men remain unknown, there is little doubt that some Anglos along the border see Mexican immigrants as hostile invaders who are an unacceptable threat to traditional American culture. In the words of Glenn Spencer of American Border Patrol, there is a "wholesale invasion" of illegal migrants from Mexico that is being orchestrated "with hostile intent" to subvert the United States.[17]

Mainstream media discussions of these border killings have rarely placed them in the long history of conflict and violence between Anglos and Mexicans in the United States. By contrast, contemporary discussions of hate crimes against blacks have almost always situated such crimes in the long history of antiblack mob violence in the United States. To be clear, contemporary violence against Mexicans is not identical to the violence that Mexicans suffered in the nineteenth and early twentieth centuries, just as contemporary hate crimes against blacks are not identical to the earlier violence to which African Americans were subjected. Yet, to many Mexicans, contemporary violence between Anglos and Mexicans can never be divorced from the bloody history of the Borderlands. They remember even if the rest of the country does not.

This persistence of racial conflict along the border was not the impetus for our writing this book, but it does underline the importance of a history of mob violence against Mexicans in the United States. Such a study provides a clearer contextual understanding of modern-day hate crimes, placing them within the longer history of Anglo violence against Mexicans while also helping better illuminate what makes contemporary violence ultimately different than that of the nineteenth and early twentieth centuries. This book not only seeks to recover the "forgotten dead" but also offers lessons from the past for those concerned with persisting conflicts arising out of race and immigration.

I

Manifest Destiny and Mob Violence against Mexicans

DON TORIBIO LOZANO was an educated and wealthy ranch owner with holdings in both Mexico and the United States. Although a Mexican citizen, Lozano duly paid taxes on his property in Texas. In 1873, he had eight thousand sheep and goats near Corpus Christi in south Texas. He spent time in both countries, but he left the day-to-day care of his flocks in the hands of several shepherds, most of whom were also Mexican citizens.

At 4:20 p.m. on December 4, 1873, a telegram for Lozano arrived in Monterrey, just a few miles from his home at Agua Fria in the state of Nuevo Leon. Lozano's Rancho La Chuza, his Duval County property, was entirely deserted, it reported. His flocks were scattered, and, worst of all, seven of his employees had been killed. The rest of his workers were missing, presumably in hiding. Lozano suspected that Native American raiders were involved and immediately made plans to travel to Texas to investigate, recover his property, and demand justice for his murdered employees. Fearing for his safety, he made arrangements for nine men to accompany him to Texas and for three more to follow later. Before reaching the border, Lozano learned that several more Mexicans had been killed at another nearby ranch in Texas called Haramusco.

Upon arriving in Texas, Lozano discovered that things were not what he expected. Indians had not killed his shepherds, but the assassins were instead a band of Anglo vigilantes from nearby Dogtown and Stone Bridge. Local authorities did not recover the bodies for over a week, allegedly due to fear of Indian attack. The coroner finally convened an inquest on December 5, seven days after the attack. Lozano acquired a copy of this report from which he learned some of the grisly details. The shepherds were found hanging from several trees near a creek, one mile from a sheep pen on La Chuza. They ranged in age from twenty-two to fifty years old. Two brothers—Filomeno Rios and Epifanio Rios—hung from one limb. The oldest of the men, Jorge Rodríguez, was found swinging from another branch of the same tree. Hanging nearby was the corpse of a fourth victim, Blas Mata. Further away, some twenty yards distant, were the bodies of the two youngest shepherds, Leonardo Garza, 22, and José Maria Reinas, 32. One final victim, Vicente Garcia, dangled a few yards beyond. Some of the victims had their hands tied behind their backs. Although a week had passed, the report noted that the hats of some of the victims still tumbled around their feet. The investigators determined that a trail of at least a dozen horses led off toward the Nueces River. The six members of the inquest concluded that the seven men "were found hung to trees by parties unknown." Although they signed the document on December 8, 1873, it took seven more weeks for the form to reach the Clerk of the District Court.[1]

Lozano burned with anger and spent considerable time, money, and energy over the next two years investigating the crime and seeking redress and justice for his lynched employees and their families. He faced an almost impossible challenge. The specific identities of mob members were usually shrouded in secrecy and almost impossible to recover by outsiders. Lozano may have understood that identifying the murderers and bringing them to justice was a Herculean task, but he hoped that his efforts would at least publicize the dangers faced by Mexicans resident in Texas.

As Lozano learned, determining the motives of a mob is often far easier than identifying the perpetrators of a lynching. The mob's motivations are, at least from a certain perspective and in some cases, very clear. For example, historians are often able to find evidence about a crime that provoked the lynching (see Table 1.1).

Such crimes were regularly—if not always—described in detail in local newspapers, a factor that in and of itself could galvanize mob action. In typical cases, a mob of local residents would form, break into the local jail, remove the accused, and hang him (sometimes her) for the alleged offense. Lynchers sometimes spelled out their motives on placards, which they then pinned to their victims, but they often assumed that the general public understood what had motivated them to kill. Other times the lynchers left little direct evidence of their thinking. The persons who killed the seven shepherds, for example, left no note.

Even in those cases where mobs proclaimed their motivations, there are good reasons to believe that additional impulses went unstated. Not every gruesome murder or horse theft, for example, was met with lynching.

Table 1.1 Crimes or Offenses Allegedly Committed by
Mexican Victims of Mob Violence, 1848–1928.

Alleged Crime or Offense	Number of Victims
Murder	303
Theft	97
Alleged outlaw or bandit	35
Being "thieves, informers, spies, and murderers"	15
Sexual assault or transgression of sexual mores	13
Unknown	13
Murder and train wrecking	10
No specific offense (victim of riotous racial violence)	9
Murder and sexual assault	7
Attempted murder	7
Murder and "resisting arrest"	6
Pursuing legal action against friend of mob	5
Theft and assault	4
Giving refuge or aid to outlaws	4
Refusing to cooperate with vigilantes, protesting lynching, or attempting to prevent lynching	4
Witchcraft	3
Kidnapping	2
Theft and attempted murder	1
Killing a cow	1
Theft and rumor of past murder	1
Breaking vigilante code of silence	1
Being a "desperate character"	1
Shouting "¡Viva Diaz!"	1
Mistaken for outlaw	1
Assault	1
Accomplice to murder	1
Fighting	1
Total	547

At times, additional motivations and underlying tensions are central to understanding a lynching, such as that of the seven shepherds in 1873. This lynching case, like so many others involving Mexicans, requires an understanding of the broad patterns of violence against Mexicans in Texas and beyond.

This chapter assesses the characteristics and the causes of the lynching of Mexicans in the United States, beginning with an overview and chronology of that violence and a related discussion of the critical importance of the US-Mexican border. This is followed by an exploration of the most common justification put forward defending the actions of vigilantes in the West, namely the weakness of legal institutions along the frontier. In the final analysis, as the second half of the chapter demonstrates, the two most important factors explaining mob violence against Mexicans are the intertwined issues of economic competition and racial prejudice.

The Chronology of Mob Violence against Mexicans in the United States and the Importance of the US-Mexican Border

Mob violence against persons of Mexican descent in the United States occurred with greatest frequency during the 1850s, then again in the 1870s, and once again in the second decade of the twentieth century. One of the reasons that the history of Mexican lynching victims has been little studied or remembered is that this chronology does not align with those of most previous lynching studies. Most works on lynching—both popular and academic—focus on the period between the end of Reconstruction and World War II. This focus is entirely defensible, given the great number of lynching episodes during that period. Yet, such decisions often have unintended consequences, and, in this case, one of those has been the underestimating of the depth of anti-Mexican mob violence in the United States.

Here, as elsewhere, a comparison with African American lynching victims is helpful. Almost all scholarly works on African American lynching hold to the same rough time frame, 1880–1930.[2] Although part of the reason for this focus is the lack of reliable data on the earlier period, the concentration on this period makes perfect sense for scholars interested in the legacy of slavery and the rise of Jim Crow in the American South. Yet, because this time frame became the de facto time frame for lynching studies in general, the extent to which mobs lynched Mexicans in the United States was obscured. Any study of the lynching of Mexicans that confined itself to the period after 1880, for example, would be severely limited.[3]

These striking differences suggest the need to rethink the traditional chronology of lynching. Why did mob violence against Mexicans peak in the 1850s and 1870s and why did this not coincide with peak periods of mob violence against African Americans? The answer lies in part in the international boundary between the United States and Mexico.

Unlike Mexicans, most African Americans had no recollection of any kin in their ancestral homeland of Africa. Most Mexicans in the US during the nineteenth and early twentieth centuries had family living in Mexico. This was true not just of recent immigrants. Even those individuals who had long been located in the parts of Mexico that were absorbed by the United States, often retained family connections south of the Rio Grande. The largely failed efforts of the American Colonization Society to return freed slaves to Africa by settling them in the English-speaking colony of Liberia stands in sharp contrast to the experience of Mexicans in the United States who needed no such company to help them relocate in far greater numbers.

That Mexicans were relatively easily able to return to Mexico does not change the tragedy of Mexicans being banished from their own homes, of Americans turning Mexicans into "strangers in their own lands." The border was never far from the minds of Anglos and Mexicans, and this fact shaped the actions of both groups. The border simultaneously shielded Mexicans from Anglo-American mobs and provoked those mobs into spasms of extreme violence. In all three peak periods of mob violence, international tensions between the United States and Mexico exacerbated tensions on both sides of the border and led to increased levels of extralegal violence against Mexicans caught on the US side of the border.

Mexican immigrants recognized that political control of the Southwest had changed after the Treaty of Guadalupe Hidalgo in 1848, but they did not see this as putting the region off limits. The new government had no immigration restrictions. For native Californios, the treaty had provided them with US citizenship and secured their property rights. For both Mexican nationals and Mexican Americans, the border was a mere political boundary and not a line separating two distinct cultures from one another. They had kin, spoke Spanish, and worshipped in Catholic churches on both sides of the border.

For many Anglo-Americans entering the gold fields, the conclusion of the US-Mexican War meant something very different. For these prospective gold seekers, the war meant the fulfillment of the nation's manifest destiny and the acquisition of California and the Southwest for use by white men. Many Anglos believed that the war had stripped any rights that Mexicans had to the Southwest. They were less than pleased to find so many Mexicans crossing the border into California. Most desired that they return from whence they came, and some employed violence to encourage such an outcome. The high number of mob murders in the 1850s can largely be attributed to the clashes in the California gold fields. The contrasting meanings of the border were never reconciled but Anglo violence and declining yields in the gold fields tipped the demographic balance by the end of the 1850s overwhelmingly to the side of the Anglo-Americans.

California was not the only place where Anglos and Mexicans clashed over the meaning of the US-Mexican War and the border that it created. In Texas, the border played more than a symbolic role because so many Mexicans lived so close to it. Unlike California, where the gold fields drew Mexicans hundreds of miles away from the border, most Tejanos in the 1850s lived relatively close to the border and crossed back and forth frequently. In California, recrossing the Mexican border usually meant that a Mexican was quitting the goldfields. In Texas, Mexicans might flee Anglo aggression, but this flight into Mexico was usually temporary and, in any event, did not place them at great distance from their home on the US side.

In the 1870s, bands of raiders began to exploit the US-Mexican border and the tensions between the two countries. American authorities raged against Mexican raiders whom they believed, quite correctly, used the Mexican border as both a staging ground and a secure retreat for their raids into the United States. These American authorities, of course, gave somewhat less attention to the fact that American raiders employed the border in exactly the same manner, though in the reverse direction. Both governments conducted investigations and attempted to limit the raiding from their respective sides. Their efforts achieved mixed results, but tensions clearly dissipated in the border region in the last two decades of the nineteenth century, something that is evident in the precipitous decline of lynchings of Mexicans in the 1880s and 1890s.

While mob violence declined, mistrust and anger between Anglos and Mexicans in Texas did not fade away. In the early twentieth century, the economy of south Texas was transformed by the arrival of the railroad. Thousands of Anglo farmers and ranchers moved into the area, unsettling its relatively calm atmosphere. Many Tejanos, heirs to a tradition of uprising and protest, recoiled at these changes.

Meanwhile in Mexico, anger at the regime of longtime President Porfirio Díaz boiled over, based in part on perceptions that he was too friendly to the United States and American businessmen in Mexico. When the Mexican Revolution began, Texas became a refuge for various groups of armed insurrectionists planning their next move. Anglo-Texans were frustrated at this use of the border by Mexicans but did not react with widespread vigilantism even after the discovery of the "Plan de San Diego," a radical plot to free the Southwest from United States control. Anglo leaders reconsidered their dismissal of this manifesto when south Texas ranchers began to suffer actual raids orchestrated by Tejano insurrectionists. Once Anglo-Texans believed that an organized rebellion against US rule was actually underway, they responded fiercely, killing thousands of Mexicans, most of whom had no direct connection in the raids. The US-Mexican border served as a launching pad for the raids into Texas by radical Mexicans and as a refuge for thousands of Tejanos fleeing mob violence on the Texas side.

The end of the Mexican Revolution and of the violence by both sides in Texas led to a new era of relative calm along the border. Although tensions never completely disappeared, the decline of mob violence in the 1920s indicated the start of a new era of rapprochement. This new period, if not scarred by thousands of Mexican deaths, was still marked by segregation, land dispossession, and the increasing economic marginalization of Mexicans in south Texas. If Tejanos had survived the worst of the storm, they still found themselves buffeted by terrible winds as they struggled to rebuild their lives in south Texas.

"Frontier Justice" and the Weakness of Courts in the American West

During the nineteenth century, Mexicans found the world that they had inhabited for generations increasingly upturned by racially prejudiced Anglo immigrants who often cared little for those whom they were displacing. For their part, many Anglos were risking their lives and banking their families' future on a new start in a new country. They were often surrounded and outnumbered by Mexicans, and they were unable to speak the local language. Under such conditions and as the inheritors of a tradition of vigilantism and popular justice from the eastern states, it is hardly surprising that Anglos allowed their frustrations to explode into mob violence. These frustrations, so evident to historians as factors motivating mob action, were rarely cited by the perpetrators of that violence or their defenders. Instead, lynchers consistently defended their actions as rational responses to the ineffectual state of the frontier courts.

In the first month of 1851, a vigilance committee hanged an alleged horse thief near Hick's Ranch in northern California. "The excuse given," reported the *San Francisco Daily Evening Picayune*, was "the inefficiency of the present laws of the State to stop wholesale horse, mule, and cattle stealing."[4] Justifications emphasizing the weakness and inadequacy of local authorities were among the most common defenses legitimizing the actions of lynch mobs. Such thinking convinced mob leaders, newspaper editors, and contemporary observers (and later historians of the American West) that "frontier justice" was indeed necessary in newly settled communities. According to this perspective, vigilantes were civic-minded individuals forced by circumstances to abandon their traditional regard for the legal process. John Eagle, a California gold miner, exemplified this transformation. He wrote to his wife Margaret in 1853: "I am opposed to Capital Punishment in communities when they have prisons to keep murderers secure for life, but in new settlements, and new countries, like California where there is little or no protection from the hands of such monsters in human shape, it becomes necessary to dispose of them by the shortest mode, for the safety of the community."[5]

Gold Rush California was critically important in the national dissemination of this defense of vigilantism. Letter writers like John Eagle convinced family and friends back in other parts of the country that, given the proper circumstances, vigilantism could and should be condoned. The national media's attention to the most famous and best organized of the California vigilance committees—those that operated in cities like San Francisco and held mock trials complete with judges, juries, and lawyers—only reinforced the growing perception of vigilantes as virtuous men doing their best to maintain, rather than undermine, law and order.[6]

Some parts of the United States, however, were more receptive than others to Californian rhetoric about the advantages of vigilantism. Praise and defense of extralegal action found especially supportive audiences in Texas and New Mexico before, during, and especially after the Gold Rush. In 1874, the *Galveston News* echoed the justifications heard so often from the western mines. "We may theorize and philosophize as much as we please, and deprecate lynch law while here in safe quarters," remarked the editors, "but we doubt if any of us would exercise more forbearance than our Western friends have done if we were in their places."[7] In 1881, the *Las Vegas Daily Optic* praised a recent lynch mob that hanged three Mexicans, noting that the vigilantes had "done a thousand favors to New Mexico and deserve the thanks of the people." The newspaper continued, praising lynching in general, noting that it was a superior method of administering justice, and claiming that justice in the courts was, by comparison, "all hollow."[8]

Such statements were often self-serving, espoused frequently by supporters of, or even participants in, the mob violence they were analyzing. Nevertheless, there was some truth to these criticisms of the courts. In parts of the American West, the legal authorities were indeed overmatched

by the rapid expansion of frontier society and by bands of organized criminals. In the 1850s, California was flooded with gold seekers. If the hundreds of diaries, letters, and journals left behind by these men and women
are to be believed, the diggings turned good men into wrongdoers and
simultaneously attracted those already familiar with a life of crime. W.
M. O. Carpenter wrote from Rose's Bar on the Yuba River that California
"is a barbarous land" filled with "men of every nation, rank, and station,
name and shape, color and hue" and that these men, though often formerly "of respectable habits and standing," become "reckless and disso-
lute" in California "from want of the success they dreamed."[9] In 1854,
journalist and author Alonzo Delano was less charitable, writing that the
"vicious from all nations seemed to find a rendezvous in California, and
hordes of the most accomplished villains in the world, who had passed
through every grade of crime, found a home and congenial spirits in this
devoted land."[10]

At least in some parts of California, the courts were overwhelmed by
the conditions of the 1850s. A systematic examination of the surviving
court records of Calaveras County in the 1850s and 1860s finds that juries
rarely brought convictions against criminals. For one thing, it proved difficult to locate witnesses to crimes, either because of the exceptional mobil-
ity of frontier Californians or because potential witnesses refused to testify
due to fear of retaliation. Second, apprehending and holding those alleged
to have committed a crime proved difficult in early California. Jails were
nonexistent or poorly constructed, and it was difficult to secure competent
law officers, given the lure of gold and fortune.[11] "For a peace officer to
bring a criminal to justice, he had to take time and energy from the hunt
for a mine and risk his life," remembered Oscar Waldo Williams, a lawyer
and surveyor. Moreover, "he exposed himself to danger from the criminal's resentment, without any disposition on the part of any other citizen
to aid, or even to sympathize with him."[12]

Outside of the California gold fields, the courts functioned somewhat
more competently but indictments still vastly outnumbered convictions
in many parts of the Southwest during the nineteenth century. In Los
Angeles County, the surviving court records suggest that the courts functioned, if only relatively, more effectively than in Calaveras County. In
a study of nearly one hundred defendants, thirty-three had their indictment dismissed before a trial could begin, while sixty-five individuals
received a verdict (with forty-eight being found guilty and seventeen being
found not guilty). The courts of Texas's McLennan County, like those of

Los Angeles County, were more effective than those of Calaveras County. However, the early Texas courts were plagued by difficulties and often had trouble convicting alleged criminals. Many cases from the middle of the nineteenth century never came to trial for the same reasons common in Calaveras County. It was not until the late nineteenth century that the courts in this central Texas county seemed fully capable of administering justice. In Arizona's Pima County, judging from the surviving records of the 1860s, 1870s, and 1880s, only a fraction of the indictments involving Mexicans—as few as one out of four—resulted in a verdict.[13] In 1872, the *Arizona Weekly Citizen* reasoned that murders committed in Arizona during the past ten years have "never been legally punished," and this "non-enforcement of statute law tends to excite mob law."[14]

Many critics of western legal process also believed that judges, juries, and executive officials—even when convicting defendants—were too merciful with frontier lawbreakers. In 1850, a former municipal official in Monterey, Walter Colton, expressed a common sentiment: lynch law "may at times be hasty, and too little observant of the forms of law, but it reaches its object" and "it leaves the guilty no escape through the defects of an indictment, the ingenuity of counsel, or the clemency of the executive."[15] Such criticisms were echoed throughout the Southwestern Borderlands, where local citizens often despaired of the courts. On July 12, 1873, an Arizona newspaperman defended a recent lynching by arguing that it was "a bad way to hang a man without legal process," but it was understandable because "citizens sometimes lose their patience" when the "legal process will not hang men" who deserved execution.[16]

Defenders of lynching also criticized the expenses incurred through judicial proceedings, for which they often blamed lawyers. After the 1872 lynching of Pancho Blanco and Cipriano Guerrero, two "robbers of great notoriety," the *Brownsville Daily Ranchero* declared that it approved of the lynching "of all suspicious characters the whole length of the frontier for the following reasons: If they are taken they remain imprisoned at the expense of the county for three or five months" and "they have no difficulty in being cleared by means of chicanery or by the cunning of their lawyers." The editor continued that many "of them have been tried more than once" and their easy escape from punishment "resulted in their thinking that they might continue their business with perfect impunity."[17]

Observers also regularly criticized juries for failing to appropriately assess severe punishments. In 1877, a letter to the editor of the *Santa Fe Daily New Mexican* complained that it "is notorious that here in New

Mexico, killing constitutes no murder" and that violent crimes "bring down the lightest punishment." Outraged by the verdict of a recent court case, the author of the letter concluded that "there can be but little doubt the result of the trial will be to still further encourage criminals and for this the jury are directly responsible."[18] In 1890, New Mexico's *Silver City Enterprise* wrote that Grant County "juries have been too lenient in the past" and "bad men have come to the conclusion that they can kill a man in this county and either come clean or get off with a year or so." The editor concluded with an ambiguous final line: "Let a few *judicial* hangings occur, and the shooter will give this county the go-by."[19]

Thus, from the perspective of at least some Westerners, the many failures of the courts fully justified the use of extralegal action. What form this extralegal action would take, however, was not so readily agreed upon. Should would-be vigilantes do their best to mimic due process and judicial proceedings in the absence of effective courts, merely supplementing more practical methods while keeping the traditional structure of the legal system? Or should they dispense with legal formalities entirely and enact swift justice?

Those that mimicked the courts often styled themselves vigilance committees rather than lynch mobs. At times, vigilance committees did indeed proceed methodically and dispassionately, or at least as much as some of the legally functioning courts in the Southwestern Borderlands. In 1851 and again in 1856, vigilance committees in San Francisco hanged a number of alleged murderers after appointing advocates to present their defense and putting them on "trial" before a jury composed of selected vigilance committee members. Although the executions of the San Francisco vigilantes are the most infamous ones from that era, there were other examples of orderly vigilance committees at work in Gold Rush California. Many of these methodical lynchings involved the hanging of alleged criminals of European descent, but there were also cases of carefully staged executions involving racial or ethnic minorities. In 1851, the mining community of Shaw's Flat near Sonora formed a vigilance committee to punish the men who robbed, stabbed, and mortally wounded a man identified in the newspapers as Captain Snow. Five Mexicans were arrested for the murder. Three, however, were released after testimony was given of their innocence. The other two were convicted by two separate vigilance committees and given the punishment of hanging. After they were executed before an orderly crowd of three thousand miners, the crowd voted to bury the two Mexicans.[20]

Executions by orderly vigilance committees were, however, far from the norm. The treatment of Snow's killers was the exception rather than the rule, especially in episodes involving Mexican lynching victims. Among the hundreds of summary killings of Mexicans that we have uncovered, there is very limited evidence of the cool, dispassionate dispensing of justice. The line between the supposedly rational actions of vigilante courts and the frenzied actions of lynch mobs is so often blurred as to disappear.

In the early 1850s, a California mob apprehended a Mexican they accused of horse theft. Although some members of the mob were in favor of shooting the victim immediately, one of them proclaimed that, "to shoot those Greasers ain't the best way. Give 'em a fair jury trial, and rope 'em up with all the majesty of the law." Persuaded by this eloquence, the mob elected a vigilance committee that retired to a room to debate the case. When they emerged with a verdict of "not guilty," a mob leader told them that the decision was "wrong" and asked them to reconsider. After resuming discussion for a half hour, the vigilance committee emerged with a verdict of guilty. The mob leader proclaimed the decision "right" and revealed that the Mexican had already been hanged an hour earlier. According to an observer, the primary goal of the mob had never been to find and execute the guilty Mexican, but rather to send a message to the larger Mexican community. One of the mob leaders made the goal of the lynching clear following the hanging: "Mexicans'll know enough to let white men's stock alone after this."[21]

This case was exceptional. The vast majority of vigilance committees returned quick, guilty verdicts and recommendations for hanging. This was, however, not the only case where the "verdict" of a vigilance committee was predetermined or overturned by the waiting mob, nor was it the only case where the goal of the vigilance committee or a lynch mob was as much to "send a message" as to punish the alleged offender. These characteristics of vigilance committees also appeared in the hanging of Reyes Feliz. In late November 1852, a "jury of the people" in Los Angeles County detained Feliz on a charge of murdering an Anglo named T. H. Bean. The vigilance committee concluded that Feliz did not participate in Bean's killing, but nevertheless voted unanimously to hang him on Prospect Hill after "evidence was adduced" that his "general character was that of a robber and murderer."[22]

Some vigilance committees did not even go as far as Feliz's executioners. A number of Anglo vigilantes made no attempt at all to distinguish between law-abiding and criminally inclined Mexicans, a major factor in exacerbating ethnic tensions. In 1851, gold miner Enos Christman wrote that a "strong feeling of hostility" existed between Americans and Mexicans. Christman believed that many Mexicans were "good citizens and favorably disposed toward the Americans" but he feared that all Mexicans would be subject to expulsion and mob violence. Although he knew that such vigilantism had "many advocates," he disagreed because it would be "making the innocent suffer with the guilty." Christman correctly predicted that such indiscriminate actions by Anglos would lead to a cycle of violence and that "no little blood will be spilled."[23]

Memoirist Pringle Shaw confirmed the carelessness and errors made by Anglo vigilantes when punishing Mexicans. Shaw remembered that hundreds of Spanish speakers were "murdered, or ruthlessly driven from their homes, for acts of depredation committed by Americans." Shaw claimed that the moment a crime was committed, "suspicion falls immediately on some unfortunate Mexican or Chileno." In these vigilante courts, Shaw continued, "where the people become the executive, the accusers are by no means expected to prove the victim guilty." Instead, Shaw concluded that the accused was "commanded to establish his innocence."[24]

Ironically, the recklessness of vigilance committees is also apparent from the lynchings that were prevented. In the summer of 1850, a mob of Anglos from the mines around Sonora seized four Mexicans who were in the process of burning two bodies. The investigation proceeded rapidly and the men were about to be hanged before a crowd of two thousand miners when a small group of citizens led by a county judge intervened. They had just obtained a report from the coroner testifying that the bodies had been dead for a long time. This confirmed the story given by the Mexicans themselves that they were merely disposing of unknown corpses found on their claim. Enos Christman remembered that "the ropes were thrown over the limbs and fastened around the necks of the prisoners" when the judge and his allies intervened. "Had the authorities delayed one minute longer," Christman concluded, "doubtless four innocent men would have met with an ignominious death, by the hands of an angry populace." Although the four men were not killed, a mass meeting of Anglos held in the immediate aftermath of the episode declared that all foreigners were to surrender their firearms and leave Tuolumne County within 15 days unless engaged "in permanent business and of reputable character."[25]

The excesses and errors of vigilance committees were known at the time and were a challenge to those who insisted the weakness of the courts was the principal cause of mob violence against Mexicans. Lynch law

Table 1.2 Mexican Descent Victims of Mob Violence by
Decade, 1848–1928.

Time Period	Victims of Mob Violence
1848–1850	4
1851–1860	146
1861–1870	41
1871–1880	153
1881–1890	68
1891–1900	18
1901–1910	5
1911–1920	107
1921–1928	5
Total	547

proponents often conceded that vigilantism was imperfect but defended it as the only remedy available to combat crime in the American West. For such observers, the key question centered on whether or not the decision to lynch was made in the presence of a genuine alternative to vigilantism.

The inventory of Mexican victims of mob violence sheds some light on this question. If the key factor in vigilantism against Mexicans was the absence of effective courts, and the courts are presumed to have grown increasingly effective over time, one would predict that the number of cases of vigilantism and mob violence would slowly decline over time. Yet, the data suggest no such pattern (see Table 1.2). Instead, mob violence against Mexicans cycled between highs and lows, cresting in the 1850s, the 1870s, and the second decade of the twentieth century, while ebbing in the 1860s, the last fifteen years of the 19th century, and the first decade of the twentieth century.

While the maturation of the legal system no doubt played a role in sty-mieing some vigilantism, the data suggests exploring Anglo mistrust of the western legal system more deeply. It is clear that the animus felt by many western lynchers for the courts, especially in cases involving Mexicans, did not stem solely from the absence or paucity of legal institutions. In many instances, Anglos were also upset that the existing structures were unfamiliar and allowed Mexicans too much influence or control. When the United States acquired California from Mexico in the Treaty of Guadalupe Hidalgo, a legal system existed but it was the system put in place under Mexico. According to the lawyer Elisha O. Crosby, "Spanish law was in operation here then and the only way it could be enforced was through the Military Governor and the Prefects and Alcaldes holding office under him. It was an unknown system to our people and we were absolutely in a state of chaos."[26] Americans were not only ignorant of Mexican law but contemptuous of it as well. Writing in 1849, San Franciscan resident C. V. Gillespie affirmed that, "every decent white man here is convinced" that Mexican law "is inapplicable to Americans."[27]

Even years after the transition to the American legal system, Anglos living in predominantly Mexican areas remained greatly frustrated with Mexican influence over local government. In 1855, Cornelius R. V. Lee created the Santa Barbara Mounted Rifles in the wake of his defeat in the mayoral race to Pablo de la Guerra. Although the Mounted Rifles claimed to be a vigilante group targeting the area's criminals, historian Louise Publos claims that they threatened to lynch de la Guerra and another Mexican leader and that the "real target of the Mounted Rifles was not Santa Barbara's outlaw element but the Democratic machine itself."[28] Lee and his men sought revenge and political control but portrayed themselves as "vigilantes" because the word conjured images of rough justice instead of an antidemocratic power grab.

Four years later, the tensions between Mexicans and Anglos in Santa Barbara exploded. On August 23, 1859, thirteen miles outside of Santa Barbara, an Anglo mob lynched fifty-nine-year-old Francisco Badillo and his sixteen-year-old son after they were acquitted of cattle theft by a predominantly Mexican jury. In response to the hanging of the Badillos, Mexicans hunted down and killed an Anglo who they alleged was part of the mob. Four Mexicans who participated in this retaliatory attack were then almost lynched, only to be saved by the arrival of Pablo de la Guerra who shuttled them out of town.[29]

The US Army was forced to intervene to ensure peace. Captain James Carleton, a veteran of the US-Mexican War, investigated the incident. Carleton had written several important reports before arriving in Santa Barbara, one of which chronicled the infamous Mountain Meadows massacre in Utah in which Mormons with the aid of Mohawk Indians massacred a caravan of Missouri immigrants, killing all but the very young whom they then adopted into Mormon families. Carleton's completed report of the Badillo hangings was astonishing. He noted that difficulties had existed between Anglos and Mexicans since the two came into contact. He estimated that Mexicans outnumbered Anglos four to one and thus controlled the local government and courts. Sympathetic to the Anglo population's criticism of this control, he noted that he believed Mexicans were not adept at self-government and were by "training and education" deceitful. Still, he concluded that local battles between Mexicans and Anglos had produced among the Anglo population a hatred of Mexicans so powerful that it had become "almost a monomania." He concluded that the Anglos in Santa Barbara were "morally insane."[30]

Frustration with Mexican control over local politics and county courts was not limited to California. In the 1880s, historian Frances Leon Swadesh noted that Anglos in the northern New Mexico county of San Juan distrusted local Mexicans who controlled the courts in the county seat of Tierra Amarilla and "tended to see legal matters differently from Anglos." San Juan County Jury Commissioner William B. Haines declared that it "is a decided fact that no more prisoners will go to Tierra Amarilla to be tried by Mexican Penitentes and get off." In response, a group of vigilantes formed the "Stockmen's Protective Association," a militia group with seventy-three members, which would dispense their own justice and insure that the balance of power in the region rested with Anglos and not with those of Mexican descent.[31]

In the end, it is difficult to separate the argument that the criminal justice system was "weak" from arguments that the courts were too influenced by Mexicans. According to our research into the criminal court records, Mexicans appear to have actually been more likely than Anglos to be punished severely by Western courts.[32] Many Anglos did not make relative judgments, however, and instead argued that those juries that failed to deliver swift and severe punishments to Mexicans accused of murder or robbery were by definition "weak." Mexican sheriffs and jurors may indeed have been sympathetic and forgiving to some Mexicans accused of crimes by Anglos, but the cumulative evidence suggests that what Anglos in the West truly wanted was complete control over the dispensing of justice. Criticizing the "weakness" of the courts was often a mere pretext to justify extralegal violence that served other purposes.

Evidence abounds of mobs claiming legal or vigilante status as a cover for their own brand of lawlessness and criminality. In 1850, the *Alta California* reported on the existence of a band of men "acting as they pretended under the authority of the law" near Roger's Bar on the Tuolumne River. The paper noted that many "persons of Spanish origin, against whom there had not been a word of complaint, have been murdered by these ruffians," while others have "been robbed of their horses, mules, arms, and even money."[33] Gold miner Andrew Stone wrote to his parents on May 8, 1853, that he greatly feared the mobs of men calling themselves "enlightened Americans" because they were "not one smite better than the fiends of Hell."[34] In 1881, New Mexico's leading paper, the *Santa Fe Daily New Mexican*, reported that Farmington was "at the mercy of a mob of the most thorough and cowardly ruffians to be found in the United States." This mob, the paper continued, was led by two men formerly from Lincoln County and "known as the vigilance committee." The leaders of the band were "as may be said of most members of the gang" engaged "in the cattle business, and by a systematic course of plunder have become enriched." According to the paper, within "the past year not less than sixteen murders have been committed by this lawless band" and these "crimes are committed openly but no sheriff or peace officer can dare venture to make an arrest."[35]

Stories such as this confirm that contemporary defenses of vigilantism paint a false picture of anti-Mexican violence in the Borderlands. Just as southern historians have disproved the assumption that a surge of black criminality necessitated the lynching of African Americans, traditional frontier violence theories are inadequate in accounting for the extralegal killing of Mexicans. The weaknesses of western courts did indeed play a role in encouraging the lynching of Mexicans, but this public justification was but one factor among several responsible for the wave of mob violence against Mexicans in the nineteenth and early twentieth centuries.

The Economic Dimension of Mob Violence against Mexicans

Although the particular sources of friction differed from region to region within the Southwest, the two most important factors in generating conflict between Mexicans and Anglos were economic competition and racial prejudice, which were inextricably intertwined. In case after case, the backdrop to so much violence between Anglos and Mexicans can be tied to the struggle for gold, to the seemingly constant conflict over land and livestock, or to the battle over terms and conditions of labor.

Throughout the nineteenth and early twentieth centuries, the raising of livestock was a key economic industry in the American West. As more and more Anglos moved into the region, it is hardly surprising that they came into conflict with Mexican ranchers and their workers. They clashed over markets, over grazing lands, and over key locations such as creeks and ponds. Adding to these tensions was the fact that numerous criminals—both Mexican and Anglo—took advantage of the situation and became organized stock thieves.

In 1857, near the ironically named Live Oak, Texas, eight Mexicans and one Anglo were found hanging from a tree, apparently dead and forgotten for three weeks. A newspaper speculated that they were horse thieves and concluded approvingly: "We hope the good citizens may succeed in driving from their midst all horse-thieves and other vagabonds, and thus set other counties a good example, that the horse thieves and murderers that now infest the country may be completely exterminated."[36]

In Bakersfield, California, on December 22, 1877, one hundred men including some of the town's "leading" citizens used axes to break down the doors to the county courthouse. They sought five Mexicans who had allegedly raided nearby Caliente and stolen horses. The mob took the men from their cells, hustled them upstairs to the courtroom, and held a mock trial complete with twelve members of the mob serving as jurors. The men were "convicted" and sentenced to hang. The punishment was meted out on the courthouse lawn where the mob improvised a gallows by hanging a wooden beam between two trees.[37]

In 1881, the *Las Vegas Daily Optic* reported on the killing of two Mexican horse thieves by a small posse of Anglos. After trailing the thieves to Cow Creek outside of Otero, New Mexico, the Anglos recovered their property. According to the source quoted by the *Optic*: "They brought back the horses and saddles, but had no use for the thieves, so of course, left them. They proved to be Mexicans. I am thinking they will never report to their families, but will always be counted among the missing," and "we hope" that they are feeding "the buzzards with their dirty carcasses."[38]

In each of these cases, no steps were taken to prosecute the men who murdered the Mexicans. Tolerance, if not outright praise, for posses or mobs that murdered alleged Mexican horse and cattle thieves was common across all parts of the American West. Beyond this point of unity, however, there were significant regional patterns of mob violence against Mexicans, much of which can be traced to the disparate economic histories of the territories and states of the American West.

California

California was sparsely populated before the Gold Rush began in 1849. The lure of gold brought tens of thousands of immigrants from all over the world. No place, apart from the eastern United States, furnished more immigrants than did Mexico. As many as twenty-five thousand Mexicans migrated to the mining regions of California between 1848 and 1852. Many

Anglos resented having to compete with these immigrants. Mexicans arrived in the mines earlier than many white prospectors and brought with them superior expertise and skills from the mines of northern Mexico. Chilean gold miner Ramon Gil Navarro recalled that Americans would "burn with anger and greed" at Mexicans who occupied the richest diggings through their superior skill at both placer and quartz mining.[39] The rapid prosperity of Mexicans aroused the bitter animosity of whites who believed that they were entitled to control California and its newly discovered riches. As the *Alta California* observed, whites reacted to "the superior and uniform success" of their ethnic rivals "with the feeling which has for some time existed against the Mexican miners, one of envy and jealousy."[40] Anglos also resented the efficiency and perceived clannishness of Mexicans. German traveler Friedrich Gerstäcker quoted a typical American miner as saying: "Those people consume nothing; they have no needs, and even then the little money that they spend remains almost all in the hands of their fellow-countrymen."[41]

These resentments fueled acts of intimidation and violence. Efforts to expel Mexicans began shortly after gold was discovered. At Sutter's Mill, the place where gold was first unearthed, mobs forced the removal of all Spanish speakers in April 1849. During that same spring, notices were posted in the camp known as Dry Diggings that ordered all non-US citizens to leave within twenty-four hours. By the summer, mobs had also ordered Mexicans off of the Tuolumne, Mokolumne, and Stanislaus rivers.[42]

Working in the Sierra foothills, miner Chauncey Canfield wrote in his diary in December 1850 that when whites learned of the success of the Mexicans, "It made them mad to think that a lot of 'greasers' were getting the benefit of it, so they organized a company and drove them away by threats and force."[43] Such actions by mobs did drive away thousands of Mexicans, but some refused to leave the mines entirely and others continued to arrive. Efforts to expel Mexicans from the mines would continue for several years.

Although mob violence was a critical component in the campaign to evict Mexicans, Anglos sought to embolden and legalize their actions by passage of the Foreign Miners' Tax. On April 13, 1850, the California legislature passed a tax requiring non-American born miners to pay a fee of twenty dollars per month to remain in the gold fields. The tax, called "unduly oppressive" by the *Alta California*, was not designed so much to raise revenue as to force Mexicans to leave the mines. Thomas Jefferson Green, author of the tax bill and chairman of the California Senate Finance

Table 1.3 Reported Expulsions and Attempted Expulsions of
Mexicans from California Mines, 1849–53.

Place	Date
Sutter's Mill	April 1849
Dry Diggings (a.k.a. Hangtown and Placerville)	Spring 1849
Stanislaus River	Summer 1849
Tuolumne River	Summer 1849
Bullard's Bar	Summer 1849
Mokelumne River	Summer and Fall 1849
Sherlock's Diggings	September 1849
Chilean Camp in Calaveras Diggings	December 1849
Sonora	July 1850
Mormon Camp	July 1850
Mariposita	August 1850, June 1852
Bear Valley	1850
Around San Andreas	January 1852
Martinez	April 1852
Rough and Ready, Nevada County	May 1852
Grass Valley	May 1852
Foster's Bar	May 1852
Atchison's Bar	May 1852
Auburn	May 1852
Horse Shoe Bar	May 1852
Ferry's Bar	May 1852
Agua Fria	June 1852
Murphy's Camp and various other locations in Calaveras County	January 1853

Committee, had spent time in a Mexican prison and afterwards had written an anti-Mexican tirade. Green was doubtless motivated by a desire to avenge the wrongs he had suffered. He boasted that he could "maintain a better stomach at the killing of a Mexican than at the crushing of a body louse."[44] Green's report of March 15 stated that the foreigners in the mines were the "worst populations" from their home countries and declared that a history of "vice and crime" made "these people irredeemably lost to all social equality or national advantage."[45]

The Foreign Miners' Tax did serve to drive away some foreign miners. The *Illustrated London News* reported on October 16, 1850, that a "large number of Chileans and Mexicans have left the country in consequence of the laws requiring them to take out licenses to mine."[46] In addition, the tax was followed by a wave of violence in the California mines. Sometimes, this violence was the direct result of the tax. At Tulletown, one Mexican was shot dead by tax collectors when he resisted paying the monthly fee.[47] More often, however, the tax indirectly contributed to the rise in violence since it gave Anglos the cover they needed to lynch Mexicans miners.

That said, most of the Anglo miners did not embrace mob violence immediately but used the threat of violence to intimidate Mexicans and frighten them into abandoning the mines. Typically, the American miners called for a mass meeting to discuss the problem of "foreign" miners. Sometimes, these mass meetings involved non-American miners of European descent because the problem of "foreign" miners usually meant the presence of Spanish-speaking miners and Chinese miners, not miners of European descent no matter where they were born or what language they spoke. These meetings almost inevitably resulted in a resolution that "foreign" miners must vacate the mines by a certain time or face retributive violence.

Recounting the expulsion of Mexicans from the north and south forks of the American River in 1849, gold miner William Redmond Ryan recalled a mass meeting of the "Oregon men and some of the Yankees" at Sutter's Mill. The "strongest arguments" were made for expulsion of foreign miners: "Chilians, Sonoreans, Peruvians, and Mexicans particularly designated as having no right to work in the mines." The meeting concluded that these groups were to be given notice and time to abandon the gold fields. If they failed to leave, the resolution threatened that the Americans would "drive them away by force of arms." Ryan remembered that the resolution and its threats worked and the Spanish speakers "immediately took their departure."[48]

Even when such resolutions failed to drive away all Mexicans, they had an impact. In search of gold, Antonio Coronel moved from Los Angeles to the California mining region in 1849. Born in Mexico City, Coronel had lived in Los Angeles since 1834 and was a naturalized US citizen. In what was then called Hangtown (later Placerville), Coronel learned of a notice posted in town that threatened violence against all noncitizens who failed to leave within twenty-four hours. When some foreigners refused to leave and armed themselves in defense, Coronel remembered that vigilantes arrested a Frenchman and a Spaniard on a spurious charge of theft. In an attempt to free the prisoners, Coronel offered to give gold from his own pocket exceeding the amount allegedly stolen, but his offer was refused. The men were placed in a cart, and a charcoal warning was placed on its side, promising death to anyone who interfered with the prisoners. The lynchers led the cart to an oak tree where they hanged the men. Unnerved,

Coronel soon left for other diggings. Although he found a great deal of gold in 1849, he found the situation in the other mining areas even worse because claims discovered by Mexicans and Spanish speakers were constantly being jumped by bands of Anglos, and he soon returned to Los Angeles.[49]

Resolutions barring Mexicans from the mines (see Figure 1.1) were so common that an anonymous author crafted a poem entitled "The Great Greaser Extermination Meeting" that satirized the meetings:

> In Sonora, one hot and sultry day
> Many people had gathered together
> They were bound to drive the Greasers away
> And they cared not a d—n for the weather
> And I hope coming folks will take warning
> And choose (if they would their property save)
> Some American place to be born in.[50]

If most Americans favored frightening Mexicans into abandoning their claims, there were a large number of Americans who did not hesitate to use force. The line between intimidation and actual violence, however, is sometimes difficult to determine. In the summer of 1852, tensions between Americans and Mexicans had been brewing at Mariposita for weeks before the Americans formed into a mob of two hundred and violence erupted. According to one disputed report, thirty to forty Mexicans were killed. Another report claimed little violence with only twenty to thirty Mexicans captured. In any event, the result was that most Mexicans abandoned the camp. Anglos passed a formal resolution against Mexican miners on June 18.[51]

Although the level of violence in the Mariposita episode is unclear, there is little doubt that Anglos in other places did resort to force in their campaign to claim the goldfields. Violence was usually most fierce in the wake of a robbery or a murder that Americans blamed upon foreign miners. After an attack by Mexican outlaws at Phoenix Mill in 1853, for example, the "enraged people" tracked down and "disposed" of one band member. The violence, as was so often the case in such episodes, did not end there. A mob of three hundred organized to "burn the habitations of the Mexicans indiscriminately," take away their arms, and "give them all notice to quit."[52] Crimes committed by Mexicans were part of the justifications given for the expulsions of Mexicans along the Tuolumne River

LA FIEBRE DE RIQUEZAS.— Dejó el pañuelo clavado en un árbol con el arma.

FIGURE 1.1 Posting of Explusion Notice, Julio Nombela, *La Fiebre de Riquezas: Siete Años en California* (Madrid: Urbano Manini, 1871–72).

in the summer of 1850 and on the upper part of the Calaveras River in 1852.[53]

One of the most infamous examples of Mexican banditry sparking indiscriminate mob violence was the Rancheria raid of 1855. On August 6, a band of criminals identified as being composed of an Anglo, a black man, and six to ten Mexicans attacked the town of Rancheria. Targeting the town's store and hotel, the band stole goods and specie worth thousands of dollars and killed at least six people, including the hotel owner and his wife, the store owner, the store's clerk, a card player in the hotel, and a Miwok Indian bystander.[54]

When the people in the nearby town of Jackson heard of the massacre, a mob of fifteen hundred people soon gathered at Rancheria. Thirty-six Mexicans were rounded up and held in a makeshift prison one mile from town. Some in the crowd favored hanging all of the Mexicans, but a vigilance committee of twelve was appointed to determine the fate of the imprisoned men. The committee concluded that three of the Mexicans were guilty and should be hanged. One of the Mexicans named Puertanino was convicted on the evidence that an Anglo named Jim Johnson had heard him shout "Viva Mexico" before the killings. After Puertanino was hanged, Johnson took over his mining claim. The mob refused to be satisfied with the hanging of these three men. They ordered all Mexicans to leave before seven o'clock that night and then burned every Mexican house in the town, plus the dance hall. Some of the exiled Mexicans were murdered as they fled, killed at a resting place called Mile Gulch.[55] Other nearby towns decided to expel Mexicans as well. A mass meeting in Jackson passed a resolution banning Mexicans from the town. At Sutter Creek, at Gopher Flat, at Drytown, at Sonora, and at a Mexican camp called Salvada, Mexicans were chased from the area and Mexican dwellings were burned and destroyed.[56]

Meanwhile, posses were still tracking the outlaws. Numerous Mexicans were killed or lynched over the next week in revenge for the Rancheria murders. The San Francisco *Alta California*'s headline read: "The Work of Revenge Going On—Mexicans and Chileans Being Shot down like Coyotes."[57] Pursuing posses killed two Mexicans alleged to be part of the raid. Another Mexican was shot as he emerged from his tent after it was set on fire. A posse found a fourth Mexican concealed in a well but the alleged bandit committed suicide before he could be captured. One Mexican was lynched after being discovered hiding in Sutter Creek. A Jackson mob hanged an alleged bandit after he was captured by a sheriff's posse. At

Columbia, another nearby town, a mob imprisoned forty Mexicans before determining that one of the men, Rafael Escobar, was one of the outlaws. Escobar was taken to Jackson where he was hanged. According to one newspaper, it was a "war of extermination" against Mexicans.[58] The total number of Mexicans killed in the aftermath of the Rancheria raid will never be known.

The *San Francisco Placer Times* printed a defense of the vigilantes. Murders committed by Mexicans, the story argued, provoked Anglos to such an extent that they would "naturally and inevitably" seek the "annihilation or expulsion of every Mexican from that portion of the mines, if not from the State." That Anglo mobs, the paper noted, "should hang the ruthless villains upon the first tree, as they did, is nothing more than what was to be expected."[59] The *Alta California* was more critical. The paper admitted that the citizens of Rancheria and the surrounding towns had the "right" to take the law into their own hands and even had a "duty" to defend themselves, but the paper nevertheless worried that they were going to an "unpardonable extreme" by proclaiming "death against every man of Spanish extraction who does not leave." The paper worried that news of the violence would deter "law-loving people" from migrating to California.[60]

While the response to the Rancheria raid was particularly violent and bloody, the episode conformed to more general patterns in Gold Rush California. Anglo miners resented the presence of Mexican miners and took advantage of tragedies like Rancheria to employ mob violence to intimidate and frighten Mexicans into leaving the mines. By 1855, the courts in California functioned far better than they had in the earliest years of the Gold Rush. It was economic competition over the increasingly stripped mines of California, not overmatched courts, that was the catalyst.

Mining beyond California

Later conflicts in the mining camps of Arizona, Colorado, Nevada, and other western states replicated the culture of vigilantism that emerged in California. Indeed, there were often direct connections, with at least some men in these mines having spent time in California.

As in California, miners in these other states and territories frequently resorted to vigilante courts and swift justice as a response to the problems of a boom economy that overwhelmed the preexisting legal structures while simultaneously drawing immigrants from all walks of life. These vigilantes executed men of various national backgrounds, but Mexicans were again the frequent targets of mobs. Colorado in particular was the site of numerous extralegal hangings of Mexicans. For example, in the spring of 1860, a vigilance committee was formed in Colorado City to try an unnamed Mexican accused of horse theft. Three judges were selected and two "bystanders" were made into the prosecutor and the defense attorney. The case was presented to the crowd who voted for hanging over the objection of two ministers in attendance. The crowd prevented the ministers from performing any kind of service, and the mob's leaders then hanged the Mexican in a gulch.[61]

Between 1860 and 1884, mobs in Colorado lynched at least 23 Mexicans. In 1873, a Mexican named Merejildo Martínez was taken from jail and hanged in Las Animas for the murder of an Anglo named James Buchanan.[62] Five years later, in 1878, a mob removed a Mexican from a jail in Bent, Colorado, and hanged him for the murder of a cattle raiser.[63] In January 1880, in Alamosa, a mob of over one hundred men lynched a Mexican named Juan Graviel for cattle theft.[64] Like mob victims from other parts of the Southwest, these men discovered that it was dangerous to be charged with serious crimes like murder or theft while living in a territory predominantly settled by Anglos.

Mob violence in mining-influenced regions outside of California did differ in some ways from the vigilantism of the early Gold Rush. These mines were often more elaborate and arduous, requiring use of inexpensive labor to be profitable. In the early California mines, Mexicans were seen as rivals and competitors, and many Anglos favored their complete expulsion from the mines. In the mines of Arizona, Nevada, Colorado, and California, where quartz mining replaced placer mining, tensions revolved less around whether Mexicans should be allowed into the mines and more over their role in the local economy.

Extralegal violence still flourished in these mining camps, but it was less uniform, less widely supported, and often implemented haphazardly. The history of lynching in Arizona illustrates the more complicated patterns of Anglo-Mexican conflict. In May 1859, some Anglos in Arizona sought to expel Mexicans on the Gila River after the murder of Greenbury Byrd and a report of Mexican thieves attacking a local mail station. A band of Anglos told Mexicans to leave, going from ranch to ranch and from camp to camp. This mob chased fleeing Mexicans southward, killing several of them in the process. The episode known as the "Sonoita Massacre" took place near the mining camp of Tubac.[65]

While some aspects of this episode paralleled clashes in California during the previous decade, most of the Mexicans killed and expelled were not miners themselves but workers employed by Anglos. One of the bloodiest clashes occurred at a mescal distillery where reports indicate four Mexicans and one Native American were killed. Greenbury Byrd's murderers were never alleged to be Mexican miners but were instead suspected of being his own workers.[66]

Anglos in Arizona, as in California, were divided over the methods employed by the vigilantes. In Arizona, the internal division was greater because whites also disagreed about whether or not Mexicans should be welcomed or expelled from the territory. A committee formed in Tubac after the Sonoita Massacre and took action against the vigilantes. They made it clear that Mexicans were welcome in Arizona and should return. They also voted to arrest and punish the men who murdered and evicted the Mexicans. Indeed, they did arrest four of the vigilantes, an important act even though there is no record of their having been convicted.

The split in the Anglo population was not over how to treat Mexican raiders and outlaws, a group that not only Anglos but also many law-abiding Mexicans wanted expelled from Arizona. Instead, the internal debate among Anglos was whether or not some Mexicans should be allowed to remain and work in the territory. Later in the summer, on August 21, 1859, another meeting of the Tubac citizenry declared that it was the duty of "good" Mexicans "to give information of any thieves or murderers, or men of bad character" to the constable or "the American citizens generally" so that "bad" Mexicans "may be driven from the country." The committee warned that any Mexican found stealing horses would be hanged.[67]

Yet tensions remained high among Anglos in Arizona. On October 15, two Anglos, one of whom was a constable, forced a Mexican boy to look on as they killed an alleged Mexican horse thief named Rafael Polaco. After taking Polaco from jail, the men hanged the prisoner, shot him nine times, stripped the corpse, divided up Polaco's possessions, and mutilated the corpse by "cutting off his ears close to his head." His ears were taken "to Tubac as a trophy of the deed." Other Arizonians reacted with great anger at this brutal killing and the English-language *Weekly Arizonian* even called for the hanging of the two Anglos responsible for Polaco's murder.[68]

The *Weekly Arizonian* is a fascinating microcosm of Anglo attitudes toward Mexicans. The paper editorialized against brutal executions such as Polaco's, but the editor did not dismiss the usefulness of a more restrained brand of vigilantism. Most Arizona whites wanted to maintain a population of docile Mexican workers while eliminating or expelling all other Mexicans. In 1869, an editorial expressed this clearly after another period of violence and conflict: "The result of the past season's experience has been the decrease of the Mexican population" but "the most worthless are always the first to find fault, or to become discouraged" and the paper believed that there were many "enterprising men who will remain, and these have had a lesson by which they will profit."[69]

Texas

Although Texas differed markedly from western states where mining was an important part of the economy, it was the scene of numerous episodes of vigilantism against Mexicans. There, too, acts of mob violence often arose from economic tensions, but the underlying sources of economic conflict tended to be rooted in agriculture. To be sure, there were numerous episodes of lynching in states like California that can be traced to ranching or the protection of agricultural property, but the mines were the center of mob violence along the Pacific Coast and in Arizona and Colorado. In Texas, conflicts between Mexican landowners and Anglo landowners as well as violence between agricultural workers—white, black, and Mexican—were acute and took center stage.

In 1854, a vigilance committee in Austin expelled every landless Mexican "who is not vouched for by respectable citizens."[70] One of the most infamous attempts to expel Mexicans in Texas took place in 1856 when Mexicans living in Colorado County were ordered to flee after allegations were made that Spanish speakers were "exercising a mischievous influence among the slaves." The alleged conspiracy of the slaves called for the rebels to "make their way to Mexico." In the wake of the plot's discovery, Mexicans in the county were driven out.[71] Colorado County was not the only place in Texas where Mexicans were expelled during the 1850s as tensions over slavery mounted.[72]

The institution of slavery was an important factor in Anglo-Mexican relations. Protecting the institution was one of the central goals of the Texas independence movement in the 1830s, and human bondage remained critical to the Texas economy through the Civil War. Bitter Mexicans understood that enticing slaves to run away was an indirect method of undermining Anglo power in the region. Mexican interference with slavery, though blown way out of proportion by observers, nevertheless compounded Anglo fears of Mexicans as untrustworthy and further clarified Anglo racial views of Mexicans as nonwhite. One result was periodic attempts to expel Mexicans from regions of Texas with large numbers of slaves.

On the whole, however, Tejanos did not face the same threat of expulsion and intimidation as did Mexican immigrants in California. By and large, Anglo-Texans, especially those who lived in south Texas, made no attempt to expel Tejanos in the nineteenth century. Greatly outnumbered in south Texas, they probably would have been unable to force Tejanos across the border in any event, but many Anglos sought instead to build upon alliances with local Tejano elites and to employ poorer Tejanos on their ranches. In the wake of the US-Mexican War, Californian miners, by contrast, were much more likely to support expelling Mexicans with threats of mob violence.[73]

Such generalities, however, belie the geographical diversity of both California and Texas. Anglos living in southern California and regions outside of the mines were not so intent on expelling Mexicans and conformed more to the pattern of modest accommodation in early south Texas. In central Texas places like Colorado County, where the Mexican population was smaller and less integral to the local economy, Anglos could and did attempt to expel Mexicans in the 1850s.

The difference between California and Texas lay in the relative importance of these varying economic sectors. In the 1850s, the California mines were at the heart of the state's economy and miners outnumbered the good claims. This led to efforts to expel foreign miners, especially Mexicans. At the same time, Texas lands were still relatively sparsely settled, agricultural labor was in great demand, and conflicts there were often about labor. Even within Texas itself, the underlying causes of anti-Mexican sentiment and violence varied according to geography. In central Texas, tensions often centered on competition between Mexican immigrants moving into the region and the working class whites and blacks who were already living there. In south Texas, Mexican land ownership and local political power were the source of much animosity on the part of Anglos who were themselves the late arrivals and newcomers.

One of the most deadly episodes of mob violence in United States history took place near Helena, in August 1857, when a band of forty masked men attacked a group of Mexicans leading a train of seventeen carts transporting goods from the coast of Texas to San Antonio. Most of the cart men managed to escape but not before sixty-five-year-old Antonio Delgado was killed, his body riddled with fourteen bullets.[74]

The killing of Delgado was part of what was referred to as "The Cart War." During the summer of 1857, Anglo vigilantes, composed at least in part of working-class men who transported goods in the Texas interior, savagely attacked their Mexican competitors. These vigilantes not only destroyed property and disrupted business, but also hanged or shot an unknown number of their rivals. Many of the killings took place in out-of-the-way places and the bodies of the Mexicans were never found. Goliad, however, was a center of violence because it lay en route from the Gulf Coast port of Indianola to San Antonio. John Linn, an Irish immigrant who had lived in Texas since 1829, later acknowledged in a memoir that the Anglo vigilantes were based in Goliad and that they had "assassinated" a number of "innocent" Mexicans on the roads, sabotaged their carts, and then sold the goods they stole from their victims. Linn recalled that the "authorities of Goliad County seemed to regard the whole thing with supine indifference" and "made no efforts whatever either to suppress the crimes or to bring the criminals to justice."[75] A tree on the courthouse lawn in Goliad, afterwards known as the "Cart War Oak," was reputed to have been the site of a number of hangings during the conflict and has been memorialized with a roadside marker (see Figure 1.2).[76]

When the Mexican government learned of these hangings and murders, it opened an investigation and then filed several complaints with both Texas and the United States. Mexican official Manuel Robles reported to Secretary of State Lewis Cass on October 14, 1857, that "committees of armed men have been organized for the exclusive purpose of hunting down Mexicans on the highway, spoiling them of their property, and putting them to death." Robles estimated the number of Mexicans killed at seventy-five. Furthermore, Robles noted that in San Antonio itself "the residents of Mexican origin have been expelled." These families and others in the region fled for their lives to Mexico, crossing the river "in utter destitution and after suffering the hardships of a weary march on foot, compulsively undertaken for the salvation of their lives." Robles pointedly noted that the "families have been forced to abandon all the interests which they had at stake." He urged the United States to proceed with "every means" to "investigate the truth" and end the mistreatment of Mexicans because such a response is "demanded by justice, the law of nations, and the honor of the United States."[77]

The Cart War divided Anglos in Texas. A number of people supported or were at least indifferent to the mob violence. The *Nueces Valley* acknowledged that "the shooting of Mexicans is doubtless a harmless amusement"

THE HANGING TREE

SITE FOR COURT SESSIONS AT
VARIOUS TIMES FROM 1846 TO
1870. CAPITAL SENTENCES CALLED
FOR BY THE COURTS WERE CARRIED
OUT IMMEDIATELY, BY MEANS OF A
ROPE AND A CONVENIENT LIMB.

HANGINGS NOT CALLED FOR BY
REGULAR COURTS OCCURRED HERE
DURING THE 1857 "CART WAR" —
A SERIES OF ATTACKS MADE BY
TEXAS FREIGHTERS AGAINST
MEXICAN DRIVERS ALONG THE
INDIANOLA-GOLIAD-SAN ANTONIO
ROAD. ABOUT 70 MEN WERE KILLED,
SOME OF THEM ON THIS TREE,
BEFORE THE WAR WAS HALTED BY
TEXAS RANGERS.

FIGURE 1.2 The "Cart War Oak," Goliad, Texas, personal collection of Carrigan and Webb.

to many Texans.[78] But a number of newspapers, including the *Nueces Valley*, were critical of the actions of the vigilantes in the Cart War. The Austin *Southern Intelligencer* opposed the violence on the same ground that Anglos criticized vigilantism in Arizona, that it was bad for the local economy. The paper argued that the purpose of the violence was "to get rid of competition which in dispatch and cheapness excels" that of the

Anglo cart men. "Consumers," the paper despaired, "are thus enormously taxed for the benefit of the selfish, murderous butchers, who are making an exterminating war upon cheap labor." The paper concluded that this "is the sole cause of the war" and warned that it "behooves the property holders of San Antonio to put down the warfare." Instead, the paper urged that the average Anglo man find a way to live with Mexicans, making these cheap laborers "the means of his own prosperity."[79]

The US Army sent soldiers to accompany Mexican freighters transporting government goods from the coast. On November 30, 1857, the Governor of Texas, Elisha M. Pease, finally called for the Texas legislature to approve a special appropriation that would pay the militia to guard Mexican teamsters. The legislature complied, but hostilities had already declined. The Mexican cart men had not waited for government action and had carved out a new route that bypassed the town of Goliad by over a dozen miles. According to John Linn, the Anglo vigilantes who had attacked the Mexicans changed tactics after this and decided to steal the property of some white men in the region. Linn observed that "the wrong bull was being gored this time" and the leaders of the Cart War were themselves hanged by a lynch mob. Linn claimed that it was only with these final executions that "peace" returned to the region. Although the state legislature authorized the militia, Linn claimed they were never needed.[80]

In searching for the causes of the mob violence of 1857, the simple and straightforward explanation of economic competition should not be slighted. Mexican cart men had gone about their business in the border region for many years. The conflict was not about whether or not Mexican cart men could work in Texas but whether they could expand their area of influence to the interior. For whites in southern central Texas, this threatened their traditional monopoly on transporting goods in the Texas interior. This economic motivation was connected to other factors, including a generations-old prejudice against Mexicans, a rising nativism fanned by the new Know-Nothing Party, and the ongoing concern that black slaves in Texas were fleeing to the border with the aid of Mexicans. But, in the final analysis, it was the economic threat that provided the key momentum for the lawless attacks against Tejanos in 1857.

While few years would see as many attacks on Mexicans, economic competition continued to be a catalyst for mob violence. As the nineteenth century progressed, more and more Mexicans moved north into central Texas to work in the cotton fields. Anglo vigilantes, often small farmers, laborers, and sharecroppers calling themselves "white caps," used warnings and mob violence to intimidate Mexican workers who they believed depressed wages. They also used threats to deter Anglo ranchers from employing these Mexican laborers. In 1897, one hundred notices were sent, postage due, to planters in the San Marcos region warning these men to maintain traditional agreements with whites and not to hire Mexicans or blacks. The notice read: "Fire, Johnson grass and cowhides are threatened" on those who disregarded this warning.[81] In 1898, a group of vigilantes in Gonzalez posted the following warning: "Hell, Texas, Feb. 16. Notice to the Mexicans: You all have got ten days to leave in. Mr. May Renfro and brother get your Mexicans all off your place. If not, you will get the same that they do. Signed, Whitecaps."[82]

Vigilantism in south Texas more often revolved around issues of property than labor competition. In 1848, the Treaty of Guadalupe Hidalgo guaranteed the rights of Mexicans who resided within the new boundaries of the United States to vote and to own property. In the short term, this meant that the vast majority of property in south Texas remained in the hands of Tejanos and that Spanish speakers gained some local influence in the reshaped political order. In the long term, however, Anglos found ways to acquire Tejano property and to assert political control.

As the landscape architect and travel writer Frederick Law Olmsted wrote during his visit to Texas in 1854, the "Americans are very jealous" of the "few Mexican land-holders" and "frequently with injustice" accuse the Mexicans "of every crime which cannot be directly traced to its perpetrators." Olmsted noted that "valuable lands" in the region belonged to Mexican families twenty years ago but had "come into the possession of Americans" with the original proprietors "rarely, if ever, having been paid anything." He further observed that it was in vain to point out the protections afforded to these people by the laws of the United States and Texas, for the citizens of Texas believed in a "higher law," namely "the great and glorious law of selfish, passionate power—Lynch Law."[83]

Lynching was but one of the many methods Anglos wielded in their attempts to gain Mexican land. Possessing more liquid capital and greater access to credit, wealthy Anglos often took advantage of downturns in the local economy to purchase Tejano land. Many Mexican landowners, by contrast, had little cash on hand and had difficulty acquiring credit, leaving them vulnerable to economic downturns and environmental hardships. Exacerbating such difficulties was the fact that the US legal system was unfamiliar to many Tejanos. They found their lands put up for sale by unforgiving Anglo-dominated courts when they failed to pay the proper taxes or missed mortgage payments. If such legal tactics did not work, Anglos did not hesitate to use threats of violence to intimidate Mexican landowners. The case of Toribio Lozano's seven shepherds is but one example of the way that lynching was used to intimidate Mexican ranchers.[84]

New Mexico

The history of anti-Mexican mob violence in New Mexico contrasts with the rough justice practices in almost all other states of the American West. This was in part because New Mexico retained a Spanish-speaking majority far longer than California or Texas and because that majority was more divided than in other places. Spanish-speaking New Mexicans were divided by class and national origin, with the territory's native-born population consciously distancing themselves from more recent (and often poor) immigrants from Mexico. We will refer to the latter as Mexican nationals and the former as Nuevomexicanos, but this simple division belies the actual complexity of New Mexico society.

Economic tensions between Anglos and Nuevomexicanos did play a role in some of the mob violence directed at Spanish speakers in New Mexico. Particular areas of New Mexico, like Silver Springs, saw trouble in the mines, but in most parts of the territory conflicts over property rights, grazing lands, and access to water were more common. While these struggles were not always as easily divided along ethnic lines as they were in some other states, such conflicts were more likely to explode into mob violence when ethnicity exacerbated economic fissures.

One area of New Mexico that experienced prolonged ethnic conflict between Anglo immigrants and Spanish speakers was along the San Juan river basin in northwestern New Mexico. In 1882, near Bloomfield, Guadulupe Archuleta was performing his duties as a law officer when he shot and killed a white man. Lionel Sheldon, the Governor of New Mexico, dispatched the state militia to protect Archuleta and prevent a lynching. They arrived too late, finding Archuleta already hanged. The shooting and subsequent lynching of Archuleta further divided the town into a Nuevomexicano and an Anglo camp. Such division had, in fact, preceded the lynching because of an ongoing ethnic conflict between the two groups over grazing rights. Nuevomexicanos in the region tended to raise sheep, while the more newly arrived Anglos had brought cattle with them. Anglos were upset not only at having to share the land with sheep raisers but also with the fact that Nuevomexicanos largely controlled the local legal system, which pushed some Anglos to embrace vigilantism. Archuleta's killing occurred at a pivotal moment in this conflict. According to historian Frances Leon Swadesh, the lynching "effectively silenced all Hispano challenge to White strong-arm tactics along the San Juan."[85]

Despite these instances of conflict between Anglos and Mexicans in New Mexico, nationality and length of residence, as well as class background, mattered greatly in who was lynched and who did the lynching.

The Role of Racial and Ethnic Prejudice

While New Mexico was something of an exception, economic conflict was surely an essential element of the alchemy of most mob violence against Spanish speakers in the United States. Yet had mobs considered only economics, they would have been just as likely to murder or expel any ethnic group standing in their way, rather than specifically targeting Mexicans and other Spanish speakers in the Southwest. Virulent prejudice played a critical role in inciting, antagonizing, and vindicating anti-Mexican violence. Other factors—such as cultural distance, the predominance of single men on the frontier, and a culture of honor and vengeance—were also important, but prejudice must be seen as one of the foundational causes.

Negative attitudes toward Mexicans were in place long before the United States acquired Texas, New Mexico, California, and other parts of the Mexican North. The American colonists viewed Spaniards through the lens of the "Black Legend."[86] Beginning at least as early as the sixteenth century, English writers portrayed Spanish culture as rich in "cruelty, superstition, and oppression without measure."[87] The cornerstones of the English critique of Spanish culture were biased interpretations of the Spanish inquisition and of the conquest of the Americas, which English colonists brought with them to North America. American observers believed that the emergence of a Mexican mestizo culture that combined elements of the country's Spanish settlers and its indigenous peoples did nothing to dilute these dangerous, inherited characteristics.

The War for Texas Independence and the US-Mexican War greatly enflamed these preexisting prejudices. In 1835, during the buildup to the Texas Revolution, American immigrants to Texas asserted that Mexicans and Anglos were so different from one another that they "cannot mingle together."[88] The following year, Anglos in Texas rose up in revolt to secure political independence from Mexico. A wartime propaganda poster portrayed Mexicans as ruthless savages who threatened the lives and freedoms of the colonists.[89] Although some Spanish-speaking Tejanos joined the independence movement, these men and women were largely forgotten in the years that followed. Instead, Mexicans in Texas were marginalized and increasingly endangered by mob violence. In 1842, John Linn remembered that a band of Anglos executed seven innocent Mexicans. When the massacre was reported, Linn remembered that good people "were horror-stricken at the outrage, but no attempt was made to bring the criminals to justice."[90]

The US-Mexican War further fueled anti-Mexican sentiment. On April 6, 1850, the *Stockton Times* printed the following from a Mexican War veteran: "Mexicans have no business in this country. I don't believe in them. The men were made to be shot at, and the women were made for our purposes. I'm a white man—I am! A Mexican is pretty near black. I hate all Mexicans."[91] The Treaty of Guadalupe Hidalgo officially concluded hostilities but could not erase this kind of bitter enmity. On the one hand, a number of Mexicans believed that the United States had acquired Mexican territory illegitimately and Mexican outlaws were therefore "social bandits" crusading against an occupying power. On the other hand, the treaty's protections for Mexicans living in territory acquired by the United States were never fully embraced by a large number of Anglos who continued to believe that Mexicans who resisted Anglo expansion into the new territories were outlaws who deserved frontier justice. In the wake of the war, numerous Anglos believed that Mexicans were a conquered people who had no rights within the United States.[92]

Rather than dissipating over time, such sentiments, some believed, grew increasingly harsh. A decade after the end of the US-Mexican War, many Mexicans found themselves agreeing with Juan Nepomuceno Seguín, a former Texas State Senator whose dealings with Anglos had worsened. Seguín wrote in 1858 that he felt like "a foreigner in my native land."[93]

Assimilating to the new nation was challenging for Mexicans because racist stereotypes abounded in private correspondence, contemporary literature, and the popular media during the nineteenth century. The law classified Mexicans as "white," but in practice they were seldom afforded the same rights and privileges as English speakers of European descent. Mexicans were often considered to be a racial hybrid of European, Indian, and African blood that had inherited none of the good and all of the bad from their ancestors.

Mexicans were commonly portrayed as a cruel and untrustworthy people with a natural proclivity toward criminal behavior. Thus, California miner Theodore Johnson could conclude in an 1849 diary entry that Mexicans "appear to be a dark, Indian-looking race, with just enough of the Spanish blood, without its appropriate intelligence, to add a look of cunning to their gleaming, treacherous eyes."[94] The *Weekly Arizona Miner* observed in 1872 that "Bad Mexicans never tire of cutting throats, and we are sorry to be compelled to say that good Mexicans are rather scarce."[95] In 1884, Marshall T. White of Carrizo, Texas, noted that Mexicans were "dirty" but warned that they "will fight if cornered." White wrapped up his closing arguments against the Mexican race by testifying that "even wolves refuse to eat their carcasses."[96]

For many Anglos, Mexicans were weakened not only by their racial characteristics but also by an inferior religion and culture. Numerous Anglo-Americans looked disparagingly upon the religion of most Mexicans, Roman Catholicism.[97] In 1855, an Anglo mob in California burned down a Catholic Church in retaliation for a crime attributed to Mexicans.[98] In 1876, a minister distributed a pamphlet in Santa Fe that argued against admitting New Mexico to the Union largely on the basis of the Catholicism of the territory's Mexican residents. "Nearly all the natives of New Mexico are Roman Catholic," wrote Reverend G. G. Smith, which led them to be "deplorably ignorant" as well as "primitive" and prone to superstition.[99]

Attacks on Roman Catholicism compounded a more general criticism of the Mexican nation and its culture and customs. Anglos often denigrated Mexican culture by citing the superior economic achievements of Americans who moved to the West. L. M. Schaeffer echoed the beliefs of many during the California Gold Rush when he wrote: "When this country belonged to the thriftless and indifferent Mexican, these hills and valleys lavished upon the desert air their wealth and beauty. It remained for the indomitable and thorough-going Anglo-Saxon race, to bring forth the mineral and agricultural wealth of this beautiful and valuable country." Schaeffer believed that Mexicans were "sadly deficient in intellectual acquirements" and were "the most dull, thriftless, and unconcerned set of mortals I have ever encountered."[100] His opinions fit with larger American views of the nation's divinely appointed "manifest destiny" to replace the flawed Mexican culture with the culture and government of the Anglo-Saxons across the North American continent.

The final proof of the power of anti-Mexican attitudes is not so much in the words and thoughts of Anglo-Americans but in their deeds. Over and over again, Anglos treated Mexicans as if they were second-class citizens and incapable of effective self-government. The *Weekly Arizona Miner* observed that: "Anarchy and bloodshed are the only fruits of Mexican attempts at self-government." The paper declared that the sooner the "barbarians of Mexico" met their "manifest destiny" and were absorbed by the United States "the better for all concerned."[101] The alleged failures of the Mexican government combined with the conquest of the Mexican north by the United States reinforced the Anglo belief that nonwhites like Mexicans were not worthy of full political rights. As a consequence, they created obstacles to their political participation, most often by denying them the right to vote.[102] Many Anglos also refused to socialize with Mexicans.[103] Western communities segregated Mexican children from Anglo children in local schools. In 1896, Phoenix's only Catholic Church—Saint Mary's— established two schools, one for Mexicans and one for Anglos.[104]

Separation and exclusion were, unfortunately, the least of the worries for many Mexicans. They often faced much more deadly manifestations of Anglo racism, including mistreatment, abuse, and murder. In 1856, the *American Flag* of Brownsville reported: "Our population is, as is well known, divided into two classes, Americans and Mexicans; the latter are unquestionably more exposed to wrong than the former."[105] In 1878, Thomas F. Wilson testified that not much had changed in south Texas, noting that when "a Mexican has been hung or killed in the neighborhood of Brownsville, or along the frontier, there is seldom any fuss made about it."[106] A story, almost certainly apocryphal, sums up the attitude of many Texans toward Mexicans. In 1915, the *La Grange Journal* admiringly reported that the infamous Judge Roy Bean had once fined a white man ten dollars for *not killing* two alleged Mexican outlaws when he was presented with the opportunity.[107]

Prejudice against Mexicans existed throughout the United States. South Carolina Senator John C. Calhoun wrote that the people of Mexico were a "colored" race that had mixed with Indians and he blamed the downfall of Spanish America on this history of miscegenation and intermarriage.[108] But Texans were almost universally regarded as possessing the greatest animosity toward Mexicans. In 1859, a former mob member recalled a vigilance committee punishing a Mexican suspected of spying for a ring of horse thieves and concluded that "suspicion with a Texan amounts to guilt."[109] According to the unpublished manuscript of an

Arizona doctor named John Miller, Sheriff George Stevens of Graham County used animosity between recently arrived Texans and Mexicans to his advantage. "He well understood the enmity between the Texans and Mexicans. If a Mexican were suspected of a crime Little Steven sent a Texan posse, knowing that there would be a fight and some Mexicans, probably guilty, would be killed." Miller concluded approvingly that the "sheriff got rid of a great number of bad men on both sides this way."[110] In 1894, Mary Jacques commented in her account of *Texas Ranch Life* that "it is difficult to convince these people that a Mexican is a human being. He seems to be the Texan's natural enemy; he is treated like a dog, or perhaps not so well."[111]

The immigration of Anglo-Texans to a community in the American West, historians have long noted, often led to confrontations with resident Mexicans. For example, a greater level of racial violence existed in the southern mines of Gold Rush California than in the northern mines, which has been linked to both the greater number of Mexicans in the diggings and to the arrival of a number of Texans in the southern mines. The Texan immigrants, including former Texas Rangers and veterans of the US-Mexican War, lived near El Monte and were called the "Monte Boys." They allegedly played a role in some of the most deadly episodes of anti-Mexican mob violence, particularly associated with the reprisals following the Rancheria raid of 1855 and the murder of Sheriff Barton and his posse in 1857.[112]

In New Mexico, Texas immigrants were also blamed for the so-called Horrell War that took place in and around Lincoln County. According to reports, Mexicans were frustrated with various acts of violence committed by Anglos in Lincoln County and were pushed over the brink by the killing of a Mexican constable named Juan Martínez. In late 1873, Mexicans shot and killed two Anglos, one of them a recent immigrant from Texas named Ben Horrell. Over the next several weeks, the Horrell family went on a bloody vendetta against Mexicans in the region. They left behind them a string of killings, including the murder of four innocent Mexicans at a dance, the execution of five Mexican teamsters waylaid on the road, and the corpse of an Anglo man whose crime was being married to a Mexican woman. The *Santa Fe Daily New Mexican* reported that, "an unfortunate war" had emerged "between Texans and Mexicans" and that the "Texans were on a general spree."[113] The *Albuquerque Republican Review* worried about the emergence of "guerilla warfare between the Texans and Mexicans throughout the section."[114] Historian C. L. Douglas described the episode as a "racial feud" that claimed nearly fifty Mexican victims and he included it in his 1930s survey of Texas feuds, even though much of the violence took place in New Mexico.[115] The Horrells eventually left New Mexico and returned to Texas. Although racial peace did not follow their departure, New Mexico never again witnessed the level of racial warfare in Lincoln County in early 1874.[116]

The most compelling evidence that racial prejudice against Mexicans was strongest in Texas lies in the fact that anti-Mexican mob violence in the Lone Star State was greater in scope and longer in duration than anywhere else in the United States. According to our data, Texans executed more Mexicans than any other state. Of the victims listed in the inventory of Mexican victims of mob violence in the appendix, nearly half (232 of 547) died in Texas.[117] Whereas other states like California saw mob violence against Mexicans peak in the 1850s and slowly decline over the course of the nineteenth century, mob violence against Mexicans in Texas followed a circular pattern, peaking in the 1850s, declining during the 1860s, peaking again in the 1870s, declining in the late nineteenth century, and peaking yet again in the second decade of the twentieth century, before declining again in the 1920s. During the twentieth century, Texans executed 108 of the 117 Mexican victims listed in the inventory. Indeed, it is the duration of mob violence against Mexicans in Texas, more than the absolute number of victims, that is the strongest testimony of a deep-seated racial prejudice on the part of Anglo-Texans.[118]

The complexities of prejudice against Mexicans do not stop with geography. Although usually critical, white attitudes toward Mexicans differed depending upon class, national origin, ethnic background, and skin color. Variations in how Anglos perceived upper and lower class Mexicans can be seen from at least 1848 onwards. The earliest Anglo settlers to the Southwest often saw the native ruling elite as a superior racial group to the mass of Mexican laborers. Travelers such as Richard Henry Dana asserted that the ruling classes could trace a direct line of descent from the Spanish colonists of the seventeenth century. Their racial purity elevated them above the Mexican population. As Dana put it, "each person's caste is decided by the quality of the blood, which shows itself, too plainly to be concealed, at first sight."[119] As historian Tomás Almaguer has written, wealthy Mexicans and Spanish speakers from other Latin American nations were sometimes considered "white" by Anglo-Americans, a decision that encouraged and made easier intermarriage between Anglo men and the daughters of elite Mexican families.[120]

Anglos in the West were often very touchy on the subject of intermarriage and the divisions that were made between Mexicans on the basis of class. When an observer ridiculed the marriages of Mexican women and Anglo men, the *Weekly Arizonian* assailed the critic, calling him a "contemptible scribbler" and a "scrub" who had made "untruthful and vicious" statements. The *Arizonian* conceded that lower-class Mexican women were indeed "fat, bulky, bull looking" and deserved little respect because they associated with "Negro minstrels, stage driving and robbing" and "invariably" worked in lewd houses or in a "whisky saloon." The paper, however, argued that the women of elite Mexican families made wonderful wives for Anglo men, saying of one in particular that "the Lord never made a better woman."[121]

The fact that Anglos sometimes distinguished elite Mexicans from other Spanish speakers allowed those elites to escape the worst aspects of prejudice in the Southwest. In 1855, for example, a Mexican described as a "worthy man" was able to escape lynching at Islip's Ferry on the San Joaquin River in California. The mob alleged he was guilty of cattle theft, but he was saved through the intervention of an Anglo friend.[122] This episode also reveals one of the most important factors in determining a Mexican's chances of suffering mob violence, the existence or lack of Anglo patronage.

No matter how highly regarded a Spanish speaker might be due to his or her class status or elite background, however, whites reserved the prerogative to deny them basic citizenship rights. To begin with, there was always an element within the Anglo community that refused to distinguish among Mexicans according to class. Traveler T. J. Farnham summed up the view of many when he wrote: "That part of the population which by courtesy are called white, are the descendants of the free settlers from Mexico," but their "complexion" is "not white, as they themselves quite erroneously imagine" and instead "is a light clear bronze" which is "not remarkably pure in any way."[123]

Many Anglos actually paid very little attention to the significant differences between Spanish speakers. They often could not identify Mexican immigrants from Spanish-speaking natives of the states or territories in which they resided. There is strong evidence that they could not, or did not care to, learn how to distinguish Mexicans from Spanish-speaking immigrants from other parts of the world such as South America. The *Alta California* noted that Peruvians were often lumped together with Mexicans by Anglo miners.[124] A local historian of Sonora wrote that many "of the early sheriffs, deputies, and constables" made "little effort to discriminate between Mexicans and Chileans."[125] Chileans and Mexicans indeed were often misidentified in reports of murders and lynchings.[126]

In addition to suffering this kind of discrimination, wealthy Mexicans were also subjected to mob violence by Anglo mobs, albeit more rarely than poorer Mexicans. In March 1881, three members of the wealthy Baca family, two brothers named Abran and Onofre and a cousin named Antonio, murdered a newspaperman named A. M. Conklin in Socorro, New Mexico. Anglos believed that the Mexican sheriff and the Mexican-influenced courts would never convict the three prominent Mexican locals. Socorro's Anglos decided to organize an extralegal association to insure justice. Some participants insisted that the group be called the Committee of Safety, but most Anglos referred to them as the Vigilantes of Socorro. Mexicans called them "Los Colgadores," or the "Hangers." The fears of local Anglos were realized when two of the three men were initially able to escape arrest. The one who was arrested, Antonio, died in a controversial alleged escape attempt from the jail. Abran was subsequently captured in El Paso, transported back to Socorro, and imprisoned awaiting trial. The other alleged murderer, Onofre, escaped to Mexico, but he was captured illegally in a raid across the border by a Texas Ranger and returned to Socorro. The Committee of Safety seized Onofre and hanged him from a beam in the courthouse yard. With two of the three Mexicans killed, the vigilantes allowed the remaining prisoner's case to come to trial. As many Anglos worried, an all-Mexican jury acquitted Abran Baca. Although many Anglos were incensed at the verdict, there was no attempt to lynch Abran. Public sentiment against the vigilantes had grown in the many months since the shock of Conklin's murder, and the Committee of Safety was forced to disband in 1883. The story of the Bacas demonstrates the steps Anglos would take when they lacked control over the judicial system. Moreover, it underlines the degree to which the privileges of class could mitigate but never erase the danger of the lynch mob.[127]

The antipathy directed at Mexicans differed in kind and character from the usual animus that existed between competitive frontiersmen, and proof of this can be gleaned from the composition of lynch mobs in the West, especially in diverse Gold Rush California. In the mines, lynch mobs executed numerous men of varying backgrounds, but the evidence is clear that it was far more common for Anglo-Americans and European immigrants to unite in mob action against Spanish speakers than it was for Spanish speakers to join mobs of Anglo-Americans bent on lynching fellow Anglos or immigrants from western Europe. In 1849, the *Placer Times* wrote: "We have been informed that hostilities have been commenced against those who only speak the Spanish language and who cannot speak English, and not only are the English, French, Dutch, Italians, Portuguese, & etc. reported to have been unmolested, but we are informed that they actually composed a part of the expelling force."[128] Miner William Downie remembered the irony of this episode, noting that this attempt to drive away "foreigners" from Bullard's Bar was led by Irishmen, non-English-speaking Dutchmen, and Germans, as well as Anglo-Americans.[129]

Prejudice was not the sole cause of mob violence against Mexicans, but such feelings made it easier for Anglos to consider lynching as a solution to their problems. The toll of this racism can be found in both the sheer number of Mexicans lynched and in the number of innocent Mexicans harassed and sometimes executed by overly hasty mobs. In 1855, the *Georgetown News* of California confessed that Mexicans had been blamed for crimes that they did not commit. "Some months ago," wrote the paper, "horrible and mysterious murders" took place in Calaveras, El Dorado, and Placer Counties. It was "universally believed" that the murderers "were Mexicans," but the paper reported that an Anglo man had confessed to committing the crimes with the help of two other Anglos. The guilt of these white men, the paper noted, was beyond doubt due to the details of the confession.[130] What is unusual about this report is not the fact that some Mexicans were blamed for crimes they did not commit but that the true story emerged so quickly and that details of the error were published.

One of the most powerful condemnations of Anglo racism and mistreatment of innocent Mexicans came from a young newspaper editor in Los Angeles, Francisco P. Ramírez. In 1855, at the age of just seventeen, Ramírez founded his own newspaper, *El Clamor Público* (The Public Outcry). He was often a moderate voice who openly admired American laws and urged Anglos and Californios to work together. On July 3, 1855, he published and translated the Declaration of Independence, appending biographies of the founders. Later that summer, on August 28, Ramírez wrote a column noting that the American government was "formed by men of such greatness and wisdom that they have no parallel in history." As late as June 18, 1859, Ramírez urged his Spanish-speaking readers to claim California as their native land and simultaneously to "divest" of bygone "traditions" and "become Americanized." He urged his readers to educate their children and contended that instilling knowledge of English would be "the best patrimony, the best inheritance."[131]

Yet, over the next four years, a series of violent attacks on innocent Mexicans increasingly embittered Ramírez. Long a critic of American slavery, Ramírez's editorials took on an increasingly strident tone after 1856 when he reported on the massacre of Chileans and Mexicans in the gold fields. Ramírez urged the authorities to protect innocent Mexicans from lynching and mob violence. In 1858, he condemned the lynchings of three Mexicans in San Luis Obispo and attempted to aid local authorities by publishing a list of suspected participants.[132] Ramírez grew increasingly frustrated with law enforcement in such matters, and months later called the authorities "deaf, dumb, blind, and paralyzed."[133]

Another strategy he supported was for Mexicans to use their voting power to effect change. But when local Mexicans continued to vote for the Democratic machine, against what Ramírez perceived to be their interests, the young editor lashed out, calling these Mexicans "cowardly and stupid" and "inspiring nothing but disdain."[134] Although still urging Californios to learn English and to adapt to American ways, he also now urged those Mexicans who could do so to leave. He followed his own advice in 1860, shuttering his paper and moving to Sonora. He later returned to the United States in 1862, calling for all Spanish speakers to unite in resistance to Anglo discrimination, but his dreams were never realized. Ramírez was nonetheless an important figure in the history of resistance against Anglo violence who will be discussed in greater detail later.[135]

California Assemblyman Joseph Lancaster Brent of Los Angeles accused Ramírez of "disseminating sentiments of treason and antipathy among the native population." The editor of the *Los Angeles Star* accused Ramírez of exaggerating the plight of the Californios and stirring up racial animosities. Were these Anglo critics correct? Did Ramírez overstate the violence faced by the average Mexican living in California?[136]

The guilt or innocence of mob victims is often difficult to determine, but the testimony of Anglo observers confirms Ramírez's claims. Lynch mobs certainly did, at times, murder innocent Mexicans. Horace Bell recalled that an innocent Mexican named Joe was lynched by an Anglo mob after the murder of an Anglo sheriff in Los Angeles County. Joe worked for Bell's friend, Bill Rubottom, and had been sent on an errand by Rubottom when he was taken by the mob, decapitated, and mutilated beyond recognition. Rubottom told Bell that when he discovered Joe's body, he "felt paralyzed" and "gasped for breath" for there "was a great roaring in my head." Rubottom recovered Joe's head, which had been severed and sent to Los Angeles, and gave Joe a Christian burial, but he estimated that none of the Mexicans ("No, not one!") killed in the aftermath of the murder of the sheriff were actually guilty of the crime.[137]

To argue that vigilance committees and lynch mobs sometimes killed innocent Mexicans is not to say that all Mexicans summarily executed were free of guilt. Sometimes, Mexican sources and Anglo sources agree on the crimes of the accused, even when disagreeing over the appropriate method of punishment. In the 1850s, Mexican leader Antonio Coronel agreed to serve on a vigilance committee investigating three Mexicans for the murder of an Anglo. Coronel believed that the evidence pointed toward past criminal activity by all three men but that none of them seemed to have been involved in the particular murder being investigated. The committee concluded that the evidence against all three men was insufficient for the death sentence, but the waiting mob nevertheless hanged all of them.[138]

Explaining mob violence against Mexicans must begin with the acknowledgment that Mexicans were often lynched in sparsely settled regions of the United States with a developing legal system. While important, this explanation has been overemphasized and is not sufficient to explain the long and varied history of mob violence against Mexicans in the United States. Explanations must also recognize economic tensions and conflicts in the American West. But this too is incomplete unless combined with an understanding of the prejudice and racism that existed against Mexicans, beliefs that helped fuel, expand, and extend the lynching, murder, and expulsion of Mexicans.

And so we return to the case of Toribio Lozano and his seven shepherds. Although the lynchers left no note for him, Lozano believed he knew the motivations behind the attack on his shepherds. According to Lozano's sources, white cattlemen had organized a series of retaliatory assaults on shepherds they accused of stealing livestock. South Texas was indeed rife with thieves, but Lozano's witnesses charged that these so-called vigilantes were nothing more than criminals themselves. In collusion with state authorities, they used any pretext to murder Mexicans and steal their stock. When local authorities refused to cooperate in his quest to bring these men to justice, Lozano turned to the Mexican government.

The intervention of Mexican diplomats on behalf of Lozano led to a lengthy correspondence with American authorities. With the aid of the Mexican government, Lozano was able to gather four witnesses who testified to the lynching of the seven shepherds. These men included thirty-eight-year-old Santos Mendez, thirty-two-year-old Rafael García, forty-year-old Bartolomé Garza, and thirty-year-old José Sendejo. They claimed to have heard testimony from a boy who escaped the Haramusco massacre with which Anglos from Dogtown and Stone Bridge were involved. Further, they noted that it was public knowledge that local authorities condoned and made no effort to thwart the lynchings. Signed copies of these testimonies were provided to Texas officials. Lozano charged that the inactions of the local authorities were the result of their desire to force all Mexicans to leave Texas. He demanded state or federal action.[139]

Law enforcement officials in Texas did indeed sympathize with the lynchers. Prominent leaders such as Texas Ranger captain Warren Wallace defended the lynching on the false grounds that Lozano had provoked local ranchers by grazing his stock without owning property or paying taxes in Texas. Reporting to the Adjutant General, Wallace argued that Lozano "had his flocks here for the last fourteen years, never owned a foot of land, and never paid any taxes or bore any of the burdens of our Government." Men such as Lozano, Wallace charged, are "intruders" who employ "irresponsible" and "worthless" shepherds whose camps become "a place of rendezvous or a hiding place for fugitives, robbers, and thieves." Wallace concluded that this "naturally creates hatred and ill feeling" and such Mexicans "are generally made to pay the penalty for their misdeeds by loss of life."[140] Not surprisingly, the local authorities asserted there was "no means of discovering the murderers."

Lozano refused to accept the inaction of the Texas government. He demanded indemnities for the families of the slain men, twenty thousand dollars for each man lynched. He and Mexican diplomats interviewed the widows and provided vivid testimony of the state of destitution into which they had been plunged by the deaths of their husbands. Despite the efforts of Lozano and diplomats like Ignacio Mariscal and Manuel Téllez, nothing could facilitate the course of justice. A letter from the Mexican consul in San Antonio to Governor Richard Coke went unanswered for three months. When Coke did reply, his only comment echoed Wallace, noting that Mexican shepherds should avoid trouble by staying on their side of the border. Mariscal concluded that it was "useless" to continue corresponding with Coke. Coke and Wallace's inactions were intended to further intimidate Mexican landowners into selling their property and abandoning Texas. Lozano calculated his total losses in Texas at over eighteen thousand dollars. Yet he felt as though he had no choice but to sell his land and retreat to Mexico.[141]

The attack on his ranch must be understood as part of a campaign by Anglos in south Texas to acquire property owned by Mexicans like Lozano. While they could not seize the land directly, they had numerous other methods to intimidate landowners. In Lozano's case, his property rights meant little without protection by local authorities. When the Texas Rangers, the government of Texas, and local officials ignored his pleas and those of the Mexican government, Lozano understood that the protections guaranteed by the Treaty of Guadalupe Hidalgo were indeed paper-thin.

The men who killed the seven shepherds appear to have cared little about their victims' guilt or innocence. In this, they were aligned with numerous other Anglo-Texans who believed all Mexicans were by their biological and cultural dispositions natural thieves. While they were often careful to conceal this underlying motivation in their writings, the hunger for Tejano lands seems to be an indisputable backdrop to the lynching of the seven shepherds. Similar to many other cases in the American West, Toribio Lozano's shepherds were lynched because a deep-seated racial prejudice against Mexicans helped Anglos justify the violence that was needed to intimidate and strip Tejanos of their lands.

Lozano's failure to bring about justice for his men was no doubt anticipated by many Mexicans living in Texas. As Ignacio Mariscal noted, the relatives of the victims of the Haramusco massacre made no attempt to obtain redress due to "ignorance, terror, or some other cause." The result of their inaction is that the number and names of Mexicans killed at Haramusco have been lost to history. Lozano's efforts, if nothing else, ensured that the names of his shepherds were enshrined in the diplomatic records of the United States and Mexico.[42]

Readers will not be surprised to learn that Anglo-Americans viewed Mexicans with suspicion and prejudice, but the extent, virulence, and transformation of these racial attitudes have not been widely appreciated. To be sure, race was not the only factor at work. The weakness of the courts in the American West and the battle for economic resources would have led to mob violence against Mexicans regardless, but the number of incidents, the deadly character of that violence, and the contemporary public's reaction to these events would have been wholly different had Mexicans been perceived without racial prejudice.

Judge Lynch on the Border

TWO HOURS PAST midnight, on January 28, 1918, a band of Texas Rangers and masked ranchers arrived at the home of Manuel Morales in the Presidio County village of Porvenir. A recent Christmas day raid on the Brite Ranch consumed their thoughts. Mexican outlaws had attacked the ranch, in the process killing several Anglos and Mexicans, robbing the store, and stealing numerous horses. The Rangers and local ranchers believed that residents of Porvenir were acting as spies and informants for Mexican raiders who lived across the border. The investigators rounded up approximately two dozen men and searched their houses. What happened next is a matter of dispute, but a later investigation concluded that the Rangers and ranchers marched fifteen men of Mexican origin to a rock bluff near the village and coolly executed them. As a result of this mass lynching, 140 residents of Porvenir fled to Mexico, leaving the village abandoned. The widows of the slain men carried their bodies to Mexico, where they were buried. A local grand jury returned no indictments in the case, but Texas Governor William Hobby later disbanded Company B of the Texas Rangers and fired five men for their actions in the affair.[1]

The Porvenir massacre, orchestrated largely by duly-appointed law officers, is one of the most unusual episodes in the history of mob violence in the United States, and it underlines the degree to which collective violence against Mexicans had its own peculiar patterns and could differ in profound ways from mob attacks on other groups in the United States. This chapter emphasizes the distinctive forms, dynamics, and characteristics of mob violence against Mexicans.[2]

How Mobs and Vigilantes Justified the Killing of Mexicans

Lynchers most commonly alleged that their victims deserved execution because they had committed murder. In this, mobs targeting Mexicans

Table 2.1 Alleged Crimes of Lynching Victims

Alleged Crime	African Americans (%)	Mexican Americans (%)
Murder	37.3	61.1
Violations of Sexual Norms	33.6	2.4
Rape and Murder	1.9	1.3
Nonsexual Assault	9.8	2.4
Theft or Robbery	4.0	17.9
Other	10.3	12.6
Unknown	3.2	2.4

were little different than other vigilantes. Yet, far more interesting is the second most common charge leveled against Mexican victims of mob violence—theft. This is one of the most significant differences between mob violence against Mexicans in the United States and the lynching of African Americans (see Table 2.1). While African Americans were also lynched for property crimes, Mexicans were significantly more likely to be killed for alleged crimes such as horse and cattle theft. According to the data compiled for this book, mobs seem to have been motivated by property crimes in the killings of Mexicans in nearly one-fifth of cases. By contrast, Stewart Tolnay and E. M. Beck found that property crimes were the justification for the lynching of blacks in only four percent of cases.[3]

This data supports what we find in the qualitative sources and highlights the relative importance of theft in the story of mob violence against Mexicans. The extent to which the alleged property crimes of Mexicans dominated the concerns of Anglo mobs, however, cannot be fully appreciated by these numbers alone. Allegations of theft played prominently on the minds of Anglo mobs when they organized to punish Mexicans. Sometimes suspected Mexican thieves were killed; sometimes they were merely branded or banished. When mobs did kill Mexicans, the lynchers often characterized their victims as "bandits," inferring that they were not only thieves but murderers and accomplices to murder as well.

The importance of theft and robbery in motivating Anglo mobs can be seen in various acts of nonlethal collective violence against Mexicans. Sometimes alleged Mexican thieves received punishments such as whipping, branding, or banishment instead of death. These nonlethal punishments were applied in all manner of cases involving theft, including horse and cattle stealing. In 1851, the *San Joaquin Republican* reported that an alleged Mexican horse thief had been tried by a vigilance committee and sentenced to be given 150 lashes and branded with the letters "H.T." After

the sentence was passed, the Mexican confessed, and the vigilantes com-
muted his sentence to one hundred lashes with no branding.[4]

Mobs also accused Mexicans of other forms of larceny, notably stealing
from mine claims. As with horse or cattle thieves, sometimes mobs killed
for such an offense and at other times inflicted less than lethal sentences
like whipping. In 1856, the Georgetown News recommended the hanging
and whipping of Mexican trespassers in the California mines. "We would
advise our mining friends," the News stated, "to keep a sharp look out
for 'hombres' who are in the habit of visiting such claims by moonlight
and panning out." If the miners managed to catch these thieves, the News
urged that they "string them up and apply the lash freely," which the paper
guaranteed would prompt the Mexicans to "vamoose."[5]

Many of the Mexicans executed for murder were also accused of being
horse or cattle thieves. In 1852, two Mexicans were hanged in San Gabriel,
the lynching being explained on the grounds that the men were "known
to have belonged to the notorious band of robbers and murderers, who for
a long time have infested this portion of the country."[6] Murder, not theft,
was punishable by death in the courts, and many vigilantes felt it was
important to accuse their victims of a capital crime, even if only indirectly.
Vigilantes who charged their victims with "banditry" often assumed that
everyone within an outlaw gang was guilty of murder without attempting
to distinguish who within the band might actually have committed a specific crime. Sometimes, there was no attempt to connect a particular killing to a particular group of "bandits" at all. Instead, the vigilantes simply
assumed that somehow the men they were executing were responsible for
at least some of the area's unsolved murders and disappearances.[7]

Although there was significant regional variation in patterns of
anti-Mexican mob violence, Anglo frustration with suspected Mexican
thieves is one of the unifying threads in the history of mob violence against
Mexicans. During the second half of the nineteenth century and throughout all regions of the West, lynch mobs routinely accused their Mexican
victims of robbery or theft. In 1855, a "party of citizens" in the territory of
New Mexico broke into the jail at Doña Ana and hanged four Mexicans
accused of robbing a storeowner named Louis Gerk.[8] Nearly a decade
later, in 1864, a mob in California's Merced County led by a man named
McAmicks hanged two Mexicans near Snelling. One of the victims was an
alleged horse thief, while the second man was hanged for his attempt to
prevent the lynching.[9] In 1871, a Colorado mob hanged a Mexican, something that the Rocky Mountain News hoped would be a "terrible warning

to horse thieves."[10] Five years later, a posse killed a Mexican man alleged to have stolen two horses near Omaha, Nebraska.[11] In 1886, the *Dallas Morning News* reported that horse theft had grown "wearisome" to farmers in Nueces County, Texas, and, as a result, a mob had rounded up two Mexicans alleged to be horse thieves and hanged them along Losoloma creek, approximately forty miles from Corpus Christi.[12] That same year, a mob hanged a "young man of Spanish descent" named Gus Kernwood near Stinking Watercreek in Wyoming. Kernwood was alleged to have been behind an eighteen-month spree of stock stealing in the region, as well as the murder of his own partner. According to reports, the "body hung for a number of days exposed, until an old hermit living in the Washakie mountains cut it down and buried it at the foot of the tree."[13]

Thus, allegations of property crimes were a dominant thread in the history of mob violence against Mexicans and such charges provided a link across time and space for mobs executing Mexicans. This was not true for African American mob victims. While horse and cattle theft figured prominently in the minds of mobs lynching Mexicans, mobs executing African Americans were much more likely to be focused on allegations of sexual assault. This was the second most common justification given by mobs that lynched African Americans, accounting for nearly one-third of all cases. Mexicans, by contrast, were rarely charged with sexual offenses. Indeed, out of the hundreds of cases we researched, mobs only lynched thirteen Mexicans for such crimes.[14]

Among the reasons for this disparity is the fact that Anglos did not perceive Mexican men as being as great a sexual threat as they did African American men. As one Texas farmwife affirmed, "You are more safe with them than with the Negroes." An explanation for this phenomenon is to be found in the gendered construction of Mexican racial identity. The dominant discourse of the nineteenth century drew distinctions between "masculine" and "feminine" races. Mexicans were classified according to the latter category.[15] Anglo stereotypes of Mexican males therefore emphasized their supposed lack of traditional masculine virtue. Mexican men were denied the attributes of honor, honesty, and loyalty. Instead they were defined as unprincipled, conniving, and untrustworthy—negative stereotypes of poor female behavior. Where white men were brave and honest, Mexicans were cowardly and treacherous. This gendered construction of racial identity was clearly articulated by Theodore Roosevelt in his work *The Winning of the West*. Roosevelt saw western settlement as the triumph of manly whites over more "effeminate" races. In this survival of the fittest,

Mexicans who attempted to resist the civilizing influence of Anglo settlers were inevitably crushed under heel.[16] The feminization of Mexicans
encouraged Anglos to accuse them of such crimes as cheating at cards or
cowardly acts of murder. At the same time, it also diminished their sexual menace to whites. Four decades after Roosevelt's publications, scholar
Paul Schuster Taylor testified to the continued power of this perception,
noting that Mexicans were less commonly seen as carnal predators than
African Americans.[17]

That Anglo men saw Mexican males as less sexually threatening than
African American men did not prevent mobs from lynching Mexicans on
such grounds. Anglo men undoubtedly regarded physical contact between
white women and Mexican men as morally undesirable. Mexicans who
transgressed the sexual boundaries imposed by Anglos could endure brutal retribution. Among those who suffered such a fate was a fifteen-year-old
Mexican boy named Francisco Cota. On October 17, 1861, a mob caught
and charged Cota with the murder and rape of an Anglo woman. The mob
placed a rope around his neck and dragged him along Alameda Street in
Los Angeles, beating and mutilating his body along the way. Although
nearly dead by the time the mob reached the spot for his execution, he was
nevertheless hanged "as a warning to other malefactors."[18]

In 1867, a Mexican immigrant and an unnamed Native American
"boy" were captured by a posse in California and charged with the rape
of an Anglo woman they had met while she was out searching for lost
sheep. The mob took a vote on what was to be done with the two men. Ten
mob members voted to hand them over to the authorities, but twenty of
the vigilantes declared for hanging. The majority's decision was promptly
carried out.[19] Another Mexican punished for a sexual assault was a gam-
bler named Juan Alvarid. On August 16, 1882, an "immense crowd" led by
members of the Socorro Vigilance Committee overpowered the jailer and
removed Alvarid from his cell where he had been placed for the alleged
rape of an eight-year-old Anglo girl named Edna Warden. The mob dragged
Alvarid before the victim who identified him as her assailant and then
hanged the Mexican from a tree in front of the Windsor hotel. According
to one historian, the next day Alvarid's innocence in the assault was "fully
established."[20]

One of the most brutal killings of a Mexican for sexual assault was that
of Aureliano Castellón on January 30, 1896. Castellón had persisted in
courting a white girl despite the angry objections of her family. Seized by
a mob, the Mexican was shot eight times, his body burned, and his corpse

left near a post office outside of San Antonio. This lynching resembled acts of mob violence against African Americans in many essential aspects, particularly the accusation that the victim had transgressed prescribed sexual boundaries and the bodily mutilation of the corpse.[21]

While the Castellón case suggests obvious parallels with the lynching of blacks in the late nineteenth-century South, the infrequency of such cases involving Mexican victims suggests that Anglo mobs did not begin their work predetermined to suspect Mexican men of sexual deviance. This point is reinforced by the fact that Anglo mobs sometimes employed nonlethal mob violence against Mexicans. As early as 1853, a posse of California Rangers and local citizens captured Isidro Albitro, who was alleged to have broken into the home of the Temple family and raped an Anglo woman named Margarita Temple. The posse gave Albitro 250 lashes, cropped his hair, and expelled him from the mines upon threat "that if ever he returns he will be hanged."[22] While it is true that Anglo mobs did not always respond in the same way across space and time to charges of African American rape, the surviving sources strongly suggest that Anglos did not regard the two crimes as equally dangerous to the social order.[23]

The Impact of Lynching on Women of Mexican Descent

Most Mexican victims of lynch mobs were—like most targets of mob violence—young men. The relatively small number of lynching cases involving Mexican women did not mean, however, that mob violence had little or no impact on them.

One important element adding to the intimidation of Mexican women by lynch mobs was the simple fact that on occasion Anglo mobs did in fact lynch Spanish speaking women. Although there were relatively few Mexican women lynched in the United States, the execution of one Spanish speaking woman garnered great attention at the time and thereafter.

On July 5, 1851, a crowd of over two thousand men gathered along the riverbank at Downieville, California, to witness the hanging of a Mexican woman named Juana Loaiza. She had been convicted by a vigilance committee of murder. A day earlier, the citizens of Downieville had joined in the national celebration of Independence Day. That night, an intoxicated Australian miner named Frederick Cannon wandered from door to door, demanding that local residents share a drink with him. In his drunken stupor, Cannon succeeded in smashing the front door of the cabin where

Juana lived with her husband José. Juana and Cannon exchanged angry insults at one another before the miner staggered home. The following morning, the three individuals again got into an argument that ended at the Loaiza home. The Loaizas demanded payment for the damage Cannon had caused the night before. Cannon denounced Juana as a whore and attempted to enter the cabin. At this moment, Juana reached for a knife and stabbed him to death.[24]

In 1851, there were five thousand citizens in the gold rush boom town of Downieville. In these frontier conditions, the administration of law and order rested in the hands of a vigilance committee, and Juana was made to stand before it. The platform constructed to celebrate Independence Day was turned into a makeshift courtroom. Only one witness spoke in defense of Juana, a physician named Cyrus Aiken, who claimed that she was pregnant. However, the crowd that had gathered around the court-room was clearly intent on revenge. Aiken was kicked and beaten for his audacity in attempting to protect the defendant. Three other doctors were called to examine Juana. None confirmed the diagnosis that she was preg-nant. Asked whether she had anything to say in her own defense, Juana calmly responded that she would not hesitate to act the same way in pro-tection of her honor.[25]

The court took only a few minutes to find the defendant guilty of mur-der. According to contemporary accounts, she met her fate with solemn dignity, refusing to be escorted to the gallows, but walking alone with her head held high. At the place of execution, she bound her skirt around her ankles and straightened her hair, before placing the rope around her own neck. "Adios señores," she declared to the crowd of onlookers. Two men then cut the ropes that held the platform underneath Juana. As her body hurtled toward the water below, the noose tightened around her neck. Her lifeless form hung suspended in the late afternoon light. Although not convicted of any offense, José was also ordered to leave town within twenty-four hours or suffer the consequences.[26]

Frederick Douglass, one of the first black leaders to comment on the lynching of a Mexican, wrote that if Loaiza had been white she would have been lauded for her deed instead of hanged for it. He concluded that she was executed because of her "caste and Mexican blood."[27] Such comments suggest that African Americans were cognizant of the parallels between Anglo attitudes toward Mexicans and blacks very early, at least since the time of the US-Mexican War.

The attention of Frederick Douglass is also an indication of the notoriety of this episode. Indeed, it is probably the most infamous and most studied Mexican lynching. Juana's story endured and became infamous because it did stand out—the victim was a woman, the size of the crowd was unusual, and the victim displayed impressive dignity in the face of her impending doom. Yet, in many ways, Juana stood for all victims of Gold Rush mob violence. Anglo feelings about Juana mirrored the vacillating attitudes toward mob violence that existed more generally. Most Anglos viewed lynching as a "necessary evil" at best and were simultaneously attracted and repulsed by the carnival nature of some executions. Such ambivalent feelings were captured in a poem written in the nineteenth century about Juana's lynching entitled "The Hanging of the Mexican Woman":

> 'Twas long ago—a July morn—
> The stars paled in the early light;
> A man lay stark and dead at dawn,
> His life ebbed with the shades of night.
> A woman wronged by brawler's strife,
> Bravely took the avenger's part;
> One swift-aimed blow her glist'ning knife,
> Plunged deep into a miner's heart.
> Men gathered, then, from near and far,
> And left to silence many a mine,
> On many a far-off creek and bar,
> Then shaded by the oak and pine,
> And rushed to swell the surging throng,
> Like gath'ring streams in onward flood;
> Men thus were wildly borne along,
> Who shrank from shedding human blood.
> The hot sun shone above the scene,
> The river murmured in its bed,
> The hills were clothed in summer green,
> And birds were fluttering overhead.
> Friends tried to shield her—all in vain—
> They brought her forth with wildest jeers;
> The die was cast, her blood must stain,
> The annals of the Pioneers.

Published in 1893 and authored by a writer identified only as "Miner," the poem evokes the complicated emotions that emerged soon after the lynching. The poem portrays Juana as "wronged" but also as a murdering "avenger." The author suggests that most of the mob were mere witnesses to the lynching, caught up in an "onward flood" and "wildly borne along" to the site of the hanging. Right or wrong, the poem concludes, the lynching was inevitable. Efforts to stop it were "all in vain" because the "die was cast." The reference to the episode entering the "annals of the pioneers" suggested what many Californians hoped, that the complicated and dubious practice of lynching and mob violence had receded into their state's past.[28]

Unlike hundreds of other Mexican lynchings in the United States, Juana's death is remembered today not only through this poem but also through a historical marker in Downieville and the reproduction of sketches drawn by artists of the time (see Figure 2.1). Yet Juana was not the only Mexican woman who suffered at the hands of vigilantes. Like Juana, whose actions were judged not "ladylike" enough for the male miners, Mexican women found themselves most in danger when they transgressed prescribed gender norms. In 1852, an Anglo vigilance committee tried a Mexican woman in the California gold mines after the murder of an American named Tom Somers. She was the "first" Mexican tried by the committee and the accusations rested principally upon the fact that she "has always worn male attire, and on this occasion, [was] armed with a pair of pistols." Although some of the vigilantes wanted to hang her, the committee fixed her punishment at banishment. It went on to try a half-dozen Mexican men, whipping two of them and banishing the rest.[29] This was probably not the only instance of vigilantes punishing a Mexican woman for theft. According to another account, a mob took a Mexican woman described only as a "game little vixen" from jail along with her six fellow prisoners, all Mexican men, and hanged them for alleged banditry in San Luis Obispo, California, in September 1853.[30]

Mexican women were punished not only for "banditry," but also for a number of alleged offenses that affronted community sensibilities. A startling episode of vigilantism involving a Mexican woman occurred near Trinidad, Colorado, in 1873. A white couple known as the Richardsons had been killed, arousing the anger of the local citizens. In late August, a gang of masked men intercepted law officers transporting the two Mexicans who had been arrested for the murder and hanged them. Shortly thereafter, a Mexican woman was found hanged. According to one report, she had reportedly revealed the location of the two Mexican men before they

HANGING OF THE MEXICAN WOMAN.

FIGURE 2.1 The Hanging of Juana Loaiza, July 5, 1851, Downieville, courtesy of the Huntington Library, San Marino, California.

were captured. Who murdered this Mexican woman remains a mystery. Perhaps the mob members were fellow Mexicans intent on punishing someone who broke ethnic ranks. Alternately, they may have been Anglos who considered her to have been guilty by association, believing that her knowledge of the men's whereabouts indicated she had somehow aided and abetted the two Mexican men in their crime.[31]

What motivated the Trinidad mob will probably never be known but what is certain is that Mexican women were endangered by Mexican mobs as well as by Anglo ones. In May 1880, Refugio Ramírez, his wife Silvestre Garcia Ramírez, and their sixteen- or seventeen-year-old daughter María Ines Ramírez were lynched in Collin County, Texas, for allegedly bewitching their fellow townspeople.[32]

Mexican women, it is clear, were not exempted from mob violence on the basis of chivalric honor. Yet, it is still true that Mexican women were seldom the primary targets of lynch mobs in the West. The stereotypes that helped justify the lynching of Mexican females did not apply to all Spanish speaking women. Indeed, Anglo men living on a frontier region populated by few potential brides often went to great lengths to portray "Spanish" women living in the Borderlands as chaste and beautiful. In the Southwest, views of Mexican women and men fluctuated from place to place and time to time as the context warranted. If an Anglo mob wished to justify summary violence against a Mexican woman, the mob could employ ready stereotypes of degraded Mexican women forsaking the proper place of women in society. If they wished instead to justify the marriage of an Anglo man to a Mexican woman, ready stereotypes of the "Spanish" lady were also available.

While views of Mexican women fluctuated, in the end, mobs rarely tended to lynch females. Anglo mob leaders, however, often cared little about the harm done to Mexican women in the process of capturing or executing Mexican men. In 1858, the wife and children of the reputed Mexican outlaw Pio Linares were nearly burned alive when their house was set on fire by a mob seeking to kill him.[33]

Even when they were not directly endangered, Mexican women were victimized by lynch mobs. The mobs that rampaged throughout the gold mines of California expelling Mexicans did not insist that Mexican men alone leave but demanded the withdrawal of all Mexicans from the mines. More Mexican men than women had flocked to the gold fields, but there were numerous Mexican women living in and near the mines. Some Mexican women, like some Mexican men, were protected by Anglo patrons and managed to avoid expulsion, but any such exceptions might be revoked, as the lynching of Loaiza herself proved.

Anglo intimidation of Mexican women was even greater beyond the California gold fields where Mexicans were more likely to live in extended families. Lynch mobs inflicted fear in Mexican women as surely as they instilled terror in Mexican men when they killed fathers, husbands, and sons. In 1874, a Brownsville mob hanged two Mexican men for theft and left the bodies on display. A paper noted that "many" Mexicans—including "men, women, and children"—saw the bodies and became emotional.[34]

During the wave of violence that swept south Texas from 1915 to 1919, Mexican women endured a terrible toll as their male relatives fled, were killed, or were forced into hiding. On October 1, 1915, the bodies of fourteen Mexicans were discovered at Ebenezer's crossroads near Donna in Hidalgo County. Allegedly killed by Rangers about a week earlier, the relatives and friends of the victims had been too afraid to recover the bodies and bury them, fearing that to do so would endanger themselves or their male family members.[35] The story of the executions of the Mexican men and boys at Porvenir underlines the harm done to the families and friends of lynching victims. Forced to recover the bodies of their slain men, the Tejanas of Porvernir were too scared to bury their fathers, sons, and brothers near their homes. Instead, they chose to cross over to Mexico and to restart their lives on the opposite side of the Rio Grande, alive but traumatized and exiled.

Table 2.2 **Multiple Victim Lynchings**

Number of Victims	African American Lynchings (%)	Mexican Lynchings (%)
1	85.8	60.8
2	9.4	17.9
3	2.8	10.3
4	1.3	3.3
5	0.4	2.2
More than 5	0.3	5.5

Why Mexican Mob Victims Rarely Died Alone

Mexican lynching victims often died together in small groups. This contrasted sharply with other victims of mob violence, particularly African Americans. Tolnay and Beck studied 2,018 lynchings involving African American victims that took place in ten southern states between 1882 and 1930. Of these, only 286, or approximately one out of seven, involved more than one victim. Our own data suggests that the proportion of Mexican mob victims killed in groups of two or more was markedly higher. Indeed, two out of every five cases involving Mexicans were multiple lynchings (see Table 2.2).[36]

An examination of the mob murders of Mexicans in one year will help illuminate these statistics and reveal the extent to which mobs targeted groups of Mexicans and not individuals. The year 1881 was, for reasons not entirely clear, a particularly brutal year for Mexicans in the Southwest. Over two dozen Mexican men were summarily executed by mobs or outlaw gangs. The first lynching recorded that year took place on January 29 in Nevada Territory. A lynching party took Matías Alcantar—described as a "typical frontier desperado"—from the Grantsville jail, where he was imprisoned on charges of murdering a fellow Mexican named S. E. Mirales, and hanged him.[37]

Two days later, this single execution was followed by a much more expansive wave of vigilantism in New Mexico. On October 14, 1880, a band of Mexicans murdered and robbed census collector Charles Potter. Over the next several months, posses pursued the gang. Two men were lynched on December 28, 1880, just before the new year. In late January, three more of the men were captured and placed in the Albuquerque jail. On the evening of January 31, 1881, a band of masked men took the three assassins and hanged them in the Albuquerque plaza. On February 24, vigilantes captured and hanged a sixth member of the gang at the same location. The alleged leader, Mariano Leyba, was not killed until he was gunned down by deputized sheriffs on a mountain trail south of Santa Fe in March 1887.[38]

In the midst of these executions, in early February, three men, two of them Anglos and the other Mexican, were hanged near El Paso, Texas. They were alleged to have murdered and robbed two visitors from Boston.[39] On March 1, a small posse tracked down two Mexicans accused of horse theft in Colfax County, New Mexico. They returned with the horses but would say nothing of what had happened to the fugitives.[40]

In the middle of March, two Mexican men disappeared near Wilcox in Arizona Territory. One of them, José Ordoña, was later found hanged. Even after the intervention of the Mexican government, the other Mexican, Rafael Salcido, was never found. Both men had been accused of being thieves.[41] At the end of March, Onofre Baca was hanged by New Mexico vigilantes in Socorro because he was suspected of being one of the three men accused of murdering an Anglo newspaperman.[42]

During the summer of 1881, there was one individual lynching in New Mexico and an explosion of indiscriminate mob violence in Arizona. On June 10, a mob broke into the jail at Taos, New Mexico, and hanged Narciso Montoya for murder.[43] At the end of July, in Cochise County, Arizona, a feud between Mexicans and the so-called "Cowboys" led to the killing of an undetermined number of Mexicans leading a pack train. Earlier, a different band of Mexicans had killed members of the Cowboys whom they alleged were stealing stock in Mexico. Hungry for revenge, these Mexicans and their pack train were at the wrong place at the wrong time. According to various reports, some of the Mexicans were killed immediately, while others were captured and tortured to death. The total number of Mexicans killed by the Cowboys may have been over a dozen.[44]

Mob violence declined in the second half of 1881, but, in October, several more Mexicans were killed in New Mexico. In the southeast, a mob broke into the Lincoln County jail and disappeared with a Mexican prisoner accused of stealing the horses of local Anglos. The prisoner's body was never discovered and he was presumed killed.[45] In the north, a mob broke into the jail at Los Lunas and hanged three Mexicans accused of murdering a saloon keeper on the banks of the Rio Grande.[46]

No single year is completely typical of anti-Mexican mob violence. The year 1881 was unusual in that most of the Mexicans killed died in New Mexico and Arizona as opposed to Texas and California, the two states with the greatest number of overall victims. Still, 1881 is illustrative of the ways in which Mexicans often died in small groups. During the year, there were twelve different episodes of mob violence involving twenty-eight total victims. Of those, seven cases involved a single Mexican victim; the other five cases accounted for the remaining twenty-one. Throughout the Southwest, and not just in 1881, Mexicans found themselves being hanged in groups of twos and threes or even larger groups. Why did Mexicans, unlike African Americans and Anglos, so often die in groups of two or three or more?

First, most Mexicans in the United States lived and worked with other Mexicans. Whether in the gold mines of California or on the cattle ranches of Texas, Mexican labor often involved a dozen or more people. By contrast, African Americans in the late nineteenth and early twentieth centuries were primarily sharecroppers who worked in single family units. Lynch mobs seeking victims were thus likely to find several Mexican men at the same time but might come across black men one at a time.

A second factor is related to racial stereotypes. Sexual assault, a crime that whites often accused blacks of committing (but rarely Mexicans), is usually considered the act of a single individual. Theft and robbery, crimes for which Mexicans were often lynched, can be regarded as group crimes. Thus, the varying racial stereotypes of blacks and Mexicans, which led lynch mobs to associate different crimes with each group, played a role in the greater incidence among Mexicans of multiple victim lynchings.

Third, Mexicans were more likely to be lynched in large groups because of the greater cultural distance between whites and Mexicans as compared to whites and blacks. A considerable gulf, even a fundamental divide, existed between white and black culture in the South. Yet, whites and blacks in the American South shared the same language, the same religion, and a history of close contact for centuries. While closeness did not bring about harmony or even understanding, the comparison with Mexicans is telling. Not only did Mexicans and Anglos speak a different language, but also each practiced what the other perceived as a very different religion. Most whites and Mexicans had little contact until the middle of the nineteenth century. Some scholars have argued that cultural distance plays a key role in motivating mob violence. There is little doubt that the unfamiliarity of most Anglos with Mexican culture, especially the Spanish language, made it difficult for them to conduct legal and extralegal investigations. Mobs seeking Mexicans accused of a crime often found it difficult to determine who among a group of Mexicans was guilty of an alleged transgression. Frustrated with the necessity of translation, unable to decide who was really "guilty," and fueled with racist feelings against persons of Mexican descent, Anglo mobs often chose to indiscriminately lynch whole groups of Mexicans.[47]

Fourth and finally, many Anglos did not want to live alongside Mexicans but instead wanted to expel them completely from the United States. Anglo mobs in the California mines and in the Rio Grande Valley often believed that Mexicans were neither needed nor wanted. The explicit goal of much mob violence against Mexicans was to initiate an exodus of Spanish speakers, leaving their mining claims and their lands behind for Anglos.

Mobs lynching African Americans in the South, by contrast, were not as focused on acquiring black property or expelling blacks. African Americans historically had little access to property, but they did possess *de jure* constitutional rights. The need to maintain strict maintenance of social control and *de facto* second-class citizenship consequently underpinned antiblack violence. Southern mobs by and large did not want to force blacks out of the region but instead to discipline blacks and to force them to conform to the system of racial hierarchy and deference that whites had imposed after Reconstruction. Many white southern farmers, as they had for centuries, depended upon black labor and were interested in shaping black behavior, not eliminating African Americans altogether.[48]

Interestingly, in this regard, it is antiblack violence in the North that might be a better comparison with anti-Mexican violence. Whites in the North did not have a lengthy history with a large population of African Americans, and they often regarded blacks migrating from the South as unwanted interlopers competing for their jobs. When white northerners struck out with mob violence, they often did so in race riots as opposed to southern-style lynch mobs. They hoped, like their counterparts in the West, to frighten the new arrivals to leave and to discourage more from coming.[49]

Why Mexicans Were More Likely To Be Shot Than Other Victims of Mob Violence

In the popular media, lynching is commonly associated with hanging. Borderlands mobs targeting Mexicans were not limited, however, to this iconic method of execution. While vigilantes in the American West did hang many of their victims, mobs lynching Mexicans tended to execute their victims by shooting far more often than did their counterparts in other areas of the United States. Indeed, observers frequently associated

Table 2.3 Modes of Execution

Modes of Execution	Number of Episodes
Hanged	345
Shot	129
Tortured and then hanged or shot	11
Burned as part of execution	9
Hanged and shot	6
Dragged as part of execution	5
Decapitated as part of execution	3
Beaten and then hanged	3
Whipped and then hanged or shot	3
Beaten to death	2
Clubbed to death with rifle	1
Beaten to death with clubs	1
Executed with axe	1
Throat slit	1
Stabbed to death	1
Shot and fed to hogs	1
Shot and ears cut off	1
Trampled to death by horse rider	1
"Lynched"/"killed"/"murdered"/"tortured"/not reported	23
Total	547

the pursuit and shooting down of victims by posses with Mexicans. In 1926, the *New York Times* reported on the lynching of three blacks at Aiken, South Carolina. The *Times* noted that a mob took the three men out of jail and then the "victims were released in a wood, and in Mexican style, shot down as they ran."[50]

Despite this association, most mobs executing Mexicans actually preferred to hang their victims. Hanging possessed a rich symbolic history and colored the perception of an execution, suggesting that the hanged man was not only guilty but also dishonorable.[51] Hangings accounted for approximately two-thirds of the Mexicans killed in our study (see Table 2.3). With some relish, the *Goliad Express* reported under the headline, "An Oak Tree in Full Bearing," on the hanging of nine men in 1857. The *Express* surmised that the eight Mexicans and one Anglo were horse thieves and noted: "That's carrying on the game of hanging by the flock" and is "a severe test of the strength of one little oak."[52]

The symbolic importance of hanging can be seen in an unusual episode involving Captain John Boling, the Sheriff of Arizona's Mariposa County. In 1855, while transporting two Mexican prisoners from Bear Valley to

Mariposa County, the captives made an attempt to escape. Boling shot and killed one during the escape, but in the process he was severely wounded. Nevertheless, he took time despite his injury to hang the still-living second prisoner.[53]

While most mobs preferred to hang their Mexican victims, vigilantes did often execute Mexicans by shooting rather than hanging. In fact, mobs dispatching Mexicans were far more likely to shoot their victims than were vigilantes executing African Americans. For one thing, the Borderlands were far less wooded than the American South, and trees tall enough to hang men are rare in many parts of the American West. One of the reasons that Mexicans were so frequently lynched near creeks and rivers was the presence of large trees along these vital water sources. Mobs coming into possession of their victims at a significant distance from such trees often made the decision to dispense with the traditional mode of lynching, hanging, and expedite matters with their guns.

One of the symbolic reasons that mobs preferred hanging was that the corpse might serve as a warning to other potential thieves and malcontents. Yet, in parts of the thinly settled American West, there were no guarantees that anyone other than the lynch mob itself would see a swinging corpse for days, weeks, or even months. During the California Gold Rush, bodies were frequently discovered days after death even though there had been no attempt to conceal the corpses.[54] In 1881, while gathering wood a few miles south of Tucson a Mexican discovered by accident the corpses of two Mexicans, decayed from several days' exposure. According to one report, one of the bodies was hanging and the other had been decapitated.[55] Much of the American West remained into the twentieth century a sparsely settled place that could hide dead corpses for long stretches.[56]

Mexicans and "Spectacle" Lynchings

In the popular mind, lynching is often associated with what scholars call "spectacle lynchings"—public executions attended by hundreds and sometimes thousands of spectators and which often involved torture, burning, and corpse mutilation. The vast majority of lynchings did not follow this pattern, but the lynching of African Americans did often reach this "spectacle" level in the early twentieth century. By contrast, it appears that such cases were rare among Mexican lynching victims.[57]

Recent studies of lynching have focused on lynchings of African Americans that drew crowds in the thousands. In 1893, Henry Smith was lynched in view of a crowd estimated at ten thousand in Paris, Texas. In 1899, Sam Hose died before a mob of two thousand people in Newnan, Georgia. In 1911, a mob of some five thousand saw Zach Walker lynched in Coatesville, Pennsylvania. In 1916, a crowd estimated at fifteen thousand watched as Jesse Washington was burned alive in Waco, Texas. Mobs executing Mexicans in most parts of the West failed to match such numbers of spectators.

The contrast between the lynching of Mexicans and blacks on the issue of spectacle lynchings can, however, be overdrawn. While less likely than African Americans to be the victims of spectacle lynchings, Mexicans did upon occasion suffer the same kind of brutal executions that blacks faced. On several occasions, mobs dismembered, burned, and brutalized Mexicans before throngs of people.

Especially in Gold Rush era California, several Mexicans were lynched before large crowds. On June 15, 1851, a crowd estimated at three thousand viewed the hanging of Patricio Janori and Antonio Cruz for murder at Shaw's Flat.[58] In 1857, a crowd again numbering around three thousand witnessed the lynching of Juan Flores, the man accused of orchestrating the attack on Sheriff Barton and his posse.

The size of the crowds attending California lynchings, however, declined after the Gold Rush. Indeed, time and space matter very much when comparing blacks and Mexicans on this issue. Before 1890, it is possible to argue that Mexicans were at least as likely to die as blacks in mass lynchings. After 1890, this is simply not the case, with African American mob violence becoming more frequent and increasingly ritualized while anti-Mexican mob violence declined in both number of victims and size of mobs.

Even during this period of decline, however, Mexicans still faced the danger of public execution by large mobs. Texas, the scene of numerous "spectacle" lynchings of African Americans, played host to two of the most brutal lynchings of Mexicans in US history. On November 3, 1910, a mob in Rock Springs apprehended a Mexican national named Antonio Rodríguez who was accused of murder of a white woman. The mob leaders tied Rodríguez to a mesquite tree, poured kerosene on him, and burned him alive. The crowd viewing the burning was reported by the *El Paso Times* to number in the thousands.[59] The exact size of the mob that gathered to watch Rodríguez burn is unknown but whatever the number it was almost unbelievably large given its location in sparsely populated Edwards County. There is little doubt that the deliberate

burning of Rodríguez was imbued with symbolic meaning akin to similar "spectacle" executions of African Americans. Mob leaders who had
chosen the execution site ahead of time and spread the word about their
plans clearly hoped that the lynching would be observed by as many folks
as possible.[60]

Few lynchings of Mexicans matched Rodríguez's in size of mob or in
brutality, but one such lynching took place just a year later. In 1911, another
young Mexican was lynched by a mob in Texas. On June 19, the son of a
local migrant worker named Antonio Gómez stabbed and killed Charley
Zieschang, the owner of a garage in Thorndale, Milam County. Mob leaders intercepted Gómez after he was arrested. The mob beat and disfig-
ured Gómez, and the leaders placed a chain around his neck. The crowd
then dragged him behind a horse ridden to the center of town where a
crowd estimated to number between one and two hundred had gathered.
Gómez, who according to one report was a boy of twelve years old, was
finally hanged around nine p.m.[61]

Although the Gómez lynching did not draw the number of spectators
that viewed the Rock Springs lynching, his killing was also meant as a
public spectacle. The dragging of the body through the town paralleled
a key element to many of the spectacle lynchings of African Americans.
The long, slow deliberate execution of the young man was a blunt ges-
ture of the power of the mob leaders and a clear warning to Mexicans
about the dangers of seeking revenge on Anglos. As with so many African
American spectacle lynchings, the symbolic and ritualistic elements of
the Gómez lynching undermine any argument that the killing was necessary because of a slow or ineffective court system. However, Gómez's
lynching ignited protests from Mexican officials that brought unwanted
attention to Thorndale and led to the end of one type of mob execution.
Numerous Mexicans would be killed in the coming decade in south Texas
but never again would there be a public execution akin to those meted out
to Antonio Rodríguez and Antonio Gómez.

The lynchings of Rodríguez and Gómez confirm that Anglo mobs did
indeed execute Mexicans in ritual-like killings akin to the experience of
some African American lynching victims. Fear, racism, and the need to
make a public statement about the dangers of criminal behavior combined
to create the mobs that killed Rodríguez and Gómez, as those forces had
and would continue to combine to kill numerous African Americans.

In the end, however, Rodríguez and Gómez stand apart from most
Mexican lynching victims, because of the way that they were executed.

The vast majority of Mexican victims of mob violence did not die in ritualized, daylight public killings but in the middle of the night or in remote ranchlands, hidden gulches, and deserted roadsides.

One factor working against the spectacle lynching of Mexicans was the presence of the Mexican border. In many of the best attended lynchings of African Americans, the execution of the alleged criminal was delayed for a short time. The delay allowed time for greater publicity of the crime, the resultant enflaming of local passions, and the window of opportunity needed for planning a massive event involving thousands of spectators. In the case of Jesse Washington, the lynching site and time were so well known that the photographer arrived well before the victim in order to set up his equipment.[62]

In the case of Mexican prisoners, vigilantes were often uncomfortable with even short delays because they worried about their captives escaping due to the poor quality of western jails and the proximity of the border. The result was a tendency of mobs to lynch Mexicans at the first opportunity. This speediness sometimes led to smaller and less brutal executions. In Tucson, for example, a newspaper lamented the quick execution of a Mexican. "It has just been found out that one of the Mexicans hung at Tucson, some time ago, had a hand in the terrible massacre of the Baker family in which case hanging was too good for him."[63]

Concern over federal intervention may also have dimmed enthusiasm for the spectacle lynchings of Mexicans. Mexico had long protested the lynching of its citizens on US soil, and public executions of Mexicans made their protests much harder for American officials to ignore. Knowing that Mexico would certainly pressure the State Department to investigate and bring charges against lynch mob leaders may have limited the number of spectacle lynchings of Mexicans in the late nineteenth and early twentieth centuries.

One final factor to note is simple population density. Although the American South was not densely populated in the early twentieth century compared to the American Northeast, the American West was even more thinly settled. Perhaps Mexicans would have been lynched by mobs comparable in size to those lynching African Americans if the West was more populous. Certainly, the executions of Antonio Rodríguez and Antonio Gómez suggest that such mob violence was possible. That their executions remained relatively rare almost certainly had little to do with the depth of anti-Mexican prejudice, which remained very significant as events in Texas demonstrated after 1915.

The Role of Law Officers in the Lynching of Mexicans

The Porvenir executions that began this chapter culminated a period of intense and bloody vigilantism that deserves special attention. There are few parallels between the mob violence of the years 1915 to 1919 and with extralegal violence at any other time in US history. The chief reason for this is the fact that duly appointed law officers played such a prominent role in leading and encouraging the era's numerous extralegal executions. To be sure, there were instances in the American South when policemen or other law officers could be found participating in mob actions or aiding mobs in their efforts to secure their victims. Yet, the leadership of the Texas Rangers and other officials in the violent reaction to the Plan de San Diego was something altogether different. After one episode in which Texas Rangers had killed fifteen Mexican outlaws, a local Anglo remembered that the "bodies of the dead thieves were brought into Brownsville and displayed like so much cordwood on the old market square as a warning to others of their ilk."[64]

Neither the intervention of the Texas Rangers into border affairs nor criticism of that action was new. Indeed, for a half century before the Plan de San Diego, the Texas Rangers had been actively involved in south Texas. In 1875, the *San Antonio Express* published a scathing indictment of the role of state officials and the Texas Rangers in fomenting anti-Mexican mob violence along the border. Governor Coke, the writer began, "sent a band of men to the Rio Grande frontier to kill Mexicans" and the "outrages committed by [Warren] Wallace's men in the summer of 1874 have led in a great measure to the recent bloodshed on the Rio Grande." According to the editorialist, this state-sanctioned violence encouraged Anglos to heightened levels of vigilantism in South Texas. "The white people of the frontier," the author concluded, "have caught the inspiration emenating [*sic*] from the capital and there seems to be a determination on their part to bring on a collision with Mexico, to force it, in fact, by acts of violence."[65] There is little doubt that the violent response of the Rangers to Mexican raiders gave encouragement to vigilantes.[66] The evidence is clear that Texas Rangers sometimes played a supporting role in mob violence against Mexicans in the 1870s. At the same time, however, Rangers targeted Anglo outlaws who disturbed relations between Mexico and the United States by raiding into Mexico. They punished Anglos who killed and intimidated innocent Mexicans, especially those allied with south Texas Anglos. On the one hand, their actions exacerbated racial and ethnic tensions along the border and indirectly, if not directly, led to mob vio-lence against Mexicans. On the other hand, their campaign against out-laws was not solely limited to Mexican outlaws and their breaking up of Anglo gangs that preyed on Mexicans contributed to the decline of mob violence that took hold in the 1880s.

The Rangers were, as Robert Utley ably demonstrated, a complicated group that contained a diversity of characters, some honorable and some flawed.[67] Unfortunately, for those living along the border, the Rangers were rarely at their best when interacting with Mexicans. Between 1915 and 1919, they were sadly at their worst. During those years, south Texas erupted into what was described as a "race war" between Anglos and Mexicans.[68] The Rangers, though bolstered by a small number of Tejano allies, were the blunt instrument of Anglos in this ethnic conflict.

In January 1915, police acting on a tip-off from informants arrested Basilio Ramos in McAllen, Texas. In his possession was a revolutionary manifesto drafted by Mexican insurgents from a prison in Monterrey, Nuevo León. The "Plan de San Diego" proposed that on February 20 a "Liberating Army for Races and Peoples" would rise up against Anglos to reannex for Mexico lands ceded under the Treaty of Guadalupe Hidalgo, including the states of Arizona, California, Colorado, New Mexico, and Texas. To secure victory, the plan called for the slaughter of all Anglo males over the age of sixteen. In return for supporting the uprising, the revolutionaries further vowed to secure territory for other racial minorities victimized by Anglos: six more states for African Americans to establish an independent republic and the restoration of Native American ancestral lands.

The insurrection failed to materialize. Indicted for sedition, Ramos posted bail and promptly disappeared across the border. Yet the matter was far from over. On the day scheduled for the uprising, a second plan appeared. Even more overreaching than the original conspiracy, it called for the conversion of a larger area of the United States that now included Utah and Nevada into a sovereign collectivist state. "Enough of tolerance!" exclaimed the revolutionary authors. "Enough of suffering insults and contempt! We are men, conscious of our acts, and who know how to think as well as they, the 'Gringos,' and who can and will be free." The fact that their ambition completely outmatched their resources may have doomed the seditionists to failure, but in contrast to the false alarm sounded by the first plan, this time around they converted words into action. In July and August 1915, raiders led by Aniceto Pizaña and Luis de la Rosa launched a series of assaults on the economic infrastructure and transport and communications networks of the Lower Rio Grande Valley, destroying railroad lines and raiding post offices and ranches.[69]

The Plan de San Diego amounted to a declaration of race war that allowed Anglos to legitimate as acts of self-defense the slaughter of innocent civilians. Pizaña and de la Rosa's raids unleashed a bloody torrent of retaliatory action. In a climate of intense paranoia, Anglos committed countless atrocities on Mexicans who they mistakenly and sometimes willfully suspected of collusion with the insurrectionists. As one scholar has suggested, "open season" was declared "on any Mexican caught in the open armed or without a verifiable excuse for his activities."[70] One journalist recalled an incident in which Anglos came across what they thought was a heavily armed force of raiders and sent an urgent appeal for protection to Texas Rangers and the US Army. The "bandits" turned out to be pick-handling farmers digging soil. "All this sounds very harmless," observed the reporter, "but it isn't, as a good many innocent people—most of them Mexicans—have been killed."[71] Estimates of the number of Mexicans indiscriminately massacred by Anglos vary from hundreds to thousands. According to the San Antonio Express, "the finding of dead bodies of Mexicans ... has reached the point where it creates little or no interest."[72] The Texas Rangers, as ever, led by example. As Ranger John Peavey later observed of the summary executions carried out by his fellow officers, "People were shooting first and not talking afterward."[73] The arbitrary execution of Mexicans in South Texas culminated in the killing of fifteen people, primarily elderly men and boys, at Porvenir.

The raids also consolidated Anglo economic control of the Lower Rio Grande Valley through the forced displacement of thousands of Mexicans who fled for their lives across the border. In a cruel irony, many of these Mexicans had settled in the region as sanctuary from the revolutionary violence in their home country. Those who remained in south Texas endured a severe curtailment of their civil liberties including the dispossession of all firearms.

Mexicans in South Texas refer to the years from 1915 to 1919 as the "Hora de Sangre" (Hour of Blood) because so many Mexicans died at the hands of vigilantes and Texas Rangers.[74] The number of Tejanos killed in reaction to the Plan de San Diego will never be known. Benjamin Johnson, author of the most recent book on the uprising, estimates the number in the "low thousands."[75] While the sheer number of murdered Mexicans is disturbing, the participation by state and local authorities, particularly the Texas Rangers, in what Walter Prescott Webb has called "an orgy of bloodshed," is even more so. Harbert Davenport, a lawyer and prominent civic leader from Brownsville, argued that one of the Ranger companies sent to South Texas to put down the uprising was composed of "mere murderers." Davenport described the company's commander as a "blood-thirsty" leader and noted that the company's members openly "boasted of their work as executioners" and defended their killing because it would have been, they believed, impossible to obtain evidence for conviction. Davenport stated that many innocent Mexicans were slain on "hear-say testimony" from Anglos that were likely themselves criminals.[76]

The company that so angered Davenport was no doubt Company D, headed by Henry Lee Ransom. Historians have described Ransom's policy in South Texas as "when in doubt, shoot." Furthermore, the Ranger commander "felt that not only should bandits be summarily killed, but even those who *looked* like bandits, as well as anyone who had guilty knowledge of crimes or who sheltered bandits."[77] Virgil Lott, a newspaperman from South Texas, summed up the violence of the era years later: "How many lives were lost can not be estimated fairly for hundreds of Mexicans were killed who had no part in any of the uprisings, their bodies concealed in the thick underbrush and no report ever made by the perpetrators of these crimes."[78]

Why did Texas authorities play such a prominent role in so many of the cases of mob violence against Mexicans? The general enmity that many Anglos felt toward Mexicans was often heightened for those who had fought in the US-Mexican War and had lost friends and comrades in that conflict. This prejudice festered long after hostilities concluded and was passed down from lawman to lawman for generations. Additionally, many of the Texas Rangers assigned to the border were not from south Texas and did not want to be there. In 1886, a Ranger wrote in a letter: "I arrived here [Rio Grande City, Texas] yesterday evening and found this to be a hell of a hole, nothing but Mexicans, everybody was surprised that Rangers are to be stationed here there is nothing going on here."[79] The conditions along the border strained and tested many law officers, especially those without a working knowledge of Spanish. The language barrier hampered their ability to investigate crimes and made it more difficult to distinguish between law-abiding and lawbreaking citizens. Such a problem might have been overcome by working closely with Spanish speaking local sheriffs, but historian Harold Preece has written that the Texas Rangers regarded Mexican

sheriffs "as being but one degree above 'bandits' and disliked even minimum dealings with them."[80]

As critical as these issues were, however, the responsibility for the
lynching and vigilante executions of alleged Mexican criminals by Texas
Rangers and other lawmen must be attributed, in part, to the tacit support
of state and federal governments. By failing to prosecute, fire, or even condemn officials who summarily killed Mexican criminals, the state of Texas
encouraged and reinforced such actions. When the federal government,
even though pressured by Mexico, failed to put significant pressure on
state and local officials to act in cases of anti-Mexican mob violence, the
result was to embolden and legitimize lynching. The best evidence for this
argument is the history of anti-Mexican mob violence after 1919, when
a serious investigation led by Texas State Representative José T. Canales
investigation reversed this trend.

When Mexicans Lynched Mexicans

Despite the prominence of interracial lynching in both the popular media
and academic analysis, mobs frequently lynched members of their own
racial and ethnic group during the nineteenth and early twentieth centuries. White-on-white lynchings are best known, and black mobs sometimes lynched alleged black criminals. Thus, it is not surprising to find
that mobs composed of persons of Mexican descent occasionally murdered men and women of Mexican descent.[81]

Mexicans could not help but be influenced by the majority culture's
endorsement of lynching. This was perhaps especially true for Mexicans
who lived in the American West where the ethic of rough justice and vigilantism was especially strong. The courts in certain parts of the West,
as has been seen, were unable to secure indictments and convictions of
alleged criminals. In those cases, evidence suggests that indicting and
convicting Mexicans of crimes against Anglos was easier than indicting
and convicting Mexicans of crimes against other Mexicans. Even in cases
where Mexicans were convicted of crimes against other Mexicans, punishments were often relatively light.[82]

Additional evidence gleaned from diaries, newspapers, and other
sources aligns with this reading of the court records. In 1853, for example,
a Mexican got up from playing cards, confronted another Mexican who
had just entered, and then stabbed and killed him in front of multiple witnesses. He turned himself into an Anglo judge who refused to prosecute

him. According to the *Marysville Herald*, the killer "had greatly aided the Americans in detecting horse thieves."[83] It is not difficult to imagine the Mexican community taking justice into its own hands in cases such as this one.

Something more than these two broad factors, however, was at work. Mexican-on-Mexican mob violence was even greater than black-on-black mob violence. Mexicans were nearly twice as likely as blacks to be murdered by a mob composed, at least in part, of their own ethnic group. Among cases of mob violence against Mexicans, sixty were composed of mobs that included Mexicans. In about half of those cases, the mobs contained both Mexican and Anglo members. In the other half, the mobs were composed entirely of Mexicans.

These numbers are somewhat conservative, as there are numerous cases in which we have not been able to confirm the composition of the lynch mob. Most of the time the key sources for a lynching make no direct mention of the ethnic background of the participants, and such information must be surmised from the context. It is apparent in many such cases that the mobs consisted largely, if not solely, of Anglos, but there are still cases of significant guesswork. When Mexicans made up a significant portion of the mob or the viewing crowd, however, Anglo newspapers usually noted their presence as a way of suggesting that the community's support for the executions was not limited by ethnicity. Newspapers were also apt to report when mobs consisted almost solely of Mexicans, though the motives for doing so varied. Sometimes a newspaper used such cases to illustrate the broad acceptance of lynching across racial lines. At other times, the press published such episodes to criticize the lawlessness of Mexicans as a people. Given that discussions of the ethnic background of lynchers depend upon a series of assumptions about the imperfect surviving sources, we have been particularly cautious in our conclusions.

Despite the difficulties of the sources, the historical record is clear on some matters. From the Gold Rush era through the turn of the twentieth century, there were numerous cases of Mexicans lynched by other Mexicans. In 1852, a mob reported to include "principally Mexicans" hanged three of their fellow countrymen near Santa Cruz for horse theft.[84] In 1876, in the largely Mexican town of San Diego, Texas, a crowd alleged to constitute the "whole people" took Anastacio Perez, Ponciano Lerma, and Emilio Gonzales from jail and dragged them a mile and a half to a tree where they hanged them for allegedly having murdered Dionicio Garcia, Pedro Gonzalez, and two peddlers.[85] In 1897, the "outraged Mexican population"

of Clifton, Arizona, broke into the jail and removed Marcello Tijares. The
mob was infuriated because Anastacio Bernal had been found behind the
Arizona Copper Mine Company's smelter with a bullet through his head.
Preliminary evidence pointed to Tijares. By two o'clock in the morning,
the mob had forced the keys from the jailer, taken Tijares outside, and
shot him dead.[86]

While some of the mobs lynching Mexicans consisted solely or principally of Mexicans, there were a substantial number of mixed or interracial mobs. This is not wholly surprising. The large crowds that were
drawn to view lynchings in the diverse American West often contained
a greater mix of peoples—Mexicans, Chinese, Native Americans as well
as Anglos—than was the case in the American South.[87] At times, the
number of Mexicans in these crowds was substantial, either due to the
demographics of the area's surrounding population or the local Mexican
community's particular interest in the lynching. In 1852, a diverse mob
reported to number between eight hundred and one thousand and containing "all classes and sexes" executed Carlos Esclava on Mokelumne
Hill in Calaveras County for murder.[88] Nine years later, in 1861, a mob
containing primarily Anglos and Mexicans lynched José Claudio Alvitre
in Los Angeles for the murder of an elderly Mexican couple. The *Alta
California* reported that Alvitre's "countrymen took the lead" in the hanging.[89] In 1872, at Stanwix Station, in Arizona, a mob reported to contain both Mexicans and Anglos executed an unknown Mexican man who
allegedly killed a Mexican boy.[90]

While Mexicans did join with Anglos in impromptu lynch mobs, they
were also included at times in the more enduring vigilante organizations
of the American West. On July 24, 1852, a Los Angeles vigilance committee
composed of Mexicans and Anglos executed thirty-five-year-old Doroteo
Zabaleta of California and twenty-year-old Jesús Rivas of Sonora for the
murder of two Americans traveling from Los Angeles to San Diego.[91]

This was not an isolated case. In 1858, the Vigilance Committee of
San Luis Obispo contained many Mexicans. Before the committee disbanded, fully sixty-two of the 148 vigilantes were of Mexican descent. This
fact alone would make this committee worth further investigation, but
there is another reason to focus on the vigilantes of 1858. They left behind
unparalleled records of the committee's inner workings, including reward
notices, transcribed testimonies of witnesses, confessions and final statements of the accused, voluminous minutes recorded by the vigilantes, and
documents testifying to the judgments rendered by the committee.[92]

The first recorded lynchings of Mexicans in San Luis Obispo date from 1853. According to Horace Bell's memoirs, in the autumn of 1853, a mob took seven members of a suspected thieving ring from the civil authorities and hanged "them to the first tree that presented itself" in San Luis Obispo.[93] Other accounts differ with Bell's in the details. Newspapers reported that a peddler had been robbed in San Juan by a band of perhaps ten individuals and that a posse had gone out in pursuit, in the process killing one of the Mexicans and capturing four or five others, all of whom were men and all of whom were eventually hanged by vigilantes.[94] The *Los Angeles Star* reported that the work of the vigilance committee in 1853 was supported by both Mexicans and Anglos in the region: "Our informant states that there is but one voice among the Americans and Californians of San Luis Obispo in regard to the hanging of the men, who committed the murder, and that is, that they deserved and well merited their fate."[95]

Another lynching followed in 1854. Mateo Andrade escaped from San Quentin Prison on July 24. Andrade, a native of Mexico who had been a baker at one point in his life, was in the midst of serving an eleven-year sentence for grand larceny and robbery when he made his break for freedom. He did not live long. Perhaps easily identified because he was missing his left eye, Andrade was captured and lynched in San Luis Obispo later that year.[96]

Following Andrade, no lynchings were reported in San Luis Obispo until 1858 when the murder of two Frenchmen prompted locals to organize an even larger vigilance committee than had existed in 1853. San Luis Obispo and the surrounding areas had been the scene of robberies and murders throughout the 1850s. Most of the robberies and violence had been directed at Anglos and orchestrated by Pio Linares, the son of a prominent local family. Linares once claimed that he had "taken up" the revolution against the Anglos on behalf of his fellow Californios.[97] By the time that the two Frenchmen were gunned down in May by an outlaw band, however, Linares and his fellow gang leader, the Irish-born Jack Powers, had made many enemies amongst the region's Anglos and Mexicans.

On May 20, a mass meeting was held in San Luis Obispo and the new vigilance committee was unveiled to the public. It was led by an English-born veteran of the Mexican War named Walter Murray who was a local newspaperman and lawyer. Only two Mexicans agreed to join in this initial stage, but more soon signed on to the committee's rolls. One of the reasons that they did so was the effectiveness of the vigilantes in breaking up the outlaw gangs. From the very first day, they signaled that they meant to punish the outlaws with death. After organizing themselves, as they put it in their minutes, for the "repression and punishment of crime by all means," they passed a death sentence on Joaquin Valenzuela. He was, according to most accounts, innocent of the recent murders but was deemed guilty of past crimes. After a makeshift gallows was constructed, the vigilantes hanged him "in full sight of the whole people of San Luis, in broad daylight."[98]

After Valenzuela's execution, the vigilantes began raising monies that would be needed for reward notices and other expenses likely to be incurred in an extended campaign against the outlaws. They also began posting notices in Spanish addressed to "all horse runners" that warned them to "quit said business" and leave the country within twenty days "under penalty of death." The notices were posted in San Luis Obispo and Santa Margarita, and they were personally delivered to four individuals.[99] The highly organized campaign exacted swift justice in the coming weeks. During May and June, vigilantes or posses hanged or shot eight more men connected to Linares's outlaw gang.[100]

One of the reasons that the vigilantes were so successful is that they were able to slowly win the support of some of the region's Mexican population. Many of the best trackers and riders in coastal California were Mexicans who had for many years given little aid to Anglos in their searches for Mexican outlaws. In 1858, something changed. Numerous Mexicans signed on to the vigilance committee and donated money to the organization's coffers. Most importantly, state senator Romualdo Pacheco led a posse of Mexicans in pursuit of some of the gang, chasing some of them all the way to Los Angeles. There, Pacheco captured Nieves Robles and sent him back to San Luis Obispo on a steamer. He was taken from the ship and soon hanged by the vigilantes.

The motivations behind the participation of Pacheco and the other Mexicans who participated in the vigilance committee's work were no doubt complex. Law-abiding citizens with significant holdings in the region, they stood to benefit from the stability likely to emerge from the end of Linares and his gang. By 1858, Pacheco had a solid foundation in the political Mexican community but was also connected with Anglo politicians and leaders. According to one account, Pacheco's involvement with the vigilantes was spurred by an editorial in an Anglo newspaper that was critical of Californios for not doing more to put down the lawlessness. In any event, Pacheco's actions on behalf of the vigilantes no doubt won him support among the Anglo population. He was later appointed a brigadier general in the Union Army, served a brief term as California's twelfth governor, and was elected to the US House of Representatives in 1878 and again in 1880.[101]

Pacheco and his fellow Californios on the San Luis Obispo vigilance committee likely remained exceptions among the mass of Mexicans in California. According to two local historians of San Luis Obispo, the "majority of the native Californians either resented or resisted punishing the criminals." The vigilance committee was forced to use extralegal violence because, even with the aid of Pacheco and his Mexican allies, they could not be certain of convictions in the courts.[102] Thus, the vigilantes of San Luis Obispo might have been an interracial force, but they did not represent the will of the Mexican people of San Luis Obispo, a community that was obviously divided on what to do with Mexican outlaws who preyed on Anglos.

California was not the only place in the American Southwest where Mexicans lynched, or helped to lynch, other Mexicans. There are cases in every state, but New Mexico saw a much higher percentage of intraracial Mexican lynchings than any other state or territory in the American West.

The prevalence of such activity in New Mexico can only be understood in the broader context of racial and ethnic relations in the state, in particular the process of cultural and political accommodation between the state's Anglo and Nuevomexicano elites. Anglos initially settled New Mexico in small numbers. As late as 1900, there were only fifty thousand Anglos in the territory, compared with one hundred twenty-five thousand Nuevomexicanos. As a result, many early pioneers intermarried with the Nuevomexicano population, accounting by 1870 for ninety percent of the married Anglo men in Las Cruces; eighty-three percent in Mesilla; and seventy-eight percent in Doña Ana. This cultural interaction muted racial and ethnic tensions between the two peoples. The overwhelming size of the Nuevomexicano population also constrained Anglos from assuming hegemonic control of the political system. While Mexicans in many areas of the southwestern states were effectively disfranchised, the Nuevomexicano elite in New Mexico wielded political power on a scale unparalleled in any other part of the Southwestern Borderlands. Although Anglos attained control of the territorial legislature in 1886, Nuevomexicanos continued to hold elected office at all levels of government. As late as 1909, Nuevomexicanos constituted eleven of the twenty-one representatives in the New Mexico House. Four Nuevomexicanos also served as governor before 1920: Donaciano Vigil (1847–48), Miguel Otero (1897–1906), Ezequiel Cabeza de Baca (1918), and Octaviano Larrazolo (1918–19). A similar arrangement of "racial power sharing" operated within the criminal justice system. While Anglos monopolized the most eminent positions within the legal hierarchy, Nuevomexicanos controlled important elected offices such as sheriff. The active participation of Nuevomexicanos in the political and legal systems protected against the unrestrained power of Anglos and promoted racial and ethnic cooperation over conflict. As historian Charles Montgomery affirms, Anglos and Nuevomexicanos were "locked in a precarious balance of power, a sometimes cooperative though always suspicious relationship that redounded to all levels of New Mexico society."[103]

The ties between the Anglo and Nuevomexicano elites were strengthened during the campaign to attain statehood for New Mexico. New Mexico remained a territory under federal jurisdiction until 1912. Congressional opposition to statehood rested on the racist assumption that only a white majority population could be entrusted with the responsibility of self-government. One pamphlet distributed in Santa Fe argued that the "Territory should not be admitted as a State because the majority of its inhabitants" were "catholic" and a "mixture of peons and Indians" and therefore "a people unworthy to live in the great American Republic."[104] The Nuevomexicano elite attempted to establish their claim to a white racial identity and the political privileges that this bestowed by calling themselves "Spanish Americans," a name that invoked their common European heritage with Anglos. The Anglo elite supported Nuevomexicanos in their assertion of whiteness since it represented the best strategy of securing statehood (while simultaneously validating the whiteness of their wives and children). Finally, but perhaps most importantly, the Nuevomexicano elite and the Anglo elite were often joined by mutual class interests, since they were property owners amidst a mass of landless shepherds and itinerant ranch hands. In this and other respects, the elites shared common class and political interests that transcended ethnic antagonism.[105]

The cultural, political, and economic interaction between Anglo and Nuevomexicano elites impacted the pattern of mob violence in New Mexico. Lynching protected the economic interests of the propertied classes, both Anglo and Nuevomexicano. The Nuevomexicano elite consciously distinguished itself from the majority Mexican population and was prepared to orchestrate acts of mob violence in defense of its socially and economically privileged status. In 1893, for instance, Cecilio Lucero, a member of a notorious gang, was arrested in Las Vegas for the murder of a ranch hand who had caught him stealing sheep. Members of the community seized Lucero from his prison cell and hanged him. According to the *Las Vegas Optic*, the "mob was said to number 1000 with 900 being Hispanic."[106] Although Mexican mobs lynched Mexicans in other parts of the Southwest Borderlands, such intra-ethnic violence was far more common in New Mexico.[107]

Alliances between Anglos and Mexicans were particularly strong in New Mexico in large part because of the territory's majority Mexican population. Yet, in other states of the borderlands, Anglos and Mexicans also formed alliances based on similar grounds, especially mutual class and political interests. The widespread existence of such networks is a final contrast between the lynching of African Americans and the lynching of Mexicans. In the American South, legal segregation reinforced the line dividing white and black and held in check the kinds of fluidity that one sees in the history of mob violence against Mexicans in the American Southwest. The line between blacks and whites was not impassable, as numerous historians have suggested. Yet, the contrast with Anglos and Mexicans is a reminder of just how different the African American experience was in the United States.

Nothing illustrates these differences better than the numerous episodes in which Mexicans, by themselves or with the aid of Anglos, lynched other Anglos. In California, on January 27, 1854, a mob of Mexicans with the approval of local Anglos hanged a man named Brown for murder. According to a newspaper's account, Brown requested that he be hanged by "white men," but his request was refused.[108] Three years later, an Anglo man named Dean was hanged by a presumed Mexican mob after the fatal shooting of a seventeen-year-old Mexican boy.[109] In 1870, a mob of thirty Mexicans seized an Anglo man named Gray for shooting and killing an unarmed Mexican named Jesus Cordova. The Mexican mob hanged Gray and then, seemingly, escaped legal punishment for doing so.[110] That Mexicans in the American West, on multiple occasions, lynched Anglos for crimes against Mexicans without producing a strong reaction from other Anglos in the region testifies to the complex character of the lynching in the American West.[111]

Even stronger evidence that the history of Mexicans and lynching defies simple categorization comes from the number of cases of Anglo mobs lynching Anglos for committing crimes against Mexicans. In 1854, in Laredo, Texas, US soldiers hanged and then mutilated the corpse of an Anglo doctor for the murder of Pedro Carera, the Mexican bandmaster of their regiment.[112] In 1863, in San Antonio, a vigilance committee led by Asa Mitchell lynched Ben Franks who was alleged to have robbed three Mexicans, killing one of them in the process.[113] While there are a few cases of white mobs lynching whites for crimes against African Americans, these cases are powerful evidence that mob violence against Mexicans followed its own particular dynamics and forms.

The lynching of white men by white mobs for the killing of Mexicans is an important story that underscores the great variations that took place in the practice of vigilantism and lynching in the United States, but such episodes were rare exceptions. Most Anglos in the American Southwest cared very little for the welfare of Mexicans in the United States. They made no effort whatsoever to protect Mexicans from mob violence, to investigate the actions of lynchers, or to hold mob leaders accountable. Instead, they willfully ignored or cruelly celebrated the mob violence that led Mexicans to be expelled from their own lands, to be stripped of their property, and to be killed without trial or legal process.

Mexicans understood very soon, some even before the ink had dried on the Treaty of Guadalupe Hidalgo, that Anglos in the West would neither abide by nor live up to the protections guaranteed in that document. This realization led many Mexicans to conclude that effective resistance to anti-Mexican mob violence would not come from Anglos at any level—local, state, or federal. Instead, aggrieved Mexicans devised, with varying results, their own strategies of resistance against Anglo discrimination and violence. Most dramatically, some would turn to self-defense, meeting violence with violence.

3

Mexican Resistance to Mob Violence

ANGLOS' RELIANCE ON violence to consolidate their social and economic power demonstrates that their domination of Mexicans was a continual process of struggle. Moreover, while mob brutalities may have facilitated Anglo control of the region, they also fostered further acts of resistance from Mexicans. While Mexicans endured widespread repression they were not the passive victims of Anglo violence. On the contrary, they implemented numerous strategies to counteract the incursions of the mob. These measures occurred both within and without the institutional framework of government and the law, ranging from the lobbying of public opinion and promotion of legislative reform to armed self-defense and retaliatory violence. What follows is an analysis of the strengths and limitations of the diverse ways in which Mexicans resisted Anglo intimidation and extralegal violence. Although Mexican defiance of mob rule had a definite impact on Anglos it was neither consistent across time nor always to the positive advancement of relations between the two peoples. Occasionally, these acts of resistance succeeded in securing redress for specific crimes committed by Anglos. Yet at other times, they had the unforeseen consequence of ensnaring Mexicans in a seemingly endless cycle of violence and retribution. Ultimately, what Mexicans in the United States were unable to accomplish was the creation of a coordinated campaign to combat the broader regional phenomenon of mob violence.

Anglo Opposition to Mob Violence

Mexican resistance to Anglo mob violence was not a straightforward story of an oppressed people heroically defending themselves against tyrannical adversaries. Relations between Anglos and Mexicans were more fluid and complex than such a dichotomy will allow. Throughout the nineteenth and early twentieth centuries there were Anglos who contested the use of mob violence as a means to enforce their racial dominion over the American

West. Despite sharing a common belief in the manifest destiny of the
Anglo-Saxon race to conquer the region, they opposed the brutal means by
which some of their fellow settlers dispossessed and displaced the indigenous Mexican population. In 1853, prospector Andrew Stone wrote home
to his parents that the atrocities perpetrated in the gold mining region of
California "are mostly committed by people calling themselves enlightened Americans. You mentioned me to keep away from Indians, but I
should feel myself more safe with them than with a large portion that call
themselves Americans for in fact they are not one smite better than the
fiends of Hell."[1]

Mob violence against Mexicans not only stirred the consciences of
individual prospectors such as Stone, but also encouraged collective
action against those who used force to press their claims to the mines.
Miners meeting at Roger's Bar on the Tuolumne River in August 1850,
for instance, approved a resolution condemning the abuse and murder
of Mexicans. "Many persons of Spanish origin, against whom there had
not been a word of complaint, have been murdered by these ruffians,"
they declared. "Others have been robbed of their horses, mules, arms, and
even money, by these persons, while acting as they pretended under the
authority of the law."[2] Seven years later, the townspeople of Goliad in central Texas issued a similar resolution deploring the slaughter of as many
as seventy-five Mexican cart men by Anglo competitors envious of their
economic success.[3] Newspapers, particularly in the metropolitan areas of
the state, also denounced the murders. "Lynch law is a dangerous institution," declared the *Galveston Civilian*, "and we apprehend that this violence
towards Mexicans has been encouraged by the high-handed measures the
people of the West have lately thought necessary to adopt towards others.
Public laws and officers to enforce them are the best guarantees against
injustice and wrong in the long run."[4]

Editorials such as this illustrate the opposition of some elements of
the Anglo press to mob violence against Mexicans. It is true that many
Anglo newspapers acted as mouthpieces for lynch mobs. The editorial
pages of these publications portrayed vigilantes as righteous citizens who
assumed responsibility for protecting their communities from dangerous
outlaws in the face of an ineffectual criminal justice system. Although
their voices were more seldom heard, the dissenting opinion of some
Anglo newspapers did occasionally penetrate the protective walls erected
around the perpetrators of mob violence, as press reaction to the Texas
Cart War demonstrates.

In October 1859, the *Weekly Arizonian* reported the removal of a Mexican from a jail cell by a police constable and his accomplice who supposedly sought his help in tracking down the other members of a gang of horse thieves. The two men repeatedly shot their captive, stole his possessions, and sliced off his ears as souvenirs. According to the newspaper, the barbarous criminality of someone supposed to uphold the law warranted his hanging by the local citizenry.[5]

More astute newspaper editors understood that such vengeful measures served only to legitimate further acts of lawlessness. They encouraged greater respect for the due process of law as the means to liberate their communities from the otherwise endless cycle of violence and retribution. One publication that acted as the conscience of its community was the *Monterey Republican,* which in May 1870 published several outspoken editorials condemning a mob that lynched three Mexicans and other members of the community who conspired to conceal their identities. The more serious a crime of which a suspect was accused, asserted the paper, the greater the need for a formal court of law to prove conclusively their guilt. Those who preempted the decisions of the proper authorities surrendered any claim to the moral high ground. As the paper exclaimed, "Men who try to conceal their villainy behind a painted mask are no less murderers than those whom they pronounce and unauthorizedly punish as such and are legally as well as morally responsible. If the present offenders are not made an example of, who knows when their bloody programme will end."[6]

Anglo opposition to mob violence against Mexicans stemmed not only from a practical concern to promote law and order in frontier communities, but also personal relations between individuals who transcended the tribal animosities between the two peoples. White planters in the southern states, acting out of a sense of paternal responsibility or economic self-interest, sometimes shielded African American laborers from lynch mobs. The ties between individual Anglos and Mexicans similarly mitigated broader group hostilities. Anglos in numerous instances proved willing to protect Mexicans with whom they had developed personal or professional relationships from lynch mobs. In February 1855, residents of Islip's Ferry, a settlement on the shore of the Stanislaus River in California, arrested a Mexican on suspicion of harboring an escaped horse thief. An Anglo named A. F. Rudler, "knowing the Mexican to be a worthy man," convinced the deputy sheriff to help him "prevent the commission of violence." The two men succeeded in dissuading the mob from hanging their captive.[7]

The role of the deputy sheriff in averting violence demonstrates the pivotal role of law enforcement officers whose action or inaction often determined whether or not a lynching would take place. Although Anglo law enforcement officers in many instances colluded with lynch mobs, there were other occasions on which they resolutely discharged their duty to protect prisoners from vigilantes. One such incident occurred in September 1892 when San Antonio police increased protection of the city jail to prevent the lynching of Sixto Flores and Patricio Lopez, who were under arrest for the murder of two Anglo ranchers.[8] Some law enforcement officers pursued a more offensive policy against vigilantes, pursuing, capturing, and sometimes killing Anglos who victimized Mexicans. The Texas Rangers had a deserved reputation for administering the law with blatant racial partiality. Despite this discrimination, there were occasions when the Rangers forcefully repressed Anglo vigilantism. In May 1875, for instance, the Texas press praised Rangers for breaking up an Anglo gang that had murdered innocent Mexicans in retaliation for a bandit raid on Corpus Christi.[9] Even though such cases were exceptional, they emphasize the complexities of relations between Anglo authorities and Mexican citizens across time and place.

Anglo authorities also managed in rare instances to bring suspected mob leaders to trial. The racial prejudices of Anglo judges and juries stacked the odds against prosecutors securing conviction of a defendant accused of lynching a Mexican. Although the prospects of success were limited, Anglo authorities at least tried on occasion to use the power of law to punish lynchers. In February 1869, for instance, the *San Antonio Herald* reported the trial of vigilantes accused of lynching Mexicans for the murder of an Anglo family near Boerne, Texas. The outcome of the case is, however, unclear.[10]

A more fully documented case, although one that ultimately led to frustration for prosecutors, occurred six years later. On October 30, 1875, vigilantes in the New Mexico boomtown of Cimarron lynched Cruz Vega for the murder of itinerant Methodist minister Franklin J. Tolby. The incident dramatized the sadistic cruelty with which Anglos enforced rough justice on Mexicans. According to one description of the corpse left hanging on public display from a telegraph pole, "Clusters of hair torn from the scalp and other signs of torture were manifest."[11] The following day, armed Mexicans intent on revenge converged on the town. A relative of Vega named Francisco Griego confronted Clay

Allison, whom he accused of having led the mob. Allison, however, had a deserved reputation as a dangerous gunfighter. When Griego pulled a weapon on him, Allison responded by shooting his assailant dead. There was still more violence to come. On November 6, local authorities arrested Manuel Cardenas whom they charged as an accomplice of Vega in the murder of Reverend Tolby. As Cardenas reached the entrance of the county jail under armed escort, a gunman shot him in the head. Samuel Beech Axtell, the governor of the New Mexico Territory, declared Cimarron in a state of "riot and anarchy" and dispatched an armed force to restore order. However, the presence of African American soldiers within the ranks only inflamed racial hostilities further. Civilians murdered two black members of the militia before finally ceding control of the town.

Grand jury investigations of lynching routinely reached the conclusion that the victim had died at the hands of persons unknown. Nonetheless, in April 1877 a grand jury indicted Reverend Oscar P. McMains for the murder of Cruz Vega. The potential partiality of jurors persuaded state prosecutors to petition for the relocation of the trial outside of Colfax County. As a result, McMains appeared before a district court in neighboring Mora County on August 23.[12] McMains did not deny his involvement in the lynching but claimed his motivation was to uphold rather than to undermine civic order. "We are not a mob of lawless men, as has been reported abroad, bent upon violence and defiance of law," he proclaimed, "but on the contrary, have assembled legally and quietly for the purpose of securing the doings of justice and the punishment of crime."[13] Since the defendant had admitted his role in the lynching the jury could not legitimately acquit him. His eloquent defense nonetheless swayed them to find him guilty only of murder in the fifth degree, an offense for which the court fined him three hundred dollars. McMains ultimately escaped even this punishment when the judge, for reasons that remain unclear, granted a motion to set aside the verdict of the jury. Although he granted the prosecution a new trial, this was later dismissed on the grounds of lack of evidence. Given that McMains had admitted to leading the lynch mob, this ruling seems to contain more than a hint of corruption. Clay Allison also eluded the law. Although arrested for the murder of Francisco Griego, authorities later dropped the charge, ruling the shooting justifiable homicide.[14]

The limitations of the criminal justice system sometimes led Anglos intent on punishing lynchers to take the law into their own hands. The most dramatic expression of Anglo sympathy for Mexican victims of racial violence was the retributive murder of those who committed such crimes. A vigilante company in San Antonio hanged Bob Augustin for harassing local Mexican women in 1863, an incident that reveals some Anglo men believed it was not only their own womenfolk who possessed virtues and honor in need of protection.[15]

Stories such as this demonstrate the permeable nature of the color line in the American West. Yet despite the many and varied instances in which Anglos broke ranks by supporting Mexican victims of mob violence, such actions did not constitute a coordinated strategy of opposition. Ultimately, it was Mexicans themselves who on numerous fronts fought a sustained resistance to the tyranny of mob rule.

Armed Resistance

"It is evident from all that I can gather," declared a correspondent from Corpus Christi to the *Galveston News* in April 1875, "that these Mexicans have been goaded by the 'Gringos' until they are compelled in self-protection to arm and assemble."[16] Long after the cessation of war, Mexicans continued to resist Anglos' use of violence to enforce their dominion over the territories ceded under the Treaty of Guadalupe Hidalgo. The American Southwest remained a battleground between Anglo settlers and displaced Mexicans.

Mexicans were not exceptional in arming themselves against lynch mobs. African Americans used similar tactics to repel white vigilantes. "A Winchester rifle should have a place in every black house," asserted the crusading black journalist Ida B. Wells, "and it should be used for that protection which the law refuses to give." Other African American editors, among them John Mitchell of the *Richmond Planet* and T. Thomas Fortune of the *New York Globe*, similarly advocated armed self-defense as not just a right but also a duty of blacks confronted by the persistent threat of mob violence.[17] African Americans did often act on this instruction, establishing a tradition of armed defense later built on by the radical protests of the Black Power era. Most dramatically, blacks sometimes organized militia groups to safeguard against lynch mobs attempting to seize prison inmates from their cells. Such incidents not only saved lives but also set an inspirational example for other African Americans.[18] Armed responses were nonetheless uncommon since the superior resources of whites allowed them to exact extreme retaliation. Although African

Americans were not the passive victims of mob violence, the risk of white reprisal led them for the most part to pursue more covert forms of resistance to the lynch mob.[19]

In contrast to African Americans, Mexicans engaged more frequently and forcefully in acts of armed resistance. African Americans may have harbored fantasies of revenge against white lynch mobs, but Mexicans actually succeeded in several instances in exacting murderous retribution.

Numerous factors account for Mexicans' engagement in direct confrontation with Anglo vigilantes. The code of masculine honor that was an intrinsic element of Mexican culture impelled many men to respond reciprocally to Anglo violence. Mexicans in the Southwest who were not citizens of the United States may not have always known how to file proper criminal complaints with local authorities. Those who did might in any case have recognized the futility of relying on conventional legal channels because of the indifference or hostility of Anglo officials.[20]

Mexicans also possessed numerous advantages over African Americans that facilitated armed challenges to Anglo mobs. The sparse settlement of many areas of the Southwest made it relatively easy compared to the more densely populated South for Mexicans to elude pursuit by law officers and citizens' posses, an advantage made all the greater by the opportunity for escape across the border. In much of the Southwest—including the southern regions of Arizona and Texas and most of New Mexico—Mexicans also outnumbered Anglos. Anglo control of these areas relied on the cultivation of cordial relations with Mexicans. Retaliation against armed resistance risked escalation into a race war in which Mexicans would hold the advantage of superior numbers.

In addition to these factors, Mexicans not only had more access to firearms than African Americans but the existence of an economically independent middle and upper class within their community also provided superior resources and opportunity to organize resistance. Anglos on occasion learned the tactical error of using force against a local Mexican population that possessed superior numbers and resources. During the early 1850s, for instance, rancheros José del Carmen Lugo and Andres Pico restrained an Anglo gang terrorizing Mexicans in El Monte, California, by threatening to retaliate by burning the town to the ground.[21] An incident in Rio Grande City similarly demonstrates the potential power of Mexicans acting on their retaliatory instincts. In July 1888, Mexican political dissident Catarino Garza published an article in his newspaper

El Comercio Mexicano accusing customs inspector Victor Sebree of murdering Abraham Reséndez, a criminal suspect in his custody. An incensed
Sebree responded by shooting and wounding his accuser. Local Mexicans
threatened to lynch Sebree, pursuing him to Fort Ringgold where he had
fled for protection. Despite distorted news stories of a riot, the mob complied with an order to disperse.[22]

Mexicans retaliated against not only vigilantes, but also against law
enforcement officers who abused their authority. In July 1856, Los Angeles
Deputy William Jenkins shot dead a Mexican named Antonio Ruiz while
attempting to execute a writ. Newspaper reports affirmed that Jenkins
had fired at Ruiz even though he offered no resistance. Despite Jenkins'
apparent guilt, his position as a law enforcement officer guaranteed his
protection by the criminal justice system. Local authorities placed him
under arrest but imposed no restrictions on his freedom of movement.
Prosecutors also charged him with manslaughter rather than murder but
failed to secure a conviction even for this lesser offense. The local Mexican
community reacted with outrage. Following a public meeting at the
funeral of Ruiz, more than two hundred Mexicans assembled on horse-
back for an assault on Los Angeles' Anglos. An initial skirmish resulted in
one of the city marshals suffering a gunshot wound. Tensions eased only
after local authorities recruited armed support from surrounding communities. Anglos subsequently formed a vigilance committee to safeguard
against further insurrection.[23]

The formation of the committee demonstrated a refusal on the part
of Anglos to accept that Mexicans had legitimate grievances. In many
instances, this disdain of Mexican dissent only fuelled further discontent.
In February 1857, a mob seized a suspected murderer named Anastacio
García from a jail cell in Monterey and hanged him. According to the
Alta California, such was "the rancor that has grown up between the
lower classes of Californios and our people that the former bitterly complain if one of their number is subjected to punishment, however much
they have deserved its infliction." Although the editorial conceded that
Anglos were in part culpable for the mutual animosity and mistrust
between themselves and Mexicans, it can only have compounded these
problems by claiming that a man who had never stood trial was a guilty
criminal who warranted hanging by vigilantes. Even if local Mexicans
knew that García had committed murder, their anger at his lynching
still demonstrated a greater adherence to due process of law than the
Anglo press.[24]

Although the rage over the lynching of Anastacio García did not spill into violence, it was inevitable that Mexicans would eventually avenge the victims of mob savagery. In some instances, they succeeded in hunting down and executing the perpetrators.[25] For example, in April 1861, Anglos in Mesilla, New Mexico, hanged a Mexican accused of theft. Ygnacio Orrantis, a local alcade, led public protests at the lynching. When Anglo authorities ignored these remonstrations, members of the Mexican community decided to take the law into their own hands, tracking down and shooting those they believed responsible for the hanging. According to the local newspaper, "The circumstances connected with this terrible affair are such as to leave no doubts in the mind of our citizens that the foul deed was committed by Mexicans from this place to avenge the death of the thief." Far from casting doubts on the merits of mob law, the retaliatory action taken by Mexicans seems only to have strengthened Anglos' faith in the moral integrity of the lynchers.[26]

Mexicans intent on retribution were not always able to locate those responsible for committing a lynching. In such cases, they sometimes settled for dispensing their own summary justice on any Anglo who committed a crime against their community. The latter form of reprisal occurred in Rio Grande City during June 1856 following the lynching of an accused Mexican thief and his Anglo accomplice. Mexicans on the other side of the border struck back by hanging a gang of Anglos charged with horse stealing.[27] Acts of revenge such as this that Mexicans directed against any or all Anglos included assaults on property as well as persons. In May 1870, a mob snatched three Mexicans charged with the murder of a local tanner from a jail in Watsonville, California, and hanged them over the side of a railroad bridge spanning the Palero River. The lynching met with widespread approval among Anglo townspeople, including an editorial in the local newspaper that avowed, "the three greasers found hanging to the bridge deserved all they got." Such was also the attitude of friends and relatives of the victims toward the lynch mob. Some months after the lynching, a local hotel burned to the ground. A second blaze two weeks later destroyed six buildings. Anglos concluded that the fires were the work of Mexican arsonists. "It is well known," commented the Watsonville newspaper, "that the friends of the men hung at the bridge uttered threats of vengeance against the entire community."[28]

The Watsonville lynching was the work of the Pajaro Property Protective Society, a vigilante group founded under the leadership of Matt Tarpy. Tarpy had been engaged in longstanding conflict with local Mexicans since his involvement in the lynching of a suspected horse thief in the late 1850s. Hostilities intensified further in the years that followed as he led mobs that murdered fifteen Mexicans and Indians. Although local Anglos perceived Tarpy as dutifully defending their property rights against the criminal advances of other races, they finally turned against him in March 1873 when he shot dead a white woman in a property dispute. After Tarpy turned himself in to local authorities, a mob seized the prisoner from his cell and hanged him. What distinguished the incident from most other lynchings was the interracial composition of the crowd. Mexicans not only participated with Anglos in hanging Tarpy but the honor of tying the noose around his neck was also bestowed to one of their number. The incident further demonstrates that when mob violence afflicted all elements of a community, Anglos and Mexicans could temporarily set aside their differences to combat a common enemy.[29]

Mexicans armed themselves not only to avenge victims of mob violence but also to avert further assaults from Anglos. In December 1914, a force of 150 Mexicans assaulted a jail in Oakville, Texas, after learning that law enforcement officers intended to hand over two inmates to a lynch mob. They were able to protect one of the men, Francisco Sánchez, but not his associate, Ysidro Gónzález. More successfully, in March 1925, a band of seventy-five armed Mexicans surrounded a jail in Elko, Nevada, to protect Guadalupe Acosta from a mob intent on lynching him for the murder of a local police officer.[30]

Those responsible for committing acts of armed retaliation against lynch mobs were usually the friends and relatives of the victims. Retributive action nonetheless eventually spread far beyond the immediate localities in which lynchings occurred. Fostered by widespread media coverage, mob violence against Mexican nationals in the United States by the early twentieth century became a focus of mounting anti-Americanism in Mexico. One particular incident, the lynching of Antonio Rodríguez in Rocksprings, Texas, in November 1910, sparked assaults on American entrepreneurs and their commercial properties nationwide. This included the shooting dead of an American civil engineer named James Reid by a police officer in Mexico City "who sought, by taking the life of an American, to avenge the burning of Antonio Rodríguez by a mob in Texas."[31] Localized acts of resistance may have allowed Mexicans to settle scores with Anglo vigilantes but had no repercussions for federal government policy on mob violence. When such confrontation reached a scale that threatened the millions of American dollars invested in Mexico, Washington would have to intervene.

Social Banditry

Most acts of armed resistance by Mexicans against Anglos were localized and ephemeral. Once the perpetrators had accomplished their purpose to correct an abuse of justice, their forces dispersed and community order returned. Yet occasionally the cumulative impact of white violence stirred such bitter resentment as to incite a larger and longer-term counteroffensive. The most infamous exponents of armed retaliation against Anglos were the outlaw leaders who aroused fear and hatred among their adversaries at the same time as hope and pride in the hearts of their fellow Mexicans. Disparaged as unscrupulous criminals by the dominant Anglo culture, they were celebrated within the Mexican community as courageous champions of the poor and oppressed. In contrast to criminals motivated solely by the desire for self-gain, the actions of such "social bandits" were seen as a form of social and political protest. Far from being wanton acts of criminality, the depredations committed by Mexican brigands were conscious acts of retaliation against Anglos for the injustices they committed. Villains to their Anglo adversaries, they were heroes to Mexicans who aided and abetted them in eluding the clutches of the law.[32]

The most notorious Mexican bandit was Joaquín Murieta. While the numerous accounts of his life contain many discrepancies, there are core elements common to all. Murieta was one of the thousands of Mexicans lured to California by the prospect of discovering gold. Although cordial toward Anglos he suffered numerous injuries at their hands. Forcibly displaced from his claim, he attempted to establish an honest trade around the camps as a merchant, only to be accused of horse theft and severely whipped. Their ire unabated, his assailants then hanged his half-brother and raped his wife. And so a decent but downtrodden man turned to violence. Murieta swore revenge against Anglos not only for the cruelties he had suffered but all the injustices inflicted on Mexicans in the gold mines.[33]

During the early 1850s Murieta led a gang that menaced Anglos, plundering ranches and mining camps, and murdering their occupants. Reacting to public pressure, California governor John Bigler on May 17, 1853, approved "An Act to authorize the Raising of a Company of Rangers" under the command of Captain Harry Love. A little more than two months later, on July 25, the Rangers confronted Murieta at his camp on the Arroyo Cantúa, situated near the Coast Range Mountains on the Tulare plains. The Rangers shot dead Murieta and three members of his gang.

As evidence that they had captured and killed the outlaw they severed his head and the hand of his accomplice Three-Fingered Jack and preserved them in alcohol for public display.[34]

Memories of Joaquín Murieta were still raw in the minds of many Anglo Californians when another Mexican outlaw leader struck renewed outrage and terror. Tiburcio Vásquez was born on April 10, 1835, into a respectable middle-class family in Monterey, California. He became embroiled in crime while still in his teens, having fallen under the influence of an outlaw named Anastacio García. In September 1854, the two men were involved in a saloon fight that led to the death of Constable William Hardmount. Although they fled from the scene of the incident, a mob captured and lynched their associate José Higuera. García eventually suffered the same fate when in February 1857 vigilantes seized the former fugitive from a jail cell following his arrest and hanged him, an incident reputed to have intensified the hatred Vásquez felt for Anglos. Vásquez himself eluded the law until August 1857 when the authorities arrested and convicted him for horse theft. Sentenced to five years in San Quentin State Prison, he escaped in June 1859 and remained on the loose for two months. Refusing to recognize the legitimacy of his incarceration, Vásquez attempted three further prison breaks before his formal release in August 1863. Despite seeking employment as a livestock herder, he soon resumed his criminal activities. Convicted of theft, he served a further term in San Quentin between January 1867 and June 1870. This second experience of prison proved no more effective than the first in rehabilitating him. Following his release he returned to crime with renewed audacity. During the next several years he attained widespread notoriety as the leader of an outlaw gang that executed a series of daring bank heists and stagecoach robberies. By 1874, state authorities offered a reward of eight thousand dollars for his capture alive. Vásquez for months frustrated the many posses on his trail but finally suffered capture at Rancho La Brea near Los Angeles on May 13, 1874. A court in San Jose found him guilty of murder and sentenced him to death. Following the failure of an appeal for clemency, on March 19, 1875, authorities carried out the execution of their calmly composed prisoner.[35]

California was not the only western state where racial conflict between Anglos and Mexicans gave rise to coordinated acts of armed resistance. The most powerful symbol of militant opposition to Anglo power in Texas was Juan Cortina, leader of an armed force of between four hundred and five hundred men that threatened revolution in the borderlands.

Juan Nepomuceno Cortina was born into an aristocratic family in Camargo, in the Mexican state of Tamaulipas, on May 16, 1824. Having served as a cavalryman during the US-Mexican War, he settled in the Lower Rio Grande Valley, managing some of his family's extensive ranch lands and participating actively in local politics. Cortina came into repeated conflict with Anglos. Disputes over land grants led to the loss of a substantial share of the family estate. Friction with other ranchers also led on two separate occasions to his indictment for horse theft.[36]

On July 13, 1859, Cortina witnessed an event that would change his life. When a drunken Mexican resisted arrest by Brownsville city marshal Robert Spears, the incensed law enforcement officer beat him repeatedly over the head with a pistol. Cortina, recognizing the Mexican as a former employee on his family ranch, attempted to intervene. When Spears refused to heed his warning gunshot, Cortina fired a second bullet that wounded the city marshal in the shoulder. He then rode off with the Mexican he had rescued across the border to the safety of Matamoros. Cortina later attempted to compensate Spears for his injury, but the two men could not settle on an appropriate sum.[37]

Escalating tensions between Cortina and Brownsville authorities culminated in a violent confrontation. On September 28, 1859, a band of armed horsemen under the command of Cortina stormed into Brownsville, shattering the predawn calm with the cry "Mueran los Gringos! Viva la República Mexicana!" The raiders caused chaos, looting stores and liberating inmates from the city jail. Most dramatically, they hunted down Anglos who they accused of murdering Mexicans "and in the most brutal and ruthless manner began to shoot them down and in several instances to mutilate their persons in a most beastly manner."[38]

Cortina maintained his occupation of the town for more than forty-eight hours until persuaded to leave by a delegation of dignitaries from Matamoros led by his friend General José María Carbajal. Fearful of a renewed assault, Brownsville leaders formed a Committee of Safety that wrote to Governor Hardin Runnells requesting armed support. While the townspeople awaited word of reinforcements, barricades went up across the streets and were watched over day and night by an armed guard.[39]

The restoration of order proved short-lived. On October 12, a posse led by Sheriff James Browne captured Tomás Cabrera, a close associate of Cortina involved in the Brownsville raid. When local authorities received a threat from Cortina that he would burn the town to the ground unless they released Cabrera, they responded by establishing a militia named

the Brownsville Tigers. On October 25, the Tigers launched an assault on
Rancho del Carmen, only to be routed by Cortina and the rapidly growing army under his command. Relations between Anglos and Mexicans
deteriorated further with the arrival in Brownsville of Texas Rangers
led by Captain William G. Tobin. On November 13, the Rangers incited
a mob to seize Cabrera from his prison cell and lynch him in the market square. When word reached Cortina of what had happened, he retaliated by hanging three Anglo captives. Several days later, the Cortinistas
engaged the Rangers in a gun battle, killing three of them and wounding
four others.[40]

State authorities responded by dispatching a second company of
Rangers under the command of John Salmon Ford. Further reinforcements in the form of 165 troops led by Major Samuel P. Heintzelman
arrived in Brownsville on December 6. Having carefully accumulated
as much information on Cortina as he could, Heintzelman engaged his
adversary in conflict for the first time on December 15, inflicting heavy
casualties that forced the rebels into retreat upriver. Heintzelman scored
an even more decisive victory on December 27 when his forces overran
their opponents' camp outside Rio Grande City, slaughtering large numbers of Cortinistas and forcing the survivors into flight across the river to
Mexico. Sporadic fighting continued for a month. Cortina emerged from
hiding to launch an attack on the Rancho La Bolsa on February 4, 1860,
but endured another crushing defeat. He remained at his retreat in the
Burgos Mountains of Mexico until May 1861, by which time Texas had
joined the Confederacy. Cortina launched a failed effort in support of the
Union cause to capture the town of Carrizo in Zapata County. Cortina
remained active in border politics but, despite a renewed series of raids in
1870, never again posed a serious threat to Anglos. Under pressure from
the United States, Mexican authorities ordered his arrest for revolutionary
activities in 1875 and he died in prison on October 30, 1894.[41]

Although the initial catalyst for Cortina's rebellion was a desire to settle
a score with the city marshal who mistreated one of his former employees, Cortina, more than any other Mexican leader of armed insurrection,
consciously embraced the role of avenging the injustices inflicted on his
people. Two days after his occupation of Brownsville, he issued a proclamation of his intention to secure justice for oppressed Mexicans. "All
has been but the baseless fabric of a dream, and our hopes having been
defrauded in the most cruel manner in which disappointment can strike,
there can be found no other solution to our problem than to make one

effort, and at one blow destroy the obstacles to our prosperity."[42] In a second proclamation of November 23, 1859, Cortina emphasized his moral purpose by portraying himself as an earthly instrument of divine retribution against sinful Anglos. "Mexicans! My part is taken; the voice of revelation whispers to me that to me is entrusted the work of breaking the chains of your slavery, and that the Lord will enable me, with powerful arm, to fight against our enemies, in compliance with the requirements of that Sovereign Majesty, who, from this day forward, will hold us under His protection."[43] This promise of salvation, not simply in the next life but the here and now, made Cortina an irresistible magnet to Tejanos desperate for greater self-determination. As Texas Ranger John Ford put it, "to the poor who heard him, Cortina was a sign of hope in a land where hope heretofore had no meaning."[44]

Although Cortina fulfils the ideals of the social bandit, the same cannot be said of all the Mexican outlaw leaders valorized as folk heroes. To Mexicans who knew him only by reputation, Vásquez may have been a folk hero but closer scrutiny reveals that he was an equal opportunities criminal who committed depredations not only against Anglos but also his own people. Although Vásquez claimed the animating impulse for his crimes was "A spirit of revenge and hatred" against Anglos, none of his later declarations, including a last statement of contrition written while awaiting execution, articulate a desire to secure justice for oppressed Mexicans.[45] Whatever his motivations, Vásquez was at least a man made of flesh and bone, which is more than can be said of Joaquín Murieta.[46] "Joaquín Murieta" was a composite character created in the fevered imaginations of Anglos fearful of the many robberies and murders committed in the California diggings during the early 1850s. The identity of this outlaw was so nebulously defined that the act authorizing creation of a company of rangers named no less than five different gang leaders who shared the same forename, none of whom the press believed to be the notorious outlaw. Moreover, there is no substantial evidence that any of these outlaws acted out of a desire to defend their fellow Mexicans from murderous Anglo gold seekers.[47]

Yet the lived experience of Tiburcio Vásquez and Joaquín Murieta is in many respects less important than their symbolic meaning. What their fellow Mexicans believed them to be was more important than what they actually were. Confronted by the relentless assertion of Anglo supremacy, Mexicans found solace and inspiration in stories of courageous men engaged in defiant acts of guerrilla fighting. As Manuel Gonzales so aptly puts it, the elevation of even undeserving bandit leaders to the status of folk heroes addressed "a psychic need" on the part of Mexicans, providing a brutally repressed people with a sustaining source of empowerment.[48]

The reason why the myth of Joaquín Murieta resonated so strongly in the imaginations of many Mexicans was that they could identify both with his victimization and with his thirst for revenge. Anglos imposed control of the California gold mines by robbing, beating, and murdering their Mexican competitors. In this sense, there were not only "five Joaquíns" but hundreds if not thousands of them, men wishing to strike back against the Anglos who had forcibly displaced them from the land where thought they would secure their fortunes. As a contemporary newspaper report asserted, "when the object of their longing desire is snatched away when almost within their reach" it was no wonder that many formerly "peaceful and industrious" miners turned to "rapine and murder." Mexicans who fled without fight from the mines could also take a vicarious pleasure in the stories of Murieta exacting his vengeance on greedy and aggressive Anglos. Those unable to defend themselves fulfilled their fantasies of revenge by placing their faith in a daring champion of the poor and oppressed.[49]

The daring actions of outlaw leaders may have psychologically empowered Mexicans, but in practical terms they proved counterproductive. Far from stemming the tide of Anglo violence, they unleashed a relentless torrent. Anglo authorities utilized the full enforcement power of the law in response to these raids, beating, arresting, and murdering suspected criminals and their supposed accomplices.[50]

Whatever the reality behind the myth of Joaquín Murieta, Anglos exacted brutal retribution on Mexicans whom they suspected of being members of the gang that terrorized their communities. This occurred, for instance, following a bandit attack on the Phoenix Mill in Calaveras County in January 1853. Anglos attributed the incident to Murieta and organized a posse in pursuit of the outlaw. The vigilantes captured one of the gang members who they identified from a gunshot wound inflicted during the raid and returned him to their settlement, where he was "disposed of by the enraged people." Within a week Anglos had captured and hanged two more suspected bandits. The following month a posse also lynched a Mexican at San Andreas who they accused of providing shelter for the gang and stabling their horses. Although newspapers reported that the Mexican confessed to his criminal association, there is certainly a possibility that he made the declaration under duress. The reaction to the raid on the Phoenix Mill also demonstrates how a climate of escalating paranoia led Anglos to turn on innocent Mexicans who had no connection with the outlaws but were believed to be furtively abetting them. At a mass meeting in Double Springs on January 23, 1853, Anglo miners "resolved to burn the habitations of the Mexicans indiscriminately, deprive them of the arms they might have in possession, and give them all notice to quit."[51]

The raids launched by Juan Cortina likewise provoked arbitrary acts of retaliation against Mexicans in south Texas. Although Anglos were right to suspect many Mexicans in the Rio Grande Valley of supporting the Cortinistas, they reacted to the raiders with indiscriminate acts of violence. By his own admission, the forces commanded by Major Samuel P. Heintzelman executed a scorched earth policy in pursuit of Cortina, systematically burning to the ground every Mexican home or ranch they encountered. A Mexican investigative committee documented how Tejanos, regardless of whether they had any connection with the Cortinas, were "murdered without pity, their families compelled to fly and their property stolen."[52] Following the clash between the forces led by Cortina and Heintzelman at Rio Grande City, for instance, three Mexicans suspected of supporting the insurrectionists were taken under armed escort to Brownsville and hanged, their bodies left on public display as a warning.[53] In an effort to preempt the spread of Cortina's influence, Anglos far from Brownsville also launched crackdowns on their local Mexican communities. An order issued in Corpus Christi required all Mexicans who were not residents to declare themselves to the authorities who then appropriated any weapons in their possession.[54]

Nor were Anglos the only victims of the violence inflicted by the Cortinistas. During their initial raid on Brownsville, they murdered a Mexican named Viviano García for refusing to surrender the jailer R. L. Johnson, who had sought refuge in his home.[55] Cortina later expressed remorse over the incident and his army subsequently does not appear to have targeted other Mexicans. This did not, however, prevent many victims from being caught in the crossfire during their gunfights with Anglo forces.[56]

Whatever the shortcomings of armed struggle, it represented to many Mexicans who had little or no access to other resources the only means by which to restore their political agency and redress the violent attacks committed against their people. The privileged position of middle-class Mexicans, however, provided them with greater social, material, and political capital that enabled them to pursue alternate forms of resistance.

The Pen as a Political Weapon

During the late nineteenth and early twentieth centuries, Mexican journalists both individually and collectively voiced some of the most trenchant
and persistent political protest of Anglo mob violence. With some honorable exceptions, English-language newspapers in the American West
responded to the lynching of Mexicans either by excluding coverage from
their pages or, when such incidents were already public knowledge, exonerating the actions of the mob. A cluster of crusading Spanish-language
newspapermen reacted to the complicity of the mainstream media, producing stories and editorials that exposed mob violence to the public glare
and thereby pressured the authorities to take more interventionist action
to protect the rights and lives of Mexican citizens. The impact of their journalism in stemming Anglo aggression is difficult to assess, but their determined criticism provided an important counternarrative to mainstream
media representations of mob violence. Several of these newspapermen
were also pioneers of organized protest against lynching, founding pro-
to-civil rights groups that attempted, often in the face of hostile opposition, to protect and promote the interests of oppressed Mexicans.

The pioneer Mexican activist journalist was Francisco P. Ramírez.
Born in Los Angeles on February 9, 1837, he embarked on his career
at the age of fourteen. Having initially worked as a compositor for the
Los Angeles Star, he pursued a circular route that took him to the offices
of the *Catholic Standard* in San Francisco and from there to the *California
Express* in Marysville before returning to his original employer as editor
of its Spanish-language section. In 1855, still shy of his eighteenth birth-
day, he established his own newspaper, *El Clamor Público* (The Public
Outcry).[57] An ardent liberal advocate of equal rights, Ramírez championed the cause not only of Mexicans but also other racial minorities.
El Clamor Público called for the emancipation of African American slaves
and opposed efforts to exclude free blacks from California. "Is it fair to be
punished because they committed the crime of not being born white?"
he asked rhetorically. "Is this civilization? Is this Christianity?"[58] Ramírez
similarly condemned the mistreatment of Chinese immigrants. His most
outspoken and persistent editorials were nonetheless motivated by the
brutal mistreatment of his own people.[59]

Initially moderate in tone, the newspaper became more vociferous
as Anglo violence against Mexicans escalated. Two events in particular
served as catalysts for this radicalization. The first act of injustice was the

decision of a grand jury not to indict Los Angeles Deputy William Jenkins for the murder of Antonio Ruiz, a Mexican on whom he was attempting to implement a repossession order. In an editorial denouncing the discriminatory treatment of Mexicans by the criminal justice system, Ramírez lamented how "It is becoming customary to assassinate and outrage Mexicans with impunity."[60] Worse was to follow. The second incident that incited Ramírez to action was the brutal retaliation Anglos inflicted on Mexicans for the murder of Los Angeles County Sheriff James R. Barton by outlaw leader Juan Flores. Captured by a posse, Flores faced trial before a vigilance committee, which found him guilty and ordered his execution. A crowd of three thousand turned out for the hanging on February 14, 1857. The death of Flores, however, did not silence public demand for revenge on his entire gang. Posses roamed the Los Angeles basin in pursuit of their prey. Historian Edward Escobar describes the indiscriminate slaughter of Mexicans that followed as "an orgy of lynchings."[61] One source calculates that Anglos murdered 158 Mexicans. The most shocking of these incidents occurred when a posse mutilated and decapitated a young Mexican who had no ties to the Flores gang at the San Gabriel Mission.[62]

Ramírez prevailed on Anglo authorities to take preventive action against mob violence through moral suasion, blending petitions to individual consciences and community spirit with implicit threats. His editorials castigated Anglos for their wrongdoing while encouraging what he considered their capacity for good. Ramírez hoped to persuade Anglos to fulfill the "magnanimous and grandiose ideals" of the Founding Fathers by according Mexicans all the freedoms and protections of citizenship. *El Clamor Público* therefore anticipated the later rhetorical strategies of twentieth-century black civil rights activists who pressured whites to address the disparities between the principles and practices of American democracy. The tone of the newspaper was nonetheless seldom conciliatory. Ramírez's anger and frustration led him to denounce Anglos as liars and hypocrites for their failure to abide by their own principles of governance. As he asserted in a caustic editorial of May 1855, "The North Americans pretend to give us lessons in humanity and to bring to our people the doctrine of salvation so we can govern ourselves, to respect the laws and conserve order. Are these the ones who treat us worse than slaves?"[63]

Ramírez prefigured the language of black civil rights activism in a further respect. His editorials demanded restitution through the law but warned that, if this failed to happen, Mexicans would themselves resort to

armed violence. Ramírez opposed armed self-defense as a means to protect Mexicans from Anglo mobs because it would further inflame racial
hostilities. "Mexicans are growing tired of being run over and having
injustices committed against them;" he argued in an editorial of July 1856,
"but to take up arms to redress their grievances, this is an act without
reason. We desire to reestablish peace: those misguided Mexicans should
return as before to their homes and we hope for an immediate reform
to take place."[64] At the same time, his entreaties to Anglos contained the
implicit threat that their failure to restrain mob violence would inevitably
lead Mexicans into bloody armed revolt. Here was the iron fist in the vel-
vet glove: beseeching Anglos to live up to the egalitarian ideals on which
their nation was founded while warning of dire consequences if they
refused. "If every individual American have the authority, just by wishing it, to sentence to death and assassinate in secret our countrymen,"
Ramírez affirmed, "we would have equal right to use similar measure
and then who would be responsible for such ill-fated consequences?"[65]
Echoes of Ramírez can be heard in Martin Luther King Jr.'s "Letter from a
Birmingham City Jail," in which he warned whites that failure to support
nonviolent solutions to racial injustice and inequality would mean "millions of Negroes will, out of frustration and despair, seek solace and security in black nationalist ideologies—a development that would inevitably
lead to a frightening racial nightmare."[66]

Whatever unease its portents of possible racial warfare caused,
El Clamor Público used an even more confrontational tactic in its campaign
for justice. Ramírez attempted to compel otherwise indifferent authorities
into taking action against vigilantism by publishing the identities of suspected mob leaders. In June 1858, for example, El Clamor Público listed the
names of seven men purportedly responsible for lynching three Mexicans
in retaliation for the murder of two French ranchers in San Luis Obispo.
Similarly, the following January the newspaper listed the members of a
grand jury investigating the lynching of two Mexicans accused of stealing
livestock in Santa Barbara in the hope that public pressure would coerce
them into indicting those responsible.[67]

Despite all these efforts, El Clamor Público was in many respects a failure, both as a publishing venture and as a political tool. A lack of subscrip-
tions led to its closure after less than four years. Nor can the newspaper be
said to have ameliorated the plight of Los Angeles' Mexican community.
The outspoken editorials published by Ramírez proved counterproductive, antagonizing rather than tempering the racial hostilities of Anglos.

City Assemblyman Joseph Lancaster Brent accused him of "disseminating sentiments of treason and antipathy among the native population." The *Los Angeles Star* even claimed that it was actually Ramírez who fuelled animosity between Anglos and Mexicans by embellishing the truth about discrimination and violence, an argument that suggests the newspaper editor had made the local political structure less rather than more inclined to address racism. Political circumstances also rendered it difficult for the newspaper to succeed. The local Mexican elite sought accommodation with Anglos and were unwilling to risk confrontation. At the same time, Ramírez's eschewal of armed retaliation and advocacy of adaptation to American cultural practices as a means to ameliorate discrimination aggravated the more militant lower classes.[68]

Despite its deficiencies, the very existence of *El Clamor Público* established a tradition of crusading political journalism on which other Mexican newspapermen would build in the long struggle against Anglo oppression. One of the most influential journalists to follow Francisco Ramírez was Carlos I. Velasco, a man described by one historian as "the conscience of the Mexican community." As publisher and editor of *El Fronterizo*, he protested Anglo violence and the racial stereotyping of Mexicans that acted as one of its catalysts. Velasco was born into an elite family in Hermosillo, Sonora, on June 30, 1837. His professional rise was rapid. Having trained as a lawyer, he set up a successful practice that led to his appointment at age twenty as a superior court judge and subsequently to a seat in the Sonora legislature. Political troubles in his native state resulted in his leaving Mexico temporarily in 1865 and then permanently in 1877, resettling across the border in Tucson, Arizona. After initially pursuing a career in the retail business, he sold his store and used the funds to purchase a printing press, publishing the first weekly edition of *El Fronterizo* on September 21, 1878.[69]

In one of his earliest editorials, Velasco identified the agenda of the paper as serving as "a zealous defender of the interests of the Mexican people in both countries, expressing their point of view, and directing their initiative along the path leading to their moral perfection and material progress." To this end, he took a strong moral stand against mob violence. "That lynch law is cruel and unjust there can be doubt," Velasco asserted in an editorial of February 1880. "Cruel because it deprives the victim of the right to a proper defense; and unjust, because it applies the death penalty to all classes of crime without any distinction." Those who defended the actions of the lynch mob may have seen them as upholding civilized society but, according to Velasco, such abuse of the law "makes people regress to primitive times." It also perpetuated an endless cycle of violent reprisals. The actions of the mob fuelled the desire for revenge among friends and relatives of their victims, "coming thus to increase the number of more and more horrible and shameful murders and other criminal acts committed day after day." This last observation attests to the prevalence of armed self-defense on the part of Mexicans confronted by Anglo mobs.[70]

Velasco not only preached in support of Mexican rights but also took practical action. On January 14, 1894, he, together with businessman Pedro C. Pellón and territorial legislature representative Mariano G. Samaniego, founded the mutual aid society Alianza Hispano Americana. The organization was not the first of its kind in Tucson, as a similar organization had been founded in January 1875.[71] Membership in the Aliana Hispano Americana nonetheless reached an unprecedented scale, with lodges established across the Southwest. The principal purpose of the organization was initially to provide low cost insurance but it also promoted political rights and cultural pride.[72]

The promotion of organized protest against the specific problem of mob violence owed to the efforts of several Mexican community activists. In June 1911, for instance, Doneciano Dávila and Emilio Flores founded La Agrupación Protectora Mexicana in San Antonio with the purpose to "come out for its members in the courts where outrages are committed with them, such as cold-blooded murders, lynchings, and so forth, or the taking of their homes or crops." Activists in Phoenix formed another civil rights organization, La Liga Protectora Latina, in February 1915.[73]

The most ambitious of these initiatives in creating a nascent Mexican civil rights movement came from the activist journalist Nicasio Idar. Idar was born in December 1855 in Port Isabel, Texas.[74] After working for the railroads in North Mexico he moved in 1880 to Laredo, where he became active in Mexican community organization. As publisher and editor of the newspaper *La Crónica*, he articulated the plights and hopes of ordinary Tejanos that were otherwise unrepresented by the media, targeting such social and economic ills as school and residential segregation, low wages and limited work opportunities, and lynching.[75]

One particular act of mob violence convinced Idar of the need not only for words, but also action. As narrated earlier on November 3, 1910, a mob seized Mexican laborer Antonio Rodríguez from a prison cell in Rocksprings following his arrest for murdering the wife of an Anglo rancher and burned him at a stake.[76] Idar published a scathing editorial in which he lamented the fate of Mexican migrants driven by destitution from their homeland in search of better opportunities in the United States. "There they have the probability of dying of hunger; here of dying ignominiously burned alive or at least lynched like rabid dogs." Affirming that Mexicans were tired of lies, the editor demanded justice. "We want revenge, we want the criminals punished in accordance with the law."[77]

No matter how stirring, Idar knew these words were not enough. Determined to avoid a repeat of the Rocksprings incident, he organized a conference to address Anglo discrimination against Mexicans, recruiting support through his newspaper and the network of Masonic and mutual aid organizations across the state. Four hundred representatives from twenty-four communities attended El Primer Congreso Mexicanista in Laredo in September 1911. The delegates agreed on resolutions denouncing the inequities and oppression endured by Mexicans, including land dispossession, labor abuse, substandard schooling, and mob violence.[78] It was, in the words of Reverend Pedro Grado, their intention "to strike back at the hatred of some bad sons of Uncle Sam who believe themselves better than the Mexicans because of the magic that surrounds the word white."[79] To further this agenda, the delegates formed a statewide federation they named La Grán Liga Mexicanista de Beneficiencia y Protección, adopting as its slogan "por la raza y para la raza" ("by the people and for the people"). Idar's daughter Jovita, herself a regular contributor to *La Crónica*, inspired women representatives to found an affiliate organization, La Liga Femenil Mexicanista.[80]

Within a short time, however, the energy generated by the conference had waned. Far from being a sustainable vehicle of protest, La Grán Liga Mexicanista de Beneficiencia y Protección sank almost immediately under withering assault from Anglos. Although Idar continued to campaign for justice through the pages of *La Crónica* until his death in April 1914, El Primer Congreso Mexicanista proved to be not only the first but also the last meeting of its kind.[81] Nonetheless, the Congreso Mexicanista represented the first occasion on which Mexican activists had assembled on such a scale to coordinate organized resistance to racial discrimination.

La Crónica was not the only publication to protest the lynching of Antonio Rodríguez. The incident was a seminal moment in which the disparate voices of campaigning newspapermen coalesced into a powerful refrain against Anglo violence. These expressions of outrage united from across both sides of the border. Some publications opportunistically used the incident as a means to assail the faltering administration of Porfirio

Díaz, claiming that the lynching symbolized the president's failure to protect Mexicans from American tyranny. Yet even those newspapers that acted out of ulterior motives could still be sincere in their moral outrage at the lynching. The anarchist periodical *Regeneración*, edited by Ricardo and Enrique Magón, had since its first publication in 1904 fervently denounced Anglo oppression of Mexicans.[82] An article written for the newspaper by Praxedis Gilberto Guerrero concluded of the lynching of Rodríguez that for all their material progress, Americans were still barbarians with an atavistic craving for violence. The mutilation and murder of an innocent man had occurred "In the model nation, in the land of freedom, in the home of the brave...in the tenth year of the century. In the age of airplanes and dirigible airships, of the wireless telegraph, of the wonderful rotary press, of the congresses of peace, of the humanitarian and animal societies."[83]

In meeting the challenges of racial discrimination and violence during the 1920s and beyond, the Mexican press in the United States drew on the tradition of outspoken political dissent established by pioneering activist journalists like Francisco Ramírez, Carlos Velasco, and Nicasio Idar. Mexican newspaper editors were forthright, for instance, in their condemnation of the Ku Klux Klan. While in the southern states the Klan directed most of its animus toward African Americans, further west its hatred focused more on Mexicans. The Klan perceived Mexicans as a triple threat to their idealized Anglo-Saxon Protestant republic. A mongrel race that could contaminate white racial purity, their Catholic faith and supposed adherence to communism further menaced the institutional and ideological foundations of the United States.[84]

Mexican journalists performed an important role in mobilizing popular opposition to this reactionary doctrine. A. C. Torres, editor of *El Defensor de Pueblo* in Socorro, New Mexico, attempted to mobilize grassroots resistance by encouraging the regional network of Mexican fraternal societies "to condemn and combat this anti-American plague of masked bandits."[85] The editorial employed a cunning rhetorical tactic that inverted the historical representation of Mexicans, positioning them as the respectable members of mainstream society threatened by a violent criminal element. Even more confrontational was El Paso editor Rafael Ramírez. The title of his newspaper, *El Azote* (The Whip), captured the way he used words. In an editorial of January 1923, Ramírez denounced the falsehood of Protestant clergymen who provided theological support for the Klan. "These supposed ministers who always have the Gospel on their lips, while in reality they are destroying and falsifying it," had disgraced their pulpits by championing an organization "that has committed many crimes and unheard of cruelties...disruptive of the public order, of the peace, of the law and of the public and private welfare."[86] The combative tone of the editorial seemed almost to channel the spirit of his namesake, Francisco Ramírez. Like *El Clamor Público*, it was also not long before the last issue of *El Azote* rolled off the press, the paper ceasing publication later that year.

Although it seldom flourished financially, radical journalism continued to confront Anglo abuse and murder of Mexicans. In the late 1920s, for instance, a San Antonio printer named Jesús Gonzales published numerous exposés of the mistreatment of Mexican laborers. The reports, which appeared in periodicals on both sides of the border, documented "That they are treated by the American authorities with great cruelty, imprisoned arbitrarily, thus attacking their personal liberty, imposing very heavy fines for supposed crimes, and that occasionally some prisoners have mysteriously disappeared between nightfall and dawn."[87]

What impact these and other protests had in restraining mob violence is ultimately difficult to determine. Mexican newspapers not only had small circulations—subscribers usually numbered in the hundreds rather than thousands—but being published in Spanish also had little or no Anglo readership. For these reasons they had only a limited ability to influence the opinions of those who committed or endorsed lynching. In the case of Francisco Ramírez, outspoken criticism of vigilantism served only to inflame further the antipathies of Anglos. Not once did the remonstrations of Mexican journalists secure the arrest and conviction of the leader or member of a lynch mob. While there may have been some correlation between newspaper campaigns and the prevention of further violence, it is impossible to demonstrate a clear causal relationship.

Some activist journalists paid a harsh price for their political dissent. Anglos treated with disdain the supposed constitutional protection of freedom of speech when newspapermen used their First Amendment rights to criticize the abuse and murder of Mexicans. In June 1915, Texas Rangers shot dead Carlos Morales Wood, editor of the Valentine newspaper, *La Patria Mexicana*. Wood had aroused the ire of law enforcement officers by issuing a call to arms against them for their abuse and murder of Mexicans. According to the Rangers, he had resisted arrest on a charge of incitement to riot. Although officers were arrested for murder, local Anglos rallied around them in a show of racial solidarity. One newspaper preempted the outcome of the trial with a headline ruling "Rangers Kill Bad Mexican." The jury reached the same conclusion and acquitted them.[88]

Despite the difficulties they faced, campaigning journalists performed an integral role in mobilizing resistance to mob violence. Editors who used their newspapers as a platform to defend the rights of Mexicans provided an oppressed people with a representative public voice otherwise denied them. In assuming leadership for the creation of protective associations, they also laid the foundations of organized civil rights protest.

Newspapermen also provided an important source of information to, and sustained pressure on, diplomatic officials investigating alleged abuses of Mexicans. Diplomats attempting to reconstruct the narratives of crimes against Mexican citizens frequently encountered the indifference or obstructionism of local officials, many of whom sought to conceal their own complicity. Anglo newspapers were similarly unsupportive in helping elucidate the identities of mob leaders. Mexican editors therefore provided important assistance to diplomats in uncovering what the rest of the media attempted to conceal. In November 1880, *El Fronterizo* called to the attention of the Mexican consul in Tucson a report of a Mexican who had come close to being lynched in Tip Top, Arizona. When the Mexican refused to pay an inflated price for a bottle of brandy, Anglos beat him and placed a rope around his neck, although they did not carry out the threatened hanging. While the paper expressed some skepticism about the story, it believed the best course of action was for the consul to investigate and, if necessary, help secure punishment of those responsible.[89]

Reforming the Rangers

Activist journalists were integral to the antilynching campaigns not only of Mexicans but also of African Americans. Francisco Ramírez, Carlos Velasco, and Nicasio Idar had their counterparts in the likes of William Calvin Chase, Timothy Thomas Fortune, and Ida B. Wells. Yet Mexicans had the advantage of another form of political leadership denied to African Americans. In the southern states, the disfranchisement and exclusion from public office of African Americans rendered them without representation in local, state, or national government. Although Mexicans suffered many restrictions on their political rights, they retained a participatory role in many southwestern electoral districts. Mexicans therefore benefited from being able to push for reform within the political system rather than having, as African Americans did, to mobilize pressure from without.

The most important instance of a politician using his access to power to promote greater protection of Mexicans is the campaign of J. T. Canales to reorganize the Texas Rangers. In some respects, the fight ended in failure. The measures eventually enacted by the state legislature fell far short of the radical changes proposed by Canales, an outcome that left him so disillusioned he abandoned politics. In exposing the abuses suffered by Mexicans to public view Canales nonetheless succeeded in tempering the worst excesses of the Rangers. His accomplishment in securing implementation of legislative reform to restrain racial violence is without parallel in the experience of southern blacks.

José Tomás Canales was born on March 7, 1877, near Kingsville in Nueces County, Texas. He practiced law in both Corpus Christi and Laredo before taking up a position at the county assessor's office in Brownsville in 1904. A year later, he entered politics, winning election to the state house of representatives as representative of the ninety-fifth district. Canales owed his position in part to the support of the Cameron County Democratic machine but broke from it when he championed the prohibitionist cause, running unsuccessfully as an independent candidate for county judge in 1910. Returning to the Democrats, he served as Cameron County's superintendent of public schools and as a county judge, before returning to the state legislature in 1917.[90]

Far from being a political radical, Canales appeared to embody the acculturationist strategy of many middle-class Mexicans. A photograph of Canales shows an urbane gentleman, smartly attired and clean shaven. His appearance matched his mainstream politics. A convert from Catholicism to Presbyterianism, Canales encouraged Mexicans to claim the full rights of citizenship by emulating Anglo cultural practices. As superintendent of the Cameron County School District, for instance, he insisted that students should speak exclusively in English, not only in the classroom but also during recess. The political purpose of this strategy is evident from his recommendation that schoolchildren sharpen their linguistic skills by learning patriotic songs. Canales also attempted to promote the American citizenship of Tejanos by helping prevent their escape across the border to evade the draft during World War I.[91]

Yet Canales appreciated that adaptation to Anglo cultural norms was not sufficient to secure equality for Mexicans: improvements in race relations had to be a reciprocal process. This led to his confrontational stand against one of the most notorious instruments of Anglo violence against Mexicans, the Texas Rangers. During 1916 and 1917, Canales commanded a company of mounted scouts that gathered intelligence for the US Army regarding Mexican raiders crossing the border into Texas. What he witnessed of the Rangers' excesses resulted in his lobbying for an investigation by the state legislature. On January 16, 1919, Canales introduced a bill to the Texas House of Representatives with the purpose of reorganizing the Rangers to restrain their criminal activities. The bill attempted to improve the character of recruits by providing that they should be at least twenty-five years old, have two years' experience as a law officer, and provide evidence from a commissioners' court of their moral temperament. To guarantee their continued good conduct it further provided that Rangers must post bond: fifteen thousand dollars for captains, twelve thousand dollars for sergeants, and five thousand dollars for privates. The bill further subordinated Rangers to the authority of local civil authorities, requiring them to transfer prisoners to the custody of the sheriff of the county where they made the arrest, and rendering them criminally liable for any abuse of office including the mistreatment of detainees.[92]

Canales made it clear from the outset that his purpose was to improve rather than impair the Rangers by purging them of corruption within their ranks. Despite this conciliatory language the radical content of the bill aroused fierce resistance. Canales placed himself in serious danger by confronting the Rangers. Even before he introduced the legislation, his outspoken criticism had provoked Ranger Frank Hamer to threaten him with physical violence. When a fearful Canales sent his wife Anne to complain to the Speaker of the House, he offered to redeploy one of the Rangers as a bodyguard without any apparent sense of irony. Politicians supportive of the Rangers also mobilized in opposition to the bill, attaching numerous amendments that led to its referral for further study.[93]

Although the Rangers and their allies closed ranks against Canales, he succeeded in securing the creation of a joint House-Senate committee to investigate the force in 1919. As prosecuting attorney, Canales introduced nineteen charges relating to the maltreatment, torture, and murder of criminal suspects. He directed his accusations against not only the Rangers who allegedly committed these abuses, but also their superiors in the office of the state adjutant general who conspired to conceal the crimes that had taken place. Many of the witnesses called by Canales provided disturbing testimonies of Ranger violence against Mexicans, none more so than the massacre of fifteen men from Porvenir on January 28, 1918.[94]

Canales may have won the battle to expose what he described as the "desperate character of men on the Ranger force" but he lost the fight to hold them fully accountable for their abuses of authority.[95] Although Canales had demonstrated the need for reform, the investigating committee recommended a much weaker set of measures than those he proposed. The substitute bill removed radical proposals such as the need for Rangers to post bond and imposed only limited control of the force by local authorities. Canales attempted to convince his fellow legislators that the bill was a "whitewash" but could not prevent the House from approving the committee report by an overwhelmingly majority of eighty-seven to ten.[96]

The bitter experience of defeat alienated Canales from the local Democratic machine and discouraged him from seeking reelection when he completed his term of office in 1920. His campaign nonetheless amounted to more than a heroic failure. The public exposure of abuses committed by the forces convinced the adjutant general to rescind the appointments of Special Rangers. Recruited to bolster law enforcement during the turbulence of the Mexican Revolution, few of these officers had undergone a rigorous screening process and it was from within their ranks that much of the worst violence against Mexicans was committed. Several companies of the regular Ranger force were also disbanded. While tensions between Texas Rangers and Mexicans persisted, the reforms that Canales initiated had a positive impact. By the early 1920s, state authorities could entrust the Rangers, long the scourge of the Mexican community, to act as their protectors against violence from Anglo civilians.[97]

Lost Opportunities for Alliance

Canales may have eschewed public office after the ordeal of his efforts to reform the Texas Rangers, but he remained a prominent advocate of Mexicans' liberties and rights. He was a founding member in 1929 of the League of United Latin American Citizens (LULAC), writing much of its first constitution and later serving as its fourth president. LULAC proved a more enduring civil rights organization than its predecessors. In one important respect, however, its story is also one that exposes the limitations and lost opportunities of antilynching protest.

Despite their shared status as victims of white mob violence, Mexicans and African Americans pursued separate paths in their pursuit of justice. LULAC attempted to secure full constitutional protections for Mexicans by promoting their white racial identity. To facilitate this process, LULAC members encouraged their members not to associate with African

Americans. In promoting the rights of one oppressed minority, the organization therefore reinforced prejudice against another.[98]

The absence of coalition building between Mexicans and African
Americans resulted in them pursuing separate campaigns to combat racial
violence and discrimination. Civil rights protest therefore developed along
parallel lines that seldom, if ever, converged. This is particularly apparent
from the lack of participation by Mexicans and African Americans in each
other's civil rights organizations. Unlike LULAC, the National Association
for the Advancement of Colored People (NAACP) had no policy of racial
exclusion. In practice, however, Mexicans were involved neither in the
organization's leadership nor in its local branches. The membership rolls
of the NAACP reveal that local branches throughout New Mexico—in such
cities as Albuquerque, Las Cruces, Gallup, and Raton—had no Mexican
members. Membership lists from Texas cities with large Mexican populations, such as El Paso and Corpus Christi, indicate not one person with a
Mexican surname.[99]

The lack of cooperation between Mexican and African American political activists diminished organized protest against mob violence. Yet
Mexican defense agencies also struggled to recruit support from within
the ranks of their own communities. In an interview conducted during the
late 1920s, Arizonan mutual aid society worker Manuel Lomelí detailed
how Anglo authorities undermined grassroots mobilization. "They beat
one up while talking; they haven't any more than told one something than
they hit one with a pistol barrel."[100] The observations of a LULAC organizer underscore the difficulties of enlisting support, especially in small
towns and remote rural areas. Like many of his colleagues, this activist
faced a paradoxical problem. The only way to prevent further lynchings
was for Mexicans to rally in protest. Yet it was the very fear of mob violence that frightened them into silence. "The Mexican people were afraid
of coming into town for a meeting," he observed, "because they thought
they were going to be shot at or lynched if we had our meeting at the courthouse. The courthouse to them was just a medium or a means of being
punished. Most of the time, even when they were innocent of what they
were being accused of, somebody would just find a goat for something,
and the goat would be a Mexican."[101]

The limitations of Mexican protest within the United States had significant consequences. Most obviously, it restricted their ability to coordinate
resistance to mob violence across the American West. While there were
many expressions of opposition to Anglo tyranny, Mexican activism was

too disparate to withstand the forces of repression. Mexicans were also unable to create broader public awareness of their victimization in the same way as African Americans. There was no Mexican equivalent to the antilynching campaign of the NAACP, which raised national and international consciousness of racial violence. How then do we account for the more rapid demise of mob violence against Mexicans? Mexicans may have struggled to build and sustain a domestic antilynching movement but they benefited from an additional resource that provided an incomparable advantage over African Americans.

4

Diplomatic Protest and the Decline of Mob Violence

ALTHOUGH MEXICANS CREATED and sustained a vibrant culture of resistance against Anglo oppression, there were limitations to the effectiveness of their tactics. Those who took up arms sporadically succeeded in avenging the deaths of victims of mob violence but more often incited further repression from Anglos. Others who wielded a pen articulated the anger of Mexicans who lacked a public voice, but because of linguistic barriers had only a limited influence on the broader English-speaking community. Activists who founded defense organizations found it difficult to recruit members because of a pervasive fear of retaliation.

The most effective means by which Mexicans confronted mob violence was diplomatic protest. From the early 1850s to the late 1920s, consular and ambassadorial officials persistently pressed the case for greater government action against lynch mobs. They investigated violent crimes against Mexican nationals in the United States, recovering the actual narratives of events that had been deliberately distorted by the local press and law enforcement, and lobbied state and federal authorities for the arrest of the perpetrators and payment of compensation to the relatives of their victims. The efforts and effectiveness of diplomatic officials ebbed and flowed according to the strength and stability of their government and its broader relationship with the United States. Although the pressure they placed on American authorities was not entirely consistent, over the course of eight decades their protests had a cumulative impact in promoting remedial and preventive action against mob violence.

Mexican diplomats emphasized the moral imperative for government intervention against vigilantism but they also understood that their protests would have more influence by appealing to the self-interest of American authorities. From the late 1870s, when Porfirio Díaz became president of Mexico, American entrepreneurs invested millions of dollars south of the border. Mob violence against Mexican nationals threatened the stable diplomatic relations between the two nations on which these economic ties depended. As the United States assumed a more prominent role on the world stage, its government also sought to protect against the damage done to its international reputation when mobs murdered foreign nationals. Mexican diplomats pushed both of these points in support of their demands for justice.

The story of Mexican diplomatic protest is not a triumphant tale. Diplomats were endlessly frustrated at the refusal or failure of American authorities to prosecute those who murdered Mexican nationals and make reparations to bereaved relatives. The fact that lynching was not a federal crime rendered it impossible for diplomats to force compliance with the demands made to the State Department. Local courts and law enforcement officers colluded in protecting murderers from punishment. Diplomatic protest was nonetheless decisive in encouraging stronger public censure of Anglo vigilantes. Ultimately, the intervention of diplomats ensured that mob violence against Mexicans declined more rapidly than was the case for African Americans, a situation not lost on black antilynching campaigners.

Decades of Disappointment

The resolution of the war between Mexico and the United States heralded a short period of diplomatic cooperation in which the impact of mob violence on their mutual border was at least contained. A case in point is the aforementioned Texas Cart War. In October 1857, the Mexican Minister to the United States (the title of the position did not change to ambassador until the 1890s), Manuel Robles Pezuela, reported to Secretary of State Lewis Cass that hordes of Mexican families had fled across the border from Texas in response to the violence. He urged him to proceed with "every means" to "investigate the truth" and end the mistreatment of Mexicans, such a response being "demanded by justice, the law of nations, and the honor of the United States."[1]

Cass wanted to placate Mexican protest but it proved difficult to coordinate action among federal, state, and local authorities. Texas Governor Elisha M. Pease complied with a request to help restore cordial relations between Mexico and the United States by offering a five thousand dollar reward for the arrest of the criminal teamsters. Pease also personally travelled to San Antonio to assess the situation. Despite the tone set by his administration he discovered that city authorities had taken no action either to apprehend the teamsters or prevent them from fomenting further violence. Although the indifference of local officials helped deny justice for the families of the murdered Mexican cart men, Pease secured an appropriation from the state legislature to pay for a militia to protect them from renewed Anglo attacks. By that time the violence had subsided.[2]

The 1860s were a period of relative calm for Mexicans in the American Southwest. Politicians on both sides of the border struggled, however, to suppress the resurgence of mob violence in the 1870s. Persistent raids by both Anglo and Mexican raiders had created a climate of violent disorder in the borderlands. In response to criticism from the United States, the Mexican government established a commission to investigate the causes and consequences of these raids. The *Report of the Mexican Commission on the Northern Frontier Question*, published in 1873, attributed the anarchic lawlessness along the border to Anglo criminals and documented numerous atrocities committed against Mexicans. In retaliation, a US congressional committee issued a report four years later that completely contradicted the Mexicans' findings. It concluded that the lax law enforcement policies of the Mexican government facilitated criminals in conducting "a perfect terrorism" against American citizens. The failure of the two governments to reach consensus on who was responsible for the violence on the border rendered it impossible for them to agree on a proposed solution.[3]

This mutual recrimination eased after the United States granted diplomatic recognition to the administration of Porfirio Díaz in May 1878. Díaz promoted the economic development of his nation through foreign investment. American corporations poured millions of dollars into Mexico, seizing monopolistic control of key industries including mining, railroads, and petroleum. The closer economic ties forged between Mexico and the United States led diplomatic officials from the two countries to collaborate more closely in pursuing complaints of racial violence along their mutual border. American companies placed increasing pressure on the State Department to promote peace and security with the purpose of protecting their investments in Mexico.[4] Mexican diplomats also appealed to American economic self-interest in lobbying for federal action against mob violence. As the Mexican Minister to the United States, Manuel de Zamacona, advised Secretary of State James G. Blaine in 1881, "such repression will doubtless have a beneficial influence upon trade between the two Republics, as well as upon the relations between the inhabitants of the frontier districts."[5]

The American system of federalism nonetheless continued to frustrate efforts to secure the arrest and prosecution of lynch mob leaders. Local law enforcement officials proved particularly obstructive, not least because in many cases they were concealing their own involvement in acts of mob violence.

An incident in the Arizona Territory during the early 1880s epitomizes the uncooperativeness or outright opposition of local officials. On March 15, 1881, horse thieves raided ranches along the Gila River. A posse pursued and captured two Mexicans, José Ordoña and Rafael Salcido. Ordoña died after being hanged from a tree. Forced to witness the death of his companion, Salcido consented to show where he and Ordoña had hidden the stolen horses. This act of compliance did not prevent him from suffering the same fate as Ordoña, although how he died is uncertain since the authorities never found his corpse.

Although local law enforcement officers failed to recover the dead body, this did not mean that they did not know where to look. When Mexican consular officials exhorted Sheriff R. H. Paul to investigate the lynching, he not only refused but also defended the actions of the posse in a manner that implied his own participation. According to Paul, the local area had "been under the control of the worst and most desperate class of outlaws, both American and Mexican, and an example was needed in order to put an end to so deplorable a state of affairs. I do not know of a single instance in which an innocent person has been hung or killed by good and law-abiding citizens."[6] The sheriff's complacent tone infuriated Manuel de Zamacona. "I should insult the Department of State by pointing out the absurd and alarming character of such a view of the case," he informed Blaine, "and the necessity of not permitting said view to impair the guarantees that should be enjoyed by Mexican citizens residing in Arizona, according to the general principles of law, and to the treaties between Mexico and the United States."[7]

Blaine attempted to appease the minister but without accepting his claim that the arrest and prosecution of the criminals was the federal government's legal and moral responsibility. Although the constitutional constraints on federal power forbade the direct involvement of the State Department, he would apply pressure on territorial authorities to launch a proper investigation of the case.[8]

The outcome of this strategy was predictable. Blaine encouraged the governor of the Arizona Territory, John C. Frémont, to provide the Mexican government with a "full and satisfactory answer." It was not forthcoming.

Frémont was at the time far from Arizona in pursuit of eastern investors to the territory, and responsibility for pursuing the matter was delegated to acting governor John J. Gosper. While more conciliatory in tone, his conclusions were little different than those of Sheriff Paul. Gosper conceded that there was little respect for due process of law in the territory, but reasoned that justice had been served because of the likely guilt of the lynching victims. The way in which local communities closed ranks in such cases meant that even if the authorities had arraigned suspects, "it was doubtful if there could be found a witness to appear before the magistrate to testify against them." While it was unfortunate that the lynchers had not relied on the criminal justice system to punish Ordoña and Salcido, Gosper implicitly condoned their actions by reasoning that "the two men in question were probably outlaws." Evidently the acting governor accepted a lesser burden of proof than beyond reasonable doubt for putting suspected criminals to death. Without his cooperation, however, Mexican diplomats had no further recourse to pursue the case.[9]

The reluctance of local authorities to arrest and prosecute lynch mob leaders contributed to the further deterioration of relations between Mexicans and Anglos in the southwestern borderlands. Mexican state governments retaliated by similarly refusing to extradite criminal suspects who eluded American law enforcement officers by fleeing across the border. In September 1881, at a time when Sheriff Paul had stalled investigation of the Ordoña and Salcido lynchings, the Governor of Chihuahua, Mariano Samaniego, declined to hand over the men accused of murdering American prospector Samuel Carr in Eagle Creek, Arizona.[10] The governors of other Mexican states subsequently adopted a similar policy of noncompliance, citing their American counterparts' lack of reciprocity.[11]

This collapse of diplomatic cooperation created a downward spiral in relations between Mexicans and Anglos along the border. Criminals from both sides believed they could act with impunity in committing depredations on foreign soil. Mexican and American authorities proved unwilling to assist one another in stemming the tide of racial violence they helped create, further accelerating the decline of conditions in the borderlands. "The mob is supreme," declared one Arizona newspaper that believed such troubles could provoke war between Mexico and the United States, "and it exists everywhere, generally in the worst form, composed of thieves, renegades, and murderers." Such editorials failed to concede that the Anglo press was itself responsible for provoking nativist prejudices by publishing hostile editorials about Mexican state authorities without level-ing similar blame against their American counterparts.[12]

The bloody chaos on the border between Arizona and Sonora, coupled with the mutual suspicion and mistrust of authorities from both sides, caused Mexican consular officials ongoing difficulties and frustration. During the summer of 1881, Arizona authorities received constant corre-spondence from diplomats protesting the assault and murder of Mexicans in the territory. These incidents included attacks by an Anglo gang on three separate parties of Mexicans: one in which nine of the victims disap-peared and were feared dead, another in which three men were murdered on a public highway in open daylight, and a confrontation that resulted in four more fatalities.[13]

The efforts of Mexican diplomats to secure redress for these crimes became ensnared in an endless bureaucratic circle. When a communica-tion from the Mexican consul in Arizona received an insufficient response from the territorial governor, he raised the matter with the Mexican Minister to the United States in Washington. The minister contacted the US Secretary of State, who subsequently forwarded the correspondence to his counterpart at the Department of the Interior. He in turn referred the matter to the same territorial governor who had done nothing about it in the first place.[14]

Mounting frustration with the inaction of local and state officials led the Mexican government to recruit alternate allies in their pursuit of jus-tice. When diplomats failed to penetrate the wall of silence surrounding a lynching in southeastern Nebraska, they decided to employ a private detective. In August 1884, masked men captured Luciano Padillo from a sheriff who had arrested him for the rape of a thirteen-year-old girl. The vigilantes conveyed their victim to Cheese Creek, a remote location six miles outside Lincoln, where they allowed him to pray before tying a rope around his neck and hanging him. A grand jury investigation of the crime concluded that Padillo had met his death at the hands of persons unknown. The Mexican Embassy was unwilling to accept that this was the end of the matter. Mexican Minister to the United States Matías Romero hired William A. Pinkerton of the Pinkerton National Detective Agency to conduct an independent investigation.[15]

Pinkerton overcame the anxieties of intimidated witnesses and, over the course of ten days, submitted seven reports that pieced together the story. The detective interviewed anyone who had been associated with Padillo, from the employees who worked alongside him at a local laundry;

to the warden at the state penitentiary where he served as an inmate for a previous offense; to the coroner who conducted the postmortem on his murdered corpse. Some of the people with whom he spoke had received warnings of reprisals should they disclose what they knew about the lynching. From their testimonies, Pinkerton firmly identified four of the men who had abducted the Mexican. He further concluded that the father of the dead girl fastened the rope around Padillo's neck.[16]

Despite his thorough investigation, there was no chance of a court using Pinkerton's evidence to convict the criminals. The attorney hired to represent Padillo, R. D. Stearns, informed Pinkerton that the grand jury had not indicted anyone for the lynching because "the members of the mob were for the most part prominent citizens and had public sympathy on their side." The uncovering of evidence against the vigilantes would do nothing to improve the prospect of their conviction since the local community knew their identities and approved their actions. Stearns made his pronouncement with regret; others who shared his evaluation did so with satisfaction. One local laborer, for instance, admitted to knowing who had murdered Padillo but opined that he was "a Mexican and deserved hanging."[17]

The employment of the Pinkerton National Detective Agency demonstrates the determination and resourcefulness of Mexican diplomats in their struggle against American mob violence. The fact that the firm identification of those responsible for the lynching of Luciano Padillo was insufficient to secure their arrest and conviction can only have compounded Mexican officials' frustration with the American political and legal systems. Since lynching was not a federal crime, prosecution of perpetrators remained the responsibility of local and state authorities who, as in the case of Padillo, seldom expended serious effort in pursuit of justice. Political circumstances would have to alter before Washington was willing to enact remedial measures for the benefit of families of mob victims. Mexican diplomats endured another decade of disappointment before that change occurred.

Breakthrough

Not until the turn of the century did Mexican diplomatic officials score their first success in the struggle to secure justice for the families of lynching victims. In 1898, President William McKinley recommended that Congress authorize payment of an indemnity to the heirs of Luis Moreno, a Mexican national murdered by a mob in northern California.

LEARNING THE ROPES.

FIGURE 4.1 The Yreka Lynchings of 1895, Mexican national Luis Moreno pictured second from the right, courtesy of the California State Library, Sacramento, California.

To understand why Washington, having rebuffed previous protests from Mexican officials, succumbed to diplomatic pressure, it is necessary not only to reconstruct the lynching but also to look at the larger forces that shaped the period's foreign relations.

Shortly after midnight on August 26, 1895, a mob of more than two hundred masked men stormed the jailhouse in the mining town of Yreka, Siskiyou County. Using sledgehammers to smash the cell doors, the intruders seized four inmates awaiting trial and hauled them to the courthouse square. The mob tied ropes around the necks of the kidnapped men and hanged them one at a time from an iron rail suspended between two locust trees. A note attached to the body of one of the victims read, "Caution! Let this be a warning, and it is hoped that all cold blooded murderers in this county will suffer likewise. Yours Resp'ly, TAX PAYING CITIZENS." Photographs of the lynching were later sold as souvenirs (see Figure 4.1).[18]

Northern California newspapers endorsed the lynching as a necessary act of rough justice. Occasional comments concerning circumstantial evidence aside, editorial writers uncritically accepted that the victims were guilty of the crimes for which the mob hanged them. Echoing the sentiment of the note pinned to the corpse of one of the victims, they concluded that the townspeople had a right to expect their tax dollars would pay for a properly functioning court system. The deficiencies of the criminal justice system, however, meant dangerous criminals would go unpunished unless ordinary citizens took the law into their own hands. "Is not even lynch law preferable to a failure of all law?" the Fresno Expositor asked its readers. "Can the act of the lynchers in Yreka do one-tenth as much harm to the good repute of the Golden State as has been done by the failure of juries to send red-handed assassins to the gallows?"[19] Although the townspeople of Yreka had hanged four men illegally, they had done so only because of the failure of the courts to use their power to convict and sentence dangerous felons. "There is an easy way to stop lynching," affirmed the San Francisco Examiner. "Let the courts do their duty in protecting society against the criminal, let the State give the murderer a speedy trial, a sure conviction if he is guilty, and short shrift if he is convicted, and we will hear no more of midnight mobs and mysterious lynchers."[20] The local press also sought to protect the reputation of their region from outside criticism by pointing out that problems with the enforcement of justice plagued the entire country. That the shortcomings of the criminal justice system drove many decent citizens to desperate acts was evident from a recent spate of lynchings in Illinois.[21]

The episode may have passed into obscurity, dismissed as another sordid example of frontier lawlessness, were it not for the identity of one of the dead men. Three of the men murdered by the mob were Anglos named L. H. Johnson, William Null, and Garland Stemler, who were awaiting trial on separate murder charges. Stemler, an eighteen-year-old migrant from Arkansas, had allegedly robbed and murdered storeowner George Sears before also shooting to death Casper Mierhaus when he attempted to intervene. The fourth victim of the mob was Stemler's supposed accomplice, a forty-year-old sawmill worker named Luis Moreno. Although Moreno's nationality was initially uncertain, Mexican diplomats made immediate inquiries into the lynching. The official who coordinated the investigation was Mexican Minister to the United States Matías Romero.[22]

Romero was approaching the end of a long and illustrious political career at the time of the Moreno lynching.[23] He commanded considerable influence and respect in Washington circles, at one time counting among his personal friends and political allies Secretary of State William H. Seward and President Ulysses S. Grant. He was a tireless advocate for his country, having lobbied successfully for the support of the United States during the Franco-Mexican War and attempted as the author of numerous works to dispel the negative stereotypes that many Americans had of their southern neighbor. "My experience in dealing with two peoples of different races," he wrote, "speaking different languages and with different social conditions, has shown me that there are prejudices on both sides, growing out of want of sufficient knowledge of each other, which could be dispelled, and by so doing, a better understanding be secured."[24]

By May 1896, Romero had secured evidence that Moreno was a Mexican national, born in Saltillo, Coahuila, and that he therefore had authority to intervene in the case. Romero accordingly wrote to Secretary of State Richard Olney to demand punishment of the lynchers and payment of an indemnity to the family of Moreno. Olney in turn exhorted California Governor James H. Budd to pursue the matter. Budd responded by publicizing a five hundred dollar reward for information leading to the successful prosecution of the mob leaders. He also instructed Siskiyou County sheriff W. L. Hobbs to investigate the incident.[25]

The sheriff's report not only failed to disclose the identities of the men who murdered Moreno, but more or less exonerated them. Hobbs filled four of its five pages with circumstantial evidence supposedly establishing that Moreno had murdered Sears and Mierhaus, including several of the storeowner's possessions found in the Mexican's pockets when a posse captured him. The sheriff produced only one paragraph that addressed the intended purpose of the investigation, concluding perfunctorily that it was impossible to determine the names of the mob leaders.[26]

Although it cannot be proven that Hobbs knew who murdered Moreno, the local citizenry rallied to protect their identities from public disclosure. A grand jury failed to indict anyone for the lynching. Nor did anyone step forward to claim the reward offered by Governor Budd. "From the complete arrangements of the mob and the profound secrecy with which such a number of persons conducted the affair," Hobbs concluded in an updated report to Budd, "I do not think it is within the bounds of possibility that any one connected with the affair will ever divulge it."[27]

Mexican diplomats were unwilling to accept this as the end of the matter. Skeptical from the outset that local or state authorities would arrest any suspects, Matías Romero had ordered the local Mexican consulate to launch an independent investigation of the lynching. Although this probe proved no more successful in exposing the identities of the mob leaders, it convinced Romero that Moreno had killed Sears and Mierhaus in self-defense. He cited in particular a letter published in the *San Francisco Examiner*, written by an unknown author using the alias "John Doe," who claimed to have witnessed the incident. According to this correspondent, Sears had assaulted Moreno and Stemler, attracting the attention of Mierhaus who rushed into the brawl on the side of the storeowner.[28]

Despite its inconclusiveness, the report produced by the local Mexican consulate raised serious concerns about the shortcomings of the criminal justice system in Siskiyou County, both in terms of the disregard for due process by the mob and the subsequent efforts at concealment by law enforcement officers. For months Romero pressured the State Department to redress the matter. Where the intermittent diplomatic protests of the past half-century had failed to elicit a positive response, Romero's insistent lobbying finally forced an act of appeasement from the US government. On January 18, 1898, President William McKinley wrote to Congress with a recommendation that it authorize payment of a two thousand dollar indemnity "out of humane consideration, without any reference to the question of liability" to the family of Luis Moreno.[29]

The positive response of the federal government owed not only to Romero's persistence but also to the United States' troubled relationships with Mexico and the rest of the world. By the late nineteenth century the United States faced criticism from governments across the globe for its failure to protect foreign nationals on its soil. The indemnity paid to the family of Moreno was consistent with a strategy by American politicians to protect their country's international reputation. Although it continued to insist that it had no authority to intervene in the affairs of individual states, the federal government had for the past decade endeavored to resolve incipient diplomatic crises by providing financial compensation to the families of lynching victims. This occurred after the massacre of Chinese miners at Rock Springs, Wyoming, in 1885, and again following three separate mob attacks on Sicilians in Louisiana during the 1890s.[30]

Mexican diplomatic officials drew inspiration from the actions of their Chinese and Italian counterparts to secure justice for the families of foreign nationals lynched in the United States. Matías Romero closely monitored the diplomatic repercussions from the lynching of eleven Sicilians in New Orleans in March 1891, an incident that led the Italian government to threaten severing diplomatic ties with the United States and brought the two countries to the brink of war. One of his many reports on the hostilities to the Mexican Ministry of Foreign Affairs contained the transcription of a telegram sent by the Italian Premier, the Marchese di Rudinì, to the State Department in Washington. Romero underlined one sentence in which Rudinì proclaimed the unquestionable right of his country "to demand and obtain the punishment of the murderers and an indemnity for the victims." Here was an instructive example for the Mexican government, a point made all the more persuasive when Romero later reported that the United States had paid twenty-five thousand dollars in compensation to the families of the murdered men.[31]

The importance of diplomatic protest by other countries to the Mexican campaign for justice became even more apparent following the payment of a further indemnity to the Italian government for the lynching in 1896 of three Sicilians in Hahnville, Louisiana. For Washington not to pay similar indemnities to the families of other foreign nationals lynched by American mobs would expose the United States to accusations of double standards. Romero alluded to this in his correspondence with State Department officials, drawing their attention to the remedial action taken in the Hahnville case. His efforts yielded the desired result. When President McKinley recommended Congress approve the indemnity for Moreno, he cited as a precedent the payment made to the families of the three Sicilians.[32]

The federal government revealed that its motivation in paying the indemnity was less enlightened principle than political expediency and economic self-interest. The earlier response to the Rock Springs massacre was influenced by a desire to protect the United States' lucrative trade links with China.[33]

Mexico was also an important economic partner that Washington could not afford to alienate. When Porfirio Díaz became President of Mexico in 1877, the United States initially refused to grant his administration diplomatic recognition. Corporate interests eager to invest in Mexico successfully lobbied Washington to ameliorate its aggressive stance. Once closer relations between the two countries were established, Díaz courted American investors in the hope of stimulating Mexico's bankrupt economy. By 1910, Mexico attracted more than half of all American overseas investments. A damaging diplomatic incident could potentially put this capital at risk, a predicament that Romero was in an ideal position to highlight since he had in his previous role as treasury secretary been responsible for directing investment in the first place.[34]

Broader foreign policy considerations also impacted on the decision to pay the indemnity. The Mexican press accused the US government of hypocrisy for supporting the Cuban struggle against Spanish colonial rule but tolerating the violent repression of foreign nationals on its own soil. By the time the federal government authorized payment of the indemnity, the United States was within months of declaring war on Spain following the sinking of the USS Maine in Havana's harbor. "America's public men should exercise their sentiments of humanity at home," asserted one Mexican periodical with reference not only to Moreno but also to the broader phenomenon of mob violence, "by putting a stop to lynching and the burning of people at the stake in the presence of applauding mobs, instead of making such loud demonstrations of sympathy for the cruelties practiced upon the Cubans."[35]

The payment of an indemnity to the family of Luis Moreno opened the door to further compensation claims by relatives of other lynching victims. Although mob leaders continued to elude the law, these indemnities provided not only material relief to immediate kin but also a symbolic recognition of the larger Mexican community's struggle for the rights and protections of American citizenship. A case in point was the federal government response to the lynching of Florentino Suaste.

On October 11, 1895, a band of armed men snatched Suaste from a prison cell in Cotulla, Texas. They proceeded to shoot and then hang their captive. Acting on a communiqué from Matías Romero, Secretary of State Olney asked the governor of Texas to investigate the incident.[36] The events that led to the lynching soon became clear. A rancher named Saul accosted a gang of Mexicans stealing and killing his cattle. Saul and Deputy Sheriff Norman Swink set off in pursuit of the fleeing criminals. When the two men caught up with their quarry, there was an exchange of gunfire. The precise chain of events later proved a matter of dispute, but there was no doubt that by the time the shooting stopped, Saul and one of the Mexicans lay dead. After seeing his wife wounded and his son killed during the shootout, Florentino Suaste was captured, incarcerated, and executed.[37]

The search to uncover what happened in Cotulla followed a course similar to the investigation of the Moreno lynching. Mexican consular officials exposed a deliberate attempt by local authorities to conceal the identities of the murderers. The grand jury that examined the incident placed its proceedings under seal, allowing for no public disclosure, after failing to return a single indictment. When the local district attorney ordered the disclosure of the written testimony taken by the grand jury, the court-house in which they were contained caught fire and burned to the ground. The timing of the blaze was either a remarkable coincidence or an act of arson.[38]

The lynching of another Mexican on American soil and the inability of local authorities to prosecute those responsible constituted a further embarrassment to the federal government. Citing the precedent established by the Moreno case, William McKinley announced on December 7, 1900, the payment of a two thousand dollars indemnity to the surviving members of Suaste's family.[39] Matías Romero did not live to see the outcome of his protests to the State Department. Shortly after being appointed the first Mexican ambassador to the United States, he died suddenly of appendicitis on December 30, 1898.[40]

Popular Unrest and Diplomatic Protest

The success of Mexican diplomatic protest contributed to the marked decline of mob violence in the first decade of the twentieth century. Payment of indemnities to the families of Luis Moreno and Florentino Suaste received widespread and supportive press coverage in the United States. This included newspapers throughout the Southwest whose editorial writers responded to mob violence within their communities with expressions of embarrassment and contrition. The decade of disorder unleashed by the Mexican Revolution nonetheless awakened the dormant spirit of the lynch mob. Diplomatic protest assumed renewed urgency as the Mexican government attempted to contain popular unrest over its relationship with the United States, which critics saw as an abandonment of national sovereignty.

On November 3, 1910, as briefly mentioned in Chapter Two, a mob snatched one of the inmates of a jail in Rock Springs, Texas, and burned him to death. The victim was a twenty-year-old Mexican laborer named Antonio Rodríguez. Law enforcement officers had arrested him for the murder of Mrs. Lemuel Henderson, a rancher's wife who had refused him when he appeared at her doorstep to ask for food. Although there was no evidence he had committed a sexual assault, the brutality of his death implied that this was a rare instance of retaliation against a Mexican suspected of raping a white woman. One newspaper report affirmed that local citizens commended the actions of the mob "as the lives of the ranchers' wives had been unsafe because of the attempted ravages of Mexican settlers along the Rio Grande."[41]

A coroner predictably concluded that Rodríguez had died at the hands of persons unknown. If the local community considered the case closed, they would soon be shocked out of their complacency.

On November 8, rioting erupted on the streets of Mexico City. Fuelled by press reports of the lynching, protesters took retaliatory action against American persons and property, smashing the windows of businesses, stoning cars carrying schoolchildren, and tearing and spitting on an American flag.[42] More widespread unrest occurred three days later. Angry demonstrators in Guadalajara destroyed up to ten thousand dollars of American property. The US Consul in Ciudad Porfirio Díaz, Luther T. Ellsworth, fled across the border to El Paso when a mob stormed his offices. And on the streets of Chihuahua, mobs pelted Americans with stones as they cried "Remember Antonio Rodríguez!"[43] Across the country, newspaper editorials demanded a boycott of American imports. Rumors that Mexico was even willing to go to war with the United States induced Texas Rangers to assemble at strategic points along the border in order to repel an armed invasion.[44]

Although hundreds of Mexicans had died at the hands of American lynch mobs, none had elicited such an outpouring of popular protest. Rodríguez's death was characterized by unusually violent cruelty even when compared with other lynching victims. This alone, however, cannot account for the anti-American violence that swept through Mexico in response to his murder.

The lynching of Antonio Rodríguez may have been the immediate catalyst for the rioting, but there was another underlying cause. "The lynching of an alleged Mexican was only incidental," concluded US Consul Samuel E. Magill of the unrest in Guadalajara, "and a large proportion of the populace engaged in the riots knew little and cared less about it." Even though his tone was unnecessarily dismissive given the extensive press coverage of the case, Magill was not entirely mistaken.[45]

By this time, US corporate interests controlled thirty-eight percent of foreign investment in Mexico. The Díaz administration struggled to withstand mounting criticism of its perceived surrender of Mexico's economic sovereignty even from within its own ranks. Although opponents accused the president of reducing his country to the status of a colonial satellite, he felt powerless to impose tighter regulations on American entrepreneurs, especially after they had helped save the country from bankruptcy during the financial crisis of 1907.[46]

Antonio Rodríguez became a potent symbol of Mexican victimization by the United States. Some protesters may not have been interested in the lynching per se but all could sense that the same unrestrained American aggression that had led to the death of one man could determine the fate of the entire country.

The Díaz administration desperately needed to stem popular unrest. Political expediency as well as a principled desire for justice consequently motivated Mexican diplomatic officials to demand that American authorities arrest and punish the mob leaders. Díaz personally appealed to President William Howard Taft to secure criminal convictions.[47] US Secretary of State Philander C. Knox responded to similar entreaties from the Mexican Embassy by instructing Texas governor Thomas M. Campbell to investigate the case and provide protection for consular officials conducting their own inquiry.[48]

Despite these efforts to uncover the truth, there were numerous acts of deception intended to derail official inquiries. One rumor claimed Rodríguez was not a Mexican national but rather born in the United States and that foreign diplomats therefore had no jurisdiction to investigate his murder. A further one blurred responsibility for the crime by claiming that local Mexicans had colluded in the lynching. Still another asserted that the supposedly dead man had publicly reappeared alive and well. A grand jury that almost certainly included members or associates of the mob failed to return any indictments.[49]

The outpouring of Mexican anger impressed upon the more progressive elements of the American press the need to protect diplomatic relations through tougher federal action on lynching. "Foreign governments cannot be expected to recognize the peculiarities of our constitutional system," affirmed the *Philadelphia Inquirer*, "and when a treaty is broken to be satisfied with the explanation that the Washington administration couldn't help it. One of these days, if nothing is done, the country will become involved in serious trouble through a case of this kind." The implication was that the country would face military conflict unless the federal government assumed greater jurisdiction to arrest and punish lynch mobs. According to *The Independent*, the violent unrest in Mexico was sufficient to constitute the "serious trouble" warned of by the *Philadelphia Inquirer*. "It is right that all Mexicans should arise in righteous wrath," asserted the periodical, "and we make no complaint that they talk of reprisal by boycott, and that they rise in a mob and insult the official representatives of our country among them."[50]

Mexican diplomats were nonetheless unable to use the threat to American investments in their country as sustained leverage over the US

State Department. On November 19, little more than ten days after the riots erupted, Francisco Madero issued his Plan de San Luis Potosi calling for the revolutionary overthrow of the Díaz regime. As consular officials became consumed with reinforcing their faltering government, the campaign to secure justice for the family of Antonio Rodríguez was swept aside.[51]

Yet far from being forgotten, the incident taught state and federal officials a lesson that to protect the fragile security of the borderlands they must take more decisive action against lynching. When little more than six months later another Texas mob murdered a young Mexican, the authorities moved with unprecedented resolve to arrest and punish the perpetrators.

As recounted earlier, on June 19, 1911, a mob in Thorndale, Texas, seized a suspected murderer named Antonio Gómez from a jail cell and hanged him from a telephone pole.[52] Although the press uncritically accepted that Gómez had stabbed a local storeowner to death, his own brutal murder attracted embarrassed outrage because he was only fourteen years old. According to the *Dallas Morning News*, the lynching of a "child victim" compelled state authorities to overcome their customary "attitude of indifference and supinity."[53]

The same newspapers that demanded justice nonetheless adopted a fatalistic attitude that officials would fail to take action against the mob leaders. "While indignation is running high it is a ten to one shot nothing is ever done to them," the *Beaumont Daily Enterprise* concluded.[54] If the men who lynched Antonio Gómez were to evade the law it would not be for lack of effort. Determined to avert further diplomatic repercussions, state authorities collaborated with Mexican officials to secure the arrest and conviction of the mob leaders. In return for the support he received from the assistant attorney general, consul Miguel Diebold dissuaded local Mexicans from holding a mass meeting that could compromise the legal process by further inflaming tensions. This newfound reciprocity proved immediately productive. Within four days, local police had arrested four men for the lynching: Z. T. Gore, Garrett F. Novack, Ezra W. Stephens, and Henry Wuensche.[55]

Gore was the first of the four defendants to stand trial. On November 14, a district court in Cameron found him not guilty.[56] The outcome of the case exposed the complicity of the local townspeople who served on the jury. Perhaps influenced by the need to place prosecution witnesses under protection during the trial, the judge granted a motion for a change of venue to Georgetown for the trial of the other three men.[57] Underlining his determination to secure justice, he also denied the defendants bail. The trial started on February 27, 1912. Despite the attempt to make the proceedings properly impartial, it took the jury only twenty minutes to acquit the alleged mob leaders.[58]

The failure to convict the defendants does not detract from the historical significance of the trial. In May 1916, thousands of townspeople in Waco participated in the burning to death of a black teenager named Jesse Washington; not one of them came before a court of law.[59] In contrast to the apparent powerlessness of African American community leaders, Mexican consular officials had through their collaboration with state prosecutors moved a decisive step forward in their struggle against mob violence. The Gómez case established an important precedent for future cooperation. It would, however, be fifteen years before anyone was convicted for lynching a Mexican. This loss of political momentum owed to the revolutionary upheavals that destabilized Mexican government.

Diplomatic Protest during the Revolutionary Era

The Mexican Revolution had a disastrous impact on diplomatic efforts to secure redress for the victims of American mob violence, severely undermining the stability, resources, and status of consular and embassy officials. The same political turbulence that precipitated a storm of racial violence in the southwestern borderlands rendered diplomats all but powerless to support the victims. The rapid rise and fall of the presidencies of Francisco I. Madero, Victoriano Huerta, and Venustiano Carranza caused a constant turnover in consular staff that prevented sustained investigation of violent crimes against Mexican citizens in the United States.[60] Since each successive administration had to struggle for diplomatic recognition by the United States, there were also periods when Mexico had no ambassador in Washington to protest mob violence at the highest levels of government. Even when the United States did recognize a new Mexican administration, the countries' relationship remained tense and fragile. For instance, although the Wilson administration granted diplomatic recognition to the Carranza government in October 1915, numerous events—including the Punitive Expedition, a military operation led by General John J. Pershing against Mexican rebel leader Francisco "Pancho" Villa between March 1916 and February 1917, and the inclusion of economically protectionist provisions in the Mexican constitution of 1917—threatened to undo ties at any moment.⁶¹ The broader instability of diplomatic relations curtailed cooperation between the Mexican Embassy and US State Department in prosecuting lynch mob leaders and compensating the families of victims.

Despite the dramatic upsurge of mob violence in the southwestern borderlands during the revolutionary era, neither the Madero nor Huerta administrations made strong representations to the US State Department. The effectiveness of diplomatic maneuvers against mob violence did not measurably improve under Venustiano Carranza, who assumed the presidency of Mexico in May 1917. A case in point is the failure to secure the arrest of those responsible for the lynching of two Mexicans in the steel town of Pueblo, Colorado. Less than two weeks before the incident occurred, Carranza had delivered an address at the opening session of the Mexican Congress in which he detailed numerous actions taken by his administration to address violent crimes committed against Mexicans in the United States. Occurring so soon afterward, the Pueblo lynching rapidly contradicted this rhetoric by exposing the deficiencies of diplomatic protest.⁶²

On September 13, 1919, a band of masked men seized two inmates from the city jail in Pueblo. They had created a diversion by phoning police headquarters with a false report of a riot. With most of the local force dispatched to investigate the alleged incident, the vigilantes had no difficulty raiding the undermanned prison cells. Their victims were two Mexicans, Salvador Ortez and José Gonzales, awaiting trial for the murder of a local police officer. The mob bundled the suspected criminals into the back of an automobile and drove them to a bridge on the city limits, tied ropes around their necks, and hanged them.⁶³ The Mexican Embassy in Washington instructed local consul A. J. Ortiz to launch an investigation. Although Ortiz did not discover the identities of the mob leaders, his inquiries established that the dead men were entirely innocent.⁶⁴

Broader diplomatic relations between Mexico and the United States at the time potentially facilitated efforts to secure redress for the lynching. In recent months the State Department had imposed increasing pressure on the Carranza administration to control border raids by Mexican outlaws and improve protection of American citizens in Mexico. This stance exposed the federal government to accusations of hypocrisy if it failed to do everything in its power to help prosecute those who perpetrated crimes of racial violence against Mexicans in the United States and provide compensation for their families. The more sensitive and astute elements of the American press accepted the argument that the United States had to honor the same standards it imposed on other countries. According to the *Houston Post*, any failure to do so would surrender the moral high ground in future diplomatic disputes with Mexico. "After the stern warnings our government has sent to Mexico against further outrages on our citizens, it is going to be humiliating in the extreme for our government to receive similar complaints from the Mexican government making charges against our people who have claimed to be so much higher in the scale of civilization."[65]

Mexican officials nonetheless failed to press this argument to their advantage. At the time of the Pueblo lynching the Wilson and Carranza administrations had sharpened their mutual criticism to the point that there were widespread rumors of an imminent American invasion of Mexico. The deterioration of diplomatic relations made local authorities in the United States less, rather than more, inclined to cooperate with Mexican consular officials. The inability of Mexican diplomats to sustain pressure on Washington also suggests their focus was more on the internal convulsions within Mexico that within months led to the violent overthrow of the Carranza administration.[66]

The Decisive Decade of the 1920s

Not until the 1920s did Mexican diplomats once more place sufficient pressure on state and federal authorities in the United States to force their intervention against vigilantism. This enhanced cooperation owed much to the broader improvement in relations between the two countries. The diplomat credited with having done more than anyone else to establish a cordial relationship between Mexico and the United States was Manuel C. Téllez.[67] Born into a middle-class family in Zacatecas, Téllez had pursued a career in journalism before joining the Mexican foreign service, rising to Chargé d'Affaires of the Mexican Embassy in Washington and then ambassador. Téllez brought personal charm and political conviction to the ambassadorship, resulting in his eventual appointment as dean of the diplomatic corps in Washington. His considerable investment of time and energy in the pursuit of justice secured an unprecedented level of federal intervention against mob violence.[68]

One of the most important means by which diplomats improved their representation of Mexican citizens was through the creation in the early 1920s of La Comisión Honorifica. From its foundation by the Mexican consulate in Texas, chapters of the organization soon opened across the United States. The comisiónes served as an important communications link between consuls and Mexican citizens, facilitating action to address poverty, labor exploitation, and racial discrimination. Their role in protecting Mexicans from Anglo violence was particularly important in south Texas where a resurrected Ku Klux Klan commanded considerable political influence. This was certainly the case in Bishop, Nueces County, where the local comisión—known as "La Norifica"—succeeded in driving the Klan out of town. Its members mobilized in reaction to the lynching of an African American physician, Dr. J. G. Smith, burned to death by a mob after his car broke down and the white woman whom he asked for help accused him of assault. The Mexican townspeople expressed interracial solidarity with African Americans, understanding that as a despised minority themselves they faced a similar threat of becoming targets of Klan violence. As the son of one of the founders of the Bishop comisión recalled his father saying, "Anybody that got hurt, there's going to be twice of them going to get hurt, and there's no telling who."[69]

Despite the improved effectiveness of Mexican diplomatic protest, the struggle against Anglo vigilantism was slow and arduous. Mexican officials could not enforce preventive measures against mob violence but rather reacted to events. The federal system of government in the United States also frustrated the efforts of Téllez and his fellow Mexican diplomats to secure justice for the families of lynching victims. Although they secured the support of State and Justice Department officials in Washington, state and especially local authorities resisted what they saw as interference in their jurisdictions, especially when it threatened to expose their complicity in promoting and protecting the actions of the mob. One illustration of this is an event that occurred in the Texas oil town of Breckenridge.

On November 16, 1922, a mob of around three hundred armed men paraded through the streets of Breckenridge, shouting a demand that local Mexicans leave the city by nightfall. When representatives from the Mexican community appealed to the mayor for protection, he replied that he could not guarantee their safety.

Manuel Téllez requested that the State Department intervene in the matter. He asserted that the incident was symptomatic of the abuse suffered by Mexicans throughout Texas. According to Téllez, the last twelve months had witnessed the "indiscriminate killing" of between fifty and sixty Mexicans across the state.[70] Sympathetic press coverage of these claims increased the pressure on federal officials. The *New York Times* asserted that while "It may seem too extravagant to say that there is an open season for shooting Mexicans in unpoliced districts along the Rio Grande," unprovoked acts of murder were "so common as to pass almost unnoticed."[71]

While the *Times* supported federal intervention as a solution, it mistakenly attributed racial violence to the frontier conditions it assumed still existed in south Texas. On the contrary, as the local Mexican Consul, Enrique D. Ruíz, emphasized, the issue was less the absence of a criminal justice system than the discriminatory manner in which it was enforced. As he asserted, "local officials have either had some responsibility in connection with these cases, or else have actually taken part in it." Although the Mexican government had spent thousands of dollars on lawyers' fees it had failed to secure the indictment of a single person suspected of participating in mob violence. In one of the more shocking incidents recounted by Ruíz, the shooting to death of a fourteen-year-old Mexican girl in Hidalgo County by vigilantes searching for bootleggers, local authorities had refused even to launch a criminal investigation.[72]

The most recent lynching had occurred only five days before unrest broke out in Breckenridge. Police in the south Texas town of Weslaco had arrested Elias Zarate for fistfighting a fellow construction worker. A mob of about fifteen men seized him from jail and shot him through the heart. The reaction of local authorities conformed to the broader pattern of complicity in and concealment of violent crimes against Mexicans. When Consul Ruíz tried to investigate the incident, his own life was threatened. Téllez concluded that those entrusted with protecting the rights of Mexican citizens were themselves responsible for covering up or actually carrying out the abuses. In his words, "It is alleged that in some instances the Mexicans were killed by American local officers, that practically no attempt was made to break down allegations that the killings were in self-defense."[73]

Téllez insisted to Secretary of State Charles Evans Hughes that the suspected collusion of local authorities in the abuse and murder of Mexicans necessitated federal mediation. Not for the first time, the intervention of the federal government was motivated as much by economic self-interest as by moral outrage. American financial assets in Mexico had been adversely affected by a decade of revolutionary violence. The US government sought compensation for damage to American property in the country and guarantees of protection for future investment. Washington was at the time of the Breckenridge disorder within months of signing the Bucareli agreements, which would grant diplomatic recognition to the administration of Álvaro Obregón in return for financial damages and restoration of American property rights in Mexico. American officials did not want to compromise their relationship with the first stable administration in Mexico since the outbreak of the revolution by repeating the diplomatic imbroglio brought about by the lynching of Antonio Rodríguez twelve years earlier. Mexican revolutionaries had seized on the incident not only to assault American businessmen and smash their property but also to try to bring down their own government.[74]

These broader strategic interests helped persuade federal officials to act promptly in response to Téllez. Although the State Department did not have the jurisdiction to intervene directly, Secretary Hughes convinced Texas Governor Patt Neff to deploy a detachment of Texas Rangers in Breckenridge. Neff took this decision over the objection of Mayor C. H. Fulwiler, who claimed the media had misrepresented the revelries of a few local "roughnecks" as an orchestrated assault on the Mexican community.[75]

Despite the obstructive attitude of local authorities, the Rangers strove to prevent further unrest by uncovering those who had committed the earlier acts of intimidation and violence. At the request of Ranger Frank Hamer, the FBI sent agent J. P. Huddleston, fresh from investigating a notorious Klan murder of two men in Mer Rouge, Louisiana, to Breckenridge.[76] Hamer and Huddleston determined that a white vigilante organization known as the White Owls was responsible for the attempted expulsion of Mexicans from the town. Founded with the purpose to protect and promote the interests of Anglo workers, the White Owls resented the recruitment of cheap Mexican labor by local employers because they believed it undercut wages at a time when the oil industry was already in recession. Their terrorizing of Mexicans was therefore "designed to boost the price of labor and drive other laborers from the field."[77]

The arrest of a radical labor activist led to press speculation that the attempted expulsion of Mexicans was part of a larger conspiracy. G. C. Blesingame was an organizer for the International Workers of the World (IWW) from Chicago. Newspaper claims that the IWW was responsible for the racial unrest in Breckenridge made little sense, however, since it contradicted the rigorous efforts made by the organization to promote biracial unionism. Blesingame denied any association between the IWW and the White Owls and a local county judge swiftly ordered his release from custody. Rather than furthering the aims of the IWW, the vigilantism of the White Owls demonstrated the difficulties labor organizers faced in promoting the common class interests that united Anglo and Mexican workers across the racial divide.[78]

The Rangers made no further arrests following the release of Blesingame. Within two weeks of their arrival they and FBI agent Huddleston withdrew from the town. In some respects the episode exposed the limitations of state and federal authorities' intervention in localized racial disturbances. The Rangers and the FBI failed to expose the leaders of the White Owls and they did not secure the arrest and prosecution of those responsible for the attempted expulsion of Mexicans from Breckenridge or the lynching of Elias Zarate. Nonetheless, the presence of state and federal law enforcement officers was sufficient to stem acts of violence and intimidation and restore order. Two months later Mexican diplomatic officials issued a statement that there had been no renewal of racial unrest. The incident demonstrated a new commitment on the part of the Rangers to administer the law in a more professional and impartial manner, acting as instruments of Mexicans' protection rather than oppression. Four years after State Representative J. T. Canales had exposed their brutal abuse of Mexicans, the Rangers began to put more racially progressive policies into practice.[79]

More important still was the success of Ambassador Téllez in persuading federal authorities to assist in the prosecution of those responsible for the lynching of three Mexicans in Texas. The case was of particular significance since the principal perpetrator was a local law enforcement officer.

In the early morning hours of September 5, 1926, a gunshot rang out on the streets of Raymondville, a small but bustling trading center in southern Texas. The shot appeared to come from a Saturday night dance held by and for the local Mexican community. A band of law enforcement officers went to investigate. Whether they sensed they were walking into a trap is unknown, but when the officers reached the scene more gunfire broke out, killing Deputy Sheriff Louis Mays and Deputy Constable Leslie Shaw.[80]

Sheriff Raymond Teller, a popular and respected thirty-one-year-old World War I veteran, took immediate action to identify those responsible and restore order.[81] Yet, his reaction to the murders would result in federal authorities treating the war hero as a villain and the man supposed to embody the law had to stand trial as a defendant.

Teller made a number of arrests, including three Mexicans and an Austrian who reportedly confessed to the crime and consented to showing the sheriff where they had hidden a cache of arms. According to the sheriff, when the prisoners, accompanied by the father of two of the suspects, led him and his officers to a remote area of brush land, it turned out to be another ambush. A band of armed Mexicans laying in wait opened fire. The rescue attempt, however, was a fiasco. When the shooting stopped, all of the prisoners lay dead.[82]

The local Mexican community immediately disputed the sheriff's narrative of events. They denied that the prisoners had admitted to murdering the two law enforcement officers and claimed instead that Teller and his men had beaten them in the cells before taking them out into the countryside where they were shot without any witnesses. A rumor circulated that the sheriff and his associates had even decapitated one of the men, Tomás Nuñez.[83]

Mexican consular officials contacted Ambassador Téllez, who insisted that the US State Department take action. Federal authorities contacted Texas governor Miriam Ferguson who launched an inquiry into the incident. State investigators, however, concluded that the victims were, with the exception of the Austrian Matt Zauder, American citizens and the Mexican government therefore had no jurisdiction in the matter.[84]

Dissatisfied with the thoroughness of Texas authorities, Mexican diplomats hired a detective agency to investigate. Their inquiries uncovered evidence that contradicted the claims made not only by state authorities but also the sheriff. Tomás Nuñez was, it transpired, a Mexican citizen, who had relocated across the border from his native home in Matamoros. Although Teller had arrested his sons José and Benancio, Tomás was only at the jail in order to bring them food. The notion that he had been the victim of an indiscriminate act of revenge for the murder of the two law enforcement officers gained greater substance when authorities exhumed the bodies of the dead Mexicans. While the decapitation rumor proved unfounded, the disinterment corroborated claims that the slain men had suffered beatings before dying of bullet wounds.[85]

Mexican diplomats liaised with US Justice Department officials to put a stop to the brutal and corrupt regime of Sheriff Teller. On December 12, 1926, a grand jury indicted Teller and fourteen other persons for conspiracy to enforce peonage during the cotton-picking season. The sheriff secured his release on a seven thousand dollar bond.[86] Within a month, however, the authorities had detained him on even graver charges. On January 7,

1927, Teller was one of eight men arrested for murder and accessory after the fact.[87] The sheriff dismissed the charges as a cynical attempt by prosecuting attorneys to secure a conviction in the peonage case by maligning his reputation among potential jurors. "It's pure politics," he proclaimed to reporters, "we are absolutely innocent. I never in all my life have seen so much bunk about nothing."[88]

Behind the bluster, however, the sheriff was evidently unnerved. His allies in the community did their utmost to undermine the legal process, intimidating numerous prosecution witnesses. Teresa Nuñez, who had lost her father and brothers in the shooting incident, testified that within hours of swearing out complaints against Teller and his associates, law enforcement officers arrested her for vagrancy and threatened to release her only if she signed a statement that she had been coerced into making the charges. The defense counsel also denounced newspapers that sympathetically reported the claims of witness tampering. Teller's attorney in particular accused the *Houston Chronicle*, which had insinuated the sheriff was part of a Ku Klux Klan conspiracy, of acting as a mouthpiece for the Mexican government.[89]

The tactics succeeded. On January 24, a grand jury returned no indictments in the murder case. If Teller and his officers thought the decision placed them above the law, however, they were wrong.[90] On February 1, the sheriff and his fellow defendants stood trial on the peonage charge in the US District Court in Corpus Christi. Mexican officials appointed San Antonio lawyer Manuel C. Gonzales to serve as special prosecutor. Judge Joseph Hutcheson warned he would punish any person who came to the courtroom armed with a pistol. Even so, Teller resorted to his old tricks by arresting Samuel H. Compton, the special agent who helped prepare the prosecution case, on the spurious charge of seduction. His attorney also besmirched Gonzales by accusing him of representing a "bolshevik government."[91]

Prosecution witnesses testified that Teller and his deputies colluded with local cotton farmers to exploit the local workforce. These laborers were predominantly Mexican but also included Anglos and African Americans. When they tried to leave the farms on which they worked, the sheriff arrested them for vagrancy and returned them to the fields where they resumed their picking, this time under armed guard. The defendants countered these accusations by claiming they had performed a duty to the public by taking preventive action against persons who would otherwise engage in acts of lawlessness. Teller even asserted that he had acted out of benevolence by providing his prison cells as a welcome place for homeless and unemployed laborers to sleep.[92]

This time, however, Teller would not escape justice. On February 5, the court convicted the sheriff and four of the other defendants of conspiracy to commit peonage. The court deferred sentencing for a month before imposing prison terms ranging from twelve to eighteen months.[93]

The guilty verdict against Sheriff Teller was less than a resounding victory for Mexican diplomats representing the families of the lynching victims. He had after all escaped conviction for the crime of summarily executing the prisoners in his care. Moreover, his prison sentence does not appear to have ameliorated local community attitudes about the mistreatment of Mexicans. On the contrary, a crowd of cheering supporters greeted Teller on the day of his release from the penitentiary.

Teller's conviction for conspiracy to commit peonage was nonetheless of considerable consequence. For decades the almost complete autonomy of southwestern sheriffs had led to endless abuses of the law, including the violent oppression of Mexicans. The prosecution of Raymond Teller by Mexican diplomats and Justice Department officials served notice to law enforcement officers that they could no longer oversee their areas of jurisdiction as independent fiefdoms. The case was to some extent comparable to the actions of federal prosecutors to bring to justice those responsible for murdering three voter registration workers during the Mississippi Freedom Summer of 1964. Federal officials could not prosecute the local sheriff and his associates for murder since it was a state crime, so they settled instead on the lesser charge of conspiracy to deny the activists their civil rights.[94] The outcome of the Teller case was similarly bittersweet since it failed to secure his conviction for murder or the payment of financial compensation to the families of his victims. Its influence was nonetheless decisive. The intervention of federal prosecutors coupled with damaging national media coverage demonstrated an increasing intolerance for those who placed themselves above the law. While Texas had been the site of the largest number of extralegal killings of Mexicans in the United States, the Raymondville lynchings were the last of their kind.

African American Reactions

The course of Mexican diplomatic protest may at times have been slow and suffered numerous setbacks, but its effectiveness is clear when compared with the antilynching campaigns of African Americans. Diplomatic

officials provided Mexicans with institutional resources and formal political representation that gave them an advantage in their opposition to mob
violence compared to blacks' organized resistance to lynching. African
American activists attempted to mobilize international opinion against
the brutal repression of their race, most conspicuously Ida B. Wells, whose
lecture tours of the United Kingdom in 1893 and 1894 led to the formation
of the English Anti-Lynching Committee. These overseas activists did not,
however, formally represent their government. They lacked the power of
diplomats, who threatened numerous reprisals—severing of official ties,
economic sanction, military action—if state and federal authorities failed
to address their grievances. The success of Mexican diplomats in securing financial compensation for the relatives of lynching victims elicited a
complicated response from African Americans. To some, it was a source
of inspiration, to others, a cause of envy and resentment.

Black newspapers reported the payment of indemnities to the families of Luis Moreno and Florentino Suaste. Although these stories were
not accompanied by editorial comment, their newsworthiness suggests
they served as an instructive example to readers of how the federal government could be forced to recognize its financial responsibility to the
families of lynching victims.[95] For the same reason, the black press followed the diplomatic protests against the hanging of Antonio Gómez, but
lost interest in the episode when it failed to reach the same resolution.
Newspaper editorials saw in the failure of Mexican diplomats to secure
financial compensation a reflection of African Americans' own frustration with the limitations of federal jurisdiction. According to the *Cleveland
Gazette*, although President Taft had assured Porfirio Díaz his administration would do all within its power to resolve the matter, "exactly what such
a promise, if really made in set terms, would be worth, is problematical
as under the Constitution and the unvarying practice since the establishment of the Government, the Federal authorities are absolutely helpless
in the matter and must rely altogether upon the energy and good will of
the state authorities."[96]

The disappointing outcome of the Gómez case may have drawn the
sympathy of the black press, but the success of Mexican diplomats in pro-
curing compensation for the relatives of other lynching victims induced
bitterness as well as adulation. African American editorialists, for the
most part unaware of the full scale of anti-Mexican violence in the United
States, expressed anger and indignation at the fact that their government
appeared to care more about the lynching of foreign nationals than it did

of its own citizens. Blacks had demonstrated their continued loyalty to the United States by serving in the armed forces that preserved the Union, secured the West for American expansion, and aided in the creation of America's first overseas empire. African American leaders therefore protested that the federal government did less to protect their people than it did Mexicans, a people whom they believed had done far less to establish their loyalty to the United States. They accused their government of a double standard—that federal officials urged state and local authorities to track down those responsible for lynching Mexicans while ignoring the more frequent murders of blacks by white mobs.

In May 1899, a lynch mob in Mexico murdered seven black railroad workers, four of whom were American citizens. The incident produced no protest from the State Department to the Mexican Ministry of Foreign Affairs. With Congress having paid an indemnity to the family of Luis Moreno little more than a year earlier, the failure of American diplomats to pursue the case appeared all the more outrageous to the black press. "Suppose an American mob should lynch four Mexicans, Spaniards or citizens of any other nationality," the *Afro-American Advance* asked rhetorically. "What would be the result?"[97] Such bitterness endured among black editorialists for decades. The federal response to the lynching of Elias Zarate and attempted expulsion of Mexicans from Breckenridge incited Roscoe Simmons, writing in the *Chicago Defender*, to insist that if Secretary of State Hughes "can ask Governor Neff about a lynched Mexican," why should Attorney General Harry M. Daughtery not also "ask about a lynched AMERICAN?"[98]

Simmons believed the federal government should prioritize the protection of its own citizens through enactment of antilynching legislation. At the time he wrote in late 1922, a bill first introduced to Congress four years earlier by Missouri Congressman Leonidas Dyer that would make lynching a federal felony was about to reach the floor of the Senate. In contrast to Simmons, other African American leaders hoped to turn the diplomatic tensions caused by lynching to their political advantage. The White Owls had actually attempted to expel not only Mexicans but also African Americans from Breckenridge. With the attention of the State Department focused on the Texas oil town, black activists argued that the common victim status of Mexican and African Americans meant action could not be taken to protect one but not the other. James Weldon Johnson, the executive secretary of the National Association for the Advancement of Colored People (NAACP), telegrammed President Warren G. Harding, calling his "attention to [the] international situation created by the lynching of Mexicans and Negroes" and urging passage of the Dyer antilynching bill.[99]

Although a southern filibuster defeated the proposed law, the positive measures taken by federal and state authorities to restore community order in Breckenridge encouraged a closer alliance between NAACP activists and Mexican diplomats. The following year, the NAACP requested that Ambassador Manuel Téllez provide details of Mexicans murdered in the last twelve months for inclusion in the statistics it published to pressure for reform.[100] In 1926, the organization assisted in the prosecution of Sheriff Raymond Teller by conducting an additional investigation of the Raymondville lynchings.[101] These actions, however, did not serve as the basis for sustained collaboration. The decline of mob violence against Mexicans may have meant diplomats no longer regarded alliance with black antilynching activists as being mutually beneficial.

The Power of Diplomacy

For eight decades a succession of Mexican consular and ambassadorial officials persistently labored to secure the prosecution of lynch mob members and financial compensation for families of their victims. Their victories were seldom less than hard won, the long and difficult campaigns for justice plagued not only by unsympathetic American authorities but also by their own weak and unstable government. Nonetheless, the determined action of Mexican diplomats had an incremental impact in eroding the longstanding forbearance of mob violence on the part of politicians, the press, and the general public. At the local and state level, business and civic leaders accepted that mob violence compromised the efforts of former frontier communities to overcome their historical reputations and establish themselves as modern and progressive centers of commerce and industry. Among federal government officials there was a similarly pragmatic concern to protect American investments in Mexico and the broader international reputation of the United States. The fact that practical rather than moral concerns often motivated state and federal government intervention does not detract from the thoroughness and perseverance with which Mexican diplomats conducted their investigations of mob violence and presented their conclusions to American authorities. Their influence was a decisive factor in the demise by the late 1920s of public toleration of mob violence against Mexicans. Without similar representation at the highest levels of government, African Americans continued to endure publicly condoned lynchings for decades.

Men such as Juan Cortina and Tiburcio Vásquez who used armed force to defend against Anglo aggression hold a prominent place in the pantheon of Mexican American folk heroes, their deeds the inspiration of songs and legends. In contrast, diplomats who promoted the rights of Mexicans in the United States, including Manuel de Zamacona, Matías Romero, and Manuel Téllez have been all but lost to history. Operating within the confines of bureaucratic channels rather than taking up arms, their slower and more deliberate pursuit of justice did more to promote stable race relations in the southwestern borderlands.

Conclusion

REMEMBERING THE FORGOTTEN DEAD

AT 11:15 ON the morning of Friday, November 16, 1928, four masked men marched into the San Juan County Hospital in Farmington, a remote town in northern New Mexico. The men seized one of the patients, a Mexican sheepherder named Rafael Benavides, and bundled him into the back of a pickup truck. Accompanied by a second vehicle carrying six other men, the kidnappers sped to an abandoned farm two miles north of town. Having forced their victim to stand on the back of one of the trucks, they tied a noose around his neck and fastened the rope to a locust tree. When the vehicle accelerated forward it snapped Benavides's neck. His limp body hung suspended in the air.

Contemporary press reports established in considerable detail the circumstances surrounding the lynching. On the night of Wednesday, November 14, 1928, a drunken Benavides broke into the home of a Mexican family in Aztec and attempted to assault a young girl, but the screams of her sister scared him off. Benavides then became involved in a brawl when he attempted to force entry into another house. Eventually he made his way to the ranch of a prominent Anglo farmer, George Lewis. Although Lewis was away on a hunting trip, his wife was asleep at home. Awoken by Benavides, Mrs. Lewis attempted to defend herself with a shotgun, only to discover it was empty. Benavides physically assaulted the farmer's wife and then carried her to a remote hillside, where he left her naked and unconscious. The sixty-year-old woman sustained injuries to her face and chest, including boot marks where she had been furiously kicked. When she regained consciousness some hours later, she staggered to the nearest house, and her neighbors raised an alarm. Sheriff George Blancett assembled a posse that pursued Benavides to the loft of an abandoned house near the Colorado border. When Benavides refused an order to surrender, the posse fired a series of shots into the house, one of which struck him in the abdomen. Blancett arrested the wounded fugitive and returned him to Farmington.[1] Informed that Benavides would not recover from his wound, the sheriff withdrew an armed guard on the hospital. The masked men who abducted Benavides therefore faced no resistance. According to the physicians who treated him, Benavides had only hours to live and the lynching "probably saved the criminal a good deal of suffering."[2]

In many respects the lynching of Rafael Benavides conforms to the broader pattern of mob violence against Mexicans in the United States. The men responsible for his murder acted in open disobedience of the law and with the approval of elements of the community. Moreover, no member of the lynch mob was ever brought to justice. Despite the testimony of more than fifty witnesses, a grand jury investigating the case failed to return any indictments.[3]

The Benavides case is nonetheless of crucial significance since he is the last known Mexican victim of community sanctioned mob violence in the United States.[4] Mexicans continued to live with the danger of lynching after 1928. However, these attacks took place surreptitiously rather than in open defiance of the law, and they received more public censure than support.[5] The lynching of Benavides decisively tipped the balance of public opinion toward those who advocated the application of due process to problems of social order, and away from those who favored informal methods of control such as vigilantism and mob violence. The result was that after 1928 would-be lynchers would no longer have the support of the majority of their fellow citizens. Potential lynchers could no longer count on escaping arrest by the authorities. They would have to be careful with their identities and with the location of their planned murder. Mob violence against Mexicans was clearly still possible after the lynching of Rafael Benavides, but vigilantes who had previously been protected by a widespread belief in "rough justice" now found themselves dangerously isolated from majority opinion.[6]

The Benavides lynching received considerable sanction from the New Mexico press. Some individuals and newspapers emphatically endorsed the actions of the mob. According to a letter published in the *Farmington Times Hustler*, the men who abducted and murdered Benavides performed a "noble and patriotic service" because they protected the community from further criminal incursions. The *Durango Herald-Democrat* was more blunt: "the degenerate Mexican got exactly what was coming to him."[7] Newspapers such as the *Herald-Democrat* made much of the fact that Benavides was a convicted felon. On September 5, 1914, Benavides was sentenced to a term of five to seven years in the New Mexico State Penitentiary for the rape of a ten-year-old Nuevomexicano girl.[8] Prison had apparently failed to reform him. In a blatant act of recidivism, he had drunkenly assaulted an innocent woman and left her for dead. The failure of the penal system therefore forced the people of Farmington to take preventive action against any further criminal outrages Benavides might perpetrate. The lynching of Benavides, it was believed, would also serve as a salutary lesson to other potential offenders. In the words of the *Mancos Times-Tribune*, "a more pronounced means of instilling fear into the hearts of the criminal class, was never resorted to."[9]

What is nonetheless remarkable is that many newspapers, despite their acceptance of Benavides's guilt, denounced his lynching as unjustified even under these circumstances. In a widely reprinted editorial, the *Santa Fe New Mexican* condemned lynching as "a dangerous experiment" because it claimed innocent victims, and demanded a "thorough and searching investigation" into the incident. The *New Mexican* articulated the influence of Progressive politics on public discourse about law and order. Its publisher, Bronson M. Cutting, had moved to Santa Fe from Long Island, New York, in 1910. As a former chairman of the board of commissioners of the New Mexican State Penitentiary, Cutting had a clear interest in the promotion of the criminal justice system over the lawless behavior of the lynch mob. In 1927 Cutting had also been appointed as a Republican to the US Senate following the death of the incumbent, Andrieus A. Jones. A year later, he won election in his own right. As the holder of such high political office, Cutting had to protect the reputation of his adopted state. However, he also had a reputation for actively promoting the political rights of Nuevomexicanos. These concerns informed the denunciation of the Benavides lynching in the pages of the *New Mexican*.[10]

In addition to criticism from newspapers such as the *Santa Fe New Mexican*, a number of interrelated social and political forces contributed to a decline in popular acceptance of mob violence by the late 1920s. The institutionalization of a formal legal system made a more significant impact on public opinion than did public protests by Nuevomexicanos. The Benavides incident appeared to belie the transition of the southwestern states from a remote frontier society to a more stable social order. During the early decades of western settlement many observers believed that vigilantism fulfilled a vital function of the frontier. In the absence of a fully functional legal system, the preservation of public order became the responsibility of community-minded citizens. Although not sanctioned by law, many Anglos believed these vigilance committees acted impartially and in the interest of the common good.[11]

Whether or not frontier justice had ever served a legitimate purpose, what was important was the perception that New Mexico no longer had need of vigilantes. By the late 1920s the establishment of an institution-alized legal system throughout the southwestern states undermined the legitimacy of frontier justice. An analysis of San Juan County court records between 1887 and 1928 demonstrates that the authorities commonly secured the indictment and conviction of serious criminal offenders.[12] The sentencing policy of the court appears to have been in part deter-mined by the ethnic identity of the convicted felon, evidenced by the fact that they imposed particularly harsh prison terms upon Nuevomexicanos. The minimum sentence imposed on a Nuevomexicano convicted of rape was two to three years; the maximum sentence was life.[13] By contrast, the only Anglo convicted of the offense received a one-year sentence.[14] Strong prison terms were also imposed on Nuevomexicanos convicted of mur-der. Donaciano Aguilar was incarcerated for ninety-nine years in 1909, and Edumenio Meastas for fifty to sixty years in 1927.[15] Arturo Rosales also affirms that after 1910 the use of the death penalty in New Mexico assumed a more explicitly racial dimension. The disproportionate num-ber of Nuevomexicanos executed during these years demonstrates that state authorities had to a certain extent supplanted the role of the lynch mob.[16]

Since there appeared to be indisputable evidence that Rafael Benavides committed an assault on Mrs. Lewis, the Anglo citizens of Farmington should have been confident of his conviction by a court of law. The *Santa Fe New Mexican* affirmed that the actions of the mob served no legiti-mate purpose. "In raw frontier communities where law was not yet estab-lished, Vigilantes were sometimes necessary. It is a question for San Juan county to decide as to whether she holds herself as a raw, lawless, frontier district." Although most newspapers accepted that Benavides was guilty of having committed a serious criminal offense, this did not in their opinion sanction the actions of the mob. In the words of the *Alamogordo News*, Benavides was a "miserable wretch" who had committed an almost unspeakable crime. However, he had already been arrested and would no doubt have been convicted by a court of law had he lived. Other news-papers expressed a similar sentiment that the barbarity of Benavides's crime did not in itself justify the actions of the mob. According to the *Farmington Times Hustler*, Benavides was a "beast man," the "perpetrator of the most revolting crime ever committed in the county." But he also had a right to be tried according to due process of law. Lynch mobs, "however well-intentioned, are dangerous means for dispensing justice and when less well-intentioned are a most dangerous menace to life, liberty and property."[17]

The lynching of Rafael Benavides therefore seemed to many political commentators to be an aberration, an unwelcome reversion to an era when citizens ignored due process for informal, community justice. The press acknowledged that racism had been the principal determining factor. Every one of the Nuevomexicanos convicted of a capital offense in San Juan County committed their crime against members of their own ethnic community. So long as this was the case, Anglos appear to have respected the due process of law. However, when a Nuevomexicano committed a criminal outrage against an Anglo, it inflamed a violent ethnic prejudice. The *Santa Fe New Mexican* astutely recognized this double standard. Had he survived his bullet wound, Benavides would have been tried and successfully convicted by the authorities. Those men who dispensed frontier justice could claim to have upheld the law; the mob that murdered Benavides undermined it.[18]

Many New Mexicans would have been uncomfortable with the racism in the lynching of Benavides in any event, but the shifting national perception of mob violence in the interwar era made the episode even more troubling. Americans perceived that the phenomenon of mob violence was in irreversible decline throughout the United States by the 1920s. According to the Tuskegee Institute, the principal source of information on the issue, the peak lynching decade of the 1890s claimed the lives of 1,333 people. By the 1920s, the figure fell to 321. While still disturbing, and a sign of the continued tolerance of mob law in the United States, this amounts to a decline of four hundred percent within a single generation.[19] Several forces shaped a new political climate less tolerant of the violent lawlessness of the mob. The NAACP launched an unrelenting political offensive against lynching in 1910. Less than a decade later, in 1919, the Commission on Interracial Cooperation mounted a regional campaign to mobilize southern liberal opposition to mob violence. Although the federal antilynching bill sponsored by Missouri Congressman Leonidas Dyer failed because of a southern filibuster in the Senate, the surrounding publicity stirred further popular outrage against lynch mobs. The federal government responded by assuming a more activist role in the arrest and prosecution of mob members.[20]

The Benavides lynching therefore threatened to place New Mexico out-side the pale of national opinion. Newspapers across the country reported the incident. This unwelcome publicity tarnished the reputation of New Mexico and threatened its association in the popular imagination with the violent racial intolerance of the southern states.[21] Newspapers across the state branded the lynching an act of barbarism that disgraced the people of New Mexico in the eyes of the nation. According to the *State Tribune*, "The good name not only of the county but of New Mexico is at issue."[22]

Political pressures not only within the United States but also without explain the critical reaction to the case. Mexican authorities continued during the interwar era to place unrelenting pressure on the US State Department. Mexican Ambassador Manuel Téllez undertook an investigation into the incident but had to abandon his demand for prosecution of the mob leaders when he learned that Benavides was actually an American citizen. The publicity in part generated by Mexican protest did, however, adversely impact upon state authorities. An editorial in the *Farmington Times Hustler* reflected the determination not to allow any further out-breaks of mob violence. "It will take San Juan County a long time to live down the bad name received by this lawless act," observed the paper. "The outside world will long remember the lynching but will forget the terrible crime that caused it."[23]

Protest of the lynching of Rafael Benavides by the Mexican govern-ment and condemnation of the episode by local and state newspapers and community leaders were important steps in the evolution of Anglo attitudes toward vigilantism and extralegal violence. But the newspaper-men and diplomats who criticized Benavides's lynching did not change public opinion on lynching in New Mexico by themselves. Rather, these critics of lynching succeeded in preventing future lynchings because the values they upheld were now more widely internalized among Anglos. In the nineteenth century, most New Mexicans had supported lynching as a "necessary evil" because of the frontier condition of the Territory and the weakness of its courts. As those courts improved, however, attitudes toward lynching evolved. By the twentieth century, Anglos had increas-ingly come to believe that justice should be meted out not by vigilantes but through the legal system in a deliberate and formal manner that empha-sized due process rights and procedures. In the end, the lynching of Rafael Benavides confirmed and accelerated a change in attitude that had been taking place throughout the previous quarter-century.

Lost to History

After 1928, with lynch mobs no longer acting in blatant defiance of the law, memories of the historical brutalities inflicted on Mexicans started to recede from the collective consciousness of Anglos, further clouded by a romantic nostalgia for their frontier past. By the turn of the twentieth century, lynching had become synonymous in the public imagination with the racist oppression of African Americans. Collective memories of mob violence outside the South were not entirely erased during the twentieth century. Hollywood Westerns certainly reminded the American public that mob violence shaped regions other than the South. Yet these films seldom represented Mexicans as the victims of rough justice.

Recent years have witnessed renewed interest in lynching among not only academics but also the larger public.[24] This attention has for good reason focused on African American victims of mob violence. Not only did lynch mobs murder African Americans in greater numbers than any other element of the population but, perhaps more importantly, the phenomenon also persisted long after similar outrages against other racial and ethnic minorities had ceased. Political agitation by civil rights activists further sustained public consciousness of mob violence against African Americans while other lynchings receded from collective memory. Scholars have also been drawn to the lynching of African Americans because of its power to symbolize the historical burden of racism in the United States.[25] This scholarship has performed a crucial role in restoring collective memory of black victims of white atrocities. Yet it also perpetuates assumptions that lynching was predominantly a regionally and racially specific phenomenon, a reading of the past that marginalizes or omits the victimization of other racial minorities outside of the southern states.

The academic focus on mob violence against African Americans in the South has also filtered down to high school education, as evidenced by the National Standards for History. In 1996, the National Center for History in the Schools at the University of California, Los Angeles, released a revised set of national history curriculum standards. The Center's standards and recommendations reflected a respect for both the traditional subdisciplines of political, military, and diplomatic history, as well as the more recent fields of social and cultural history. However, the history of Latinos in general and Mexicans in particular appear irregularly and infrequently in the standards. Indeed, the standards mention these groups directly in only two places: first, in relation to the Texas War for Independence and the US-Mexican War and, second, in the civil rights movements of the post-World War II era. They are indirectly included, one presumes, in a number of places where they refer to "immigrants" or "racial and ethnic minorities," but this is not completely clear. The two standards that address violence against, or the lynching of, racial minorities include explicit mention of African Americans and the Chinese but include no specific reference to Mexicans.[26] The practical result of not including direct mention of Mexicans is to reinforce popular misconceptions that they were not frequently the victims of mob violence. The particular emphasis on the South similarly compounds the assumption that lynching was a regional phenomenon, excluding other areas of the country that experienced widespread mob violence.

The exclusion of Mexicans from the master narrative of lynching is evident in contemporary politics as well as education. Renewed public interest in lynching in the late twentieth and early twenty-first centuries, led by the *Without Sanctuary* exhibit, stimulated a resolution from the US Senate in June 2005 offering a long overdue apology to the victims of mob violence and their surviving relatives for its historical failure to enact federal antilynching legislation. Both the resolution and the media response to it defined lynching almost exclusively in terms of white violence against African Americans. In the words of the resolution, "lynching succeeded slavery as the ultimate expression of racism in the United States following Reconstruction." It further stated that the victims of mob violence were "predominantly African Americans" but failed to identify other racial and ethnic minorities to whom the Senate should atone, other than the observation that lynching had led to the formation of the Anti-Defamation League, an oblique reference to the extralegal execution of Jewish businessman Leo Frank.[27] Whether sympathetic, hostile, or indifferent toward the resolution, editorial reaction also overlooked the multiracial and multiregional dynamics of lynching. For many newspapers, public reflection on past atrocities committed against African Americans provided a means to assess the extent to which the southern states and the country as a whole had overcome an historical burden of racism.[28]

Given the pervasive historical amnesia about mob violence against Mexicans, the question remains why the phenomenon has faded from collective memory. The most obvious explanation is that while mob violence against Mexicans receded after the late 1920s, the lynching of African Americans continued to hit national and international newspaper headlines. The onset of the Great Depression aggravated extralegal violence against African Americans as whites sought a scapegoat for their economic difficulties. During the 1930s, mobs lynched at least 119 African Americans, including some spectacular acts of sadism. On October 26, 1934, for instance, a mob seized black suspect Claude Neal from an Alabama jail cell and transported him across state lines to Marianna, Florida, where they tortured, mutilated, and finally hanged their victim. Shocking and highly publicized incidents such as this made lynching even more indelibly associated in the public imagination with white violence against blacks.[29]

Even when they still faced the threat of mob violence, Mexicans had been less active than African Americans in shaping popular understanding of lynching. During the late nineteenth century, crusading black journalists, foremost among them T. Thomas Fortune and Ida B. Wells, redefined public consciousness of lynching. Their relentless campaigning eroded the assumption that lynching served a legitimate function in the absence of a properly administered criminal justice system and established that it was an instrument of racial oppression used by whites against blacks. African American activists retained their role in molding and maintaining this definition of lynching during the early twentieth century, most conspicuously through the lobbying of the NAACP.[30] Although Mexican activists mobilized resistance to mob violence within their own communities, they were less assertive than African Americans in framing the broader public definition of lynching. The assimilationist strategy of Mexican civil rights organizations, such as the League of United Latin American Citizens, precluded agitation on the issue.[31]

The Selective Memory of Mob Violence

Although the decades since the lynching of Rafael Benavides saw historical memory of mob violence against Mexicans steadily erode, it did not disappear altogether. Although rare compared with representations of the lynching of African Americans, Anglos did occasionally recall the racial oppression of Mexicans, sometimes in memoirs that disclosed real crimes and in novels and films that depicted fictionalized incidents of violence. Yet even on those rare occasions when Anglos discussed anti-Mexican violence they often did so in a way that minimized the racial dimensions of the crime.

While many autobiographical accounts of life in the American West written by Anglos perpetuated popular romanticism about the frontier, some at least reminded readers of a darker historical reality. Miriam Chatelle recalled of her childhood in the Rio Grande Valley that, "There were several times that the Anglos mistreated innocent Mexican people, burning their huts, confiscating their stock and frightening them beyond all reason; this made us feel ashamed and hurt." One particular experience that still haunted her was a visit to a site where she saw the "charred remains" of three suspected Mexican criminals.[32] No Anglo author documented the atrocities committed against Mexicans in more detail than Napoleon Jennings. His confessional memoir has particular potency since he was a former Texas Ranger. Jennings recalled one specific episode in April 1875 during which "Large parties of mounted and well-armed men, residents of Nueces County, were riding over the country, committing the most brutal outrages, murdering peaceable Mexican farmers and stockmen who had lived all their lives in Texas. These murderers called themselves vigilance committees and pretended that they were acting in the cause of law and order." Moreover, those sworn to uphold the law were themselves responsible for many of the worst abuses committed against Mexicans. Jennings revealed how his Ranger company, under the command of Captain L. H. McNelly, regularly crossed the border into Matamoras under cover of dark "to carry out a set policy of terrorizing the Mexicans at every turn. Captain McNelly assumed that the more we were feared, the easier would be our work of subduing the Mexican raiders; so it was tacitly understood that we were to gain a reputation as fire-eating, quarrelsome, dare-devils as quickly as possible and to let no opportunity unimproved to assert ourselves and override the 'greasers.'"[33] Dramatic as these revelations were, such accounts were nonetheless too infrequent to disrupt the prevailing historical narrative of frontier life constructed by Anglos.

A similar assessment can be made of Anglo journalists who chronicled historical and contemporary acts of injustice against Mexicans. The most celebrated of these authors is Carey McWilliams, a passionate social justice advocate whose work exposed racial and religious discrimination against numerous minorities. McWilliams wrote extensively about Mexicans, most notably in his 1949 study *North from Mexico*.[34] In another of his books he described mob violence against Mexicans as being such a common practice in southern California during the nineteenth century that it assumed the characteristics of "an outdoor sport."[35] Yet his documenting of these atrocities had only a limited impact on popular understanding of lynching outside the region. One explanation for this is that his historical writing reached a smaller readership than his bestselling exposés of the plight of contemporary migrant laborers such as *Factories in the Field* and *Ill Fares the Land*.[36] A second reason is that other authors maintained the conception of race as a binary division between black and white. Gunnar Myrdal, whose *The American Dilemma* was published at the same time as McWilliams was writing about Mexicans, had the greatest impact on public consciousness about race. As is evident from the subtitle of the book, *The Negro Problem and Modern Democracy*, Mydral understood the contradictions between the principles and practices of American political culture in terms of black-white relations, to the exclusion of other races.[37]

Anglos depicted the lynching of Mexicans not only in factual but also fictional terms. Some of the earliest cultural representations of mob violence against Mexicans, created while mob violence was still a contemporary rather than historical phenomenon, occur in the films of D. W. Griffith. Scholars have contrasted the ambiguous treatment of Mexicans in these films with the unequivocally racist characterization of African Americans in Griffith's most famous work, *Birth of a Nation*. In *The Fight for Freedom* (1908), a Mexican who murders both a man who cheats him at poker and the sheriff who tries to arrest him flees a lynch mob but is eventually captured and taken back to town to meet his inevitable demise. His wife also dies during the chase. Another Griffith film, *The Greaser's Gauntlet* (also 1908), despite its title, provides a contrastingly sympathetic portrait of a Mexican falsely accused of theft but rescued from an extralegal hanging by an Anglo woman.[38]

The most famous literary and cinematic portrayal of mob violence against Mexicans is *The Ox-Bow Incident*. Walter Van Tilburg Clark's novel had an immediate impact on the American reading public when published in 1940, leading only three years later to a relatively faithful movie adaptation by director William A. Wellman. Set in Nevada during 1885, *The Ox-Bow Incident* is a forceful indictment of rough justice. In response to a report that rustlers have murdered a local cattleman and stolen his livestock, the citizens of a mountainous frontier community form a posse and set out in pursuit of the criminals. Eventually they come across the camp of three men, two of them Anglos and the other Mexican. Although some members of the posse become convinced of the suspects' innocence, they are too few in number to avert a lynching. As the posse men return home, however, they learn that the supposed murder victim is actually still alive and that he sold his cattle rather than having them stolen. Guilt and shame overwhelm them, most spectacularly in the case of a father and son whose conflict over the lynching leads both to commit suicide.[39]

With an antiheroic narrative that subverts the conventions of the Western genre, *The Ox-Bow Incident* brilliantly dramatizes the irrational mentality of the lynch mob. Written as the storm clouds of war gathered over Europe, Clark intended his novel as an antifascist allegory, a warning to Americans of the forces of intolerance and authoritarianism within their own midst. The inclusion of a Mexican among the lynching victims alludes to the racial supremacist ideology common to antidemocratic elements in either context. Prejudice alone does not explain the hanging of Juan Martinez. The mob does not single him out for further punishment before lynching him along with two Anglos. Yet the dignity with which he meets his death not only defies the stereotype of the cowardly Mexican but contrasts with the murderous impulses of the mob. The casting of handsome actor Anthony Quinn in the film heightens audience identification with the character. Martinez may be deceitful, not only pretending to the posse that he cannot speak English but even lying to his associates about his real name, yet in contrast to the villainous bandido of many Westerns, he is a sympathetic individual attempting to survive in a hostile environment dominated by Anglos.

An analogous depiction of a Mexican calmly and courageously meeting his death at the hands of a lynch mob appears in Niven Busch's novel *The Furies*. Published eight years after *The Ox-Bow Incident*, with a subsequent screen version shot by legendary Western director Anthony Mann, this is a Freudian tale of conflict between New Mexico cattle rancher T. C. Jefford and his headstrong daughter, Vance.[40] Jefford is ruthless in defending his estate against cattle thieves. Near the beginning of the novel we learn that whenever a robbery occurs it gives him "the excuse he wanted...for making a few coffee-colored Mexicans look for a new place to live and also, if you preferred other methods of retaliation, for rape, arson, lynching, tar-and-feathering, or any corresponding recourse."[41] This declaration anticipates a scene at the center of the novel in which Jefford orders the hanging of Juan Herrera, a Mexican who has supposedly purloined one of his cattle but more importantly stolen the heart of Vance. Herrera faces death with similar stoicism to Juan Martinez, standing straight and silently crossing himself as his executioners lead him to a noose dangling from a wagon pole. The scene solemnly encapsulates the corruption and brutality with which Anglos imposed control over the American West.[42]

Another novel less famous than *The Ox-Bow Incident* but more insightful about the motivations for mob violence against Mexicans is *The Law at Randado* by Elmore Leonard. Published in 1954, and later ineffectually filmed as *Border Shootout*, the novel is set in Pima County, Arizona, although the precise date is unspecified. It recounts the lynching of two Mexicans accused of cattle theft by a local citizens' committee. In contrast to Clark, Leonard explicitly identifies racism as a motivation for the lynching, members of the mob attempting to minimize physical contact with the "Greasers" even as they escort them to the makeshift gallows. The rationalizations offered by the leaders of the citizens' committee are also consistent with those of real-life lynch mobs. Not only will there be a delay transporting the prisoners to the county court, claims one of the conspirators, but any sentence is unlikely to meet the severity of the crime. "Chances are," he asserts, "the rustler's only given a term in Yuma and in a year or so he's back driving stock over the border again." Confronted by the inadequacies of the criminal justice system to protect Anglos from Mexican raiders, the committee appeals to the political tradition of local autonomy in taking the law into their own hands.[43]

What is missing from the narrative is any sense of how "Randado's small Mexican community" reacts to the lynching.[44] This is a novel in which Mexicans are the passive victims of Anglo violence. Leonard does not invite the reader to witness the grieving of friends and relatives of the lynching victims, let alone entertain the notion that they may seek to exact their revenge. The principal protagonist of the novel is instead Anglo Deputy Sheriff Kirby Frye who must reclaim both his manhood and the authority of his office by hunting down the mob leaders. Although the lynching of Mexicans provides the premise for the story, the subsequent struggle for control of this frontier town is between competing forces of Anglos: reactionary proponents of rough justice versus the civilizing agents of law and order. Mexicans are caught in the middle of this contest but cannot influence its outcome. Deputy Sheriff Frye duly arrests the main instigator of the lynching, Phil Sundeen, an outcome at odds with the darker historical reality in which Anglo law enforcement officers often participated in lynching or conspired in their cover-up.

Another problematic aspect of all three novels is their inclusion of a Mexican among the members of the lynch mob. In *The Ox-Bow Incident* a Mexican named Amigo (renamed Pancho in the movie) strengthens the resolve of the townspeople to pursue the cattle rustlers after claiming to have witnessed the crime. Amigo is not among the dissenters when the posse votes whether to hang the suspects. More striking still are the Mexican mob members in *The Furies* and *The Law at Randado*. In the former, it is Jefford's loyal henchman Quintinella ("El Tigre" on screen) who accuses Juan of cattle theft and tightens the noose around his neck, while in the latter the brutal Digo performs a similar role as the enforcer for his Anglo boss. To a certain extent the inclusion of these characters is consistent with the complicated intraracial dynamics of lynching. Their presence nonetheless diminishes the importance of racism as a motivating force for mob violence against Mexicans, distorting historical reality and diluting the dramatic impact of the novels individually and collectively. *The Ox-Bow Incident* may challenge readers' prejudices by having a proud and intelligent Mexican die at the hands of uncivilized Anglos, but the moral power of its message is undercut by Amigo, whose servile behavior and thick dialect ("What for you theenk I have the eyes, not to know heem; like thees") verge on racist caricature.[45] Worse still are Digo and Quintinella, characters who ironically conform to the very racial stereotype of Mexicans as sadistic criminals—"I swear all you think about is killin' people," Jefford exclaims to the latter—that historically fuelled the mob violence being condemned by their creators.[46] By contrast, it is inconceivable that a white author would write a novel about the lynching of African Americans in which the centrality of racism was not unambiguously clear.

While adaptations of all three of these novels later appeared on screen, there is also an original story produced for television in the 1950s that revolved around mob violence against Mexicans. *A Town Has Turned to Dust*, written by "Twilight Zone" creator Rod Serling and starring William Shatner, appeared as part of the Playhouse 90 series in June 1958. Set in the fictional southwestern town of Dempseyville during the 1870s, it is a story of violence and salvation. The drama opens with an angry mob taking a sixteen-year-old Mexican named Pancho Rivera from the jail cell where he is awaiting trial for allegedly robbing a store and raping an Anglo woman and hanging him. Having surrendered his prisoner to the mob, the sheriff eventually finds redemption by rescuing Pancho's brother from a similar fate.[47]

Although the production received positive accolades from critics, Serling had no particular interest in mob violence against Mexicans. His original purpose was to stage a dramatized reconstruction of the notorious lynching of African American teenager Emmett Till in Mississippi during the summer of 1955. When studio executives vetoed the proposal because they feared alienating white southern audiences, Serling substituted Pancho Rivera for Till and relocated the narrative in both time and place to the American West of the nineteenth century.[48] In constructing this surrogate storyline, he evidently drew on a historical memory of anti-Mexican violence. Yet he criticized his own use of Rivera as a proxy for Till in a way that implied a concern only for the contemporary plight of African Americans rather than the past mistreatment of Mexicans, lamenting that "By the time 'A Town Has Turned to Dust' went before the cameras, my script had turned to dust.... They chopped it up like a roomful of butchers at work on a steer." These comments may also have reflected a concern on Serling's part that his antiracist message would be lost on audiences who would associate a story set in the American West of the 1870s with frontier lawlessness rather than with white bigotry.[49]

Remembering and Recovering Mexican Victims

Although Mexicans were less successful than African Americans in molding national memories of lynching, they still wanted to remember the victims of mob violence. Rather than engaging in a spirited public debate on the issue, the nurturing of these memories occurred within their own communities, through stories and songs, usually in Spanish. These memories served to counteract racist Anglo narratives of Mexicans and strengthen Mexican resistance to Anglo discrimination but they had little impact on the English-speaking national majority who rarely heard or knew of these memories even when the most famous of the stories and legends became more accessible through translation.

The corridos sung on the southwestern border recounted the heroic acts of individual and collective resistance by Mexicans confronted with Anglo tyranny. Historical accuracy is less important than symbolic function in these musical narratives. The corridos reclaim those who took up arms against Anglos as freedom fighters rather than common outlaws. These tales of heroism enabled a disempowered Mexican population to strike back at least rhetorically against those who sought to crush ethnic dissent. The spirit of cultural resistance implicit in the corridos is reflected in a first-person narrative about the life and legend of Joaquín Murieta:

> *Now I go out onto roads*
> *To kill Americans*
> *You were the cause*
> *Of my brother's death*
> *You took him defenseless*
> *You disgraceful American.*[50]

Another ballad mythologizing Mexican resistance to Anglo tyranny is "El Corrido de Gregorio Cortez." The historical basis of the song is less contentious than is the case of the legend of Joaquín Murieta. On June 12, 1901, the sheriff of Karnes County, Texas, W. T. Morris, interrogated two ranch hands, the brothers Gregorio and Ronaldo Cortez, about a stallion they had reportedly traded to a fellow Mexican. Morris and the Cortez brothers addressed one another through one of the deputies whom the sheriff had brought along as a translator. The deputy, however, made matters worse by mistranslating several crucial points in the conversation. When the sheriff asked about the stallion, Gregorio responded that the horse he traded was a mare. The deputy, not understanding the distinction, translated the reply in a manner that incriminated Cortez. When Morris moved to arrest the brothers, Gregorio resisted. At this crucial moment, the deputy made another fateful mistake, confusing his declaration "You cannot arrest me for nothing" as "No white man can arrest me." When the sheriff drew his gun, Ronaldo lunged at him. Morris shot and wounded his assailant. Gregorio retaliated with a gunshot that killed the sheriff.[51]

Gregorio Cortez had led a life indistinguishable from that of thousands of other Mexican laborers who toiled industriously but inconspicuously in the southwestern borderlands. Born in Matamoros on June 22, 1875, while still in his teens, he had moved with his family to Texas. Married with four children, he made a modest living as a vaquero. The confrontation with Sheriff Morris nonetheless transformed him from man to legend.[52]

After shooting Morris, Cortez fled from the scene, first heading north but later turning south toward safety across the Rio Grande. He traversed around five hundred miles in ten days, pursued by hundreds of lawmen. When a posse tracked him down to a ranch on which he had sought refuge there followed a gunfight that led to the deaths of Gonzales County Sheriff Robert Glover and Constable Henry Schnabel. While he remained on the run, wildly inaccurate newspaper stories fanned the fear and prejudice of readers, Cortez mutating in the pages of the *San Antonio Express* into a marauding gang of murderers. Cortez had almost reached the border when, on June 22, a Mexican informer betrayed him to one of the posses giving chase.[53] There followed a series of trials in which Cortez faced charges of horse stealing and three charges of murder. Although a mob of three hundred men attempted at one point to lynch him, the courts ultimately determined his fate. Acquitted of killing Sheriff Morris and Constable Schnabel, Cortez nonetheless received a life sentence for the murder of Sheriff Glover. Having exhausted the appeals process, he commenced his incarceration at Huntsville penitentiary on January 1, 1905. Although pardoned by Governor O. B. Colquitt in July 1913, he had only a short time to enjoy his freedom, dying at the age of forty of pneumonia on March 21, 1916.[54]

"El Corrido de Gregorio Cortez" inverts gendered stereotypes of Mexicans and Anglos by emphasizing the masculine bravery and honor of its central protagonist in contrast to his timorous and indecisive pursuers. Cortez demonstrates great ingenuity in eluding the posse. Although law enforcement set bloodhounds on his trail, "trying to overtake Cortez was like following a star." Even when they track down their quarry, the "cowardly *rinches*" are unable to use their superior numbers to capture him. In response to Cortez's defiant declaration that he will never be arrested, the posse hopelessly concede, "If we catch up with him, what shall we do? If we fight him man to man, very few of us will return." When Cortez is eventually taken into custody it owes less to the acumen of the authorities than his own ethical concern not to endanger other Mexicans. "They say that because of me many people have been killed; so now I will surrender, because such things are not right."[55]

Despite the heroic depiction of Cortez, this narrative twist suggests that even the balladeers who mythologized Cortez conceded the futility of armed resistance against Anglos. Several Mexicans caught up in his flight from law enforcement officers did suffer the fate described in the corrido. A posse hanged until nearly dead the son of a family that had harbored the fugitive in the hope of gaining information of his whereabouts. He and his relatives also suffered imprisonment. In separate incidents during the manhunt, law enforcement officers killed three Mexicans, allegedly for resisting arrest, and wounded five others. Romanticized as the portrait of its hero may be, "El Corrido de Gregorio Cortez" also alludes to the darker consequences of Mexicans' confrontation with Anglo authorities.[56]

Since they were composed and sung in Spanish, corridos such as "El Corrido de Gregorio Cortez" did not have a substantial influence beyond the Mexican community, even when they became available in English translation. None of the corridos captured the larger public imagination in the same way as protest songs about the lynching of African Americans, including Irving Berlin's "Supper Time," Bob Dylan's "The Death of Emmett Till," and most notably Billie Holiday's heart-rending recording of "Strange Fruit."[57] The revival of the corridos by Chicano movement activists during the 1960s nonetheless demonstrates their importance as a source of political identity and empowerment, reconnecting a later generation with their heritage of racial oppression and determined resistance. This renewed interest in and enthusiasm for corridos stemmed from the publication in 1958 of *With His Pistol in His Hand* by folklorist Américo Paredes, which evocatively reconstructed the legend and reality of Cortez's confrontation with Anglo authorities. The book attracted a devoted readership on college campuses and later inspired a widely praised film. Its enduring significance has been to reclaim historical memory of racial violence in the borderlands and, in the process, invert the moral assumptions that underpin conventional narratives of the conflict between Anglo law enforcement and Mexican outlaws.[58]

Mexicans also sustained memories of mob violence through oral histories and storytelling. Testimonies collected by historians and folklorists in south Texas show how Mexicans nurtured this individual and collective consciousness by passing down reminiscences of their historical victimization from one generation to the next. These recollections privately preserved an important aspect of the history and identity of Mexicans erased from public discourses by the willful amnesia of many Anglos. Many of the Mexicans interviewed by academics drew either on their own memories or those of their parents in documenting the acts of resistance undertaken by friends and relatives confronted by Anglo violence. Ninfa Garza told of how her uncle Beto shot and wounded an abusive Anglo employer named Joe Holmes before fleeing to safety in California.[59] Mexican interviewees also preserved memories of the atrocities committed by Anglo law enforcement officers, especially the Texas Rangers. Such tales provided an important counternarrative to Anglos who repeatedly defended the actions of local and state authorities by claiming they protected the community from the violent criminality of Mexicans.[60] Celia Cuenca recalled how her father suffered permanent injury from the interrogation tactics used by the Rangers. In her words, he was "hung by the neck by the rinches to see if he would squeal on his friends."[61]

Mexicans' collective memory of mob violence informs their perception of contemporary vigilantism. Citizens' militias such as the Minutemen have been accused of numerous crimes against Mexicans illegally attempting to cross the border into the United States, including assault, kidnapping, and murder.[62] Many Mexicans contextualize these incidents within a longer historical continuum of nativist violence that dates back to the nineteenth century. A video posted on YouTube conveyed this perspective by interweaving images of current abuses committed against immigrants with older scenes of racial cruelty. The videomaker underlined the theme of historical continuity through his use of "El Corrido de Juan Cortina" as a soundtrack, evoking a tradition of heroic resistance to Anglo racism on which contemporary activists can draw.[63] In contrast to the seamless narrative of repression and resistance constructed by Mexicans, Anglos have seldom situated contemporary anti-immigrant violence within a larger historical framework, a limited perspective that allows the actions of vigilantes to be dismissed as aberrant behavior rather than an expression of brutal racial bigotry rooted in American political culture.

Reconstructing the historical reality about mob violence against Mexicans may facilitate reconciliation of these conflicting interpretations. The vigilantism committed along the border is not simply a case of history repeating itself. Although there is still a powerful strain of nativist intolerance in the United States—as evidenced by the enactment of legislation in Arizona in 2010 authorizing the stop and search of suspected illegal immigrants—contemporary militia groups do not command the same community sanction as the lynch mobs of the nineteenth and early twentieth centuries. Neither the press nor public officials have colluded in legitimating violent crimes against immigrants or concealing the identities of those who commit them. At the same time, Anglos who confine modern-day militias within a historical vacuum cannot hope to comprehend, let alone alleviate, Mexican anger. The roots of violent nativist bigotry run much deeper than post-9/11 anxieties about border insecurity. Uncovering the forgotten dead murdered by Anglo lynch mobs is therefore less a reopening of old wounds than a means to enhance mutual understanding in a nation where race remains one of the deepest fault lines.

Confirmed Cases of Mob Violence against Persons of Mexican Origin and Descent in the United States, 1848–1928

Date	Name	Closest Locality	State	Alleged Crime	Makeup, Size and Action of Mob (if Known)	Source(s)
Late 1849	Unknown	Sarage's Diggings	California	Theft	Hanged for stealing a mule.	Calif. Historical Marker 446; Weston, *Mother Lode Album*[1]
31 Dec. 1849	Unknown	Dry Diggings	California	Theft	Hanged.	*Placer Times* (Auburn), 19 Jan. 1850; *Rough Abstract of a Forty-Niner Diary*[2]
Jan. 1850	Juan Chapa Guerra	Brownsville	Texas	Theft	Whipped and then killed by a small group of men under mistaken impression that victim was Juan Chapa García.	Report of the Committee of Investigation of the Mexican Government[3]
July 1850	Francisco Flores	Brownsville	Texas	Murder	Hanged.	*Wisconsin Democrat*, 17 Aug. 1850
7 Jan. 1851	Pablo	Agua Fria	California	Murder	Hanged by a mob of 500 Anglos and 200 "foreigners."	*Sacramento Transcript*, 21 Jan. 1851
15 June 1851	Antonio Cruz and Patricio Janori	Shaw's Flat	California	Murder	Hanged for murder of Anglo before a crowd estimated to be between one and three thousand.	*San Francisco Herald*, 28 June and 1 July 1851

Date	Name	Location	State	Crime		Source
June 1851	Unknown	Jackson	California	Murder	Hanged by all-Anglo vigilance committee.	*San Joaquin Republican*, 28 June 1851
5 July 1851	Josefa Segovia	Downieville	California	Murder	Hanged by vigilance committee before crowd of 2000 miners.	John R. McFarlan Journal[4]
15 Nov. 1851	Domingo	Campo Seco	California	Murder	Hanged by mob filled with "fierce indignation."	*New York Times*, 6 Jan. 1852
22 Dec. 1851	Two unknown Mexicans	Rich Gulch	California	Murder	Hanged by vigilance committee.	*Journals of Alfred Doten*[5]
16 Feb. 1852	Patricio Chaves and Domingo Ramón Apodaca	Belen	New Mexico	Unknown	Hanged ("murieron orcados").	Archives of the Archdiocese of Santa Fe[6]; *Santa Fe Weekly Gazette*, 1 Jan. 1853
1 Apr. 1852	Carlos Esclava	Mokelumne Hill	California	Theft	Convicted by vigilance committee and hanged before a crowd "of all classes and sexes" and estimated to be between 800 and 1000.	*Alta California* (San Francisco), 3 Apr. 1852
12 Apr. 1852	Flores	Mokelumne Hill	California	Murder	Taken from officers and hanged.	*San Francisco Herald*, 3 May 1852

(Continued)

Date	Name	Closest Locality	State	Alleged Crime	Makeup, Size and Action of Mob (if Known)	Source(s)
Apr. 1852	Unknown	Rio Grande City	Texas	Murder	Hanged by the citizens in the presence of the "whole people—all concurring."	*New York Times*, 13 May 1852
Apr. 1852	Unknown	Rio Grande City	Texas	Murder	Captured in Mexico, returned to Texas, and hanged.	*New York Times*, 13 May 1852
Apr. 1852	Six unknown Mexicans	"The Wells," outside of Rio Grande City	Texas	Murder	Charged upon and shot dead by Anglos for murdering Thomas Harris "in all probability."	*New York Times*, 13 May 1852
29 Apr. 1852	Two unknown Mexicans	One hundred miles from Snelling	California	Murder	Tracked for over one hundred miles and then hanged by "Judge Lynch."	*San Joaquin Republican*, 5 May 1852; Collins, *Sam Ward*[7]
15 May 1852	John Balthus	Klamath river near Yreka	California	Theft	"Half-breed Mexican" convicted by vigilance committee and shot for theft of $800 in gold.	*Alta California* (San Francisco), 18 May 1852
10 June 1852	José Cheverino	Jackson	California	Murder	Hanged by a mob consisting principally of French goldseekers.	*Nevada Journal* (Nevada City), 16 June 1852

Date	Name	Location	State	Crime	Disposition	Source
11 June 1852	Cruz Flores	Jackson	California		Hanged "amid demoniacal rejoicings, and a spice more of severity, than is usually administered by the barbaric code of Judge Lynch."	*Sacramento Daily Union*, 12 and 14 June 1852
20 July 1852	Domingo Hernandez	Santa Cruz	California	Theft	Hanged by vigilance committee.	*Los Angeles Star*, 7 Aug. 1852
21 July 1852	Capistrano Lopez and unknown Mexican	Santa Cruz	California	Theft	Taken from jail and hanged for horse theft.	*Sacramento Daily Union*, 28 July 1852
21 July 1852	Pansa	Sutter's Creek	California	Murder	Lashed 75 times by vigilance committee, then hanged when victim died.	*Sacramento Daily Union*, 23 July 1852
24 July 1852	Doroteo Zavaleta and Jesús Rivas	Los Angeles	California	Murder	Hanged by vigilance committee.	*Los Angeles Star*, 31 July 1852
29 Nov. 1852	Reyes Feliz	Los Angeles	California	Murder	Hanged.	*Sacramento Union*, 16 Dec. 1852
12 Dec. 1852	Cipriano Sandoval, Benito Lopez, and Barumas	Los Angeles	California	Murder	Hanged.	*San Joaquin Republican*, 18 Dec. 1852

(Continued)

Date	Name	Closest Locality	State	Alleged Crime	Makeup, Size and Action of Mob (if Known)	Source(s)
Late 1852	Gabriel Luhan and José de la Cruz Vigil (Hispanicized Navajo)	Mora	New Mexico	Murder	Hanged.	*Santa Fe Weekly Gazette*, 18 Dec. 1852
Jan. 1853	Big Bill	Yankee Camp	California	Murder	Hanged.	*Sacramento Daily Democratic State Journal*, 31 Jan. 1853
Jan. 1853	Unknown	Murphy's Camp	California	Murder	Hanged.	Elias S. Ketchum Diary[9]
1 Feb. 1853	Unknown	Angel's Camp	California	Giving aid to outlaw	Hanged after he admitted to serving as a scout for Joaquin Murrieta.	Boessenecker, *Gold Dust*[10]
8 Feb. 1853	Two unknown Mexicans	Monterey	California	Theft	Taken from the authorities and hanged for horse theft.	Gonzales-Day, *Lynching in the West*[11]
15 Feb. 1853	Antonio Valencia	Jackson	California	Murder	Hanged by vigilance committee.	*Sacramento Union*, 17 Feb. 1853
20 Feb. 1853	Juan Sanchez	San Andreas	California	Murder	Hanged after confessing to be part of Joaquin Murrieta's band of outlaws.	*Placer Herald* (Auburn), 5 Mar. 1853
25 July 1853	Palonio Sanchez	Jackson	California	Theft	Seized from officers and hanged for horse theft.	*Sacramento Daily Union*, 29 July 1853

Date	Name	Location	State	Crime	Description	Source
4 Sept. 1853	José Maria Ochoa	Martinez	California	Murder	Hanged.	Gonzales-Day, *Lynching in the West*[12]
13 Oct. 1853	Bernardo Daniel, Higuerro, and three unknown Mexicans	San Luis Obispo	California	Murder	Hanged for murder of San Jose dry goods peddler.	*Los Angeles Star*, 22 Oct. 1853, 10 Dec. 1853; *Nevada Journal* (Nevada City), 4 Nov. 1853
11 Feb. 1854	Dollores and unknown Mexican	Angle	California	Murder	Hanged for murder of Anglo and left swinging from the tree "until decomposition shall take place."	*Columbia Gazette*, 25 Feb. 1854
21 July 1854	Nemesio Berreyesa	San Vicente Rancho	California	Murder	Abducted from his home and hanged.	Boessenecker, *Gold Dust*[13]
25 Aug. 1854	Unknown	Drytown	California	Murder	Hanged with a log-chain for murder of Chinese miner.	*Nevada Journal* (Nevada City), 8 Sept. 1854
2 Sept. 1854	José Higuera	Monterey	California	Murder	Hanged by vigilance committee for murder of Anglo constable.	*Placer Herald*, 9 Sept. 1854
Late 1854	Mateo Andrade	San Luis Obispo	California	Theft	Reportedly lynched sometime after his escape from San Quentin on 29 July 1854.	Gonzales-Day, *Lynching in the West*[14]

(Continued)

Date	Name	Closest Locality	State	Alleged Crime	Makeup, Size and Action of Mob (if Known)	Source(s)
22 Jan. 1855	Salvador Valdéz	San Joaquin river in Contra Costa County	California	Theft	Hanged by vigilance committee for cattle theft along with two unknown Chileans.	*San Francisco Daily Placer Times*, 27 Jan. 1855
Late Mar. 1855	Four unknown Mexicans	Doña Ana	New Mexico	Theft and assault	Taken from jail and hanged for robbing an Anglo clerk and "abusing" his wife.	*Santa Fe Weekly Gazette*, 31 Mar. 1855
22 Apr. 1855	Justo Betancour	Jesus Maria	California	Murder	Seized from magistrate's office and hanged.	*Georgetown Weekly News*, 10 May 1855
Early May 1855	Four unknown Mexicans	El Paso	Texas	Sexual assault	Hanged for "outrage on a family."	*New York Times*, 12 May 1855
7 Aug. 1855	Trancolino, Puertovino, and José	Drytown	California	Murder	Hanged by vigilance committee.	*Empire County Argus* (Coloma), 11 Aug. 1855
10 Aug. 1855	Manuel Castro	Texas Bar	California	Murder	Taken from law officers and hanged.	Secrest, "Revenge of Rancheria"[15]
15 Aug. 1855	Rafael Escobar	Jackson	California	Murder	Taken from law officers and hanged in presence of an "immense crowd."	*Autobiography of Charles Peters*[16]
Mid Aug. 1855	Unknown	Gopher Flat	California	Murder	Hanged.	Secrest, "Revenge of Rancheria"[17]

Date	Name(s)	Location	State	Crime	Description	Source
Mid Aug. 1855	Manuel García and at least six unknown Mexicans	Near Rancheria	California	Murder	Hanged by posse seeking suspects in the Rancheria murders.	Los Angeles Star, 25 Aug. 1855
19 Oct. 1855	Francisco Tapia, Jesus Pino, and Francisco Sanchez	One mile from Hill's Ferry	California	Theft	Hanged by vigilance committee along with German who confessed and implicated his Mexican partners.	New York Times, 29 Nov. 1855
1 Dec. 1855	Unknown Mexican	Corpus Christi	Texas	Murder	Taken from jail and hanged.	San Antonio Ledger, 22 Dec. 1855
24 Dec. 1855	Unknown Mexican	Snelling	California	Theft	Taken from law officer and hanged for cattle theft.	San Francisco Daily Placer Times, 30 Dec. 1855
11 May 1856	Three unknown Mexicans	Monterrey	California	Murder	Taken from jail and hanged "on rather slight proof."	Nevada Journal (Nevada City), 16 May 1856
Early June 1856	Unknown	Rio Grande City	Texas	Theft	Hanged for stealing horses and robbing a church.	Galveston Weekly News, 8 July 1856
Late Oct. 1856	José Castro	Pajaro river, near Watsonville	California	Attempted Murder	Hanged by Matt Tarpy and his vigilantes after being forcibly removed from Mexicans trying to protect him.	Santa Cruz Pacific Sentinel, 1 and 15 Nov. 1856

(Continued)

Date	Name	Closest Locality	State	Alleged Crime	Makeup, Size and Action of Mob (if Known)	Source(s)
29 Jan. 1857	Diego Navarro, Pedro Lopez, Juan Valenzuela, Miguel Soto, Juan Catabo, and two unknown Mexicans	Near Los Angeles	California	Murder	After the murder of an Anglo sheriff, a mob hanged Catabo, decapitated and shot Soto, and shot the other five.	*Sonoma County Journal* (Petulama), Feb. 20, 1857
2 Feb. 1857	José Jesus Espinosa	San Buenaventura	California	Murder	Hanged.	*New York Times*, Mar. 17, 1857
2 Feb. 1857	Encarnacion Berreyesa	Near Ventura	California	Murder	Hanged.	*El Clamor Publico* (Los Angeles), 28 Mar. and 9 May 1857
3 Feb. 1857	Francisco or Guerro Ardillero	Near Los Angeles	California	Murder	Hanged.	*Los Angeles Star*, 7 Feb. 1857
6 Feb. 1857	Three unknown Mexicans	Los Nietos	California	Murder	Two hanged, one shot.	*Sonoma County Journal* (Petulama), 20 Feb. 20 1857
14 Feb. 1857	Juan Flores	Los Angeles	California	Murder	Hanged in public ceremony for murder of Anglo sheriff.	*Alta California* (San Francisco), 2 Mar. 1857
16 Feb. 1857	José Anastacio García	Monterey	California	Murder	Seized from jail by a mob of two hundred and hanged.	Santa Cruz *Pacific Sentinel*, 28 Feb. 1857; *Santa Cruz Sentinel*, 12 May 1877

Date	Name	Location	State	Crime	Outcome	Source
Feb. 1857	Mexican Joe	Near El Monte	California	Murder	Hanged and decapitated.	Bartlett, ed., *Reminiscences of a Ranger*[18]
Feb. 1857	José Santos	Los Angeles	California	Murder	Hanged.	*Pacific Sentinel*, 21 Feb. 1857
11 Mar. 1857	Manuel Ribera	Santa Fe	New Mexico	Murder	Shot through the bars of his jail cell.	*Santa Fe Weekly Gazette*, 14 Mar. 1857
Early Apr. 1857	Eight unknown Mexicans	Near Goliad	Texas	Theft	Hanged.	*San Antonio Herald*, 18 Apr. 1857
Early Aug. 1857	Unknown	Near Escondido Creek	Texas	Killing of a cow	Hanged.	*San Antonio Ledger*, 22 Aug. 1857
13 Jan. 1858	Unknown	Brownsville	Texas	Murder	Hanged by the "inhabitants of Brownsville."	*Brownsville Nueces Valley Weekly*, 23 Jan. 1858
Feb. 1858	Jesus Anastasia	Monterey	California	Murder	Hanged.	*Nevada Journal*, 26 Feb. 1858
Late Mar. 1858	Carlos Martinez	Albuquerque	New Mexico	Assault on girl aged eight or nine years	Beaten and then hanged.	*Santa Fe Weekly Gazette*, May 1, 1858
Early May 1858	Unknown	El Moro	New Mexico	Murder	Hanged.	*Santa Fe Weekly Gazette*, 15 May 1858
13 May 1858	Santos Peralta	San Luis Obispo	California	Murder	Hanged.	*Santa Cruz Pacific Sentinel*, 26 June 1858

(Continued)

Date	Name	Closest Locality	State	Alleged Crime	Makeup, Size and Action of Mob (if Known)	Source(s)
29 May 1858	Nicanor Urdiales, Pablo Longoria, Francisco Huizan, and Felipe Lopez	Near San Antonio	Texas	Theft	Seized by band of thirty masked men from Mission San Jose and hanged.	*San Antonio Ledger*, 12 June 1858
8 June 1858	Joaquin Valenzuela and Luciano Tapia	San Luis Obispo	California	Murder	Hanged in "broad daylight."	Angel, *History of San Luis Obispo County*[19]
12 June 1858	Pío Linares	San Luis Obispo	California	Murder	Shot.	California Newsclippings[20]
14 June 1858	Miguel Blanco, Rafael Herrada, and Deiderio Grijalva	San Luis Obispo	California	Murder	Hanged.	California Newsclippings[21]
19 June 1858	José Antonio García	San Luis Obispo	California	Murder	Hanged.	*Los Angeles Star*, 12 June 1858
28 June 1858	Nieves Robles	San Luis Obispo	California	Murder	Shot.	Angel, *History of San Luis Obispo County*[22]
30 Nov. 1858	Pancho Daniel	Santa Barbara	California	Murder	Taken from jail and hanged.	*Los Angeles Star*, 4 Dec. 1858
9 May 1859	Four unknown Mexicans	Sonoita Valley	Arizona	Murder	Mob shot and killed these four Mexicans during attempt to expel Mexicans from region after murder of an Anglo.	*Tucson Weekly Arizonian*, 12–28 May 1859

Date	Name	Location	State	Crime	Description	Source
3 Aug. 1859	Rafael Polaco	Tucson	Arizona	Murder	Hanged.	Weekly Arizonian, 30 June 1859 and 20 Oct. 1859
23 Aug. 1859	Francisco Badillo and son	Near Santa Barbara	California	Theft	Hanged after elder Badillo found not guilty of horse theft.	Los Angeles Star, 3 Sept. 1859
12 Nov. 1859	Tomás Cabrera	Brownsville	Texas	Murder	Taken from jail and hanged under cover of night.	Corpus Christi Ranchero, 26 Nov. 1859
15 Oct. 1859	Unknown	Near Tubac	Arizona	Murder	Shot and then ears cut off.	Tucson Weekly Arizonian, 20 Oct. 1859
Early Spring 1860	Unknown	Colorado City	Colorado	Theft	Hanged by vigilance committee.	New York Times, 3 Sept. 1860.
26 Dec. 1860	Mateo García	Arizona City	Arizona	Murder	Hanged.	Los Angeles Semi-Weekly Southern News, 30 Jan. 1861
22 Mar. 1861	Unknown	Mesilla	New Mexico	Theft	Hanged.	Santa Fe Gazette, 13 Apr. 1861
10 Apr. 1861	Unknown	Mesilla	New Mexico	Theft	Hanged.	Mesilla Times, 23 Mar. 1861
28 Apr. 1861	José Claudio Alvitre	El Monte	California	Murder	Hanged for murder of his wife by a mob led by "his countrymen."	Sacramento Union, 6 May 1861

(Continued)

Date	Name	Closest Locality	State	Alleged Crime	Makeup, Size and Action of Mob (if Known)	Source(s)
13 Sept. 1861	F. Rameris	Near San Luis Obispo	California	Sexual assault	Hanged, rescued before dying, then seized from jail and hanged again.	*Sacramento Union*, 26 Sept. 1861
17 Oct. 1861	Francisco Cota	Los Angeles	California	Murder	Taken from authorities and hanged.	*Sacramento Union*, 17 Oct. 1851
Nov. 1862	Tom "the Spaniard"	Auburn	Oregon	Murder	Dragged down main street and hanged.	Bancroft, *Popular Tribunals*[23]
21 Nov. 1863	José Olivas and José Yreba	Los Angeles	California	Murder	Taken from jail and hanged by a mob of three hundred.	*Contra Costa Gazette* (Martinez), 28 Nov. 1863
24 Nov. 1863	Unknown	Alvarado	California	Attempted murder	Taken from jail and hanged from Alameda bridge.	*The California Farmer and Journal of Useful Sciences* (San Francisco), 27 Nov. 1863
9 Dec. 1863	Manuel Cerredel	Los Angeles	California	Murder	Taken from steamboat ready to transport him to San Quentin and hanged from yard-arm on the dock.	*The California Farmer and Journal of Useful Sciences* (San Francisco), 11 Dec. 1863
26 Dec. 1863	Luis Seyra and Cosmé Nuñez	Campo Chino	California	Murder	Taken from authorities and murdered by mob.	House Ex. Doc. #73[24]

Date	Name	Location	State	Offense	Method / Notes	Source
11 Jan. 1864	Joe Pizanthia, aka Spaniard Frank	Bannock	Montana	Murder	Corpse was burned (likely hanged before burning).	Bancroft, *Popular Tribunals*[25]
9 Feb. 1864	Patrocinio Lopez	Natividad	California	Murder	Hanged.	*Monterey Gazette*, 12 Feb. 1864
18 Feb. 1864	Jesús Arellanes	San Pedro	California	Murder	Hanged.	H. H. Bancroft, Reference Notes[26]
June 1864	José Aniceto Baldenbro and Simon Montoya	La Plata	Nevada	Refusing to cooperate with vigilantes	One man shot, other clubbed to death with end of a rifle.	*Virginia Daily Union* (Virginia City), 14 June 1864
19 Sept. 1864	Unknown	Near Snelling	California	Theft	Hanged.	*Sacramento Union*, 23 Sept. 1864
19 Sept. 1864	Unknown	Near Snelling	California	Attempting to prevent lynching	Shot.	*Sacramento Union*, 23 Sept. 1864
18 May 1865	Juan Higuera	Eight miles from Monterey	California	Murder	Son of 1854 victim, hanged for murder of a deputy.	*Monterey Gazette*, 19 May 1865
June 1866	Unknown	Golden	Colorado	Attempted murder	Hanged.	*Rocky Mountain News*, 27 June 1866[27]
Sept. 1866	Juan Valenzuela	Natividad	California	Murder	Hanged.	Reader, "Vigilantism"[28]

(*Continued*)

Date	Name	Closest Locality	State	Alleged Crime	Makeup, Size and Action of Mob (if Known)	Source(s)
1 Aug. 1867	Unknown	Near Adobe Ranch	California	Sexual assault	Hanged by vigilance committee after vote of twenty for hanging and ten for handing over to the authorities.	*Colusa Sun*, 10 Aug. 1867
Late summer 1868	Seven unknown Mexicans	Boerne	Texas	Murder	Hanged "indiscriminately."	*San Antonio Herald*, 20 Sept. 1868
30 Aug. 1869	S. Robles	LaGrange	California	Theft	Hanged.	Bancroft, *Popular Tribunals*[29]
13 Sept. 1869	Unknown	Elizabethtown	New Mexico	Murder	Taken from authorities and hanged.	*Santa Fe Weekly Gazette*, 18 Sept. 1869
20 Apr. 1870	José Ortega and Luciano García	Las Vegas	New Mexico	Theft	Taken from authorities by masked men and hanged for stealing groceries.	*New York Times*, 22 Apr. 1870
17 May 1870	Valentine Varaga, Jesus Gómez, and Gregorio Gómez	Watsonville	California	Murder	Taken from jail and hanged.	*Watsonville Parjaronian*, 19 May 1870
6 Sept. 1870	Juan de Dios Sepúlveda	Bakersfield	California	Murder	Taken from sheriff and hanged.	*Calaveras Chronicle*, 10 Sept. 1870,
26 Sept. 1870	Sacramento Duarte	Watsonville	California	Theft	Hanged in jail cell by mob.	Reader, "Vigilantism"[30]

Date	Name	Location	State	Crime	Method	Source
Oct. 1870	Unknown	Iron Springs	Colorado	Murder	Hanged.	Denver Rocky *Mountain News*, 25 and 27 Oct. 1870[31]
17 Dec. 1870	Miguel Lachenal	Los Angeles	California	Murder	Taken from jail and hanged in front of mob estimated at one thousand.	*Los Angeles Star*, 18 Dec. 1870
Jan. 1871	Donacino Sanchez	Saguache	Colorado	Theft	Hanged.	Leonard, *Lynching in Colorado*[32]
Feb. 1871	Pablo García alias Quemado and Tomás the "Chihuahuanian"	Los Lunas	New Mexico	Murder	Hanged.	*Albuquerque Republican Review*, 18 Feb. 1871
Feb. 1871	Diego Lucero	Albuquerque	New Mexico	Murder	Taken from jail and hanged.	*Santa Fe Daily New Mexican*, 19 Apr. 1871
July 1871	Unknown	Jimmy's Camp	Colorado	Theft	Hanged.	Leonard, *Lynching in Colorado*[33]
30 Dec. 1871	Pablo Padilla	Peralta	New Mexico	Theft	Hanged.	*Santa Fe Weekly New Mexican*, 16 Jan. 1872
5 Jan. 1872	Juan Sandobal	Peralta	New Mexico	Murder	Taken from authorities and hanged.	*Santa Fe Weekly New Mexican*, 16 Jan. 1872
12 Jan. 1872	Unknown	Banquette	Texas	Theft	Hanged.	Corpus Christi *Nueces Valley*, 27 Jan. 1872

(Continued)

Date	Name	Closest Locality	State	Alleged Crime	Makeup, Size and Action of Mob (if Known)	Source(s)
Spring 1872	Juan or José Castro	Watsonville	California	Theft	Hanged.	Reader, "Vigilantism"[34]
22 May 1872	Ramón Cordova	Phoenix	Arizona	Murder	Hanged.	Weekly Arizona (Tucson) Miner, 1 June 1872
18 July 1872	José Segura	Near Fort Stanton	New Mexico	Theft	Hanged and shot.	Santa Fe Weekly New Mexican, 25 July 1872
12 Oct. 1872	Unknown	Limestone County	Texas	Theft	Taken from his home and hanged by eight or nine men.	McKinney Messenger, 9 Nov. 1872
19 June 1873	Merijiilodo Martinis	Las Animas	Colorado	Murder	Taken from jail and hanged.	Denver Rocky Mountain News, 25 June 1873
28 June 1873	Domingo García	Near Tucson	Arizona	Murder	Taken from jail and beaten to death with clubs.	Weekly Arizona Miner (Prescott), 3 July 1873
3 July 1873	Mariano Tisnado	Phoenix	Arizona	Theft and rumor of past murder	Taken from jail and hanged.	Weekly Arizona Miner (Prescott), 12 July 1873
July 1873	Nine unknown Mexicans	Phoenix	Arizona	"Banditry"	Vigilantes rounded up and hanged nine men after Tisnado's lynching as concerted plant to clear region of "bandits."	Phoenix Herald, 26 Nov. 1880

Date	Name	Location	State	Offense	Action	Source
July 1873	Two unknown Mexicans	Phoenix	Arizona	"Banditry"	Two more "bandits" hanged a day after the lynching of the nine.	*Phoenix Herald*, 26 Nov. 1880
8 Aug. 1873	Leonardo Córdoba, Clemente Lopez, and Jesus Saguaripa	Tucson	Arizona	Murder	Hanged from murder of Mexican shopkeeper and his wife.	*Arizona Citizen* (Tucson), 9 Aug. 1873
Late Aug. 1873	Two unknown Mexicans	Near Trinidad	Colorado	Murder	Taken from officers and hanged.	*Denver Rocky Mountain News*, 28 Aug. 1873
Late Aug. 1873	Unknown female Mexican	Near Trinidad	Colorado	Unknown but clearly related to recent lynching in Trinidad	Hanged.	*Denver Rocky Mountain News*, 30 Aug. 1873
Late Aug. 1873	Three unknown Mexicans	Hole in the Rock on the Carson Road	Colorado	Theft	Hanged.	*Denver Rocky Mountain News*, 2 Sept. 1873
31 Aug. 1873	Lúcas Lugas	Kenyon Station	Arizona	Murder	Captured by small posse and shot in the back of the head.	*Arizona Weekly Citizen* (Tucson), 27 Sept. 1873
Early Sept. 1873	Manuel Subiate	Yuma County	Arizona	Murder	Taken from sheriff and hanged.	*Arizona Weekly Citizen* (Tucson), 27 Sept. 1873
16 Sept. 1873	Unknown	Nuecestown	Texas	Theft	Hanged.	*Houston Weekly Telegraph*, 17 Sept. 1873

(Continued)

Date	Name	Closest Locality	State	Alleged Crime	Makeup, Size and Action of Mob (if Known)	Source(s)
28 Nov. 1873	Filomeno Rios, Jorge Rodríguez, José M. Reinas, Epifanio Rios, Blas Mata, Vicente García, and Leonardo Garza	Rancho La Chuza, Duval County	Texas	Theft	Hanged.	Arias, Report on "Siete Pastores"[35]
20 Dec. 1873	Pedro Patrón, Isidoro Padilla, Dario Juan Balagan, and José Candelaria	Lincoln	New Mexico	No specific crime; victims of riotous racial violence	Shot and killed at a dance in Lincoln in revenge for the killing of Ben Horrell by Mexicans.	Albuquerque Republican Review, 10 Jan. 1874
Late Dec. 1873	Severanio Apodaca and four unknown Mexicans	West of Roswell	New Mexico	No specific crime; victims of riotous racial violence	Shot and killed on the road to Roswell in revenge for the killing of Ben Horrell by Mexicans.	Fulton, Lincoln County War[36]
2 Jan. 1874	Indian Charley	Frankstown	Colorado	Murder	Hanged.	Rocky Mountain News, 6 Jan. 1874
12 May 1874	Three unknown Mexicans	Cayman Lake	Texas	Murder	Hanged.	Galveston Daily News, 14 May 1874
17 May 1874	Tomás Valencia	North of Rio Puerco, Sandoval County	New Mexico	"The cause of the murder originated in a law suit."	Taken from his home with a rope around his neck and dragged "until his life was extinct."	San Diego Union, 3 June 1874

Date	Name	Location	State	Cause	Description	Source
17 May 1874	Juan Correro García	North of Rio Puerco, Sandoval County	New Mexico	"The cause of the murder originated in a law suit."	Taken from his home and his throat was cut with an axe.	*San Diego Union*, 3 June 1874
5 June 1874	Jesus Romo aka "El Gordo"	Near Los Angeles	California	Murder	Taken from officers by masked men and hanged.	*Sacramento Union*, 6 June 1874
7 June 1874	Juan and his two sons, Antonio and Marcelo	Refugio County	Texas	Murder	Taken from jail and hanged.	*San Antonio Express*, 12–16 June 1874
8 June 1874	Three unknown Mexicans	Refugio County	Texas	Murder	Taken from sheriff. One hanged, one body trampled by horse, throat of another victim cut.	Dobie, *Vaquero*[37]
25 June 1874	Mateo Robles	San Felipe	Texas	Unknown	Seized from his home by several men who arrived without their prisoner at Las Moras. Robles's corpse never found.	Mariscal to Fish[38]
30 June 1874	Gabriel Levya	San Felipe	Texas	Unknown	Seized from San Felipe, taken to ravine, shot, killed, and his body thrown into a river.	Mariscal to Fish[39]

(Continued)

Date	Name	Closest Locality	State	Alleged Crime	Makeup, Size and Action of Mob (if Known)	Source(s)
23 July 1874	Lupe Vaca and Isidoro Anaya	Desert Station	Arizona	Theft	Shot for stealing horses.	Arizona Weekly Citizen (Tucson), 25 July and Dec. 26, 1874; 2 Jan. 1875
27 Aug. 1874	Francisco Romirez	Near Brownsville	Texas	Unknown ("one of Cortina's men")	Hanged.	Galveston Daily News, 29 Aug. 1874
30 Oct. 1874	Unknown	Bloomfield	New Mexico	Murder	Hanged by mob led by sheriff.	Santa Fe New Mexican, 31 Oct. 1874
15 Dec. 1874	Antonio Guerra and Pedro Garza	Near Brownsville	Texas	Unknown	Hanged.	Galveston Daily News, 17 Dec. 1874
11 Dec. 1874	Ventura Nuñez	Burke's Station	Arizona	Murder	Taken from authorities and hanged.	Bancroft, Popular Tribunals[40]
Late Mar. 1875	Unknown	Corpus Christi	Texas	Murder	Captured and hanged by mob four days later.	Morris, "The Mexican Raid"[41]
Apr. 1875	Unknown	Near Corpus Christi	Texas	Theft	Killed and fed to hogs by vigilantes for horse theft.	Galveston News, 5 May 1875
1 Apr. 1875	Two unknown Mexicans	Chocolate	Texas	Unknown	Hanged.	Galveston News, 1 Apr. 1875
27 Apr. 1875	Two unknown Mexicans	Near Corpus Christi	Texas	Murder	Hanged.	House Report on Texas Frontier Troubles[42]
8 Aug. 1875	Jesus Mes, Pat Mes, Thomas Madrid, and Jermin Aguirre	San Augustin Ranch	New Mexico	Murder	Taken from authorities and shot.	Mesilla News, 14 Aug. 1875

Date	Name	Location	State	Crime	Description	Source
30 Oct. 1875	Cruz Vega	Near Cimarron	New Mexico	Murder	Tortured and hanged.	U.S. Department of Interior Papers[43]
6 Nov. 1875	Manuel Cardinas	Near Cimarron	New Mexico	Murder	Shot in the head while at door of jail under escort.	U.S. Department of Interior Papers[44]
4 Dec. 1875	R. García and J. Elvira	Campo	California	Theft	Seized from guards and hanged.	*Sacramento Union*, 6 Dec. 1875
21 Dec. 1875	José Ygarra	Hopland/Senel	California	Murder	Taken from courtroom and hanged.	Bancroft, *Popular Tribunals*[45]
23 Dec. 1875	Antone	Hopland	California	Murder	Hanged.	*Sacramento Union*, 27 Dec. 1875
Circa Jan. 1876	Pancho, Cruz, and Ramón Mes	Shedd's Ranch	New Mexico	Murder	Captured in Mexico, returned to New Mexico, and killed for murder of Oliver Thomas.	Mullin, *Lincoln County War*[46]
28 Jan. 1876	Anastacio Perez, Ponciano Lerma, and Emilio González	San Diego	Texas	Murder	Taken from jail and hanged by the "whole people united."	*Galveston News*, 5 Feb. 1876
2 Feb. 1876	Eight unknown Mexicans	Edinburgh	Texas	Murder	Hanged.	*New York Times*, 21 Feb. 1876
5 Feb. 1876	Three unknown Mexicans	Near Halletsville	Texas	Murder	Taken from officers and hanged.	Hicks to his nephew[47]
Feb. 1876	Juan Trajillo	Dry Cimmaron	Colorado	Murder	Hanged.	Leonard, *Lynching in Colorado*[48]

(Continued)

Date	Name	Closest Locality	State	Alleged Crime	Makeup, Size and Action of Mob (if Known)	Source(s)
22 June 1876	José María Miera	Near Albuquerque	New Mexico	Murder	Taken from jail and hanged.	*Albuquerque Republican Review*, 15 July 1876
28 June 1876	Melitón Cordoba, Gregorio Miera, and Juan Miera	Near Albuquerque	New Mexico	Murder	Intercepted, taken from officers, and hanged.	*Albuquerque Republican Review*, 15 July 1876
Early July 1876	Juan Buenvidas and Crespino Gallegos	Santa Fe	New Mexico	Murder	Hanged for murder of Anglo physician.	Spiegelberg Papers[49]
21 July 1876	Felipe Salazar and Jose Talmage	Cannon City	Colorado	Murder	Taken from jail and hanged.	*Colorado Weekly Chieftain* (Pueblo), 27 July 1876
Aug. 1876	Nica Meras	Lincoln County	New Mexico	Theft	Hanged for horse stealing.	Fulton, *History of the Lincoln County War*[50]
Aug. 1876	Jesús Largo	Near Fort Stanton	New Mexico	Theft	Hanged.	Fulton, *History of the Lincoln County War*[51]
3 May 1877	José Chamales and Francisco Arias	Santa Cruz	California	Murder	Taken from jail and hanged from bridge.	*Santa Cruz Sentinel*, 12 May 1877
14 June 1877	Five unknown Mexicans	Near Bonham	Texas	Murder and Sexual Assault	Executed by posse for murdering a man, a boy, and "outraging" three women.	*Bonham News*, 15 June 1877

Date	Name	Location	State	Crime	Outcome	Source
7 July 1877	Two unknown Mexicans	Near Banquette	Texas	Murder	"Made to pay the penalty of their crimes" by a posse for murdering a father and his son, a boy.	*Corpus Christi Weekly Gazette*, 14 July 1877
13 July 1877	Justin Arajo	San Juan	California	Murder	Taken from jail by masked men and hanged.	*San Francisco Chronicle*, 14 July 1877
23 July 1877	Marcos González	La Veta	Colorado	Murder	Taken from jail by 75 men and hanged from telephone pole.	*Denver Rocky Mountain News*, 25 July 1877
21 Nov. 1877	Andrés Barela	Costilla	New Mexico	Theft and attempted murder	Hanged for theft and attempted murder.	*Colorado Weekly Chieftain* (Pueblo), 22 Nov. 1877
22 Dec. 1877	Antonio Maron, Francisco Encinas, Miguel Elias, Fermin Eideo, and Bessena Ruiz	Bakersfield	California	Theft	Taken from jail by mob of 100 and hanged after a mock trial.	*Bakersfield Southern Californian and Kern County Weekly Courier*, 27 Dec. 1877
Early July 1878	Unknown	Bent County	Colorado	Murder	Hanged.	*Weekly Arizona Miner*, 12 July 1878
6 July 1878	Refugio Montallo Baca	San Jacinto	California	Murder	Taken from guard and hanged.	*Los Angeles Evening Express*, 11 July 1878

(Continued)

Date	Name	Closest Locality	State	Alleged Crime	Makeup, Size and Action of Mob (if Known)	Source(s)
Nov. 1878	Unknown	San Diego	Texas	Murder	Captured in Mexico, returned to Texas and hanged in front of crowd a hundred strong.	*San Antonio Express,* 5 Dec. 1878
4 June 1879	Manuel Barela	Las Vegas	New Mexico	Murder	Taken from jail and hanged.	*Albuquerque Republican Review,* 14 June 1879
12 June 1879	Romulo or Ramino Baca	Los Lunas	New Mexico	Murder	Taken from jail and hanged.	Santa Fe *Weekly New Mexican,* 14 June 1879
5 Dec. 1879	Francisco Sandoval	Las Vegas	New Mexico	Murder	Hanged from windmill by vigilance committee.	Stanley, *The Las Vegas Years*[52]
Jan. 1880	Juan Graviel	Alamosa	Colorado	Theft	Hanged by vigilance committee.	*Colorado Chieftan,* 8, 9 Jan. 1880[53]
Late Feb. 1880	Paz Chavez	Lincoln County	New Mexico	Theft	Hanged.	*Cimarron News and Press,* 11 Mar. 1880
Circa 10 Mar. 1880	Juanito Mes	Seven Rivers	New Mexico	Being a "Desperate Character"	Executed by vigilance committee.	Las Cruces *Thirty-Four,* 10 Mar. 1880

Date	Name(s)	Location	State	Crime	Outcome	Source
1 May 1880	Refugio Ramírez, his wife, Silvestre García Ramírez, and his daughter, Maria Ines Ramírez	Collins County	Texas	Witchcraft	Burned.	Zamacona to Blaine[54]
21 June 1880	José María Salazar	Vulture Mine	Arizona	Murder	Hanged by vigilance committee.	New York Times, 8 July 1880
Early Oct. 1880	Antonius Mestes	Heurfano County	Colorado	Murder	Mutilated and shot corpse dragged for a mile.	Rocky Mountain News, 16 Oct. 1880
26 Dec. 1880	Pantaleón Miera and Santos Benavides	Bernalillo	New Mexico	Murder	Hanged.	Las Vegas Daily Optic, 31 Dec. 1880
29 Jan. 1881	Matias Alcantar	Grantsville	Nevada	Murder	Taken from jail and hanged.	Sacramento Union, 8 Feb. 1881
31 Jan. 1881	California Joe, Escolastico Perea, and Miguel Barrera	Albuquerque	New Mexico	Murder	Hanged in Albuquerque's Old Town plaza in front of jail.	Santa Fe New Mexican, 30 Jan. 1881
Feb. 1881	Unknown	El Paso	Texas	Murder	Captured and hanged after confession.	Santa Fe Daily New Mexican, 16 Feb. 1881
25 Feb. 1881	Faustino Gutiérrez	Albuquerque	New Mexico	Murder	Note attached to chest: "Hanged by the 601—Assassin of Col. Potter."	Santa Fe Daily New Mexican, 26 Feb. 1881

(Continued)

Date	Name	Closest Locality	State	Alleged Crime	Makeup, Size and Action of Mob (if Known)	Source(s)
1 Mar. 1881	Two unknown Mexicans	Near Otero	New Mexico	Theft	Killed by posse who then left their bodies to "feed the buzzards."	*Las Vegas Daily Optic*, 4 Mar. 1881
15 Mar. 1881 31 Mar. 1881	José Ordoña Onofre Baca	Wilcox Socorro	Arizona New Mexico	Theft Murder	Hanged. Captured in Mexico, returned across border; seized by vigilantes, and hanged.	Zamacona to Blaine[55] *Las Vegas Daily Optic*, 31 Mar. 1881
10 June 1881	Narciso Montoya	Taos	New Mexico	Murder	Head "pounded" and body hanged inside courtroom.	*Cimarron News and Press*, 16 June 1881
Late July 1881	Miguel Tarazona, Joaquin Montano, José Samaniego, and Reinaldo Samaniego	Near Fronteras	Arizona	Murder	Sixteen Mexicans attacked by Clantons as part of riotous reprisal for murder of five Clantons. These four killed.	Morales to Gosper[56]
Late July 1881	Nine unknown Mexicans	Cochise County	Arizona	Murder	Bodies never found, believed tortured and executed by the Clanton gang as a reprisal for the killing of five Clantons.	Otero to Willard[57]

Date	Name	Location	State	Crime	Description	Source
Early Oct. 1881	Waken	Lincoln County	New Mexico	Theft	Mexican man seized from jail for horse theft; body never recovered.	Santa Fe *Daily New Mexican*, 7 Oct. 1881
6 Oct. 1881	Selzo Espinosa, Aristotle Noranjo, and Fernando Chávez	Los Lunas	New Mexico	Murder	Taken from jail and hanged.	*Las Vegas Daily Optic*, 7 Oct. 1881
25 June 1882	Francisco Tafoya	Las Vegas	New Mexico	Attempted murder	"Half-breed" who was hanged from telephone pole by a mob estimated to number 300.	*Albuquerque Morning Journal*, 25 June 1882
July 1882	Pedro Gomez and Pablo Aguilar	Near Laredo	Texas	Fighting and Protesting Killing of Mexican	Gomez killed by "crowd" of Americans because of participating in a fight among Mexicans. Aguilar killed by crowd for protesting Gomez's killing.	*Saint Paul (MN) Daily Globe*, 31 July 1882
16 Aug. 1882	Juan Alvarid (Elverad)	Socorro	New Mexico	Sexual Assault	Taken from jail by "immense throng" and hanged.	*La Cronica del Rio Colorado* (San Lorenzo), 19 Aug. 1882
30 Oct. 1882	Guadalupe Archuleta	Bloomfield	New Mexico	Murder	Hanged.	Albuquerque *Evening Review*, 1 Nov. 1882

(Continued)

Date	Name	Closest Locality	State	Alleged Crime	Makeup, Size and Action of Mob (if Known)	Source(s)
26 Apr. 1883	Two unknown Mexicans	Collins	Texas	Theft	Taken from law officers and hanged.	*Corpus Christi Caller,* 29 Apr. 1883
Early to mid-May 1883	Pedro Quintinilla	Rosita Creek	Texas	Theft	Hanged.	*Corpus Christi Caller,* 20 May 1883
14 June 1883	Unknown	Cotulla	Texas	Theft	Hanged.	*New York Times,* 16 June 1883.
17 June 1883	Encarnacion García	Los Gatos	California	Murder	Taken from jail and hanged.	W. F. Webb, "A History of Lynching in California"[58]
Oct. 1883	Unknown	Rosita	Colorado	Murder	Hanged.	*Buena Vista Democrat,* 1 Nov. 1883[59]
Oct. 1883	Unknown	Iron Springs	Colorado	Murder	Hanged.	Leonard, *Lynching in Colorado,* 171.
7 Dec. 1883	Four unknown Mexicans	Near Fort Davis	Texas	Murder	Armed mob seized prisoners and shot them.	*San Antonio Express,* 7 Dec. 1883
10 May 1884	Chaves	Silver City	New Mexico	Theft	Executed for train robbery.	*Southwest Sentinel* (Silver City)
3 Aug. 1884	Juan Castillo	Trinidad	Colorado	Murder and Sexual Assault	Given three hundred lashes at first, then hanged when victim died.	*Albuquerque Evening Democrat,* 4 Aug. 1884
23 Aug. 1884	Luciano Padilla	Cheese Creek	Nebraska	Sexual Assault	Hanged.	Pinkerton to Romero[60]

Date	Name	Location	State	Charge	Description	Source
26 Feb. 1885	José Trujello Gallegos	San Miguel County	New Mexico	Murder	Shot by a mob of twenty men.	*New Mexican Review* (Santa Fe), 21 Feb. 1885
23 Jan. 1886	Vicente Olivas	Susanville	California	Murder	Taken from jail, stripped of clothes, and hanged.	*San Francisco Call*, 28 Jan. 1886
14 Apr. 1886	Andres Martínez and José María Cadena	Collins	Texas	Theft	Taken from custody of constable and shot by masked men.	*Lockhart Register*, 30 Apr. 1886
30 Apr. 1886	Pedro Peña and Mateo Cadena	Duval County	Texas	Theft	Hanged.	*Dallas Morning News*, 29 Apr. 1886
Dec. 1886	Gus Kerwood	Washakie Mountains	Wyoming	Murder	This "young man of Spanish descent" was hanged as an alleged horse thief.	*Cheyenne Daily Leader*, 13 Jan. 1887
1 Jan. 1887	Three unknown Mexicans	Guadalupe County	Texas	Filing legal action against member of mob	Shot and burned by small group of African Americans.	*Lockhart Register*, 7 Jan. 1887
7 Dec. 1887	Cecilio Ybarra and Viviano Diaz	Near Rio Grande City	Texas	Kidnapping	Taken from sheriff and hanged.	*Corpus Christi Weekly Caller*, 17 Dec. 1887
10 Dec. 1887	José Maria Casas and Gerardo Contreras	Near Rio Grande City	Texas	Theft	Taken from jail and hanged.	*Beeville Bee*, 15 Dec. 1887
14 Jan. 1888	Mat Pettis and Reto	Caldwell	Texas	Murder	Mob entered jail and shot two Mexicans.	*Dallas Morning News*, 17 Jan. 1888

(Continued)

Date	Name	Closest Locality	State	Alleged Crime	Makeup, Size and Action of Mob (if Known)	Source(s)
24 Jan. 1888	Santos Salizar	Collins	Texas	Murder	Hanged.	*Dallas Morning News*, 24 Jan. 1888
20 July 1889	Two unknown Mexicans	Kelly	New Mexico	Theft	Taken from guard, riddled with bullets, then hanged.	*Santa Fe New Mexican*, 25 July 1889
9 Jan. 1890	Unknown	Georgetown	New Mexico	Attempted murder	Taken from officers, shot and hanged.	*Santa Fe New Mexican*, 9 Jan. 1890
12 June 1890	Unknown	Taylor	Texas	Sexual assault	Taken from officers, hanged, and then shot.	*Austin Statesman*, 14 June 1890
5 Feb. 1891	Jesus Salceda	Knickerbocker	Texas	Unknown	Hanged by mob from San Angelo.	*Austin Statesman*, 7 Feb. 1891
20 Aug. 1892	Francisco Torres	Santa Ana	California	Murder	Hanged for murder of foreman.	*New York Times*, 21 Aug. 1892
22 Oct. 1892	Patricio Maes	Las Vegas	New Mexico	Breaking vigilante vow of silence	Onetime vigilante hanged by vigilantes after mock trial.	*Las Vegas Daily Optic*, 22 Oct. 1892
5 Feb. 1893	Ireneo González	Ceboletta	New Mexico	Attempted murder	Taken from jail and hanged.	*El Boletín Popular* (Santa Fe), 9 Feb. 1893
7 Apr. 1893	Jesús Fuen	San Bernardino	California	Murder	Taken from jail and hanged from bridge in front of crowd estimated at 700.	*Los Angeles Times*, 7, 8, 9 and 10 Apr. 1893

Date	Name	Location	State	Accusation	Description	Source
5 May 1893	Antonio Martínez, Antonio José García, and Victoriano Aragón	Los Lunas	New Mexico	Murder	Taken from jail and hanged.	*El Boletín Popular* (Santa Fe), 11 May 1893
29 May 1893	Celio Lucero	Las Vegas	New Mexico	Murder	Taken from officers and hanged in front of crowd estimated to number 1000.	*El Nuevo Mexicano* (Albuquerque), 3 June 1893
9 Nov. 1894	Charlie Williams	West Caroll Parish	Louisiana	Murder	Taken from jail by "infuriated crowd" who shot the "half-breed Mexican."	*New Orleans Times-Democrat*, 9 Nov. 1894
26 Aug. 1895	Luis Moreno	Yreka	California	Murder	Taken from jail and hanged.	*Yreka Journal*, 27 Aug. 1895
11 Oct. 1895	Florentino Suaste	Cotulla	Texas	Murder	Taken from jail, shot, and then hanged.	*Carrizo Springs Javelin*, 19 Oct. 1895
22 Oct. 1895	James Umbra and Mexican John	Hennessey	Oklahoma	Theft	Executed for cattle stealing.	Tuskegee Lynching Records
30 Jan. 1896	Aureliano Castellán	Near Senior	Texas	"Paying attention" to white woman	Shot and burned.	*San Antonio Express*, 31 Jan. 1896
Early May 1897	Unknown	Milam County	Texas	Unknown.	Hanged.	*Austin Daily Statesman*, 20 May 1897
28 June 1897	Marcelo Tijares	Clifton	Arizona	Murder	Taken from jail and shot to death.	*Arizona Republican*, 28 Oct. 1897

(Continued)

Date	Name	Closest Locality	State	Alleged Crime	Makeup, Size and Action of Mob (if Known)	Source(s)
5 Apr. 1898	Carlos Guillen	Brownsville	Texas	Murder	Shot in jail cell by "frenzied" mob.	*Corpus Christi Weekly Caller*, 8 Apr. 1898
28 July 1901	Ignacio Rivera	Hart's Ranch	Arizona	Theft	Hanged for horse stealing.	*Arizona Gazette*, 30 July 1901
25 Aug. 1901	Felix Martínez	Near Kenedy	Texas	Unknown	Called to his door by "other Mexicans" and shot to death.	*Corpus Christi Caller*, 30 Aug. 1901
16 Feb. 1905	Carlos Muñoz	Dale	Texas	Sexual assault	Taken from officers and shot.	*Dallas Morning News*, 18 Feb. 1905
12 Oct. 1909	Michael Rodriguez	Slabtown	Louisiana	Theft	"Lynched."	*Chicago Daily Tribune*, 1 Jan. 1910
3 Nov. 1910	Antonio Rodriguez	Rock Springs	Texas	Murder and sexual assault	Seized from jail, tied to a tree, and burned alive.	*San Antonio Light Gazette*, 4 Nov. 1910
30 May 1911	Unknown	Barstow	Texas	Shouting "¡Viva Diaz!"	Surrounded and shot by Americans and Mexicans.	*New York Times*, 31 May 1911
20 June 1911	Antonio Gómez	Thorndale	Texas	Murder	Beaten and dragged behind buggy through the streets by a mob estimated at 100.	*Thorndale Thorn*, 23 June 1911
31 Mar. 1914	Adolfo Padilla	Santa Fe	New Mexico	Murder	Seized from jail by masked men and stabbed to death.	*El Combate* (Wagon Mound, NM), 11 Apr. 1914

Date	Name	City	State	Charge	Fate	Source
23 Dec. 1914	Alejos Argijo	Oakville	Texas	Murder	Tortured, hanged, and shot.	*The Beeville Bee*, 24 Dec. 1914
19 Feb. 1915	Juan Gonzalez	Omaha	Nebraska	Murder	Shot by a posse of 200 men for killing police officer.	Garza thesis[61]
19 Apr. 1915	Hilario and José Maria Leon	Greaterville	Arizona	Murder	Hanged during interrogation by police officers.	*Tucson Citizen*, 22–24, 26–29 Apr., and 3, 8, 11, 14, 18 May 1915
24 July 1915	Lorenzo and Gorgonio Manriquez	Mercedes	Texas	Murder	Shot by posse.	Frank Pierce Inventory[62]
29 July 1915	Rudolfo Muñoz	Brownsville	Texas	Murder	Taken from jail by seven or eight masked men and hanged.	*Victoria Advocate*, 30 July 1915
3 Aug. 1915	Desiderio Flores, Antonio Flores, and Desiderio Flores, Jr.	Paso Real	Texas	Murder	Shot by posse and left to rot. One body riddled with seventeen bullets.	*Brownsville Herald*, 7 Aug. 1915
8 Aug. 1915	Eusebio Hernandez	El Suaz ranch, south of Raymondville	Texas	Giving refuge to outlaws	Shot by posse.	*Nevada State Journal*, 15 Aug. 1915 and Frank Pierce Inventory
8 Aug. 1915	Abraham Salinas and Juan Tobar	Norias	Texas	Murder	Shot by posse.	Johnson, *Revolution in Texas*, 113.
10 Aug. 1915	Francisco Becanegra and unknown Mexican	Near Sebastian	Texas	Alleged outlaw	Shot.	*Dallas Morning News*, 11 Aug. 1915

(Continued)

Date	Name	Closest Locality	State	Alleged Crime	Makeup, Size and Action of Mob (if Known)	Source(s)
12 Aug. 1915	Three unknown Mexicans	Between Mercedes and Donna	Texas	Murder	Shot by posse, details obscured by "policy of secrecy" adopted by law officers.	*Dallas Morning News*, 13 Aug. 1915
18 Aug. 1915	Two unknown Mexicans	Brownsville	Texas	Murder	Shot by mob while lodged in jail during a "break" taken by the guards.	*Brownsville Herald*, 19 Aug. 1915
20 Aug. 1915	Six unknown Mexicans	San Benito	Texas	Murder	Taken from jail and hanged.	Meed, *Bloody Border*[63]
Sept. 1915	Fourteen unknown Mexicans	Near Donna	Texas	Alleged outlaws	Most shot and left where slain, at least two hanged.	Frank Pierce Inventory
2 Sept. 1915	Three unknown Mexicans	Los Cuates	Texas	Murder and "resisting arrest"	Shot.	*Brownsville Herald*, 3 Sept. 1915
2 Sept. 1915	Three unknown Mexicans	Near Edinburg	Texas	Murder and "resisting arrest"	Shot, but one of three men also decapitated, tied to a tree trunk, and thrown into Rio Grande.	*New York American*, 15 Sept. 1915
10 Sept. 1915	Ygnacio Rincones, Alejos Vela, and Angel Rivera	Between San Benito and Harlingen	Texas	Murder	Taken from jail and shot.	Investigation of the Texas Rangers[64]

Date	Name	Location	State	Alleged Offense	Disposition	Source
13 Sept. 1915	Unknown Mexican	Cameron County	Texas	Alleged outlaw	After arrest, shot and killed by "mishap" during transit to jail.	*Brownsville Herald*, 16 Sept. 1915
14 Sept. 1915	Unknown	Lyford	Texas	Theft	Shot.	*San Antonio Express*, 15 Sept. 1915
14 Sept. 1915	Unknown	Sebastian	Texas	Theft	Shot.	*San Antonio Express*, 15 Sept. 1915
14 Sept. 1915	Unknown	Lacoma	Texas	Theft	Shot.	*San Antonio Express*, 15 Sept. 1915
17 Sept. 1915	Refugio Perez	Lyford	Texas	Mistaken for outlaw	Shot.	Frank Pierce Inventory
17 Sept. 1915	Alberto Cantú	Lyford	Texas	Alleged outlaw	Shot.	Frank Pierce Inventory
17 Sept. 1915	Juan Nepemuceno Rodriguez	South Texas	Texas	Alleged outlaw	Dragged "with wire around neck" and then shot.	Frank Pierce Inventory
28 Sept. 1915	Twelve (at least) unknown Mexicans	Ebenoza	Texas	Murder	Hanged.	Investigation of the Texas Rangers and Johnson, *Revolution in Texas*
Late Sept. 1915	Jesus Bazan and Longorio	Hidalgo County	Texas	Giving refuge to outlaws	Shot.	Johnson, *Revolution in Texas*[65]
Oct. 1915	Juan Niete	Las Norias	Texas	Alleged outlaw	Captured at Lyford, transported to Las Norias and shot.	Frank Pierce Inventory

(Continued)

Date	Name	Closest Locality	State	Alleged Crime	Makeup, Size and Action of Mob (if Known)	Source(s)
19 Oct. 1915	Trinidad Ybarra, Manuel Ybarra, Severe Garcia, Santiago Salas and six unknown Mexicans	Near Brownsville	Texas	Murder and trainwrecking	Four hanged and the other six shot.	*Bonham News*, 22 Oct. 1915
Late Oct. 1915	Manuel Robles	Sebastian	Texas	Alleged outlaw	Shot in his home by vigilantes.	Johnson, *Revolution in Texas*[66]
Nov. 1915	Juan Tevar	Las Norias	Texas	Alleged outlaw	Shot after being captured and taken prisoner.	Frank Pierce Inventory
May 1916	Victoriano Ponce and José Morin	Kingsville	Texas	Alleged Outlaws	Shot after being captured and taken prisoner.	Investigation of the Texas Rangers
20 June 1916	Geronimo Lerma	Near Brownwood	Texas	Attempted Murder	Shot by posse.	*Daily Bulletin* (Brownwood, Texas), 21 June 1916

Date	Name(s)	Place	State	Charge	Description	Source
28 Jan. 1918	Bivanio, Pedro, and Sibranio Herrera, Flores Longinio, Ramon Nieves, Tiburcio Jacquez, Alberto Garcia, Macadonio Huerta, Ambrocia Hernandez, Eutemio Gonzalez, Manuel Morales, Antonio Casteneda, and Serapio, Pedro and Juan Jiminez,	Porvenir	Texas	Being "thieves, informers, spies, and murderers"	Rounded up from their village, taken to nearby hillside, and executed.	Investigation of the Texas Rangers
5 Apr. 1918	Florencio Garcia	near Port Isabelle	Texas	Theft	Taken from jail and found shot to death on the road to San Benito.	Investigation of the Texas Rangers
13 Sept. 1919	José Gonzalez and Santos Ortez	Pueblo	Colorado	Murder	Hanged by mob of 100 persons for murder of policeman.	Denver *Colorado Post*, 20 Sept. 1919
11 Nov. 1922	Elias Villareal Zarate	Weslaco	Texas	Assault	Taken from jail and hanged for fighting with a white co-worker.	*San Antonio Light*, 14 Nov. 1922

(*Continued*)

Date	Name	Closest Locality	State	Alleged Crime	Makeup, Size and Action of Mob (if Known)	Source(s)
9 Sept. 1926	Tómas Nuñez and his two sons	Raymondville	Texas	Murder	Taken from jail, beaten to death, and secretly buried.	El Cronista del Valle (Brownsville), 8 Sept. 1926
16 Nov. 1928	Rafael Benavides	Farmington	New Mexico	Sexual assault	Taken from hospital and hanged by mob of masked men.	Farmington Times Hustler, 16, 24, 30 Nov. 1928

[1] Otheto Weston, Mother Lode Album (Stanford: Stanford University Press, 1948), 30.

[2] Anonymous, Rough Abstract of a Forty-Niner Diary, unpublished manuscript, Bancroft Library, University of California, Berkeley.

[3] Reports of the Committee of Investigation Sent in 1873 by the Mexican Government to the Frontier of Texas, translated from the official edition made in Mexico (New York: Baker & Godwin, 1875), 179.

[4] John R. McFarlan Journal, 7 July 1851, Henry E. Huntington Library, San Marino, California.

[5] Walter Van Tilburg Clark, ed., The Journals of Alfred Doten, 1849–1903 (Reno: University of Nevada Press, 1973), 100–105.

[6] Nuestra Senora de Belen, Burials, 16 Feb. 1852, Archives of the Archdiocese of Santa Fe, 1851–1854, microfilm roll 35, District Court Records, New Mexico State Records Center and Archives, Santa Fe, New Mexico (SRCA); cited in Robert J. Tórrez, Myth of the Hanging Tree (Albuquerque: University of New Mexico Press, 2008), 164.

[7] Carrol Collins, ed., Sam Ward in the Gold Rush (Stanford: Stanford University Press, 1949), 164–7, quote (171).

[8] Cited in Tórrez, Myth of the Hanging Tree, 5.

[9] Elias S. Ketchum Diary, Henry E. Huntington Library, San Marino, California.

[10] John Boessenecker, Gold Dust and Gunsmoke: Tales of Gold Rush Outlaws, Gunfighters, Lawmen, and Vigilantes (New York: John Wiley and Sons, Inc., 1999), 88.

[11] Ken Gonzales-Day, Lynching in the West (Durham: Duke University Press, 2006), 212.

[12] Gonzales-Day, Lynching in the West, 213.

[13] John Boessenecker, Gold Dust and Gunsmoke, 68–69.

[14] Gonzales-Day, Lynching in the West, 213.

15 William B. Secrest, "Revenge of Rancheria," *Frontier Times* (Sept. 1968), 16–19, 59–61.

16 Charles Peters, *The Autobiography of Charles Peters* (Sacramento, CA: The LaGrave Co., 1915), 21.

17 Secrest, "Revenge of Rancheria," 59–61.

18 Lanier Bartlett, ed., *On the Old West Coast: Being further Reminiscences of a Ranger, Major Horace Bell* (New York: William Morrow & Co., 1930), 100–101.

19 Myron Angel, *History of San Luis Obispo County, California* (Berkeley: Howell-Worth Books, 1966), 296.

20 California Newsclippings, 1888–1897, Rare Book # 34549, HEH.

21 California Newsclippings, 1888–1897, Rare Book # 34549, HEH.

22 Myron Angel, *History of San Luis Obispo County, California*, 303–4.

23 Hubert Howe Bancroft, "Popular Tribunals—Volume I," in *The Works of Hubert Howe Bancroft*, vol. 36 (San Francisco: The History Company, Publisher, 1887), 630.

24 "The Condition of Affairs in Mexico," House Executive Document No. 73, US Congress, 39th Congress, 1st session, Serial Set # 1262, pp. 206, 207, 215.

25 Hubert Howe Bancroft, "Popular Tribunals—Volume I," in *The Works of Hubert Howe Bancroft*, vol. 36, 682.

26 *San Francisco Daily Alta California*, n.d., quoted in Bancroft, Reference Notes, Spring Binder no. 16, MS, Bancroft Library, Berkeley, California.

27 Cited in Stephen J. Leonard, *Lynching in Colorado, 1859–1919* (Boulder: University Press of Colorado, 2002), 55.

28 Phil Reader, *A Brief History of the Pajaro Property Protective Society: Vigilantism in the Pajaor Valley during the 19th Century* (Santa Cruz: Cliffside Publishing, 1995), posted online at www.santacruzpl.org, accessed to July 2008.

29 Hubert Howe Bancroft, "Popular Tribunals—Volume I," in *The Works of Hubert Howe Bancroft*, vol. 36, 568–69.

30 Reader, *A Brief History of the Pajaro Property Protective Society*, www.santacruzpl.org.

31 Cited in Stephen J. Leonard, *Lynching in Colorado, 1859–1919*, 54.

32 Stephen J. Leonard, *Lynching in Colorado, 1859–1919*, 169.

33 Stephen J. Leonard, *Lynching in Colorado, 1859–1919*, 55.

34 Reader, *A Brief History of the Pajaro Property Protective Society*, www.santacruzpl.org.

35 Juan D. Arias Reports, "Siete Pastores," T 312, 25 Nov. 1874, 590–699; and T 315, 29 Mar. 1875, 57–59, Matías Romero Institute, Archivo de Secretaría de Relaciones Exteriores (SRE), Mexico City.

36 Maurice Garland Fulton, *History of the Lincoln County War* (Tucson: University of Arizona Press, 1968), 21–24.

37 J. Frank Dobie, *A Vaquero of the Brush Country* (New York: Grosset & Dunlap, 1929), 71–72.

38 Ignacio Mariscal to Hamilton Fisk, 8 Mar. 1875, T 315, N. 22, SRE.

39 Ignacio Mariscal to Hamilton Fisk, 8 Mar. 1875, T 315, N. 22, SRE.

40 Hubert Howe Bancroft, "Popular Tribunals—Volume I," in *The Works of Hubert Howe Bancroft*, vol. 36, 732–33.

41 Leopold Morris, "The Mexican Raid of 1875 on Corpus Christi," *The Quarterly of the Texas State Historical Association* 4:1 (July 1900), 138–39.

42 "Texas Frontier Troubles," House Reports, 44th Congress, First Session, Report No. 343 (Series No. 1709), xx.

43 Investigation of O. P. McMains, United States Department of Interior, Appointment Papers: Territory of New Mexico, 1850–1907 (National Archives II, M750, Reel 1, Frames 207–13, 226, 507).

44 Investigation of O. P. McMains, United States Department of Interior, Appointment Papers: Territory of New Mexico, 1850–1907 (National Archives II, M750, Reel 1, Frames 207–13, 226, 507).

45 Hubert Howe Bancroft, "Popular Tribunals—Volume I," in *The Works of Hubert Howe Bancroft*, vol. 36, 732–33.

46 Robert N. Mullin, *A Chronology of the Lincoln County War* (Santa Fe: Press of the Territorian, 1966), 12–13

47 A. W. Hicks to Nephew, 6 Feb. 1876, Halletsville, Texas, Photocopy in possession of author, Printed from online scan of letter, Letter placed online for auction, 16 Oct. 2005, www.alexautographs.com.

48 Stephen J. Leonard, *Lynching in Colorado, 1859–1919*, 171.

49 Flora Spiegelberg Papers, 1919–1939, MSS 18 SC, Folder 1, Center for Southwest Research, UNM.

50 Maurice Garland Fulton, *History of the Lincoln County War*, 66.

51 Maurice Garland Fulton, *History of the Lincoln County War*, 66.

52 Francis Stanley, *The Las Vegas Years* (Denver: World Press, 1951), 127.

53 Cited in Stephen J. Leonard, *Lynching in Colorado, 1859–1919*, 57.

54 Manuel Maria de Zamacona to James G. Blaine, 30 Oct. 30, 1880; Reel 18, Notes from the Mexican Legation in the United States to the Department of State, 1821–1906, National Archives at College Park, Maryland; Zamacona to Blaine, 7 Apr. 1881, Reel 19, Notes from the Mexican Legation.

55 Zamacona to James G. Blaine, 8 Aug. 1881, Secretary of Territory Papers, Subject Group 10, Box 12, Folder 172, Arizona State Library and Archives, Phoenix, Arizona.

56 V. Morales, Mexican Consul of Arizona, to Acting Governor of Arizona, John J. Gosper, 10 Aug. 1881, Secretary of Territory Papers, Subject Group 10, Box 12, Folder 171, Arizona State Library and Archives, Phoenix, Arizona.

57 General Jose Otero to Alexander Willard, American Consul at Guaymas, Mexicao, 31 July 1881, Secretary of Territory Papers, Subject Group 10, Box 12, Folder 171, Arizona State Library and Archives, Phoenix, Arizona.

58 Warren Franklin Webb, "A History of Lynching in California since 1875" (MA thesis, University of California, 1935), 33–35.

59 Cited in Stephen J. Leonard, *Lynching in Colorado, 1859–1919*, 55.

60 William Pinkerton to M. Romero, 14 Nov. 1884, T 342, No. 793, SRE, Mexico City.

61 Michael De La Garza, "Anti-Mexican Hysteria in Nebraska, 1910–1920: The Lynching of Juan Gonzalez and the Trial of Juan Parral." (MA thesis, University of Nebraska, 2000), 25–47.

62 Frank Pierce's "Partial List of Mexicans Killed in the Valley Since July 1, 1915." Records of the Department of State Relating to the Internal Affairs of Mexico, 1910–1929, National Archives, Microfilm Publication, M274, vol. 51. File No. 812 / 17186.

63 Douglas V. Meed, *Bloody Border: Riots, Battles and Adventures Along the Turbulent US-Mexican Borderlands* (Tucson: Westernlore Press, 1992), 128.

64 Proceedings of the Joint Committee of the Senate and House in the Investigation of the Texas State Ranger Force, 36th Legislature, Regular Session, Legislative Papers, Texas State Archives, Austin

65 Benjamin Johnson, *Revolution in Texas: How a Forgotten Rebellion and Its Bloody Suppression Turned Mexicans into Americans* (New Haven: Yale University Press, 2003), 116.

66 Benjamin Johnson, *Revolution in Texas*, 116.

Unconfirmed Cases of Mob Violence against Persons of Mexican Origin and Descent in the United States, 1848–1928

Date	Name	Locality	State	Alleged Crime	Makeup, Size and Action of Mob (if Known)	Source(s)
Jan. 1849	Antoine, a "Spaniard"	Dry Diggings	California	Abetting Murder and Attempted Murder	Hanged by vigilance committee.	Alta California, 15 Feb. 1849; Buffum, Six Months[1]
10 July 1850	Four unknown Mexicans	Sonora	California	Theft	Taken from authorities and hanged by mob.	Newton and Newton[2]
Sometime in 1850	Unknown Mexican	Second Garrote	California	Theft	Hanged for robbing a sluice.	Weston, Mother Lode Album[3]
28 Apr. 1851	Five unknown Mexicans (one source suggests victims were Anglos)	Scott's Ferry on the San Joaquin River	California	Theft	Hanged for stealing cattle and horses.	Gonzales-Day, Lynching in the West[4]
21 July 1852	Unknown Mexican	Santa Cruz	California	Theft	Hanged.	Los Angeles Star, 7 Aug. 1852
Jan. 1853	Unknown Mexican	Cherokee Flat	California	Murder	Shot dead by posse during alleged escape attempt.	Boessenecker, Gold Dust[5]
Apr. 1853	Unknown	Martinez	California	Theft	Hanged for horse theft.	Bancroft, Popular Tribunals[6]
Spring 1853	Three unknown Mexicans	Southern Mines	California	Murder	Hanged on suspicion of murder.	Bancroft, Popular Tribunals[7]
Spring 1853	Seven unknown Mexicans	Southern Mines	California	Fraud	Shot for cheating at cards.	Bancroft, Popular Tribunals[8]

Date	Name	Location	State	Crime	Description	Source
Spring 1853	Two unknown Mexicans	Southern Mines	California	Theft	Hanged for robbing a claim.	Bancroft, *Popular Tribunals*[9]
12 Aug. 1853	"Spanish Charley"	Gibsonville	California	Murder	Hanged by vigilance committee.	*Los Angeles Star*, 20 Aug. 1853
Sept. 1853	Six unknown Mexican males and one unknown Mexican female	San Luis Obispo	California	Theft	Taken from authorities and hanged.	Bell, *Reminiscences*[10]
2 Jan. 1854	Unknown Mexican	Corpus Christi	Texas	Murder	Killed during a retaliatory raid by 18–20 American soldiers who were angry over the death of a comrade during a fight on New Year's Day.	Austin *Tri-Weekly State Times*, 24 Jan., 7 Feb. 1854
19 Jan. 1854	Luis Burgos	Los Angeles	California	Theft and Sexual Assault	Shot by a posse along with the outlaw Jack Wheelan after robbing an Anglo and "ravishing his wife."	*Alta California*, 3 Feb. 1854
July 1854	Unknown	Jackson	California	Theft	Hanged for horse theft.	Bancroft, *Popular Tribunals*[12]
July 1854	Unknown	Jackson	California	Attempted Murder	Hanged.	Bancroft, *Popular Tribunals*[13]

(Continued)

Date	Name	Locality	State	Alleged Crime	Makeup, Size and Action of Mob (if Known)	Source(s)
June? 1854	Manuel Gonzales?	San Antonio	Texas	Theft	Hanged "on the spot" for attempted horse theft.	Olmsted, *Journey through Texas*[14]
1854	Unknown	Manzano	New Mexico	Unknown	Hanged.	Tórrez, *Myth of the Hanging Tree*[15]
Early 1855	Unknown	Near Hawkins Bar	California	Murder	Whipped and Hanged.	Bancroft, *Popular Tribunals*[16]
1855	Eleven unknown Mexicans	Along the Nueces river	Texas	Murder and Theft	Hanged.	Acuña, *Occupied America*[17]
Apr. or May 1856	Twenty unknown Chilenos and Mexicans	Shasta County	California	Murder	Hanged in retaliation for the murder of a man named Conley.	*Galveston Weekly News*, 3 June 1856
15 July 1856	Cruz	Near Mission San Gabriel	California	Theft	Shot by parties unknown and left in a ravine.	*Los Angeles Star*, 19 July 1856
Late Oct. 1856	Juan Salazar and two unknown Mexicans	Near Watsonville	California	Theft	Shot by renowned vigilante Matt Tarpy and his men.	*Pacific Sentinel*, 1 and 15 Nov. 1856
Summer 1857	Antonio Delgado and an estimated 74 additional unknown Mexicans	Goliad and Karnes Counties	Texas	Competing with Anglos by running a freight transportation service	Delgado was shot. Details of the remaining victims are uncertain. Some were hanged, others shot.	Austin *Southern Intelligencer*, 23 Sept. 1857

Date	Name	Location	State	Crime	Outcome	Source
June 1860	Manuel	Carson City	Nevada	Sexual Assault	Shot in the middle of court by his alleged victim, Mrs. Hesse, with no attempt to stop or prosecute her for act.	Bancroft, *Popular Tribunals*[18]
Nov. 1862	Unknown	Auburn	Oregon	Attempted Murder	Shot down by mob after attempt to prevent lynching of Tom "the Spaniard."	Bancroft, *Popular Tribunals*[19]
Apr. 1863	Victorio Espinosa	Near Four Mile Creek	Colorado	Murder	Shot to death by posse.	Rockafellow, "History of Fremont County"[20]
Jan. 1864	Orosco (possibly American Indian)	Monterey	California	Unknown	Hanged.	*Monterey Gazette*, 12 Feb. 1864
21 May 1864	José Ramón Carillo	Cucamonga	California	Murder	Shot by concealed assassin for murder of Anglo.	*Los Angeles Star*, 28 May 1864
Early Aug. 1865	Unknown	LaGrande	Oregon	Theft	Hanged by "his sufferers" for stealing horses.	*Seattle Weekly Gazette*, 26 Aug. 1865
10 Jan. 1867	Three unknown Mexicans	Arroyo de San Miguel	Texas	Unknown	Shot.	*Brownsville Ranchero*, 20 Jan. 1867

(Continued)

Date	Name	Locality	State	Alleged Crime	Makeup, Size and Action of Mob (if Known)	Source(s)
28 Mar. 1869	L. García	Santa Barbara County	California	Unknown	Hanged.	Notes of Clare McKanna, in possession of authors.
Early to mid-Aug. 1869	Three unknown Mexicans	LaGrange	California	Theft	Shot by posse.	Bancroft, *Popular Tribunals*[21]
Late Feb. 1870	Francisco Redondo	San Miguel Canyon	California	Theft	Shot down during escape attempt by members of a vigilance committee called the "Pajaro Property Protective Society."	Reader, "Vigilantism"[22]
July 1870	Unknown	Near Bunty's Gulch	California	Unknown	Body found hanged.	*Calaveras Chronicle*, 16 July 1870
3 Mar. 1872	Manuel Reyes	Safford	Arizona	Threatening to kill Anglo	Shot.	Bancroft, *Popular Tribunals*[23]
May 1872	Two unknown Mexicans	Unknown	Arizona	Murder	"Promptly executed" after being discovered with stolen horses of slain men.	*Prairie City (IA) Index*, 31 May 1872
8 Aug. 1872	Unknown	Stanwix Station	Arizona	Murder	Shot by mob of Mexicans and Anglos.	Bancroft, *Popular Tribunals*[24]

Date	Name	Location	State	Alleged Crime	Description	Source
Aug. 1872	Four Unknown Mexicans	Near Brownsville	Texas/Mexico	Theft	Three Mexicans hanged on Mexican side of the Rio Grande by "Sheriff's Confederates" and fourth Mexican shot by sheriff.	*Petersburg (VA) Index*, 26 Aug. 1872
Unknown 1872	Don Francisco Gándara, Jr.	Near Blackwater	Arizona	Murder	Shot by vigilantes in his home.	Castillo and De León, *North to Aztlán*[25]
27 Sept. 1873	Unknown	Unknown	Arizona	Murder	Hanged.	Abney, "Capital Punishment"[26]
5 Dec. 1873	Seferino Trujillo and unknown Mexican	Horrell Ranch	New Mexico	Unknown	Found dead on the Horrell ranch.	Fulton, *Lincoln County War*[27]
11 Aug. 1874	N. Zapata	Las Vegas	New Mexico	Unknown	Hanged.	Tórrez, *Myth of the Hanging Tree*[28]
Mid-Jan. 1875	"Several" unknown Mexicans (3?)	King Ranch	Texas	Theft	Hanged from pasture fence, presumably for cattle theft.	*Galveston Daily News*, 28 Jan. 1875
Circa 1875	Unknown	Bee County	Texas	Refusing to play fiddle for Anglos	Murdered.	House Report on Texas Frontier Troubles[29]
5 Jan. 1876	Patricio Baca	Chimayo	New Mexico	Theft	Killed by two men who were subsequently arrested.	*Santa Fe Daily New Mexican*, 6 Jan. 1876

(Continued)

Date	Name	Locality	State	Alleged Crime	Makeup, Size and Action of Mob (if Known)	Source(s)
Aug. 1876	Unknown Mexican	Lincoln County	New Mexico	Theft	Hanged for horse stealing.	Fulton, *History of the Lincoln County War*[30]
Late Summer 1876	Juan González	Lincoln County	New Mexico	Theft	Shot.	Fulton, *History of the Lincoln County War*[31]
17 July 1877	Two Unknown Mexicans	Milquatay	California	Theft	Killed for stealing horses by posse.	House Report[32]
Late July 1877	Forty unknown Mexicans	Nueces County	Texas	Murder	At least forty Mexicans reported shot and hanged in riotous reprisal violence for murder of Lee Rabb.	House Committee on Military Affairs[33]
13 Dec. 1878	Unknown	Unknown	Arizona	Attempted murder	Hanged.	Abney, "Capital Punishment"[34]
5 Apr. 1881	Francisco Jimeno	Lompoc	California	Murder and sexual assault	Mob of 100 hanged this "Mexican" and "Full-blooded Indian."	*Sacramento Union*, 6 Apr. 1881
13 Apr. 1881	Janrequez and Sanchez	Near El Paso	Texas	Conflict over land	Killed by persons unknown but Mexican community suspected Anglos engaged in property dispute with two men.	*Galveston Daily News*, 16 Apr. 1881

Date	Name	Location	State	Cause	Description	Source
25 Nov. 1881	Francisco Jordan	Cuchilla Negra	New Mexico	Murder	Ethnicity unclear; hanged by "Mexican vigilant committee."	*Las Vegas Daily Optic*, 26 Nov. 1881
28 July 1882	Mexican Frank	Oldham County	Texas	Murder	Person of multiracial descent reportedly caught and executed by posse for murder of deputy sheriff.	*Fort Wayne (IN) Daily Gazette*, 29 July 1882
8 Aug. 1882	Augustin Agirer	Oatmanville	Texas	Taking Anglo to Court	Shot to death in front of his wife by two Anglo men for taking their friend to court over the shooting of a dog.	*Austin Statesman*, 9 Aug. 1882
20 Oct. 1883	Unknown	Gardner	Colorado	Murder	Unknown.	*Montezuma Millrun* (Summit County, CO), 27 Oct. 1883[35]
3 Dec. 1883	Silvestre García	Ranchito	Texas	Unknown	Hanged and then body thrown into river.	*Brownsville Cosmopolitan*, 10 Dec. 1883
2 May 1884	Crestino Manzaneres	Bernalillo County	New Mexico	Unknown	Twelve-year old boy hanged by parties unknown.	*Albuquerque Evening Democrat*, 12 May 1884
12 Sept. 1884	Francisco Gonzales	Tombstone	Arizona	Murder	"Lynched."	Tuskegee Lynching Records

(Continued)

Date	Name	Locality	State	Alleged Crime	Makeup, Size and Action of Mob (if Known)	Source(s)
Nov. 1884	Antonio Quiñones	Hanging Gulch	Arizona	Theft	Hanged from a tree for cattle theft by a single Anglo rancher.	Rice Papers[36]
30 Nov. 1884	Three unknown Mexicans	Live Oak County	Texas	Murder	Shot and killed by a posse.	Tuskegee Lynching Records; *Corpus Christi Weekly Caller*, 30 Nov. 1884
26 Apr. 1886	Juan Telles	Lubbock	Texas	Murder	Found with gunshot wound to the head, corpse dragged off by horse riders to "the plains."	*Galveston Daily News*, 10 May 1886
Circa 12 Oct. 1887	Nine unknown Mexicans	Starr County/ Matamoras	Texas/Mexico	Kidnapping	Captured by American posse and executed either in Starr County or on Mexican side of border.	*Beeville Bee*, 17 Nov. 1887
Late Oct. 1887	Jose Cutteriez	San Pedro County	New Mexico	Unknown	Reportedly killed by "gang of cowboys."	*Dallas Morning News*, 2 Nov. 1887
16 Jan. 1888	Pazo (or Reto)	Caldwell	Texas	Accomplice to Murder	Shot in jail cell by mob after confessing to aiding in murder of local planter.	*Fort Worth Daily Gazette*, 17 Jan. 1888; *Fort Wayne (IN) Sentinel*, 20 Jan. 1888

Date	Name(s)	Place	State	Reason	Description	Source
Oct. 1888	Three unknown Mexicans	Pueblo	Colorado	Unknown	Hanged with bailing wire.	Cairns Interview[37]
Jan. 1889	Three to five unknown Mexicans	Bonita Creek	Arizona	Herding sheep	Shot and killed by Anglos working for cattle company.	*Arizona Silver Belt,* 26 Jan. 1889
21 July 1890	Bartolo Melena and his six-year old daughter	Near Hutto	Texas	Encouraging elopement of Anglo and Mexican couple	Shot and killed along with his German wife by three Anglo men. Their six-year old daughter was also killed when a bullet intended for their teenage daughter instead struck the younger sibling.	*Austin Statesman,* 26 July 1890 and *Laredo Times,* 27 July 1890
29 May 1892	Francisco Chávez	Santa Fe	New Mexico	Physical Assault	Assassinated by four men for beating jailed Anglo.	Simmons, *When Six-Guns Ruled*[38]
16 July 1893	M. Jarzo or Juzo	Near El Paso	Texas	Murder	"Lynched."	Tuskegee Lynching Records
7 Apr. 1894	Antonio Lobato	Ponil Park	New Mexico	Unknown	Hanged.	Torrez, *Myth of the Hanging Tree*[39]
18 Feb. 1895	San Juan Miguel	Eagle Pass	Texas	Unknown	Hanged in a canvas sack after being shot and his body disfigured and mutilated by knives.	*San Antonio Express,* 8 Nov. 1895

(Continued)

Date	Name	Locality	State	Alleged Crime	Makeup, Size and Action of Mob (if Known)	Source(s)
22 Sept. 1896	Two unknown men, reportedly Mexicans	Near Fort Davis	Texas	Theft	Alleged outlaws shot by posse of Anglos while resisting arrest.	San Antonio Express, 1 Oct. 1896
28 June 1897	Juan Madera	Morenci	Arizona	Murder	Shot and killed during mob's attack on Morenci jail.	Arizona Republican, 28 Oct. 1897
Late June 1900	Unknown	Ray	Arizona	Murder	Killed by parties unknown.	Rosales, Pobre Raza[40]
15 May 1902	Ramón de la Cerda	Cameron County	Texas	Theft	Shot, dragged, beaten, and then buried.	Dallas Morning News, 18 May 1902
3 Oct. 1902	Alfredo de la Cerda	Near King's Ranch	Texas	Protesting the Texas Rangers	Shot by A. Y. Baker.	Webb, The Texas Rangers, 462–465[41]
Circa 1913	Two unknown Mexicans	Near Cuba	New Mexico	Unknown	Hanged.	Wetherill Interview[42]
15 Jan. 1915	Pedro Moliundro	Lovelace	Kentucky	Unknown	Lynched by night riders.	Tuskegee Lynching Records (find more)
7 July 1915	Two unknown Mexicans	Hidalgo County	Texas	Theft	Shot by posse.	San Antonio Light, 8 July 1915
12 Aug. 1915	Flores	Lyford	Texas	Murder	Shot by posse.	Brownsville Herald, 13 Aug. 1915
12 Aug. 1915	Unknown	Near Mercedes	Texas	Alleged outlaw	Shot by citizen's posse.	Dallas Morning News, 13 Aug. 1915

Date	Name	Location	State	Alleged offense	Notes	Source
13 Aug. 1915	Three unknown Mexicans	Santa Maria	Texas	Alleged outlaw	Shot and found in "neat pile." Ranger joked that maybe they died of "sunstroke."	*Dallas Morning News*, 14 Aug. 1915
17 Aug. 1915	Nine unknown Mexicans	Hidalgo County	Texas	Alleged outlaw	Shot by sheriff and his deputies.	Pierce, *A Brief History*[43]
26 Aug. 1915	Unknown	Raymondville	Texas	Murder	Shot by posse for attacing the Norias ranch and for "resisting arrest."	*Brownsville Herald*, 27 Aug. 1915
29 Aug. 1915	Unknown	Cameron County	Texas	Murder	Shot by posse for murder of Austens.	*Brownsville Herald*, 30 Aug. 1915
30 Aug. 1915	Pascual Orozco, Jr. and four unknown Mexicans	Green River Canyon	Texas	Alleged outlaw	Shot by posse in case of mistaken identity.	*Brownsville Herald*, 1 Sept. 1915
9 Sept. 1915	Francisco Guerra	Cameron County	Texas	Bill collector	Shot by five Mexicans.	*Brownsville Herald*, 10 Sept. 1915
Late summer/ Early Fall 1915	Felipe Falcon	Las Yescas Ranch	Texas	Murder	Shot by Rangers after being captured by U.S. soldiers.	Frank Pierce Inventory
20 Oct. 1915	Four unknown Mexicans	Near Brownsville	Texas	Murder and trainwrecking	Killed while attempting to cross the Rio Grande.	*Logansport (IN) Pharos-Reporter*, 20 Oct. 1915
10 Nov. 1915	Unknown	Near Sebastian	Texas	Unknown	Killed by a group of Americans.	Frank Pierce Inventory
Oct. 1918	Arturo? Garcia	Near Mercedes	Texas	Unknown	Taken from jail and found "shot all to pieces."	Investigation of the Texas Rangers

(Continued)

Date	Name	Locality	State	Alleged Crime	Makeup, Size and Action of Mob (if Known)	Source(s)
5 Feb. 1922	Manuel Durate	Cameron County	Texas	Unknown	Unknown.	Tuskegee Lynching Records
28 Nov. 1923	Matiax Martinez	Duval County	Texas	Unknown	Shot.	Dallas Morning News, 29 Nov. 1923
9 Sept. 1926	Two unknown Mexicans	Raymondville	Texas	Murder	Unknown.	Montgomery Advertiser, 19 Sept. 1926

[1] E. Gould Buffum, Six Months in the Gold Mines; From a Journal of Three Years' Residence in Upper and Lower California, 1847–49 (Philadelphia: Lea And Blanchard, 1850), 83–85.

[2] Michael Newton and Judy Ann Newton, Racial & Religious Violence in America: A Chronology (New York and London: Garland Publishing, Inc., 1991), 125.

[3] Otheto Weston, Mother Lode Album (Stanford: Stanford University Press. 1948), 30.

[4] Ken Gonzales-Day, Lynching in the West (Durham: Duke University Press, 2006), 208.

[5] John Boessenecker, Gold Dust and Gunsmoke: Tales of Gold Rush Outlaws, Gunfighters, Lawmen, and Vigilantes (New York: John Wiley and Sons, Inc., 1999). 88.

[6] Hubert Howe Bancroft, "Popular Tribunals—Volume I," in The Works of Hubert Howe Bancroft, Vol. 36 (San Francisco: The History Company, Publisher, 1887), 529.

[7] Bancroft, 530–31.

[8] Bancroft, 530–31.

[9] Bancroft, 530–31.

[10] Horace Bell, Reminiscences of a Ranger or Early Times in Southern California (Santa Barbara: Wallace Hebberd, 1927), 150.

[11] Bancroft, 530–31.

[12] Bancroft, 540.

[13] Bancroft, 540.

14 Frederick Law Olmsted, *A Journey through Texas; Or, a Saddle-Trip on the South-western Frontier* (New York: Dix, Edwards, and Company, 1857), 164.

15 Robert J. Tórrez, *Myth of the Hanging Tree* (Albuquerque: University of New Mexico Press, 2008), 161.

16 Bancroft, 543.

17 Rodolfo Acuña, *Occupied America: A History of Chicanos* 3rd ed. (New York: Harper and Row, 1988), 28.

18 Bancroft, 600.

19 Bancroft, 630.

20 B. F. Rockafellow, "History of Fremont County," in Ano1., *History of the Arkansas Valley, Colorado* (O. L. Baskin and Company, 1881), 576–78.

21 Bancroft, 568–69.

22 Phil Reader, *A Brief History of the Pajaro Property Protective Society: Vigilantism in the Pajaor Valley during the 19th Century* (Santa Cruz: Cliffside Publishing, 1995). posted online at www.santacruzpl.org, accessed to July 2008.

23 Bancroft, 727.

24 Bancroft, 728–29.

25 Richard Griswold del Castillo and Arnoldo de León, *North to Aztlán: a History of Mexican American in the United States* (New York: Twayne, 1996), 31.

26 David Lawrence Abney, "Capital Punishment in Arizona, 1863–1963" (MA thesis, Arizona State University, 1988).

27 Maurice Garland Fulton, *History of the Lincoln County War* (Tucson: University of Arizona Press, 1968), 21–24.

28 Robert J. Tórrez, *Myth of the Hanging Tree* (Albuquerque: University of New Mexico Press, 2008), 161.

29 "Texas Frontier Troubles: Testimony Before the Committee on Foreign Affairs," House of Representatives, No.701, 45th Congress, 2nd Session, Serial No. 1824, 85.

30 Maurice Garland Fulton, *History of the Lincoln County War* (Tucson: University of Arizona Press, 1968), 66.

31 Maurice Garland Fulton, *History of the Lincoln County War* (Tucson: University of Arizona Press, 1968), 66.

32 45th Congress, First Session, Report No.13 (Series No.1773), 202–3.

33 "Committee on Military Affairs in Relation to the Texas Border Troubles," House of Representatives, Miscellaneous Document, No. 64, 45th Congress, 2nd Session, Serial No. 1820, 230.

34 David Lawrence Abney, "Capital Punishment in Arizona 1863–1963" (MA thesis, Arizona State University, 1988).

35 Case also listed in *Chicago Tribune* and Tuskegee Lynching Files.

36 "Lynching in Cochise County," Michael Rice Papers, Box 2, Folder 26, Arizona Historical Society, Tucson, Arizona.

37 Elizabeth Cairns, "Interview with J. H. Maxey, 12 December 1933," Civil Works Administration Interviews, Pueblo County, CWA 344/3, 11, typescript in Colorado Historical Society, cited in Stephen J. Leonard, *Lynching in Colorado, 1859–1919* (Boulder: University Press of Colorado, 2002), 192n9.

38 Simmons, *When Six-Guns Ruled*, 16–19.

39 Robert J. Tórrez, *Myth of the Hanging Tree: Stories of Crime and Punishment in Territorial New Mexico* (Albuquerque: University of New Mexico Press, 2008), 161.

40 F. Arturo Rosales, *Pobre Raza!: Violence, Justice, and Mobilization among México Lindo Immigrants, 1900–1936* (Austin: University of Texas Press, 1999), appendix.

41 Walter Prescott Webb, *The Texas Rangers* (Boston: Houghton Mifflin, 1935), 462–65.

42 Marietta Wetherill Oral Interview. Pioneer Foundations Oral History Collection. Center for Southwest Studies, University of New Mexico, Albuquerque. MSS 123 BC.

43 Frank C. Pierce, *A Brief History of the Lower Rio Grande Valley* (Menosha, WI: George Banta Pub. Co., 1917), 92.

Notes

1. One infamous example of the political exploitation of the term lynching came in 1991 when Supreme Court nominee Clarence Thomas described his confirmation hearing as a "high tech lynching." Not only was Thomas not killed in his "lynching," but he was also appointed to the Supreme Court.

2. The issue of how many people must participate in an execution for that body to have been designated a "mob" is a challenging one. There is no consistent definition of "mob" in the primary documents that support this study. There are cases where a single individual was referred to as a "one-man mob" and there are multiple cases of a single individual hanging an alleged criminal. On at least one occasion, this hanging by a single person was dubbed a "lynching." We have not included such "one-man mobs" in our inventory, and most of our cases involve groups of substantial size. There are some cases, however, where the number of vigilantes is unknown or quite small. Following the standards set by studies of lynching in the American South, we have included many of these "private lynchings," as one scholar has called them.

3. As an alternative to words such as Latino, the phrases Spanish speaker or native Spanish speaker have weaknesses. Such terms are problematic because, even in the early twentieth century, some Borderlands Anglos gained fluency in Spanish at an early age and some persons of Mexican descent could not speak Spanish.

4. The difficulties that surround the collection of data on lynching make only the most general of comparisons possible. Nevertheless, we have tried to follow the same basic methods used by Tolnay and Beck, arranging our data to parallel that which they collected. In the final analysis, the data are not as compatible as we would have liked, but we still find the basic contrasts that emerged helpful. Stewart Tolnay and E. M. Beck, *A Festival of Violence: An Analysis of Southern Lynchings, 1882–1930* (Urbana: University of Illinois Press, 1995).

5. The focus on black victims and the American South was not limited to classic studies from the early twentieth century or even the pathbreaking works of Brundage and Tolnay and Beck, but continued in some of the best scholarship produced

at the turn of the twentieth century. See W. Fitzhugh Brundage, *Lynching in the New South: Georgia and Virginia, 1880–1930* (Urbana: University of Illinois Press, 1993); Leon Litwack, *Trouble In Mind: Black Southerners in the Age of Jim Crow* (New York: Alfred A. Knopf, 1998); David Grimsted, *American Mobbing, 1828–1861: Toward Civil War* (New York and Oxford: Oxford University Press, 1998); Grace Hale, *Making Whiteness: The Culture of Segregation in the South, 1890–1940* (New York: Pantheon Books, 1998); Dominic J. Capeci, Jr., *The Lynching of Cleo Wright* (Lexington: University Press of Kentucky, 1998); Mark Curriden and Leroy Phillips, Jr., *Contempt of Court: The Turn-of-the-Century Lynching That Launched 100 Years of Federalism* (New York: Faber and Faber, 1999); Monte Akers, *Flames After Midnight: Murder, Vengeance, and the Desolation of a Texas Community* (Austin: University of Texas Press, 1999), and Michael W. Fedo, *The Lynchings in Duluth* (St. Paul: Minnesota Historical Society Press, 2000).

INTRODUCTION

1. Joel Williamson, *A Rage for Order: Black-White Relations in the American South since Emancipation* (New York: Oxford University Press, 1986), 205.
2. *Amarillo Globe-News*, May 29, 1999. Our thanks to the archivist who handed us this Associated Press news clipping at the New Mexico State Library in Santa Fe.
3. Several infamous episodes of mob violence against Mexicans did not make it into the final version of the main inventory. These cases have not been included because the details surrounding the killings were deemed too incomplete. For example, despite the fact that both the US government and the Mexican government agree that in the summer of 1857 Anglo vigilantes, eager to eliminate their competition, hanged or shot at least seventy-five Mexican freight runners in Texas, most of the killings were done so secretively that they were not reported in the newspapers or other sources until much later, depriving us of names, specific dates, and specific locations. The victims in the "Cart War" of 1857 and over two hundred additional Mexican victims of mob violence are included in a second inventory, also located in the appendix, but they are not included in any of the statistical data summarized in this book. The concern that has been paid to differentiating victims and separating them into two inventories does not mean that the data in the first inventory are perfectly accurate. All data on mob violence are inescapably limited and prone to contain errors no matter how careful the compilers may have been.
4. For great insight into the connection between historical events and historical memory, as well as the example of the Holocaust, we are beholden to Michel-Rolph Trouillot, *Silencing the Past: Power and the Production of History* (Boston: Beacon Press, 1995), esp. 11–13.
5. Carey McWilliams, *North from Mexico: The Spanish-Speaking People of the United States* (1948), ed. Matt S. Meier (New York: Praeger, 1990), 123.

6. [San Francisco] *Alta California*, May 4, 1877; *Sacramento Union*, May 4, 1877; *Santa Cruz Sentinel*, May 5, 1877; May 12, 1877. Chamales is spelled Chamalis in many newspaper accounts, but we believe this is an error and that the correct spelling is Chamales.

7. In addition to the *Sacramento Union* and the previously cited *Alta California* and *Santa Cruz Sentinel*, the story was reported in the *Santa Cruz Local Item*, the *San Francisco Chronicle*, and the *San Francisco Examiner*.

8. *Sacramento Union*, May 4, 1877; May 5, 1877.

9. For a careful parsing of the strengths and weaknesses of newspapers as sources for studying lynching, see Susan Jean, "'Warranted' Lynchings: Narratives of Mob Violence in Southern White Newspapers, 1880–1940," in *Lynching Reconsidered: New Perspectives in the Study of Mob Violence*, ed. William D. Carrigan (London and New York: Routledge, 2007), 125–46.

10. Inmate Francisco Arias, #1594 and #4794, San Quentin Prison Registers, 1851–1867, California State Archives, Sacramento. Although we are fairly certain that the Francisco Arias detailed in this prison record is the same Francisco Arias who was later lynched, it should be pointed out that correlations of lynching victims and government documents is not a certainty. For example, there were many men named Francisco Arias in California in the 1870s. Another Francisco Arias was a miner who was still alive in 1880 and living in Santa Clara County. It is possible that this prison record refers to him and not the man who was lynched in 1877. If this were true, however, there would be multiple errors in the two documents. First, the ages of the two Arias men are slightly different in the prison and census records, one having him being born in 1832 and the other in 1827. Second, the prison records list Arias as a laborer whereas the census records list him as a miner. Third, newspapers confirm that the lynched Arias went to State Prison, whereas we have no such correlating information on Arias the miner. Only one Francisco Arias appears in the prison record, so we conclude that the record refers to the Arias who was later lynched. The point of this discussion is not so much to cast doubt on the information gleaned from the prison records cited above as to illustrate the difficulties of reconstructing the lives of those who were lynched in the United States. Government documents are a rich source that we could not have done without, but they have limitations and often forced us to draw conclusions that will always lack absolute certainty. See Francisco Arias, Santa Clara County, California, 1880 US Federal Census, accessed via ancestry.com, January 10, 2008.

11. One of the best books on lynching in recent years corrects this inattention to visual sources. See Amy Louise Wood, *Lynching and Spectacle: Witnessing Racial Violence in America, 1890–1940* (Chapel Hill: University of North Carolina Press, 2009). As good as this book is, however, it gives scant attention to the American West. Ken Gonzales-Day helps fill this gap by discussing in detail the visual records that document lynching in California, including the surviving photograph of the

Arias and Chamales lynching entitled "Hanged at the Water Street Bridge." See Ken Gonzales-Day's analysis, from which we learned much, in *Lynching in the West, 1850–1935* (Durham: Duke University Press, 2006), 93–98.

12. Gonzales-Day, *Lynching in the West*, 93–98.

13. Martin Espada, *Alabanza: New and Selected Poems, 1982–2002* (New York: Norton, 2003). Espada is of Puerto Rican descent and was born in Brooklyn, New York.

14. Particularly important collections of oral histories with Mexicans can be found in the archives of Texas A&M Kingsville, University of Texas Pan-American, and the University of New Mexico.

15. Tuskegee's reports were hardly the only publications misleading Americans about the multiracial history of lynching. Writers, journalists, and academics have repeated this mistake for over a hundred years. In 2002, Philip Dray published *At the Hands of Persons Unknown: The Lynching of Black America*, the first national overview of mob violence in the United States in more than a half-century. Although the book was critically and commercially well received, it is a less than comprehensive survey of extralegal violence. In its chronological focus on the post–Civil War era, its geographical focus on the South, and its racial focus on African Americans, the book betrays the field's myopic attention to one chapter in the history of racial violence. See Philip Dray, *At the Hands of Persons Unknown: The Lynching of Black America* (New York: Random House, 2002). Not as commercially successful as Dray's account but a superior history of mob violence is Manfred Berg's *Popular Justice: A History of Lynching in America* (Chicago: Ivan R. Dee, 2011). Berg's account is a much better overview of mob violence and includes a chapter entitled "Popular Justice Beyond Black and White." Another recent book that has a nuanced analysis of the multiracial dimensions of lynching is Michael J. Pfeifer, *The Roots of Rough Justice: Origins of American Lynching* (Urbana: University of Illinois Press, 2011).

16. *New York Times*, June 18, 2000.

17. *New York Times*, October 23, 2002, and June 1, 2003; *PR Newswire*, May 5, 2000, accessed via *Lexis Nexis Academic*, March 9, 2009.

CHAPTER ONE

1. Dozens and dozens of documents in English and Spanish survive for the story of Toribio Lozano's shepherds. Spanish-language originals are located in the Archivo de la Embajada Mexicana en Estados Unidos de América at the Secretaría de Relaciones Exteriores (SRE) in Mexico City. See, for example, Siete Pastores, Juan D. Arias Reports, November 25, 1874, T.312, 590–699, SRE; Siete Pastores, T.315, No. 38, 69, 71–73, SRE. English language sources are found in the National Archives. See, for example, Department of State, *Papers Relating to the Foreign Relations of the United States*, 1875, Volume II (Washington, D.C.: US Government Printing Office, 1875), 954–84.

2. See, for example, W. Fitzhugh Brundage, *Lynching in the New South: Georgia and Virginia, 1880–1930* (Urbana: University of Illinois Press, 1993); Stewart Tolnay and E. M. Beck, *A Festival of Violence: An Analysis of Southern Lynchings, 1882–1930* (Urbana: University of Illinois Press, 1995). Edward L. Ayers, *Vengeance and Justice: Crime and Punishment in the 19th Century American South* (New York: Oxford University Press, 1984); Terence Finnegan, "At the Hands of Parties Unknown: Lynching in Mississippi and South Carolina, 1881–1940" (PhD diss., University of Illinois, 1993), and Michael J. Pfeifer, "Lynching and Criminal Justice in Regional Context: Iowa, Wyoming, and Louisiana, 1878–1946" (PhD diss., University of Iowa, 1998).

3. Statistics for African American lynching victims are from Tolnay and Beck, *A Festival of Violence*, 271–72. Tolnay and Beck did not include Texas or Virginia in their statistics. They also include no data on the period before 1882.

4. *San Francisco Daily Evening Picayune*, January 22, 1851.

5. Eagle to his wife Margaret, Gold Hill, CA, September 12, 1853, John Eagle correspondence, Henry E. Huntington Library, San Marino, CA.

6. Christopher Waldrep, *The Many Faces of Judge Lynch* (New York: Palgrave Macmillan, 2004), see esp. chap. 2, "The Word and the Nation."

7. *Galveston News*, June 14, 1874.

8. *Las Vegas Daily Optic*, October 7, 1881.

9. Letters of W. M. O. Carpenter, HM 16777, Typescript of letters, 6, Henry E. Huntington Library.

10. Alonzo Delano, *Life on the Plains and Among the Diggings* (1854; New York: Miller, Orton & Co., 1857), 365.

11. Among the unsolved cases of early Calaveras County are: *California v. J. C. Bell* (1855), *California v. John Phipps* (1856), *California v. Carmelita Feliz* (1862), *California v. Paul Tibeaux, Batista Denny, Andrea Molino, and Juan Alvarez* (1864), *California v. Rafael Ochoa* (1866), and *California v. Antonio Alvarez* (1866), Calaveras County Historical Museum, San Andreas, California. The authors have done some comparative research on nineteenth century court cases in selected counties in Arizona, southern California, New Mexico, and Texas. Although the research is hardly exhaustive, it does suggest that Calaveras County and the surrounding counties were relatively ineffective compared to other parts of the West.

12. Oscar Waldo Williams, *Pioneer Surveyor, Frontier Lawyer: The Personal Narrative of O. W. Williams, 1877–1902*, ed. S. D. Myres (El Paso: Texas Western College Press, 1966), 187–93. The *San Francisco Herald* was more critical of peace officers but echoed Williams: "Acts of violence succeed each other with such rapidity, that I almost hesitate about communicating them to you. We have more gold in the hills and gulches of this town, more gamblers, more rowdies, and more murders than in almost any other section of California, and the civil authorities who are always well paid for being conservators of the peace bring no one to justice." See *San Francisco Herald*, January 1, 1852.

13. Examination of court records from *Territory of Arizona vs. Francisco Trujillo, William Green, and Antonio Feliz (1866)* to *Territory of Arizona vs. Manacio Martinez (1883)*, Pima County Criminal Court Records, Record Group 110, Microfilm Reel 85.6.9, Arizona State Library and Archives, Phoenix, Arizona.

14. In an examination of five hundred court cases in Los Angeles County over a ten-year period beginning in 1861, the authors narrowed their research by focusing on cases involving individuals, either plaintiffs or defendants, with Spanish surnames. Punishments varied depending on the charge and circumstances and ranged from fines all the way to the death sentence. The cases that made up the sample included *People v. Adolphus Sylvester*, March 9, 1861, #541; *People v. Ramon Navarro*, May 17, 1861, # 545; *People vs. Serrapio Navarro, Ramon Navarro, and Jesus Lopez*, November 7, 1861, #561; *People v. Jose Machado*, November 13, 1861, #565; *People v. Rosalio Mesa*, November 15, 1861, #566; *People v. Lorenzo Garcia*, November 16, 1861, #567; *People v. Polonia Acosta and Josefa Ybarra*, November 16, 1861, #568; *People v. Tomas Rodriguez and Perfecto Escalante*, November 16, 1861, #569; *People v. Synacio Arza*, November 22, 1861, #572; *People v. Feliciano Lopez and Cornelio Espinosa*, March 8, 1862, #579; *People v. Jose Ruiz*, March 10, 1862, #582; *People v. George McDermott*, March 20, 1862, #586; *People v. Antonio Rodriguez and Procopio Bustamente*, March 12, 1862, #585; *People v. John H. Cunningham*, November 3, 1862, #591; *People v. Serrapio Navarro*, November 7, 1862, #594; *People v. George Shears Ross*, November 13, 1862, #599; *People v. Serrapio Navarro and Procopio Bustamente*, November 14, 1862, #601; *People v. Serrapio Navarro and Manuel Ceredel*, November 14, 1862, #603; *People v. Bernardo Montalva*, November 18, 1862, #606; *People v. Juan Buelna and Luis Bojarquez*, May 18, 1863, #625; *People v. William Durgin*, September 16, 1863, #634; *People v. William Durgin*, September 16, 1863, #636; *People v. James Kellar*, September 18, 1863, #637; *People v. William Miner*, September 18, 1863, #638; *People v. Manuel Ceredel*, September 30, 1863, #641; *People v. James Caywood*, November 5, 1863, #642; *People v. Cyrus Sanford*, November 18, 1863, #648; *People v. Ramon Alvitre and Lucio Alvitre*, November 18, 1863, #652; *People v. Manual Cerradel*, December 5, 1863, #662; *People v. Anastacio Moreno*, December 5, 1863, #663; *People v. Jesus Ballastero*, March 23, 1864, #680; *People v. Bartolo Velardez*, March 23, 1864, #681; *People v. Fernando Sepulveda*, April 28, 1864, #686; *People v. George Morris*, June 1, 1864, #690; *People v. Antonio Sanchez*, September 14, 1864, #692; *People v. Jose Ybarra*, September 27, 1864, #694; *People v. Henry Wolfe*, October 8, 1864, #697; *People v. John Buckley*, December 1, 1864, #701; *People v. Rafael Barela*, January 11, 1865, #702; *People v. Jose A. Villa*, January 16, 1865, #703; *People v. Jose Antonio Villa*, April 3, 1865, #707; *People v. Jose Antonio Villa*, April 6, 1865, #709; *People v. Ynocente Garcia*, April 24, 1865, #713; *People v. Jose Domingo and Juan Napomecente*, April 5, 1865, #716; *People v. Maria Antonio Ales, Dolores Castillo Mares, Trinidad Garcia and Severo Fimbres*, September 16, 1865, #719; *People v. Manuel Bermudes*, September 20, 1865, #721; *People v.*

Theofolo Ortega, November 14, 1865, #729; *People v. Leandro Buelna*, March 17, 1866, #747; *People v. Antonio Maria*, October 20, 1866, #769; *People v. Alexander Trajio*, October 29, 1866, #771; *People v. Jose Dias and Jose Prosporo*, November 3, 1866, #733; *People v. Juan Jose*, November 3, 1866, #774; *People v. Cecelio Tapia*, March 21, 1867, #790; *People v. Horace Bell*, May 9, 1867, #793; *People v. Luis Bojorquez*, September 26, 1867, #800; *People v. Ramon Sotello and Manuel Morrilla*, December 12, 1867, #818; *People v. John Bagaman*, May 27, 1868, #835; *People v. Jose M. Aragon and Ramon Ochoa*, July 21, 1868, #841; *People v. Manuel Roe*, #852, November 14, 1868, #852; *People v. Dominguez Avilez*, January 18, 1869, #862; *People v. Librado Quiroa*, January 28, 1869, #866; *People v. Edwardo Galligo*, #870, March 13, 1869, #870; *People v. Marcus Leiba, Ramon Ballesteros, and Henrique*, March 13, 1869, #871; *People v. Miguel Soto*, March 23, 1869, #873; *People v. Ramon Ochoa*, June 14, 1869, #885; *People v. John Doe Sepulveda*, August 11, 1869, #891; *People v. Santos Cañados and Carmen Lugo*, December 15, 1868, #858; *People v. Victor Samouri*, August 9, 1869, #888; *People v. Agustin Iguerra*, January 19, 1870, #919; *People v. William Tines*, January 22, 1870, #920; *People v. Trinidad Castro*, 1-25-70, #922; *People v. F.S. Buhn*, March 18, 1870, #937; *People v. Pablo Pryor*, March 26, 1870, #938; *People v. Patrick Comody*, August 11, 1870, #972; *People v. Miguel Lachenais*, #954, July 5, 1870; *People v. Adolfo Celis*, May 11, 1870, #946; Los Angeles Area Court Records, Criminal, Court of Sessions, Case numbers 541–946, Henry E. Huntington Library; For Texas, see William D. Carrigan, *The Making of a Lynching Culture: Violence and Vigilantism in Central Texas, 1836–1916* (Urbana: University of Illinois Press, 2004), 107–9. For Arizona, see *Territory of Arizona vs. Francisco Trujillo, William Green, and Antonio Feliz* (1866), *Territory of Arizona vs. Jose Maria Parzas* (1868), *Territory of Arizona vs. Francisco Maldonado* (1870), *Territory of Arizona v. Felipe Amibisca* (1870), *Territory of Arizona v. Antonio Gallardo* (1871), *Territory of Arizona v. Refugio Marin* (1871). Murder of Mexican, *Territory of Arizona v. Juan Moreno* (1871), *Territory of Arizona v. Refugio Pacheco* (1871), *Territory of Arizona v. Jesus and Ambrosio Morales* (1871), *Territory of Arizona v. Salvador Candelario* (1871), *Territory of Arizona v. Francisco Carrillo* (1871), *Territory of Arizona v. Juan Jose Duarte et al.* (1871), *Territory of Arizona v. Pedro Rivera* (1871), *Territory of Arizona v. Alcario Torres, Margarito, Lugan and Luis Pollero* (1871), *Territory of Arizona v. Pablo Valenzuela and Casimira Ybarra* (1872), *Territory of Arizona v. Nestor Rivas* (1872), *Territory of Arizona v. Francisco Miranda* (1872), *Territory of Arizona v. Guadalupe Alcalar* (1872–73), *Territory of Arizona v. Manuel Cariaga* (1873), *Territory of Arizona v. Onofre Tores* (1873), *Territory of Arizona v. Cayetano Tabanico* (1874), *Territory of Arizona v. Charles Vince Moore and William Hall* (1874), *Territory of Arizona v. Felipe Amabisca* (1878), *Territory of Arizona vs. Jesus Sandoval* (1879), *Territory of Arizona vs. Francisco Grijalba* (1879), *Territory of Arizona vs. Cerilio Mendes Espinosa* (1879), *Territory of Arizona vs. Jose Maria Hernandez* (1879), *Territory of Arizona vs. Miguel Leavadie* (1879), *Territory of Arizona vs. Escapalo*

Navarra (1880), *Territory of Arizona vs. Jesús Ramirez* (1881), *Territory of Arizona vs. Leon Rufio and Perfecto [Doe]* (1881), *Territory of Arizona vs. Julian Perez de Senano* (1882), *Territory of Arizona vs. Francisco Rios* (1882), *Territory of Arizona vs. Louis Correa and Juan Chico* (1882), *Territory of Arizona vs. Jose Ignacio* (1882), *Territory of Arizona vs. Juan Doe* (1882), *Territory of Arizona vs. Manuel Doe and Ramon Due* (1882), *Territory of Arizona vs. Jesus Urias* (1882), *Territory of Arizona vs. Manacio Martinez* (1883).

15. Walter Colton, *Three Years in California* (New York: A.S. Barnes & Co., 1850), 393.

16. *Arizona Weekly Citizen*, July 12, 1873.

17. *Daily Ranchero*, Brownsville, no date given but perhaps February 10, 1872, quoted in *Reports of the Committee of Investigation Sent in 1873 by the Mexican Government to the Frontier of Texas*, translated from the official edition made in Mexico (New York: Baker & Godwin, 1875), 108.

18. *Santa Fe Daily New Mexican*, March 12, 1877.

19. *Silver City Enterprise* (Grant Co., NM), January 10, 1890 (italics added).

20. *San Francisco Herald*, June 26, 1851; *Sacramento Daily Union*, June 18, 1851; Richard H. Peterson, "Anti-Mexican Nativism in California, 1848–1853: A Study of Cultural Conflict," *Southern California Quarterly* 62:4 (1980): 312.

21. Clarence King, *Mountaineering in the Sierra Nevada* (Boston: J. R. Osgood and Comany, 1872), 283–7.

22. *Sacramento Union*, December 16, 1852. See also *Alta California*, December 15, 1852; *San Joaquin Republican*, December 18, 1852; Horace Bell, *Reminiscences of a Ranger or Early Times in Southern California*, (Santa Barbara, CA: Wallace Hebberd, 1927), 8–9; Hubert Howe Bancroft, "Popular Tribunals—Volume I," in *The Works of Hubert Howe Bancroft*, Vol. 36 (San Francisco: The History Company, Publisher, 1887), 492; Leonard Pitt, *The Decline of the Californios: A Social History of the Spanish-Speaking Californians, 1846–1890* (Berkeley and Los Angeles: University of California Press, 1966), 157–58; John Bossenecker, *Gold Dust & Gunsmoke: Tales of Gold Rush Outlaws, Gunfighters, Lawmen, and Vigilantes* (New York: John Wiley and Sons, Inc., 1999), 86.

23. Enos Lewis Christman Papers, Letter to Peebles Prizer, July 21, 1850, Henry E. Huntington Library.

24. Pringle Shaw, *Ramblings in California* (Toronto: John Blackburn, 1854), 17.

25. Enos Lewis Christman Papers, Letter to Peebles Prizer, July 21, 1850, Henry E. Huntington Library. See also *Sonora Herald*, July 20, 1850. A similar rescue took place in 1851. Three men—Solomon Pico, Cecilio Mesa, and William Otis—were sentenced by a "People's Court" to be hanged but were "rescued" by the authorities according to the *San Francisco Herald*, May 1, 1851.

26. Memoirs and Reminiscences of E. O. Crosby, original manuscript, 44–45, Henry E. Huntington Library.

27. C. V. Gillespie to A. H. Gillespie, July 30, 1849, Archibald H. Gillespie Papers, Special Collections, University of California, Los Angeles. Coy says that Mexican

law was ignored by forty-niners because it was both inadequate and repugnant (to the whites). They also only had a limited knowledge of it. See Owen Cochran Coy, *Gold Days* (San Francisco: Powell Publishing Co, 1929), 189–90.

28. Louise Publos, "Father of the Pueblo: Patriarchy and Power in Mexican California, 1800–1880," in *Continental Crossroads: Remapping U.S.-Mexico Borderlands History*, eds. Samuel Truett and Elliot Young (Durham: Duke University Press, 2004), 85.

29. *Alta California*, August 27, 1859; Bossenecker, *Gold Dust & Gunsmoke*, 70–71; Publos, "Father of the Pueblo," 86; Albert Camarillo, *Chicanos in a Changing Society: From Mexican Pueblos to American Barnos in Santa Barbara and Southern California, 1848–1930* (Cambridge, MA, and London: Harvard University Press, 1996), 21–22.

30. Aurora Hunt, *James H. Carleton, 1814–1873, Western Frontier Dragoon* (Glendale, CA: The Arthur H. Clark Company, 1958); James Henry Carleton, *Special Report of the Mountain Meadows Massacre* (Washington, DC: Government Printing Press, 1902). Note: This is a reprinted government documented originally presented to the House of Representatives during the 57th Congress, 1st Session; Charles Fernald, *A County Judge in Arcady: Selected Private Papers* (Glendale, CA: Arthur H. Cark, Co., 1954), 114–15.

31. Haines quoted in Frances Leon Swadesh, *Los Primeros Pobladores: Hispanic Americans of the Ute Frontier* (Notre Dame, IN: University of Notre Dame Press, 1974), 88–89. It is worth noting that the divisions in Northern New Mexico were not strictly along ethnic lines. Class and kin divisions were also prominent. Seventeen of the militiamen had Spanish surnames, including two that were "officers."

32. See, for example, *California v. Antonio Lopez* (1862) and *California v. Bartola Ortega* (1862). Additional evidence can be found in legal executions of Mexicans during this time period. See execution of Antonio Valencia as reported in *Alta California*, May 10, 1849. See also the execution over the protests of local Spanish-speakers of a Mexican soldier named Herrera in *Alta California*, February 22, 1854, Carol A. O'Connor notes that Mexicans often received harsh sentences in "A Region of Cities" in Clyde A. Milner II, Carol O'Connor, Martha A. Sandweiss, *The Oxford History of the American West* (New York and Oxford: Oxford University Press, 1994), 550.

33. *Alta California*, August 19, 1850. Numerous episodes of Anglos receiving light or no punishment for killing Mexicans can be found during the late nineteenth and early twentieth centuries.

34. Andrew J. Stone to his parents, May 8, 1853, Andrew J. Stone Correspondence, Henry E. Huntington Library.

35. *Santa Fe Daily New Mexican*, February 26, 1881.

36. *San Antonio Herald*, April 18, 1857; June 13, 1857.

37. The five victims were named Anthony Maron, Francisco Encinas, Miguel Elias, Fermin Eideo, and Bessena Ruiz. See *Bakersfield Southern Californian*

and *Kern County Weekly Courier*, "Five Mexicans Lynched," December 27, 1877; *Alta California*, December 23, 1877; and Warren Franklin Webb, "A History of Lynching in California Since 1875," (MA thesis, University of California, Berkeley, 1934), 20–22; Michael J. Pfeifer, *Rough Justice: Lynching and American Society, 1874–1947* (Urbana: University of Illinois Press, 2004), 85–86.

38. *Las Vegas Daily Optic*, March 4, 1881.

39. Ramon Jil Navarro, "California in 1849," in *We Were 49ers! Chilean Accounts of the California Gold Rush*, ed. Edwin A. Beilharzand and Carlos V. Lopez (Pasadena, CA: Ward Ritchie Press, 1976), 103–4.

40. *Alta California*, August 9, 1850. See also March 7, 1851 and March 15, 1851.

41. Friedrich Gerstäcker, *Scenes of Life in California* (San Francisco: John Howell, 1942), 111 (quote), 114, 116.

42. Bayard Taylor, *Eldorado, or Adventures in the Path of Empire* (New York: Alfred A. Knopf, 1949), 365–66; Sister M. Colette Standart, O. P., "The Sonoran Migration to California, 1848–1856: A Study in Prejudice," *Southern California Quarterly* 58:3 (1976): 340; Zaragosa Vargas, ed., *Major Problems in Mexican American History* (Boston and New York: Houghton Mifflin Company, 1999), 158.

43. Chauncey L. Canfield, *The Diary of a Forty-Niner* (New York and San Francisco: Morgan Shepard Company, 1906), 40.

44. *Alta California*, July 9, 1850; Green quoted in Richard H. Peterson, "The Foreign Miner's Tax of 1850 and Mexicans in California: Exploitation or Expulsion," *Pacific Historian* 10:3 (1976): 269.

45. Report of Thomas Jefferson Green on Mines and Foreign Miners, March 15, 1850, *Journal of the Senate of the State of California First Session* (San José: J. Winchester, 1850), 493–97.

46. Clipping in California Gold Rush Days, English Clippings, Henry E. Huntington Library.

47. *Illustrated London News*, September 15, 1855, Clipping in California Gold Rush Days, English Clippings, Henry E. Huntington Library.

48. William Redmond Ryan, *Personal Adventures in Upper and Lower California in 1848–1849* (London: William Shoberl, 1851), II: 296–97.

49. Don Antonio Franco Coronel, *Cosas de California*, trans. Diane de Avalle-Arce (Santa Barbara, CA: Bellerophon Books, 1995), 60–61; Rodman Wilson Paul, *Mining Frontiers of the Far West, 1848–1880* (New York: Holt, Rinehart, and Winston, 1963), 142–43.

50. *Sonora Herald*, August 21, 1850; cited in William Robert Kenny, "Mexican American Conflict on the Mining Frontier, 1848–1852," *Journal of the West* 6:4 (1967): 585–86.

51. *Alta California*, July 3, 1852. See also July 13, 1852 issue.

52. *Alta California*, January 29, 1853.

53. Edmund Booth, *Forty-Niner: The Life Story of a Deaf Pioneer* (Stockton, CA: San Joaquin Pioneer and Historical Society, 1953), 27; Walter Van Tilburg Clark,

ed., *The Journals of Alfred Doten, 1849–1903* (Reno: University of Nevada Press, 1973), 140.

54. *Sacramento Union*, August 10, 1855; *Georgetown News*, August 9, 1855; Bossenecker, *Gold Dust & Gunsmoke*, 52–58; Dave Demarest, "Mother Lode Massacre," *Frontier Times* 49:2 (1975): 12–13, 35–36; William B. Secrest, "Revenge of Rancheria," *Frontier Times* (September 1968), 16–19, 59–61.

55. *Alta California*, August 10, 1855; Bossenecker, *Gold Dust & Gunsmoke*, 52–58; Secrest, "Revenge of Rancheria," 16–19, 59–61; Demarest, "Mother Lode Massacre," 12–13, 35–36.

56. *San Francisco Daily Placer Times*, August 10, 1855; *Illustrated London News*, September 29, 1855, in Clipping in California Gold Rush Days, English Clippings, Henry E. Huntington Library; *Georgetown News*, August 16, 1855.

57. *Alta California*, August 11, 1855.

58. *Alta California*, August 13, 1855.

59. *San Francisco Daily Placer Times*, August 15, 1855. Innocent Mexicans, however, were defended in the same story, and the paper composed a much stronger defense in a second story of August 17, 1855.

60. *Alta California*, August 31, 1855.

61. Irving Howbert, *Memories of a Lifetime in the Pikes Peak Region* (1925; Glorieta, NM: Rio Grande Press 1970), 45.

62. *Rocky Mountain News*, June 25, 1873. Note that the victim's name is spelled "Martinis" in the newspaper but has been changed to reflect the more common spelling of this last name.

63. *Denver Tribune*, quoted in the *Weekly Arizona Miner*, July 12, 1878.

64. *Colorado Chieftan*, January 8, 9, 1880; quoted in Stephen J. Leonard, *Lynching in Colorado, 1859–1919* (Boulder: University Press of Colorado, 2002), 57.

65. *Weekly Arizonian*, September 15, 1859; Doris W. Beats, "The History of Tubac, 1752–1948" (MA thesis, University of Arizona, 1949), 129.

66. Beats, "The History of Tubac," 129.

67. Quoting a story from the *Arizonian* of September 1, 1859, *Pacific Sentinel*, September 16, 1859.

68. *Weekly Arizonian*, October 20, 1859.

69. *Weekly Arizonian*, August 28, 1869.

70. *New York Times*, November 16, 1854.

71. *New York Times*, September 18, 1856; *New York Times*, September 24, 1856; George D. Garrison, *Texas: A Contest of Civilizations* (Boston: Houghton Mifflin Co., 1903), 273–74.

72. *New York Times*, May 12, 1854, November 16, 1854; Carrigan, *Making of a Lynching Culture*, 73–74.

73. Benjamin Heber Johnson, *Revolution in Texas: How a Forgotten Rebellion and Its Bloody Suppression Turned Mexicans into Americans* (New Haven and London: Yale University Press, 2003), 7–20.

74. Austin *Southern Intelligencer*, September 23, 1857; *San Antonio Herald*, September 15, 1857; *The Eastern Texian*, October 10, 1857.

75. John J. Linn, *Reminiscences of Fifty Years in Texas* (New York: D. J. Saddler, 1883), 352–54, see esp. 353.

76. The "Cart War Oak" still stood when the authors visited the Goliad courthouse lawn in 2005.

77. Manuel Robles to Lewis Cass, October 14, 1857, Copy of Translation of Letter sent to Lewis Cass, Secretary of State of the United States, Office of the Governor, Record Group 301, Records of Elisha Marshall Pease, Box 301–26, Folder 47, Texas State Archives, Austin.

78. *Nueces Valley*, April 17, 1858, and October 10, 1857; quoted in Eugenia Reynolds Briscoe, *City by the Sea: A History of Corpus Christi, Texas, 1519–1875* (New York and other cities: Vantage Press, 1985), 160–61.

79. Austin *Southern Intelligencer*, September 9, 23, 1857.

80. Linn, *Reminiscences*, 352–54.

81. *San Antonio Express*, December 28, 1897.

82. *Waco Times-Herald*, February 17, 1898.

83. *New York Times*, May 12, 1854.

84. Patrick Carroll nicely summarizes the use of force in south Texas when he notes that "treaty rights took a backseat to might." See Patrick J. Carroll, *Felix Longoria's Wake: Bereavement, Racism, and the Rise of Mexican American Activism* (Austin: University of Texas Press, 2003), 18.

85. Swadesh, *Los Primeros Pobladores*, 95; Albuquerque *Evening Review*, November 1, 1882; *Santa Fe Daily New Mexican*, November 1, 1882.

86. On the Black Legend and the origins of Anglo prejudice against Mexicans, see David J. Weber, "'Scarce More than Apes': Historical Roots of Anglo-American Stereotypes of Mexicans in the Border Region," in *Myth and the History of the Hispanic Southwest* (Albuquerque: University of New Mexico Press, 1988), 153–67; Philip Wayne Powell, *Tree of Hate: Propaganda and Prejudice Affecting United States Relations with the Hispanic World* (New York: Basic Books, 1971).

87. Rómulo D. Carbia, *Historia De La Leyenda Negra Hispano-Americana* (1943; Madrid: Marcial Pons Historia, 2004), 38.

88. Resolution of December 22, 1835, originally published in the *Telegraph and Texas Register* (San Felipe de Austin), January 23, 1836.

89. Reprinted in Geoffrey C. Ward, *The West: An Illustrated History* (Boston: Little, Brown, 1996), 75.

90. Linn, *Reminiscences*, 324.

91. Quoted in Peterson, "Foreign Miner's Tax of 1850," 265.

92. On the role of the US-Mexican War in producing or sustaining hostile feelings, see Doris L. Meyer, "Early Mexican-American Responses to Negative Stereotyping," *New Mexico Historical Review* 53:1 (January 1978): 75–76; Lawrence I. Seidman, *The Fools of '49: The California Gold Rush, 1848–1856* (New

York: Alfred A. Knopf, 1976), 177; James E. Officer, *Hispanic Arizona, 1536–1856* (Tucson: University of Arizona Press, 1987), 229.

93. Juan N. Seguin, *A Revolution Remembered: The Memoirs and Selected Correspondence of Juan N. Seguin* (Austin: Texas State Historical Association, 2002), 103.

94. Theodore T. Johnson, *California and Oregon, or Sights and Scenes in the Gold Region and Scenes by the Way*, 4th ed. (Philadelphia: Lippincott, 1865), 290.

95. Prescott *Weekly Arizona Miner*, April 20, 1872.

96. Quoted in *San Antonio Express*, August 29, 1884.

97. William Robert Kenny, "Mexican American Conflict on the Mining Frontier, 1848–1852," *Journal of the West* 6:4 (1967): 583. Kenny noted that "Mexicans and other Latin Americans were identified in the minds of most Americans with a system of religious beliefs wholeheartedly despised in the United States." Kenny was referencing California in particular, but his statement is true for the rest of the American West as well. For example, historian A. Brophy agrees that anti-Catholicism was troublesome for Mexicans in Arizona. See A. Blake Brophy, *Foundlings on the Frontier: Racial and Religious Conflict in Arizona Territory, 1904–1905* (Tucson: University of Arizona Press, 1972), 21.

98. Bossenecker, *Gold Dust & Gunsmoke*, 52–58.

99. *Albuquerque Republican Review*, March 11, 1876. See also Nancy Gonzalez, "Untold Stories of Murder and Lynching in Territorial New Mexico, 1850–1912" (M.A. thesis, University of New Mexico, 2003).

100. L. M. Schaeffer, *Sketches of Travels in South America, Mexico and California* (New York: James Egbert Printer, 1860), 90–91, 102, 225.

101. Prescott, *Weekly Arizona Miner*, April 20, 1872.

102. Camarillo, *Chicanos in a Changing Society*, 59; Brophy, *Foundlings on the Frontier*, 19. For segregation of Mexicans in Texas, see David Montejano, *Anglos and Mexicans in the Making of Texas, 1836–1986* (Austin: University of Texas Press, 1987); Neil Foley, *The White Scourge: Mexicans, Blacks, and Poor Whites in Texas Cotton Culture* (Berkeley: University of California Press, 1998); Johnson, *Revolution in Texas*.

103. In 1855, young men of Mexican "blood" gave a ball in a large dancing room of Callaghan's store building. According to a local paper: "Judges, members elect of the Legislature and others would not take with them their wives and American lady friends, fearing, as we have reason to believe, that they would be contaminated with contact with greasers." *San Antonio Herald*, September 18, 1855.

104. Brophy, *Foundlings on the Frontier*, 101.

105. *American Flag*, Brownsville, August 20, 1856; quoted in *Reports of the Committee of Investigation Sent in 1873 by the Mexican Government to the Frontier of Texas*, translated from the official edition made in Mexico (New York: Baker & Godwin, 1875), 131–32.

106. "Texas Border Troubles," Testimony taken by the Committee on Military Affairs, Series # 1820 (Washington, DC: Government Printing Office, 1878), 285.

107. *La Grange Journal*, August 19, 1915.

108. US Congress, Senate, *Congressional Globe*, 30th Congress, First Session, 1848, 98.

109. *Colorado Weekly Chieftan* (Pueblo), May 14, 1874.

110. James M. Patton, *History of Clifton*, (Clifton, AZ: Greenlee County Chamber of Commerce, 1977), 101–2.

111. Mary J. Jaques, *Texan Ranch Life* (London: Horace Cox, 1894), 361.

112. Jorane King Barton, *El Monte* (Mount Pleasant, SC: Arcadia Publishing, 2006), see esp. chap. 2.

113. *Santa Fe Weekly New Mexican*, July 25, 1872; *Santa Fe Daily New Mexican*, December 9, 1873; *Santa Fe New Mexican*, January 27, 1874.

114. *Albuquerque Republican Review*, December 20, 1873.

115. C. L. Douglas, *Famous Texas Feuds* (Austin, TX: State House Press, 1936, 1988), 134. For a description of the Horrell War as a "race war," see also Eve Ball, ed., *My Girlhood among Outlaws by Lily Klanser* (Tucson: University of Arizona Press, 1972), 102.

116. Philip Rasch, "The Horrell War," *New Mexico Historical Review* 31 (January 1956): 223–31.

117. If additional victims that are included in Inventory B are included, the disparity becomes even greater because Texas accounted for nearly seven out of ten (193 of 279) of the victims of mob violence in that compilation.

118. Texas possessed by far the greatest number of people of Mexican descent between 1848 and 1928 and would thus be expected to have the highest number of Mexican lynching victims. We think, however, that Texas's lynching record, even when adjusted for population, has no peer as a scene of anti-Mexican mob violence largely due to the thousands of unknown victims of mob violence killed during the Plan de San Diego.

119. Richard Henry Dana, Jr., *Ten Years Before the Mast: A Personal Narrative of Life at Sea* (1840; Harmondsworth, England: Penguin, 1981), 126–27.

120. Tomás Almaguer, *Racial Fault Lines: The Historical Origins of White Supremacy in California* (Berkeley, Los Angeles, and London: University of California Press, 1994), 54–58.

121. *Weekly Arizonian*, September 6, 1879.

122. *Placerville Mountain Democrat*, February 17, 1855.

123. T. J. Farnham, *Life, Travels, and Adventures in California and the scenes in the Pacific Ocean* (New York: William H. Graham, 1846), 358.

124. *Alta California*, August 26, 1850.

125. Margaret Hanna Lang, *Early Justice in Sonora* (Sonora, CA: Mother Lode Press, 1963), 45.

126. *Sacramento Daily Union*, July 29, 1852. See also Edward J. Phillips, "Seeing the Elephant," *Pacific Historian* 189:1 (1974): 12–30.

127. *Santa Fe Daily New Mexican*, February 27, 1881, and April 1, 1881; James B. Gillett, *Six Years with the Texas Rangers, 1875 to 1881* (Lincoln and London: University

of Nebraska Press, 1921, 1976), 213–21; Claude D. Potter, "Reminiscences of the Socorro Vigilantes," ed. Paige W. Christiansen, *New Mexico Historical Review* 40 (January 1965): 23–54; Erna Fergusson, *Murder and Mystery in New Mexico* (Albuquerque, NM: Merle Armitage, 1948), 21–27; Harold L. Edwards, "Trouble in Socorro," *Old West* (Winter 1990): 42–47; Marc Simmons, *When Six-Guns Ruled: Outlaw Tales of the Southwest* (Santa Fe, NM: Ancient City Press, 1990), 2–3.

128. *Placer Times*, July 9, 1849, clipped from and quoted in *Alta California*, July 26, 1849.

129. William Downie, *Hunting for Gold* (San Francisco: California Publishing Co., 1893), 21–22.

130. *Georgetown News*, October 4, 1855.

131. *El Clamor Público*, June 18, 1859; Paul Bryan Gray, "Francisco P. Ramírez: A Short Biography," *California History* 84 (2006): 20–38, 70–71.

132. *El Clamor Público*, June 5, 1858.

133. *El Clamor Público*, January 29, 1859. For additional examples of Ramírez's frustrations after 1856, see *El Clamor Público*, November 14, 1857; January 23, 1858; June 19, 1858; June 11, 1859; September 17, 1859.

134. Quoted in Paul Bryan Gray, "Francisco P. Ramírez: A Short Biography," *California History* 84 (2006): 29.

135. Francisco Arturo Rosales, *Dictionary of Latino Civil Rights* (Houston: Arte Público Press, 2006), 376–77; Paul Bryan Gray, "Francisco P. Ramírez: A Short Biography"; Coya Paz Brownrigg, "Linchocracia: Performing 'America' in *El Clamor Público*"; and Jose Luis Benavides, "'Californios! Whom Do You Support': *El Clamor Público*'s Contradictory Role in the Racial Formation Process in Early California," *California History* 84 (2006): 20–68, 70–73.

136. Quoted in Félix Gutiérrez, "Francisco P. Ramírez: Californio Editor and Yanqui Conquest," accessed online at http://www.freedomforum.org/, July 15, 2009.

137. Lanier Bartlett, ed., *On the Old West Coast: Being further Reminiscences of a Ranger, Major Horace Bell* (New York: William Morrow & Co., 1930), 100–101, see esp. 101.

138. Don Antonio Franco Coronel, *Cosas de California*, trans. Diane de Avalle-Arce (Santa Barbara, CA: Bellerophon Books, 1995), 70.

139. Siete Pastores, Juan D. Arias Reports, November 25, 1874, T.312, 590–699, SRE; See also Department of State, *Papers Relating to the Foreign Relations of the United States*, 1875, vol. 2 (Washington, DC: US Government Printing Office, 1875), 954–84.

140. Warren Wallace to Adjutant General, August 22, 1874, Typed Transcript in Walter Prescott Webb Papers, Box 2R287, Center for American History, University of Texas at Austin.

141. Siete Pastores, Juan D. Arias Reports, November 25, 1874, T.312, 590–699, SRE; Siete Pastores, T.315, No. 38, 69, 71–73, SRE; Siete Pastores, T.315, No. 12, 19–25,

SRE; See also Department of State, *Papers Relating to the Foreign Relations of the United States*, 1875, vol. 2, 954–84.

142. Department of State, *Papers Relating to the Foreign Relations of the United States*, 1875, vol. 2, 956.

CHAPTER TWO

1. *Brownsville Herald*, December 28, 1917; Charles H. Harris III and Louis R. Sadler, *The Texas Rangers and the Mexican Revolution: The Bloodiest Decade, 1910–1920* (Albuquerque: University of New Mexico Press, 2004), 351–56, 450–51; Douglas V. Meed, *Bloody Border: Riots, Battles and Adventures Along the Turbulent US-Mexican Borderlands* (Tucson, AZ: Westernlore Press, 1992), 130–31; Glenn Justice, *Revolution on the Rio Grande* (El Paso: Texas Western Press, 1992). Proceedings of the Joint Committee of the Senate and House in the Investigation of the Texas State Ranger Force, 36th Legislature, Regular Session, Legislative Papers, Texas State Archives, Austin; *Handbook of Texas Online*, s.v. "The Porvenir Massacre," accessed July 27, 2009, http://www.tshaonline.org/handbook/online/articles/PP/jcp2.html.

2. Comparison between the extralegal execution of Mexicans and parallel attacks against other ethnic and racial groups in the United States will be employed at times to bring the entire subject of mob violence into greater focus, revealing new dimensions in the history of lynching and opening new areas for study. Although comparisons of Mexican victims of mob violence will be made with the larger universe of those lynched, the primary focus of our comparisons will be with African American victims of mob violence. There are several reasons for this, but the most important reason is that historians have devoted far more attention to the study of African Americans murdered by mobs than they have other groups, such as Chinese immigrants, Native Americans, and even victims from the Anglo majority. Texts of particular importance to us in this regard have been W. Fitzhugh Brundage, *Lynching in the New South: Georgia and Virginia, 1880–1930* (Urbana: University of Illinois Press, 1993), and Stewart Tolnay and E. M. Beck, *A Festival of Violence: An Analysis of Southern Lynchings, 1882–1930* (Urbana: University of Illinois Press, 1995).

3. Tolnay and Beck, *A Festival of Violence*, 48. Please see Chapter One for a full listing of the alleged offenses given by mobs targeting Mexicans. One important aspect to note is that Mexicans were frequently accused of being "bandits" or outlaws. In these cases, the mob victims were presumed thieves and murderers even if there was no specific episode connected to them. These thirty-three cases have been included as a separate category "alleged outlaw or bandit" in Table 1.

4. *San Joaquin Republican*, July 9, 1851.

5. *Georgetown News*, May 23, 1856.

6. *San Joaquin Republican*, December 18, 1852.

7. Mobs lynching African Americans also certainly cloaked additional motives under the charge of murder, though blacks were not stereotyped as "bandits" in the same way as were Mexicans.

8. *Santa Fe Weekly Gazette*, March 31, 1855. The paper also alleged that the Mexican men "abused" Gerk's wife, though exactly what this meant—insulting language, physical harassment, or sexual assault—is unclear. Robbery, however, was what the men were officially charged with before they were hanged, and it seems to have been the prime justification in the lynching given the newspaper's description of the hanging.

9. *Alta California*, September 23, 25, 1864.

10. *Rocky Mountain News*, July 15, 1871.

11. *Mesilla News*, September 16, 1876. According to one account, the Mexican was killed while resisting arrest.

12. *Dallas Morning News*, November 20, 1886.

13. *Cheyenne Daily Leader*, January 13, 1887. Our thanks to Michael Pfeifer for sharing this story with us.

14. Tolnay and Beck, *A Festival of Violence*, 96.

15. Gary Y. Okihiro, *Common Ground: Reimagining American History* (Princeton, NJ: Princeton University Press, 2001), 64–65.

16. Theodore Roosevelt, *The Winning of the West: An Account of the Exploration and Settlement of our Country from the Alleghanies to the Pacific*, ed. Daniel Boone, 4 vols. (New York: Putnam, 1896–1901).

17. Paul Schuster Taylor, *An American-Mexican Frontier: Nueces County, Texas* (New York: Russell and Russell, 1971), 274.

18. Harris Newmark, *Sixty Years in Southern California, 1853–1913* (New York: Knickerbocker Press, 1916), 304.

19. *Alta California*, August 7, 1867. See also *Colusa Sun*, August 3, 1867.

20. Alvarid's last name is spelled at least three different ways in the various accounts of his death, including Elverad and Alari. *Albuquerque Evening Review*, August 17, 1882; (San Lorenzo, NM) *La Crónica del Rio Colorado*, August 19, 1882; (San Lorenzo, NM) *Red River Chronicle*, August 19, 1882; Erna Fergusson, *Murder and Mystery in New Mexico* (Albuquerque, NM: Merle Armitage, 1948), 29; Claude D. Potter, "Reminiscences of the Socorro Vigilantes," ed. Paige W. Christiansen, *New Mexico Historical Review* 40, no. 1 (Jan 1965): 35.

21. *San Antonio Express*, January 31, 1896; *Dallas Morning News*, January 31, 1896.

22. *Los Angeles Star*, quoted in *Nevada Journal*, October 7, 1853.

23. An even more startling case two years later makes the same point. Stephen Alvarez, identified as Mexican, was accused of "improper conduct towards two little girls, one five and the other seven years of age." The *Placer Times* noted that the "details of the case are too filthy for publication." Although the possibility of lynching was mentioned, the surviving evidence suggests that Alvarez was

never executed by a mob and that the case faded from view. The case was at least allowed to proceed legally, being sent to a grand jury for action, something hard to imagine if a black man had been similarly accused in a public newspaper. See *San Francisco Daily Placer Times*, January 10, 1855. On the complex relationship between race and rape in the American South, see Lisa Lindquist Dorr, *White Women, Rape, and the Power of Race in Virginia, 1900–1960* (Chapel Hill: University of North Carolina Press, 2004).

24. The victim is sometimes referred to by her by the diminutive name Juanita and has also been identified as Juana. There are numerous accounts of this lynching. The best is the recent summary in Helen McLure, "'I Suppose You Think Strange the Murder of Women and Children': The American Culture of Collective Violence, 1652–1930" (PhD diss., Southern Methodist University, 2009), 155–60.

25. This summary is based on several sources, including McLure's above, but also *Alta California*, July 9, 14, 1851; John R. McFarlan Journal, July 7, 1851, Henry E. Huntington Library; Katherine A. White, comp., *A Yankee Trader in the Gold Rush, the Letters of Franklin A. Buck* (Boston: Houghton Mifflin Company, 1930), 167; Hubert Howe Bancroft, "Popular Tribunals—Volume I," in *The Works of Hubert Howe Bancroft*, vol. 36 (San Francisco: The History Company, Publisher, 1887), 577–87; William Secrest, *Juanita* (Fresno, CA: Saga-West Publishing Co., 1967).

26. Ibid.

27. October 16, 1851, Item #26171, Frederick Douglass Papers, Rochester, New York.

28. William Downie, *Hunting for Gold* (San Francisco: California Publishing Co., 1893), 196.

29. Louise Amelia Knapp Smith Clappe, *The Shirley Letters: Being Letters written in 1851–52 from the California Mines* (Salt Lake City, UT: Peregrine Smith Books, 1983), 149–51.

30. Horace Bell, *Reminiscences of a Ranger or Early Times in Southern California* (Santa Barbara, CA: Wallace Hebberd, 1927), 150. Other sources have not corroborated Bell's account that one of the victims was female, but it is hard to believe that Bell would misremember or invent such an unusual detail. The mystery of the lynching of the "vixen" may never be satisfactorily solved.

31. *Rocky Mountain News*, August 28, 1873; *Rocky Mountain News*, August 30, 1873.

32. P. Ornelas, Consul of Mexico at San Antonio, August 15, 1880; Manuel Maria de Zamacona to James G. Blaine, October 30, 1880; Reel 18, Notes from the Mexican Legation in the United States to the Department of State, 1821–1906, National Archives at College Park, Maryland; Zamacona to Blaine, April 7, 1881, Reel 19, Notes from the Mexican Legation. Also see McLure, "'I Suppose You Think Strange the Murder of Women and Children,'" 237–38.

33. *Alta California*, June 14, 1858. Not all Anglos agreed with targeting Mexican women and children, especially if they were innocent. The *Alta California* itself

held this position: "It is possible that Linares is a criminal, but, if so, this was not a proper [way to act] against him. His family, at least, were innocent."

34. *Galveston Daily News*, December 17, 1874. For essential analysis of women and lynching in the West and beyond, see McLure, "'I Suppose You Think Strange the Murder of Women and Children.'"

35. Harris and Sadler, *The Texas Rangers and the Mexican Revolution*, 289.

36. Statistics on African American multiple lynchings are from period 1882–1930 and are taken from Tolnay and Beck, *A Festival of Violence*, 274. To be completely fair, our inventory includes numerous cases of indiscriminate mob violence that borders on rioting. Since Tolnay and Beck do not include riotous violence such as the Atlanta race riot of 1906, which claimed the lives of at least twenty-five African Americans, the data do not perfectly compare. This is one of the reasons that we decided to compare lynching episodes instead of lynching victims because the difference would have been statistically starker (too stark) calculated that way. In any event, we think that even considering the large number of black victims killed in race riots, Mexicans still faced a greater danger of being lynched in small groups than African Americans.

37. *Sacramento Union*, February 8, 1881.

38. *Las Vegas Daily Optic*, December 31, 1880; *Santa Fe New Mexican*, January 30, 1881; February 1, 1881; *Cimarron News and Press*, February 10, 1881; *New York Times*, March 31, 1887.

39. *Santa Fe Daily New Mexican*, February 16, 1881.

40. *Las Vegas Daily Optic*, March 4, 1881.

41. R. H. Paul, Sheriff of Pima County, to Mexican Consul at Tucson, June 30, 1881; Manuel de Zamacona to James G. Blaine, August 8, 1881, Secretary of Territory Papers, Subject Group 10, Box 12, Folder 172, Arizona State Library and Archives.

42. Manuel Maria de Zamacona to James G. Blaine, April 19, 1881, Notes from the Mexican Legation in the United States to the Department of State, 1821–1906, National Archives; *Las Vegas Daily Optic*, March 31, 1881; *El Paso Times*, April 8, 1881; James B. Gillett, *Six Years with the Texas Rangers, 1875 to 1881* (Lincoln and London: University of Nebraska Press, 1921, 1976), 179–222.

43. *Cimarron News and Press*, June 16, 1881; *Santa Fe Daily New Mexican*, June 16, 1881.

44. General José Otero to Alexander Willard, American Consul at Guaymas, Mexicao, July 31, 1881; V. Morales, Mexican Consul of Arizona, to Acting Governor of Arizona, John J. Gosper, August 10, 1881, Secretary of Territory Papers, Subject Group 10, Box 12, Folder 171, Arizona State Library and Archives; *Arizona Citizen*, August 21, 1881; Katherine Benton-Cohen, *Racial Division and Labor War in the Arizona Borderlands* (Cambridge: Harvard University Press, 2009), 58–59; Phillip J. Rasch, *Desperadoes of the Arizona Territory* (Stillwater, OK: National Association for Outlaw and Lawman History, 1999), 29–30; *Arizona Gazette*, August 22, 1881.

45. Santa Fe *Daily New Mexican*, October 7, 1881.

46. *Las Vegas Daily Optic*, October 7, 1881.

47. For an important theoretical work on collective violence that emphasizes cultural distance, see the work of Roberta Senechal de la Roche, including *In Lincoln's Shadow: The 1908 Race Riot in Springfield, Illinois* (Carbondale, IL: Southern Illinois University Press, 2008) and "The Sociogenesis of Lynching," in *Under Sentence of Death*, ed. Brundage, 48–76.

48. Although not as common as in the case of Mexican workers, whites did use mob violence to expel black workers from the South, especially in those parts of the South outside of the cotton belt. See, for example, Kimberly Harper, *White Man's Heaven: The Lynching and Expulsion of Blacks from the Southern Ozarks, 1894–1909* (Fayetteville: University of Arkansas Press, 2010).

49. There is, however, one great problem with this comparison of the North and the West. In the North, a number of whites could claim to have been living in the region for at least some time before African Americans began arriving in great numbers in the late nineteenth and early twentieth centuries. In the West, however, it was Mexicans who had lived in the region for decades before Anglo Americans began to flood into the region. Such contrasts suggest the underlying importance of economic competition, not length of residence, as the true grindstone of mob violence in each case.

50. *New York Times*, October 9, 1926.

51. To give just one example of the symbolic power of hanging, a captured British officer during the American Revolution pleaded that he be executed by firing squad as a gentleman instead of hanged as a spy. George Washington concluded that the man was a spy and ordered him hanged over the protests of his own staff. See Joseph Ellis, *Founding Brothers: The Revolutionary Generation* (New York: Vintage, 2002), 132

52. *San Antonio Herald*, April 18, 1857.

53. *Empire County Argus*, August 18, 1855. The *Argus* actually pronounced Boling dead of his wounds, but Boling survived and lived another decade. See his obituary in the *Mariposa Free Gazette*, June 18, 1864.

54. *Marysville Herald*, October 4, 1850.

55. *Arizona Citizen*, August 7 and 14, 1881.

56. The example cited in the introduction is relevant here as well. In 1999, the body of a man in his thirties or forties went unnoticed for one or two months before it was found north of Deming, New Mexico. The body had not been hidden but rather chained to an electric pole where it had been steadily decomposing before it was discovered. See *Amarillo Globe-News*, May 29, 1999.

57. Statistics for mobs lynching African Americans are unavailable, but a reading of the relevant literature suggests the majority of lynchings resulted in hanging. However, it is equally obvious that a significant percentage of African Americans were burned, quite probably well in excess of the number of burned Mexican

victims. See Tolnay and Beck, *A Festival of Violence*, Brundage, *Lynching in the New South*, and especially Leon F. Litwack, *Trouble in Mind: Black Southerners in the Age of Jim Crow* (New York: Knopf, 1998), 280–325.

58. *Sacramento Daily Union*, June 18, 1851. See also *Alta California*, June 18, 1851; *San Francisco Herald*, June 28 and July 1, 1851.

59. *San Antonio Daily Express*, November 14, 1910; *El Paso Times*, November 4, 1910; Gerald G. Raun, "Seventeen Days in November," *The Journal of Big Bend Studies* 7 (January 1995): 157–80; Arnoldo De León, *Mexican Americans in Texas: A Brief History* (New York: Harlan Davidson, 1999), 50; Harris and Sadler, *The Texas Rangers and the Mexican Revolution*, 51–52; F. Arturo Rosales, "The Lynching of Antonio Rodriguez of 1910: An Historical Reassessment," unpublished paper in possession of the authors.

60. *Santa Anna News*, November 18, 1910; *New York Times*, November 10–18 and December 24, 1910; *The Outlook* (New York), November 26, 1910; *The Independent* (New York), November 17, 24, 1910; Douglas W. Richmond, "Mexican Immigration and Border Strategy During the Revolution, 1910–20," *New Mexico Historical Review* 57:3 (July 1982): 277–78.

61. *Thorndale Thorn*, June 23, 1911; *New York Times*, June 26, 1911; Harris and Sadler, *The Texas Rangers and the Mexican Revolution*, 73. For a recent examination of the Gómez case, see George R. Nielsen, *Vengeance in a Small Town: The Thorndale Lynching of 1911* (Bloomington: IUniverse, 2011).

62. Patricia Bernstein, *The Waco Horror: The Lynching of Jesse Washington and the Rise of the NAACP* (College Station: Texas A&M University Press, 2005), 110.

63. *Daily Arizona Miner*, February 9, 1874.

64. Virgil N. Lott Narrative, The Rio Grande Valley, Part I, 71, Center for American History, University of Texas at Austin.

65. *San Antonio Express*, June 21, 1875. The editorialist was clearly making a political attack on Richard Coke with this account of the border troubles, but there is little doubt that the state government's support for the Rangers and a general tolerance of mob violence, as demonstrated by the lynching of the seven shepherds, encouraged vigilantism just as the writer concludes.

66. It should be noted, however, that genuine violence on the part of Mexican outlaws was part of the cycle of border violence. Furthermore, the Rangers themselves did attempt to break up the Anglo vigilante groups when they were perceived to have gotten out of control in 1875. *San Antonio Herald*, May 12, 1875.

67. Robert M. Utley, *Lone Star Justice: The First Century of the Texas Rangers* (New York: Oxford University Press, 2002), and *Lone Star Lawmen: The Second Century of the Texas Rangers* (New York: Oxford University Press, 2007).

68. Oscar J. Martínez, *Fragments of the Mexican Revolution: Personal Accounts from the Border* (Albuquerque: University of New Mexico Press, 1983), 138.

69. Benjamin Johnson, *Revolution in Texas: How a Forgotten Rebellion and Its Bloody Suppression Turned Mexicans into Americans* (New Haven: Yale University Press,

2003), 72–74, 80, 88–90, 94; José A. Ramírez, *To the Line of Fire: Mexican Texans and World War I* (College Station: Texas A&M University Press, 2009), 8–9.

70. James A. Sandos, "The Plan of San Diego: War and Diplomacy on the Texas Border, 1915–1916," *Arizona and the West* 14.1 (1972): 5–24; Neil Foley, *The White Scourge: Mexicans, Blacks, and Poor Whites in Texas Cotton Culture* (Berkeley: University of California Press, 1997), 56; James A. Sandos, *Rebellion in the Borderlands: Anarchism and the Plan of San Diego, 1904–1923* (Norman, OK: University of Oklahoma Press, 1992); Emilio Zamora, *The World of the Mexican Worker in Texas* (College Station: Texas A&M University Press, 1993), 83; Alfred Arteaga, "The Chicano-Mexican Corrido," *Journal of Ethnic Studies* 13 (Summer 1985), 83–84; James L. Haley, *Texas: From Spindletop through World War II* (New York, 1993), 94, 121.

71. *Hallettsville Rebel*, October 9, 1915. Anglos' disproportionate fear of Mexicans is also described in Dorothy Lee Pope, *Rainbow Era on the Rio Grande* (Brownsville, TX: Springman-King Company, 1971), 121.

72. *San Antonio Express*, September 11, 1915. For a contemporary estimate of the number of Mexicans killed by Anglos, see *Matagorda County News*, August 20, 1915.

73. John R. Peavey, *Echoes from the Rio Grande* (Brownsville, TX: Springman-King Co., 1963), 101.

74. William Madsden, *Mexican-Americans of South Texas* (New York: Holt, Rinehart and Winston, 1964), 9.

75. Johnson, *Revolution in Texas*, 120.

76. Harbert Davenport to Walter Prescott Webb, January 30, 1935, Box 2M260; Harbert Davenport to Walter Prescott Webb, February 8, 1935, Box 2M260, Walter Prescott Webb Papers, Center for American History, University of Texas at Austin. For a biographical sketch of Davenport, see Handbook of Texas Online, s.v. "DAVENPORT, HARBERT," accessed April 12, 2006, http://www.tsha.utexas.edu/handbook/online/articles/DD/fda21.html.

77. Harris and Sadler, *The Texas Rangers and the Mexican Revolution*, 258–59.

78. Virgil Lott Narrative, Part II, 41.

79. George H. Schmitt to L. P. Sieker, November 13, 1886, Webb Papers, Box 2R 289.

80. Harold Preece, *Lone Star Man: Ira Aten, Last of the Old Texas Rangers* (New York: Hastings House Publishers, 1960), 42. The position of the Texas Rangers can be compared to that of US soldiers who served in Vietnam or, later, in Iraq. In all three instances, linguistic challenges and racial antipathies, combined with hostile and alien surroundings, led these men to abuse innocent and law-abiding citizens.

81. In 1997, E. M. Beck and Stewart Tolnay noted that not only had white mobs sometimes lynched whites but that black mobs, as well as interracial mobs, had sometimes murdered black victims. Tolnay and Beck noted that the number of blacks killed by black mobs paled in comparison to the number of African

Americans murdered by white mobs. According to their inventory, a mere 6 percent of black victims were lynched by black mobs. Such intraracial violence was nonetheless surprising to many readers, but Beck and Tolnay effectively argued that some level of black-on-black mob violence was understandable given the larger culture's general endorsement of lynching as popular justice and the white-dominated criminal justice system's erratic treatment of blacks that victimized other blacks. E. M. Beck and Stewart E. Tolnay, "When Race Didn't Matter: Black and White Mob Violence Against Their Own Color" in W. Fitzhugh Brundage, ed., *Under Sentence of Death: Lynching in the South* (Chapel Hill: University of North Carolina Press, 1997), 132–54; Tolnay and Beck, *Festival of Violence*, 93–98, 271–2.

82. See, for example, *State of New Mexico v. Teodoro Martinez*, April 1914, *State of New Mexico v. Cenon Herrera*, December 1914, Criminal Docket, San Juan County, New Mexico, No. 2, San Juan County Archives, Aztec, New Mexico.

83. *Marysville Herald*, August 22, 1853.

84. *Los Angeles Star*, August 7, 1852; *Sacramento Daily Union*, July 28, 1852; *Nevada Journal*, August 7, 1852; Bancroft, "Popular Tribunals—Volume I," 477; Ken Gonzales-Day, *Lynching in the West: 1855–1935* (Durham: Duke University Press, 2006), 210.

85. *Galveston News*, February 5, 1876.

86. *Arizona Silver Belt*, November 4 and 11, 1897; *Arizona Republican*, October 28, 1897.

87. Most descriptions of lynch mobs in the West do not clearly identify the non-Anglos in the crowd. For example, newspapers reporting the 1851 lynching of a Mexican youth named Pablo at Agua Fria in California's Mariposa County estimated the crowd to contain five hundred Anglos and two hundred "foreigners." See San Francisco *Alta California*, January 17, 1851 and *Sacramento Transcript*, January 21, 1851.

88. *Alta California*, April 3, 1852; *San Francisco Herald*, April 5, 1852; Bancroft, "Popular Tribunals—Volume I," 466; Richard Coke Wood, *Calaveras, The Land of Skulls* (Sonora, California: Mother Lode Press, 1955), 56; Ken Gonzales-Day, *Lynching in the West*, 209.

89. San Francisco *Alta California*, May 11, 1861; *Sacramento Union*, May 6, 1861; Harris Newmark, *Sixty Years in Southern California, 1853–1913* (New York: Knickerbocker Press, 1916), 147.

90. David Lawrence Abney, "Capital Punishment in Arizona, 1863–1963" (MA thesis, Arizona State University, 1988); Bancroft, "Popular Tribunals—Volume I," 728–29.

91. *Los Angeles Star*, July 31, 1852, and August 7, 1852; Lanier Bartlett, ed., *On the Old West Coast: Being further Reminiscences of a Ranger, Major Horace Bell* (New York: William Morrow & Co., 1930), 164; William Deverell, *Whitewashed Adobe: The Rise of Los Angeles and the Remaking of its Mexican Past* (Berkeley, Los Angeles,

and London: University of California Press, 2004), 13; Leonard Pitt, *The Decline of the Californios: A Social History of the Spanish-Speaking Californians, 1846–1890* (Berkeley and Los Angeles: University of California Press, 1966), 156; Richard Griswold del Castillo, *The Los Angeles Barrio, 1850–1890: A Social History* (Berkeley, Los Angeles, and London: University of California Press, 1979), 107; Gonzales-Day, *Lynching in the West*, 211.

92. The records are located in the archives of the San Luis Obispo Historical Society in San Luis Obispo, California.

93. Horace Bell, *Reminiscences of a Ranger or Early Times in Southern California* (Santa Barbara: Wallace Hebberd, 1927), 150.

94. *Los Angeles Star*, October 22, 1853, December 10, 1853; *Nevada Journal*, November 4, 1853. See also Myron Angel, *History of San Luis Obispo County, California* (Berkley: Howell-Worth Books, 1966), 294, 306.

95. *Los Angeles Star*, December 10, 1853.

96. Mateo Andrade, Number 117, San Quentin Prison Registers, California State Library, Sacramento, California; *Columbia Gazette*, July 29, 1854; John Boessenecker, *Gold Dust & Gunsmoke: Tales of Gold Rush Outlaws, Gunfighters, Lawmen, and Vigilantes* (New York: John Wiley & Sons, 1999), 84.

97. Quoted in Bossenecker, *Gold Dust & Gunsmoke*, 108.

98. Minutes of the Vigilance Committee, May 20–21, 1858, Box 9, Local History, San Luis Obispo Historical Society, San Luis Obispo, California; *Pacific Sentinel* (Santa Cruz), June 26, 1858; Annie L. Morrison and John H. Haydon, *History of San Luis Obispo and Environs* (Los Angeles: Historic Record Company, 1917), 64–65.

99. "Warning for All Horse Runners," Minutes of the Vigilance Committee, May 22, 1858, Box 9, Local History, San Luis Obispo Historical Society.

100. Minutes of the Vigilance Committee, May 20–23 and June 5–6, 12–13, 29, 1858, Box 9, Local History, San Luis Obispo Historical Society; California Newsclippings, 1888–1897, Rare Book # 34549, Henry E. Huntington Library; *Los Angeles Star*, June 19, 1858; *Pacific Sentinel* (Santa Cruz), June 26, 1858; Harris Newmark, *Sixty Years in Southern California, 1853–1913* (New York: Knickerbocker Press, 1916), 210; Morrison and Haydon, *History of San Luis Obispo and Environs*, 64–67.

101. Angel, *History of San Luis Obispo County*, 299; Boessenecker, *Gold Dust & Gunsmoke*, 116; Morrison and Haydon, *History of San Luis Obispo and Environs*, 65.

102. Morrison and Haydon, *History of San Luis Obispo and Environs*, 67.

103. Charles Montgomery, "The Trap of Race and Memory: The Language of Spanish Civility on the Upper Rio Grande," *American Quarterly* 52 (2000): 488–89; Darlis A. Miller, "Cross-Cultural Marriages in the Southwest: The New Mexico Experience, 1846–1900," *New Mexico Historical Review* 57 (1982): 341; Juan Gómez-Quiñones, *Roots of Chicano Politics, 1600–1940* (Albuquerque, NM: University of New Mexico Press, 1994), 329–30, 354; Laura E. Gómez, "Race, Colonialism, and Criminal Law: Mexicans and the American Criminal

Justice System in Territorial New Mexico," *Law & Society Review* 34 (2000):
1129–202; Charles Montgomery, "Becoming 'Spanish-American': Race and
Rhetoric in New Mexico Politics, 1880–1928," *Journal of American Ethnic
History* 20 (2001): 60.

104. *Republican Review*, March 11, 1876, quoted in Nancy Gonzalez, "Untold Stories
of Murder and Lynching in Territorial New Mexico," 8.

105. John Nieto-Phillips, "Spanish American Ethnic Identity and New Mexico's
Statehood Struggle" in Erlinda Gonzales-Berry and Daniel R. Maciel, eds.,
The Contested Homeland: A Chicano History of New Mexico (Albuquerque, NM:
University of New Mexico Press, 2000), 97–142; Montgomery, "The Trap of
Race and Memory," 480.

106. *El Nuevo Mexicano*, June 3, 1893; Las Vegas *Daily Optic*, May 31, 1893, 2; *El Boletin
Popular*, June 1, 1893; Carlos C. de Baca, *Vicente Silva: The Terror of Las Vegas*
(Las Truches, NM: Tate Gallery, 1968), 38–39; Mitchell C. Sena, "Third Rate
Henchman of a First-Rate Terror," *True West* (February 1979): 28–29, 40–44.

107. In February 1885, Jose Trujillo Gallegos was lynched in San Miguel County by
a mob of men led by Cresensio Lucero. Gallegos, it was alleged, had murdered
his family. In 1893, a mob of Nuevomexicanos hanged Ireneo Gonzalez for
attempted murder. Santa Fe *New Mexican Review*, February 23, 1889. *El Nuevo
Mexicano*, February 11, 1893; *Albuquerque Democrat*, February 7, 1893; Santa Fe
New Mexican, February 7, 1893.

108. *Placer Herald* (Auburn), January 27, 1854.

109. *Alta California*, May 29, 1857.

110. *Alta California*, September 27, 1870.

111. Did black mobs lynch whites for crimes against blacks? Stewart Tolnay and E. M.
Beck make no references to such cases existing among the 284 whites lynched
in the American South in their study. There is little doubt that such cases were
rare, but they did take place. Bruce E. Baker has indeed uncovered one such case.
In 1887, Manse Waldrop, a white man, was lynched by a black mob for raping a
black girl. Baker describes how this single case challenged basic notions about
when and who to lynch in the American South and led to a petition campaign and
a debate in South Carolina about the nature and purpose of lynching. Another
possible example of a black mob lynching a white man comes from Texas in 1891.
In this case, the public debate was not nearly as conflicted as was the case in the
Waldrop lynching. The Anglo majority was united in anger at the lynching. On
January 4, three black men shot and killed George Taylor, an Anglo they accused
of leading an earlier lynching of a black man named Charles Beall. Knowing
that local reaction to their killing would be unpopular, the three murderers fled
the region, probably to Mexico. Anglos formed a large mob to search for, and
presumably lynch the three men, but they successfully escaped. There may have
been a handful of incidents similar to these cases, but the point is the ways
in which the surrounding communities reacted to these unusual cases, with

attempted legal and extralegal punishment. The response by the Anglo community to Mexican on Anglo violence appears to have been less severe. See Tolnay and Beck, *A Festival of Violence*, 93–98; Bruce E. Baker, "Lynch Law Reversed: The Rape of Lula Sherman, the Lynching of Manse Waldrop, and the Debate over Lynching in the 1880s," ed. William D. Carrigan, *Lynching Reconsidered: New Directions in the Study of Mob Violence* (London and New York: Routledge, 2008), 47–67; William Carrigan, *The Making of a Lynching Culture* (Urbana: University of Illinois Press, 2004), 158–59.

112. *New York Times*, July 11, 1854; July 20, 1854.

113. *San Antonio Herald*, July 11, 1863, quoted in Lois Council Ellsworth, "San Antonio During the Civil War" (master's thesis, University of Texas at Austin, 1938), 109. Anglos also aided Mexicans in lynching members of other ethnic groups who committed crimes against Mexicans. For example, in 1852, a mob of "citizens" lynched a Native American for the murder of a Mexican and a Peruvian near San Jose. See *San Francisco Herald*, April 28, 1852.

CHAPTER THREE

1. Andrew J. Stone, letter to parents, May 8, 1853; Andrew J. Stone Correspondence, Henry E. Huntington Library, San Marino, CA.

2. *Alta California*, August 19, 1850.

3. *San Antonio Ledger*, August 22, 1857.

4. *Galveston Civilian* editorial, quoted in *San Antonio Ledger*, August 15, 1857.

5. *Weekly Arizonian*, October 20, 1859.

6. *Monterey Republican*, May 26, 19, 1870.

7. *Placerville Mountain Democrat*, February 17, 1855.

8. *New York Times*, September 30, 1892.

9. *San Antonio Herald*, May 12, 1875.

10. *San Antonio Herald*, September 20, 1868, February 17, 1869.

11. Arie W. Poldervaart, *Black-Robed Justice: A History of the Administration of Justice in New Mexico from the American Occupation in 1846 until Statehood in 1912* (Santa Fe: Historical Society of New Mexico, 1948), 97. For further details of the lynching and subsequent acts of violence, see *Santa Fe Daily New Mexican*, September 18, 1875; Larry Murphy, *Out in God's Country: A History of Colfax County, New Mexico* (Springer, NM: Springer Publishing Co., 1969), 74–76; Francis Stanley, *Desperadoes of New Mexico* (Denver: World Press, 1953), 192; Marcus F. Taylor, *O. P. McMains and the Maxwell Land Grant Conflict* (Tucson: University of Arizona Press, 1979), 39–55; Howard Lamar, *The Far Southwest, 1846–1912: A Territorial History* (New Haven: Yale University Press, 1966), 53–54.

12. *Territory of New Mexico vs. O. P. McMains*, Colfax County District Court Records, Criminal Cases, Box Containing Cases #351–70, New Mexico State Records and Archives Center, Albuquerque.

13. United States Department of the Interior, Appointment Papers: Territory of New Mexico, 1850–1907, M750, Reel 1, Frames 207–13, 226, 507, National Archives and Records Administration II, College Park, Maryland.

14. *Santa Fe Daily New Mexican*, August 27, 29, 1877; Poldervaart, *Black-Robed Justice*, 97; Calvin Horn, *New Mexico's Troubled Years: The Story of the Early Territorial Governors* (Albuquerque, NM: Horn and Wallace, 1963), 177.

15. Lois Council Ellsworth, "San Antonio During the Civil War" (master's thesis, University of Texas at Austin, 1938), 108–9.

16. *Galveston News*, April 30, 1875.

17. For further information on the antilynching campaigns of these black journalists, see Christopher Waldrep, *African Americans Confront Lynching: Strategies of Resistance from the Civil War to the Civil Rights Era* (Lanham, MD: Rowman & Littlefield, 2009), 13–58.

18. Paul Ortiz, *Emancipation Betrayed: The Hidden History of Black Organizing and White Violence in Florida* (Berkeley and Los Angeles: University of California Press, 2006), 82–84; W. Fitzhugh Brundage, *Lynching in the New South: Georgia and Virginia, 1880–1930* (Urbana: University of Illinois Press, 1993), 183.

19. W. Fitzhugh Brundage, "The Roar on the Other Side of Silence: Black Resistance and White Violence in the American South, 1880–1940," in *Under Sentence of Death: Lynching in the South*, ed. W. Fitzhugh Brundage (Chapel Hill and London: University of North Carolina Press, 1997), 285; Stewart Tolnay and E. M. Beck, *A Festival of Violence: An Analysis of Southern Lynchings, 1882 to 1930* (Urbana: University of Illinois Press, 1993), 183.

20. For further insight into the Mexican code of masculine honor, see Pablo Piccato, *Tyranny of Opinion: Honor in the Construction of the Mexican Public Sphere* (Durham, NC: Duke University Press, 2010).

21. Antonio Ríos-Bustamante, *Mexican Los Angeles: A Narrative and Political History* (Encino, CO: Floricanto Press, 1992), 155.

22. *Corpus Christi Caller*, July 21, September 29, 1888; Elliot Young, *Catarino Garza's Revolution on the Texas-Mexico Border* (Durham: Duke University Press, 2004), 65–70.

23. *San Francisco Herald*, July 30, August 3, 1856.

24. *Alta California*, February 21, 1857.

25. Mexicans sometimes exacted their revenge on individual murderers who acted without the support of the wider community. In May 1857, for instance, after an Anglo shot dead a seventeen-year old Mexican in a petty domestic dispute, a mob hanged him and burned down his house. Similarly, during September 1870 Mexicans at Plata Creek in California hanged an Anglo who murdered an unarmed member of their community. Mexicans also proved as willing as Anglos to circumvent the criminal justice system by capturing and executing accused murderers before they had a chance to stand trial. Such an incident occurred in October 1897 when "infuriated Mexicans" stormed a jail in Clifton,

Arizona, and shot dead one of the inmates who had allegedly murdered one of their compatriots. *Alta California*, May 29, 1857, September 27, 1870; *Arizona Republican*, October 28, 1897.

26. *Mesilla Times*, April 13, 1861.

27. *New York Times*, July 17, 1856.

28. *Watsonville Parjaronian*, May 19, November 17, 1870; *Alta California*, May 18, November 20, 1870.

29. *Watsonville Pajaronian*, March 20, 1873; John Bossenecker, *Gold Dust & Gunsmoke: Tales of Gold Rush Outlaws, Gunfighters, Lawmen, and Vigilantes* (New York: John Wiley and Sons, 1999), 42–43.

30. F. Arturo Rosales, *¡Pobre Raza! Violence, Justice, and Mobilization Among México Lindo Immigrants, 1900–1936* (Austin: University of Texas Press, 1999), 26.

31. *New York Times*, November 26, 1910.

32. Historian Eric Hobsbawm first coined the concept of social banditry in *Bandits* (London: Weidenfeld and Nicolson, 1969). For the application of this idea to Mexicans in the American West, see Susan Lee Johnson, *Roaring Camp: The Social World of the California Gold Rush* (New York: W. W. Norton, 2000), 28; Rosales, *¡Pobre Raza!*, 28; Robert J. Rosenbaum, *Mexicano Resistance in the Southwest: "The Sacred Right of Self-Preservation"* (Austin: University of Texas Press, 1981), 55.

33. Joseph Henry Jackson, *Anybody's Gold: The Story of California's Mining Towns* (New York: D. Appleton-Century Company, 1941), 118; G. Ezra Dane with Beatrice J. Dane, *Ghost town, wherein is told much that is wonderful, laughable, and tragic, and some that is hard to believe, about life during the gold rush and later in the town of Columbia on California's mother lode, as remembered by the oldest inhabitants* (New York: Tudor Publishing Company, 1948), 127–28; Albert Shumate, *Boyhood Days: Ygnacio Villegas' Reminiscences of California in the 1850s* (San Francisco: California Historical Society, 1983), 44–45.

34. *Alta California*, July 30, 1853; John Eagle to his wife Margaret, August 10, 1853, John Eagle correspondence, Henry E. Huntington Library; *Daily Placer Times & Transcript* (San Francisco), August 8, 1853; *Los Angeles Star*, September 3, 1853.

35. This brief narrative draws on some of the numerous biographies of Vasquez, including Eugene T. Sawyer, *Life and Career of Tiburcio Vásquez: The Bandit and Murderer* (Washington, DC: Office of the Librarian of Congress, 1875); Jack Jones, *Vásquez: California's Forgotten Bandit* (Carlsbad, CA: Akira Press, 1996); and John Boessenecker, *Bandido: The Life and Times of Tiburcio Vasquez* (Norman: University of Oklahoma Press, 2010).

36. There is a substantial literature on Juan Cortina. Other sources are identified in subsequent notes, but the best single volume, and our principal source for biographical information on the outlaw leader, is Jerry Thompson, *Cortina: Defending the Mexican Name in Texas* (College Station, TX:Texas A&M University Press, 2007).

37. Jerry Thompson, ed., *Fifty Miles and a Fight: Major Samuel Peter Heintzelman's Journal of Texas and the Cortina War* (Austin: Texas State Historical Association, 1998), 20–23; Charles M. Robinson III, *The Men Who Wear the Star: The Story of the Texas Rangers* (New York: Random House, 2000), 122–23.

38. Citizens of Brownsville to Hardin R. Runnells, Governor of the State of Texas, October 2, 1859, Memorials and Petitions, Texas State Archives, Austin.

39. Rosenbaum, *Mexicano Resistance in the Southwest*, 42; Eugenia Reynolds Briscoe, *City by the Sea: A History of Corpus Christi, Texas, 1519–1875* (New York: Vantage Press, 1985), 161.

40. Robinson, *The Men Who Wear the Star*, 123–24; Thompson, *Fifty Miles and a Fight*, 32.

41. Jerry Thompson, "'The Sacred Right of Self Preservation': Juan Nepomuceno Cortina and the Struggle for Justice in Texas," in *Racially Writing the Republic: Racists, Race Rebels, and Transformations of American Identity*, ed. Bruce Baum and Duchess Harris (Durham, NC: Duke University Press, 2009), 91–93; Chad Richardson, *Batos, Bolillos, Pochos, and Pelados: Class and Culture on the South Texas Border* (Austin: University of Texas Press, 1999), 8.

42. U. S. Congress, House, Difficulties on the Southwestern Frontier, 36th Congress; 1st Session, 1860, H. Exec. Doc. 52.

43. Ibid.

44. John Salmon Ford, *Rip Ford's Texas* (Austin: University of Texas Press, 1987), 309.

45. Boessenecker, *Bandido*, 46–48, 291, 303, 371–75.

46. This displacement of fact for fiction in the minds of the reading public owes in particular to the influence of John Rollin Ridge, author of *The Life and Adventures of Joaquín Murieta, the Celebrated California Bandit*. Published in 1854, the book cast Murieta in the role of heroic righter of Anglo wrongs with which he would continue to be associated in numerous songs, stage plays, and movies. Yellow Bird (John Rollin Ridge), *The Life and Adventures of Joaquín Murieta, the Celebrated California Bandit* (Norman: University of Oklahoma Press, 1955); Walter Nobel Burns, *The Robin Hood of El Dorado: The Saga of Joaquín Murrieta, the Famous Outlaw of California's Age of Gold* (New York: Coward-McCann, 1932). For further assessments of the Murieta myth, see Joseph Henry Jackson, "The Creation of Joaquin Murieta," *Pacific Spectator* 2 (1948): 176–81; Hector H. Lee, "The Reverberant Joaquín Murieta in California Legendry," *Pacific Historian* 25 (1981): 39–47

47. James W. Parins, *John Rollin Ridge: His Life and Works* (Lincoln: University of Nebraska Press, 1991), 101; Bruce Thornton, *Searching for Joaquín: Myth, Murieta and History in California* (San Francisco: Encounter Books, 2003), 69, 91, 116.

48. Manuel G. Gonzales, *Mexicanos: A History of Mexicans in the United States* (Bloomington: Indiana University Press, 1999), 89.

49. *Stockton Journal*, July 9, 1850. See also Bayard Taylor, *Eldorado, or Adventures in the Path of Empire* (New York: Alfred A. Knopf, 1949), 79; Jackson, *Anybody's Gold*, 109.

50. Douglas Monroy, "Guilty Pleasures: The Satisfactions of Racial Thinking in Early-Nineteenth-Century California," in *Race and Nation: Ethnic Systems in the Modern World*, ed. Paul R. Spickard (New York: Routledge, 2005), 49.

51. *Alta California*, February 24, 1853; *Sacramento Daily Democratic State Journal*, February 28, 1853; Walter Van Tilberg Clark, ed, *The Journals of Alfred Doten, 1849–1903* (Reno: University of Nevada Press, 1973), 141.

52. Thompson, *Cortina*, 74, 77. See also Rosenbaum, *Mexicano Resistance in the Southwest*, 43.

53. Carlos Larralde and Jose Rodolfo Jacobo, *Juan N. Cortina and the Struggle for Justice in Texas* (Dubuque, IA: Kendall/Hunt Publishing Company, 2000), 68.

54. Bruce S. Cheeseman, ed., *Maria von Blücher's Corpus Christi: Letters from the South Texas Frontier, 1849–1879* (College Station: Texas A&M University Press, 2002), 117.

55. *New York Times*, October 17, 1859; Citizens of Brownsville to Hardin R. Runnells, October 2, 1859.

56. Gonzales, *Mexicanos*, 109.

57. Paul Bryan Gray, "Francisco P. Ramírez: A Short Biography," *California History* 84 (Winter 2006–7): 20, 24–25.

58. *El Clamor Público*, March 5, 1859.

59. José Luis Benavides, "'Californios! Whom Do You Support?' *El Clamor Público*'s Contradictory Role in the Racial Formation Process in California," *California History* 84 (2006–7): 60–64.

60. *El Clamor Público*, July 26, 1856.

61. William Deverell, *Whitewashed Adobe: The Rise of Los Angeles and the Remaking of its Mexican Past* (Berkeley, Los Angeles, and London: University of California Press, 2004), 22–23, 261n35.

62. Lanier Bartlett, ed., *On the Old West Coast: Being further Reminiscences of a Ranger, Major Horace Bell* (New York: William Morrow & Co., 1930), 100–101. For other specific examples of the lynchings committed by Anglos, see Harris Newmark, *Sixty Years in Southern California, 1853–1913* (New York: Knickerbocker Press, 1916), 208–10, and Bossenecker, *Gold Dust & Gunsmoke*, 126–28.

63. Félix Gutiérrez, "Francisco P. Ramírez: Californio Editor and Yanqui Conquest," in *Profiles in Journalistic Courage*, ed. Robert Giles, Robert W. Snyder, and Lisa DeLisle (New Brunswick, NJ: Transaction, 2001), 20.

64. *El Clamor Público*, July 26, 1856.

65. *El Clamor Público*, October 9, 1855.

66. Martin Luther King, Jr., "Letter from Birmingham City Jail," in *A Testament of Hope: The Essential Writings and Speeches of Martin Luther King, Jr.*, ed. James M. Washington (San Francisco: HarperCollins, 1991), 297.

67. *El Clamor Público*, June 5, 1858, September 3, September 24, 1859.

68. Coya Paz Brownrigg, "Linchocracia: Performing 'America' in *El Clamor Público*," *California History* 84 (Winter 2006–7), 50; Gutiérrez, "Francisco P. Ramírez," 26–27.

69. Manuel G. Gonzales, "Carlos I. Velasco," *Journal of Arizona History* 25 (Autumn 1984): 265–84.

70. *El Fronterizo*, February 29, 1880.

71. *Arizona Weekly Citizen*, January 16, 1875.

72. For a more substantial organizational history, see Olivia Arrieta, "La Alianza Hispano-Americana, 1894–1965: An Analysis of Collective Action and Cultural Adaptation," in *Nuevomexicano Cultural Legacy: Forms, Agencies & Discourse*, ed. Francisco A. Lomelí, Víctor A. Sorell, and Genaro M. Padilla (Albuquerque: University of New Mexico Press, 2002), 109–26.

73. Cynthia E. Orozco, *No Mexicans, Women, or Dogs Allowed: The Rise of the Mexican American Civil Rights Movement* (Austin: University of Texas Press, 2009), 69–70; Rosales, *¡Pobre Raza!*, 114–15.

74. The sources are unclear as to the precise day in December on which Idar was born.

75. Johnson, *Revolution in Texas*, 43; Beatriz de la Garza, *A Law for the Lion: A Tale of Crime and Injustice in the Borderlands* (Austin: University of Texas Press, 2003), 80–82.

76. *New York Times*, November 10, 11, 1910. This incident is discussed in more detail in chap. 4.

77. *La Crónica*, June 29, 1911.

78. José E. Limón, "El Primer Congreso Mexicanista de 1911: A Precursor to Contemporary Chicanismo," *Aztlán* 5 (1974): 86; Francisco H. Vásquez and Rodolfo D. Torres, *Latino/a Thought: Culture, Politics, and Society* (Lanham, MD: Rowman & Littlefield, 2003), 227; Richard R. Flores, *Remembering the Alamo: Memory, Modernity, and the Master Symbol* (Austin: University of Texas Press, 2002), 6.

79. David J. Weber, ed., *Foreigners in Their Native Land: Historical Roots of the Mexican Americans* (Albuquerque: University of New Mexico Press, 1973), 250.

80. Limón, "El Primer Congreso Mexicanista," 97–98; *La Crónica*, October 19, 1910.

81. Rosales, *¡Pobre Raza!*, 27.

82. The newspaper was first published in San Antonio but suppression by the authorities led to its relocation to several other cities. Nicolás Kanellos with Helvetia Martell, *Hispanic Periodicals in the United States, Origins to 1960: A Brief History and Comprehensive Bibliography* (Houston: Arte Público Press, 2000), 21.

83. Ward S. Albro, "Práxedis G. Guerrero: Revolutionary Writer or Writer as Revolutionary," in *Recovering the U.S. Hispanic Literary Heritage*, II, ed. Erlinda Gonzales-Berry and Chuck Tatum (Houston: Arte Público Press, 1996), 209.

84. For more information on Klan activities in the region, see Charles C. Alexander, *The Ku Klux Klan in the Southwest* (Lexington: University of Kentucky Press, 1965); Sue Wilson Abbey, "The Ku Klux Klan in Arizona, 1921–1925," *Journal of Arizona History* 14 (1973): 10–30; and Carlos M. Larralde and Richard Griswold del Castillo, "San Diego's Ku Klux Klan 1920–1980," *Journal of San Diego History* 46 (2000): 68–88.

85. *El Defensor de Pueblo*, November 30, 1923.

86. *El Azote*, January 14, 1923.

87. Eliodoso Péres Rendón to Texas Governor Dan Moody, August 22, 1927, Papers of Governor Dan Moody Box 80, Folder Set 199, Texas State Archives, Austin.

88. Charles H. Harris III and Louis R. Sadler, *The Texas Rangers and the Mexican Revolution: The Bloodiest Deacde, 1910–1920* (Albuquerque, NM: University of New Mexico, 2004), 182–83, 456.

89. *El Fronterizo*, November 14, 1880.

90. Hon. Dermot H. Hardy and Major Ingham S. Roberts, eds., *Historical Review of South-East Texas and the Founders, Leaders and Representative Men of Its Commerce, Industry and Civic Affairs* (Chicago: Lewis Publishing Company, 1910), II, 995–96.

91. Benjamin Johnson, "The Plan de San Diego Uprising and the Making of the Modern Texas-Mexican Borderlands," in *Continental Crossroads: Remapping U.S.-Mexico Borderlands History*, ed. Samuel Truett and Elliott Young (Durham, NC: Duke University Press, 2004), 283.

92. Wesley Hall Looney, "The Texas Rangers in a Turbulent Era" (MA thesis, Texas Tech University, 1971), 44; Michael J. Lynch, "The Role of J. T. Canales in the Development of Tejano Identity and Mexican American Integration in Twentieth Century South Texas," *Journal of South Texas* 13 (2000): 221–22.

93. Johnson, *Revolution in Texas*, 174; Ribb, "Patrician as Redeemer," 198.

94. Texas Legislature, "Proceedings of the Joint Committee of the Senate and the House in the Investigation of the Texas State Ranger Force," typed transcript, 36th Leg., reg. sess., 1919, 2 vols., Legislative Papers, Texas State Archives.

95. Ibid., I, 269.

96. Unidentified newspaper clipping, Texas Ranger Scrapbook, Folder 2, Texas Rangers Papers, Center for American History, University of Texas at Austin; Harris and Sadler, *The Texas Rangers and the Mexican Revolution*, 459–60.

97. Johnson, *Revolution in Texas*, 175.

98. Benjamin Márquez, *LULAC: The Evolution of a Mexican American Political Organization* (Austin: University of Texas Press, 1993), 32–34; Neil Foley, *Quest for Equality: The Failed Promise of Black-Brown Solidarity* (Cambridge, MA: Harvard University Press, 2010), 14–15.

99. Membership Records, Boxes G-128, G-201, G-202, Branch Files, National Association for the Advancement of Colored People Papers, Library of Congress, Washington, DC.

100. Manuel Gamio, *The Life Story of the Mexican Immigrant* (New York: Dover, 1970), 139.

101. Ozzie G. Simmons, *Anglo-Americans and Mexican Americans in South Texas: A Study in Dominant-Subordinate Group Relations* (New York: Arno Press, 1974), 465.

CHAPTER FOUR

1. Manuel Robles to Lewis Cass, October 14, 1857, Copy of Translation of Letter sent to Lewis Cass, Secretary of State of the United States, Office of the Governor, Record Group 301, Records of Elisha Marshall Pease, Box 301–26, Folder 47, Texas State Archives, Austin.

2. Ernest C. Shearer, "Border Relations Between the United States and Mexico, 1848–1960" (PhD diss., University of Texas, 1939), 227; Eugenia Reynolds Briscoe, *City by the Sea: A History of Corpus Christi, Texas, 1519–1875* (New York and other cities: Vantage Press, 1985), 160–61.

3. "Report of the Mexican Commission on the Northern Frontier Question" in Carlos E. Cortes, ed., *The Mexican Experience in Texas* (New York: Arno Press, 1976); "Texas Frontier Troubles," Report No.343, House of Representatives, 44th Congress, Ist Session, 1877.

4. Jorge I. Domínguez and Rafael Fernández de Castro, *The United States and Mexico: Between Partnership and Conflict*, 2nd ed. (New York: Routledge, 2009), 12; Lars Schoultz, *Beneath the United States: A History of U.S. Policy Toward Latin America* (Cambridge, MA: Harvard University Press, 1998), 237–38.

5. Manuel de Zamacona to James G. Blaine, April 15, 1881, Secretary of Territory Papers, Subject Group 10, Box 12, Folder 171, Arizona State Library and Archives, Phoenix.

6. R. H. Paul to Mexican Consul at Tucson, June 30, 1881, Secretary of Territory Papers, Subject Group 10, Box 12, Folder 172.

7. Manuel de Zamacona to James G. Blaine, June 30, 1881, Reel 19, Notes from the Mexican Legation in the United States to the Department of State, 1821–1906, The National Archives, College Park, Maryland; Manuel de Zamacona to James G. Blaine, August 8, 1881, Secretary of Territory Papers, Subject Group 10, Box 12, Folder 172. For a short biography of Zamacona, see José Roselio Álvarez, ed., *Enciclopedia de México*, vol. 14 (Ciudad de México: Enciclopedia de México, 1994), 8232.

8. James G. Blaine to John C. Frémont, August 29, 1881, Secretary of Territory Papers, Subject Group 10, Box 12, Folder 172.

9. Manuel de Zamacona to James G. Blaine, November 15, 1881, *Papers Relating to the Foreign Office of the United States, 1881* (Washington, DC: Government Printing Office, 1882), 407–8.

10. George H. Stevens, Sheriff of Graham County, to Governor John J. Gosper, June 13, 1881, and September 13, 1881; Mariano Samaniego to Governor of Arizona

Territory, August 19, 1881, Secretary of Territory Papers, Subject Group 10, Box 12, Folder 171.

11. The Governor of Sonora, for example, refused to transfer murder suspect Francisco Vega to Arizona authorities. Illegible (Department of State) to Lewis Wolfley, Governor of Arizona, October 2, 1889, Secretary of Territory Papers, Subject Group 10, Box 12, Folder 173.

12. *Arizona Weekly Miner*, August 26, 1881. For an example of the unilateral editorial line taken by Anglo newspapers, see *Arizona Citizen*, March 25, 1871.

13. Luis E. Torres, Governor of Sonora, and J. P. Robles, Hermosillo, to Governor of the Territory of Arizona, June 15, 1881; General Jose Otero to Alexander Willard, American Consul at Guaymas, Mexico, July 31, 1881; V. Morales, Mexican Consul of Arizona, to Acting Governor of Arizona, John J. Gosper, August 10, 1881, Secretary of Territory Papers, Subject Group 10, Box 12, Folder 171.

14. Manuel de Zamacona to James G. Blaine, April 15, 1881; James G. Blaine to Samuel J. Kirkwood, April 19, 1881; Samuel J. Kirkwood to John C. Frémont, April 21, 1881, Secretary of Territory Papers, Subject Group 10, Box 12, Folder 171.

15. Matías Romero to Señor Secretario, December 31, 1884, including report of William A. Pinkerton to Matías Romero, November 14, 1884, T.342, No.1100, pp.891–5 Secretaría de Relaciones Exteriores Archives, Mexico City, Mexico (hereinafter cited as SRE).

16. William A. Pinkerton to Matías Romero, November 14, 15, 20, 22, 24, 26, 1884, SRE T.342, No.1100, 891–95.

17. William A. Pinkerton to Matías Romero, November 15, 26, 1884, SRE T.342, No.1100, 891–95.

18. Warren Franklin Webb, "A History of Lynching in California Since 1875" (MA thesis, University of California, Berkeley, 1934), 59–61; *Yreka Journal*, August 27, 30, September 3, 1895; *San Francisco Chronicle*, August 27, 28, 1895.

19. *Fresno Expositor* editorial reprinted in *Yreka Journal*, September 3, 1895. See also the editorial from the *Sacramento Bee*, reproduced in the same edition.

20. *San Francisco Examiner*, August 27, 1895. The paper expressed similar sentiments in its edition of the following day even though it accepted there was only circumstantial evidence of Moreno's guilt.

21. *Yreka Journal*, September 3, 10, 1895.

22. *Yreka Journal*, August 27, 30, 1895; *San Francisco Examiner*, August 28, 1895.

23. For more extensive biographical details, see undated newspaper clippings, *Expediente Personal de Matias Romero 1898–1899* (LE 1038), 157–60, SRE.

24. Matías Romero, *Mexico and the United States, A Study of Subjects Affecting Their Political, Commercial, and Social Relations, Made With A View to Their Promotion* (New York and London: G. P. Putnam's Sons, 1898), I, vii.

25. "Indemnity to Relatives of Luis Moreno: Message from the President of the United States, Transmitting a Report from the Secretary of State, With

Accompanying Papers, Touching the Lynching in 1895, at Yreka, Cal., of Luis Moreno, a Mexican Citizen, and the Demand of the Mexican Government for Indemnity," House of Representatives, Document No.237, 55th Congress, 2nd. Session (3679), vol. 51, 2, 5, 7, 9.

26. W. L. Hobbs to James H. Budd, June 15, 1896, SRE T.444, No. 143, pp. 231–35; Sheriff W. L. Hobbs to Governor James H. Budd, June 15, 1896, "Indemnity to Relatives of Luis Moreno," 11–13.

27. W. L. Hobbs to James H. Budd, August 27, 1897, SRE T.453, No.285, pp. 195–96. Secretary of State John Sherman informed Mexican officials that Governor Budd had commissioned the report from Sheriff Hobbs and forwarded a copy once it was completed. John Sherman to Matías Romero, n.d., SRE T.453, No.278, p. 184; No.285, p. 194, John Sherman to Matías Romero, n.d., SRE T.453, No.285, p. 194.; Matías Romero, report, August 1, 1896, SRE T.445, No.74, p. 162; J. M. Todman to John Sherman, September 1, 1897, SRE T.453, No.285, p. 197.

28. *San Francisco Examiner*, November 29, 1895. See also Matías Romero to Richard Olney, May 15, 1896, SRE T.440, pp. 508–9; Matías Romero to SRE, May 19, 1896, SRE T.440, No.1215, p. 547; Matías Romero to Ignacio Mariscal, May 23, 1896, SRE T.440, No.1235, p. 601.

29. "Indemnity to Relatives of Luis Moreno," 1. See also *New York Times*, January 19, 1898; Matías Romero to Ignacio Mariscal, January 18, 1898, SRE T.457 No.662, p. 133; Matías Romero to Ignacio Mariscal, January 19, 1898, SRE T.457, No.669, p. 145; Matías Romero to William R. Day, July 18, 1898, SRE T.455 (1898), No.54, p. 101.

30. Jean Pfaelzer, *Driven Out: The Forgotten War Against Chinese Americans* (New York: Random House, 2007), 209–15; Clive Webb, "The Lynching of Sicilian Immigrants in the American South, 1886 to 1910," *American Nineteenth Century History* 3 (2002), 66–68.

31. Matías Romero to SRE, March 21, 1891, SRE T.400, No.443, pp. 398–404; Matías Romero to SRE, April 1, 1891, SRE T.400, No. 494, pp. 564–6; Matías Romero to SRE, May 4, 1891, SRE, T.401, No. 673, pp. 20–22; Matías Romero to SRE, May 6, 1891, SRE, T.401, No. 679, pp. 39–43; Matías Romero to SRE, May 9, 1891, SRE T.401, No.679, pp. 39–43.

32. Matías Romero to Ignacio Mariscal, January 19, 1898, SRE T.457, No.669, p. 145.

33. Pfaelzer, *Driven Out*, 214.

34. Paul Garner, *Porfirio Díaz* (Harlow, Essex: Longman, 2001), 139–43; David M. Pletcher, *The Diplomacy of Trade and Investment: American Economic Expansion in the Hemisphere, 1865–1900* (Columbia: University of Missouri Press, 1998), 77–113; Dirk W. Raat, *Mexico and the United States: Ambivalent Vistas* (Athens: University of Georgia Press, 1992), 38.

35. Unspecified "Mexican Journal" quoted in *Omaha Enterprise*, December 14, 1895.

36. Richard Olney to Matías Romero, January 30, 1897, No. 209, p. 32, Correspondencia del Departamento de Estado 1897, T.453; Ignacio Mariscal to Matías Romero. February 9, 1897, No.703, p. 221, Correspendencia de la Secretaria de Relaciones Exteriores (1897) T.448.

37. William R. Day, to Matías Romero, June 28, 1897, No.263, p. 139; C. A. Davies to C. A. Culberson, June 16, 1897, No. 263, pp. 140–42, Correspondencia de la Legacion Mexicana en Washington 1897 T.453. The lynching attracted considerable newspaper publicity. See, for example, *Houston Daily Post*, October 8, 9, 14, 1895; *Laredo Daily Times*, October 8, 1895; and *Carrizo Springs Javelin*, October 19, 1895.

38. C. A. Davies to C. A. Culberson, June 16, 1897, No.263, pp. 140–42, Correspondencia del Departmento de Estado 1897, T.453; M. Romero, report, June 29, 1897, Correspondencia de la Legacion Mexicana en Washington 1897, T.452.

39. *New York Times*, December 8, 1900.

40. John Hay to Jose F. Godoy, December 30, 1898, *Expediente Personal de Matias Romero 1898–1899*, 177; *New York Times*, December 31, 1898.

41. *New York Times*, November 11, 1910; *Dallas Morning News*, November 4, 1910; *The Independent*, November 17, 1910; *Santa Anna News*, November 18, 1910.

42. *Hartford Courant*, November 10, 1910; *New York Times*, November 10, 1910; *The Independent*, November 17, 1910.

43. *New York Times*, November 12, 15, 1910. Swift police action prevented further riots in two other cities, Oaxaca and Tampico. Gerald G. Raun, "Seventeen Days in November: The Lynching of Atonio Rodríguez and American-Mexican Relations, November 3–19, 1910," *Journal of Big Bend Studies* 7 (1995), 168.

44. *New York Times*, November 11, 16, 17, 1910; *St Petersburg Evening Independent*, November 12, 1910.

45. Frederick C. Turner, "Anti-Americanism in Mexico, 1910–1913," *Hispanic American Historical Review* 47 (1967): 506. The US Ambassador to Mexico, Henry Lane Wilson, similarly dismissed the notion that the rioters acted out of sincere moral outrage at the lynching. *Papers Relating to the Foreign Relations of the United States, 1911* (Washington, DC: US Government Princting Office, 1918), 358.

46. Raat, *Mexico and the United States*, 82–83; Garner, *Porfirio Díaz*, 141. Popular resentment toward the United States intensified when the press reported that American authorities had arrested and surrendered critics of the Díaz administration who sought political asylum across the border. *Otautau Standard and Wallace County Chronicle*, January 10, 1911.

47. *New York Times*, November 14, 1910.

48. J. L. de la Garra to Philander C. Knox, November 9, 1910, T.33, No.281, pp. 523–24, SRE; J. L. de la Garza to Philander C. Knox, November 12, 1910, T.33 No.293,

p. 527, SRE; J. L. de la Garra to Philander C. Knox, November 12, 1910, T.33, No.294, p. 529, SRE; *New York Times*, November 12, 1910; Charles H. Harris III and Louis R. Sadler, *The Texas Rangers and the Mexican Revolution: The Bloodiest Decade, 1910–1920* (Albuquerque: University of New Mexico Press, 2004), 51–52.

49. *Lexington (NC) Dispatch*, December 21, 1910; *New York Times*, November 13, 14, 24, 1910; *The Independent*, November 24, 1910; *Los Angeles Times*, December 24, 1910.

50. *The Independent*, November 17, 1960. See also *The Outlook*, November 26, 1910.

51. F. Arturo Rosales, *¡Pobre Raza! Violence, Justice, and Mobilization Among México Lindo Immigrants, 1900–1936* (Austin: University of Texas Press, 1999), 37.

52. *Beaumont Daily Enterprise*, June 20, 1911; *Atlanta Constitution*, June 25, 1911; *New York Times*, June 26, 1911.

53. *Dallas Morning News*, February 19, 1912, June 22, 1911.

54. *Beaumont Daily Enterprise*, June 24, 1911.

55. *Victoria Advocate*, June 23, 1911; *Daily Oklahoman*, June 24, 1911; *Anacona Standard*; *Beaumont Daily Enterprise*, June 25, 1911; *Fort Worth Star-Telegram*, June 24, 25, 27, 1911.

56. *New Orleans Times Picayune*, November 7, 1911; *Cleburne Morning Review*, November 8, 1911; *The State* (Columbia, SC), November 11, 1911; *Fort Worth Star Telegram*, November 12, 1911; *Macon Telegraph*, November 15, 1911.

57. *New York Times*, June 16, 1911; *Fort Worth Star-Telegram*, November 17, 1911.

58. *Fort Worth Star-Telegram*, February 28, 1912; *Cleburne Morning Review*, February 28, 1912; *Anacona Standard*, March 3, 1912.

59. For more information on this infamous incident, see Patricia Bernstein, *The First Waco Horror: The Lynching of Jesse Washington and the Rise of the NAACP* (College Station: Texas A&M University Press, 2005); and William D. Carrigan, *The Making of a Lynching Culture: Violence and Vigilantism in Central Texas, 1836–1916* (Urbana: University of Illinois Press, 2004).

60. This is not to suggest that there were no protests against Anglo oppression of Mexicans. See, for example, Douglas W. Richmond, "Mexican Immigration and Border Strategy During the Revolution, 1910–1920," *New Mexico Historical Review*, 57 (July 1982): 277–78.

61. Raat, *Mexico and the United States*, 112–15.

62. *New York Times*, September 2, 1919.

63. *Des Moines Capital*, September 14, 1919; *Delaware Herald*, September 15, 1919; *Deseret News*, September 15, 1919; *Hartford Courant*, September 15, 1919; *New York Call*, September 15, 1919; *New York Sun*, September 15, 1919.

64. *New York Times*, September 16, 1919; *Denver Post*, September 20, 1919.

65. *Houston Post*, September 18, 1919. An editorial in the *New York Globe* of September 16, 1919, also noted the apparent hypocrisy of U.S. diplomatic protest. "When

two Americans are killed in Mexico, even though it be in a section of the country remote from any city and notoriously infested with bandits, a roar for intervention goes up throughout this country. When two Mexicans are killed in a civilized American city by a mob it is regrettable, to be sure; but, after all, they look somewhat like Negroes, and everyone knows what we do with the latter."

66. Rosales, *¡Pobre Raza!*, 40–41.

67. *New York Times*, May 24, 1937

68. Álvarez, *Enciclopedia de México*, vol. 13, 7623; *New York Times*, May 24, 1937; *Time*, May 31, 1937. The official portrait of Téllez can be seen at http://www.sre. gob.mx/acerca/secretarios/xx.html.

69. Antero and Ramon Garcia, Interview #182; Antero Garcia, Interview #158, South Texas Oral History and Folklore Collection, James C. Jerrigan Library, Texas A&M University, Kingsville, Texas. For further details of the lynching of Dr. J. G. Smith, see *The Crisis* 26, no. 6 (October 1923): 260.

70. *New York Times*, November 16, 1922; *Dallas Morning News*, November 16, 1922; *Excelsior*, November 16, 1922.

71. *New York Times*, November 18, 1922.

72. *San Antonio Express*, November 17, 1922. One of the other acts of violence protested by the Mexican ambassador was the beating and whipping of an unnamed Mexican in Charco three months earlier. *New York Times*, August 26, 1922.

73. *Philadelphia Inquirer*, November 26, 1922.

74. For more information on the Bucareli agreements, see William Dirk Raat and William H. Beezley, eds. *Twentieth-Century Mexico* (Lincoln: University of Nebraska Press, 1986), 59; and Leslie Bethell, ed., *Mexico Since Independence* (Cambridge: Cambridge University Press, 1991), 206.

75. *San Antonio Express*, November 16, 21, 1922; *San Jose Evening News*, November 16, 1922; *Fort Worth Star-Telegram*, November 20, 1922; *New York Times*, November 18, 1922.

76. *San Antonio Express*, November 19, 21, 1922; *New York Times*, November 20, 1922.

77. *Fort Worth Star-Telegram*, November 16, 1922; *Tulsa World*, December 15, 1922; *San Antonio Express*, November 16, 1922.

78. *San Antonio Express*, November 18, 19, 30, 1922; *Fort Worth Star-Telegram*, November 19, 1922; *Philadelphia Inquirer*, November 26, 1922. On the organizing efforts of the IWW in Texas, see Robert H. Zieger and Gilbert J. Gall, *American Workers, American Unions: The Twentieth Century* (Baltimore, MD: Johns Hopkins University Press, 2002), 30

79. *Dallas Morning News*, November 30, 1922, January 31, 1923.

80. *Los Angeles Times*, September 8, 1926; *New York Times*, September 8, 1926.

81. Unspecified newspaper clipping, January 10, 1927, Oliver Douglas Weeks Collection, box 1, folder 21, LULAC Archives, Benson Latin American Collection, the University of Texas at Austin.

82. *San Antonio Light*, September 8, 1926; *El Cronista del Valle*, September 8, 1926.

83. *El Cronista del Valle*, September 9, 13, 1926.

84. *El Cronista del Valle*, September 11, 1926; *Galveston Daily News*, September 19, 1926; *Syracuse Post Standard*, October 24, 1926.

85. *El Cronista del Valle*, September 11, 13, 18, 1926; *Houston Post Dispatch*, November 25, 1926; *Prescott Evening Courier*, November 26, 1926.

86. *Sheboygan Press*, December 13, 1926; *San Antonio Light*, December 15, 1926.

87. The other arrested persons were Deputy Sheriff Frank Brandt, Deputy Constable Leon Gill, Special Investigator Roy Collins, jailer Arturo Flores and three game wardens named M. F. Cowert, N. M. Ragland, and Charlie Wroten. *Appleton Post-Crescent*, January 8, 1927; *Daily Northwestern*, January 8, 1927; *Lincoln Star*, January 8, 1927; *Portsmouth Daily Times*, January 8, 1927; *St. Petersburg Evening Independent*, January 8, 1927; *Los Angeles Times*, January 9, 1927.

88. Unspecified newspaper clipping, January 10, 1927, Weeks Collection, box 1, folder 21.

89. Unspecified newspaper clipping, January 10, 1927, Weeks Collection, box 1, folder 21; *Houston Chronicle*, January 11, 12, 13, 1927.

90. *Salt Lake Tribune*, January 25, 1927; *San Antonio Express*, January 25, 1927.

91. *San Antonio Light*, February 1, 1927; *El Cronista del Valle*, January 27, 1927; *Kingsport Times*, January 9, 1927.

92. *San Antonio Express*, February 2, 3, 1927; *Salt Lake Tribune*, February 5, 1927.

93. *Abilene Morning Reporter-News*, February 6, 1927; *Los Angeles Times*, February 6, 1927; *Nevada State Journal*, February 6, 1927; *Modesto News-Herald*, February 6, 1927; *Salt Lake Tribune*, February 6, 1927; *San Antonio Express*, February 6, 7, 1927; *San Antonio Light*, February 6, 7, 1927.

94. For further information on this infamous case, see Seth Cagin and Philip Dray, *We Are Not Afraid: The Story of Goodman, Schwerner, and Chaney and the Civil Rights Campaign for Mississippi* (New York: Macmillan, 1988).

95. *Raleigh Gazette*, January 29, 1898; *Savannah Tribune*, April 13, 1901.

96. *Cleveland Gazette*, November 26, 1910. For an example of initial press interest in the case, see *The Crisis* II (August 1911), 140.

97. *Afro-American Advance* (Minneapolis), May 27, 1899. For more press coverage of the case, see *American Citizen* (Kansas City), May 27, 1899.

98. *Chicago Defender*, November 25, 1922.

99. James Weldon Johnson to President Harding, November 17, 1922, Administrative Files, Box C-338, National Association for the Advancement of Colored People (NAACP) Papers, Library of Congress, Washington, DC; *Fort Worth Star-Telegram*, November, 16, 21, 1922.

100. Assistant Secretary to Don Manuel C. Téllez, January 5, 1923; Don Manuel Téllez to Assistant Secretary, February 16, 1923, Administrative Files, Box C-339, NAACP Papers.

101. James Weldon Johnson to José A. Valenzuela, November 29, 1926; José A. Valenzuela, Consul General, to James Weldon Johnson, December 4, 1926; James Weldon Johnson to Mexican Embassy, December 9, 1926, Administrative Files, Box C-339, NAACP Papers.

CONCLUSION

1. The events surrounding the shooting and arrest of Rafael Benavides were widely reported in the press, including the following: *Farmington Times Hustler*, November 16, 1928, November 23, 1928; *Albuquerque Journal*, November 16, 1928; *Aztec Independent*, November 16, 1928; Roswell *Morning Dispatch*, November 16, 1928; *Roswell Daily Record*, November 16, 1928; *El Paso Times*, November 17, 1928; *La Prensa* (San Antonio), November 17, 1928; *Las Vegas Daily Optic*, November 17, 1928; *Santa Fe New Mexican*, November 17, 1928; *Raton Daily Range*, November 17, 1928, November 20, 1928; *Alamogordo News*, November 22, 1928; *Santa Rosa News*, November 23, 1928; *Roy Record*, November 24, 1928.

2. *Farmington Times Hustler*, November 23, 1928.

3. *Farmington Times Hustler*, December 7, 1928; *Santa Fe New Mexican*, December 5, 1928, December 6, 1928, November 22, 1928.

4. Other historians, including mob violence expert Arturo Rosales, share this assessment of the case. Arturo Rosales, correspondence with authors, August 5, 2002. Benavides was at the very least the last Mexican lynched in New Mexico. Robert J. Tórrez, "New Mexico's Last Lynching," '*Round the Roundhouse* (November 11–December 9, 2003): 6F.

5. Although Benavides was the last identifiable Mexican to be murdered by a lynch mob, lynching must be differentiated from other forms of ethnic violence. The Los Angeles Zoot Suit riot of August 1943 is a stark illustration of continued conflict between Anglos and Mexicans. While anti-Mexican violence continued after 1928, Benavides's lynching coincided with a subtle but decisive shift in Anglo attitudes. According to our research, in the years that followed, would-be mob members were discouraged by the threat of public condemnation and prosecution by the courts. *Los Angeles Times*, October 11, 1933; *New York Times*, October 11, 1933; Mauricio Mazón, *The Zoot-Suit Riots: The Psychology of Symbolic Annihilation* (Austin: University of Texas Press, 1984); Carey McWilliams, "The Los Angeles Riot of 1943" in *Violence in America; A Historical and Contemporary Reader*, ed. Thomas Rose (New York: Random House, 1969), 168–80.

6. For a convincing discussion of the cultural struggle between advocates of "rough justice" and supporters of due process throughout the United States, see Michael J. Pfeifer, *Rough Justice: Lynching and American Society, 1874–1947* (Urbana and Chicago: University of Illinois Press, 2004).

7. *Farmington Times Hustler,* November 30, 1928; *Durango Herald-Democrat* editorial republished in *Santa Fe New Mexican,* November 26, 1928, and *Farmington Times Hustler,* December 7, 1928.

8. Department of Corrections, Penitentiary of New Mexico, Record Book of Convicts, #3384.

9. *Rio Grande Farmer* editorial republished in Santa Fe *New Mexican,* November 27, 1928; *Mancos Times-Tribune* editorial republished in Farmington *Times Hustler,* November 30, 1928.

10. *Santa Fe New Mexican,* November 17, 1928. For more information on Cutting, see Richard Lowitt, *Bronson M. Cutting: Progressive Politician* (Albuquerque: University of New Mexico Press, 1992).

11. Ray Abrahams, *Vigilant Citizens: Vigilantism and the State* (Malden, MA: Polity Press, 1998), 53–54.

12. The observations below are based upon a systematic study of the county civil and criminal record books for the years 1887 to 1928: San Juan County District Court Criminal Docket No.1, New Mexico State Archives; San Juan County District Court Criminal Docket No.2, San Juan County Courthouse, Aztec, New Mexico.

13. Criminal Docket No.1, Case #379: *State of New Mexico v. Teodoro Martinez* (1914), Criminal Docket No.2, Case #150: *Territory of New Mexico v. Prudencio Trujillo* (1904).

14. Criminal Docket No.1, Case #177: *Territory of New Mexico v. Joseph Palen* (1902).

15. Criminal Docket No.1, Case #299: *Territory of New Mexico v. Donaciano Aguilar* (1909); Criminal Docket No.2, Case #516: *State of New Mexico v. Edumenio Maestas* (1924). Our conclusions about the institutional bias of the legal system against Nuevomexicano defendants are commensurate with a broader territorial study by Donna Crail-Rugotzke. Crail-Rugotzke, "A Matter of Guilt: The Treatment of Hispanic Inmates by New Mexico Courts and the New Mexico Territorial Prison, 1890–1912," *New Mexico Historical Review* 74 (1999): 295–314.

16. F. Arturo Rosales, *¡Pobre Raza! Violence, Justice, and Mobilization Among México Lindo Immigrants, 1900–1936* (Austin: University of Texas Press, 1999), 141. Robert Tórrez notes that Spanish-speakers were not executed in disproportionate numbers during the territorial period. He does state, however, that Mexican nationals were more likely to be put to death than Anglos or Spanish-speaking citizens of the United States in this period. Robert Tórrez to authors, December 31, 2002, correspondence in possession of authors.

17. *Alamogordo News,* November 22, 1928; *Farmington Times Hustler,* November 16, 1928, November 23, 1928.

18. *Santa Fe New Mexican,* November 27, 1928.

19. "Lynchings: By Year and Race," www.law.umkc.edu/faculty/projects/ftrials/shipp/lynchingyear.html, last accessed February 23, 2010.

280

Notes

20. W. Fitzhugh Brundage, *Lynching in the New South: Georgia and Virginia, 1880–1930* (Urbana and Chicago: University of Illinois Press, 1993), 248–49, 251. See also Robert L. Zangrando, *The NAACP Crusade Against Lynching, 1909–1950* (Philadelphia: Temple University Press, 1980).

21. Newspapers outside of New Mexico that reported the lynching included the *Montgomery Advertiser*, November 17, 1928; *New York Evening Post*, November 17, 1928; *Atlanta Constitution*, November 18, 1928; and *Norfolk Journal and Guide*, November 24, 1928.

22. *New Mexico State Tribune*, quoted in *Farmington Times Hustler*, November 30, 1928.

23. *Farmington Times Hustler*, November 23, 1928.

24. At the forefront of these publications are Jacquelyn Dowd Hall, *Revolt against Chivalry: Jessie Daniel Ames and the Women's Campaign against Lynching* (Columbia: Columbia University Press, 1979); Brundge, *Lynching in the New South*. Stewart E. Tolnay and E. M. Beck, *A Festival of Violence: An Analysis of Southern Lynchings, 1882–1930* (Urbana: University of Illinois Press, 1995).

25. For further insight into the symbolic power of lynching, see Amy Louise Wood, *Lynching and Spectacle: Witnessing Racial Violence in America, 1890 to 1940* (Chapel Hill: University of North Carolina Press, 2009).

26. United States History Content Standards (revised 1996), Era 4: Standard 1C: Era 9: Standard 4a, Era 10: Standard 2B, National Center for History in the Schools, UCLA, http://www.nchs.ucla.edu/Standards/us-history-content-standards, last accessed April 21, 2011. United States History Era 6 Content Standard 2b reads: "Explain the rising racial conflict in different regions, including the anti-Chinese movement in the West and the rise of lynching in the South."

27. For the full text of the Senate resolution, see http://landrieu.senate.gov/priorities/civilrights/resolution.pdf, last accessed March 28, 2011.

28. *Washington Post*, June 14, 2005; *USA Today*, June 16, 2005; *New York Times*, June 19, 2005; *Austin American-Statesman*, June 29, 2005. For one example of a newspaper criticizing the resolution, see *Augusta Chronicle*, July 22, 2005.

29. "Lynchings: By Year and Race," http://law2.umkc.edu/faculty/projects/ftrials/shipp/lynchingyear.html, last accessed May 4, 2011; James R. McGovern, *Anatomy of a Lynching: The Killing of Claude Neal* (Baton Rouge: Louisiana University Press, 1992).

30. Christopher Waldrep, *The Many Faces of Judge Lynch: Extralegal Violence and Punishment in America* (New York: Palgrave Macmillan, 2002), 103–50.

31. For more on the strategy of Mexican activists, see Neil Foley, *Quest for Equality: The Failed Promise of Black-Brown Solidarity* (Cambridge, MA: Harvard University Press, 2010).

32. Miriam Chatelle, *For We Love Our Valley Home* (San Antonio, TX: Naylor Company, 1948), 70.

33. N. A. Jennings, *A Texas Ranger* (Dallas, TX: Southwest Press, 1930), 118, 128. See also p. 126 for a further account of Ranger abuses.

34. Carey McWilliams, *North from Mexico: The Spanish-Speaking People of the US* (Philadelphia: Lippincott, 1949).

35. Carey McWilliams, *Southern California Country: An Island on the Land* (New York: Duell, Sloan & Pearce, 1946; reprint, Layton, Utah: Gibbs Smith, 1973), 60.

36. Carey McWilliams, *Factories in the Field: The Story of Migratory Farm Labor in California* (Boston: Little, Brown and Company, 1939); Carey McWilliams, *Ill Fares the Land: Migrants and Migratory Labor in the United States* (Boston: Little, Brown and Company, 1942).

37. Gunnar Myrdal, *An American Dilemma: The Negro Problem and Modern Democracy* (New York: Harper, 1944).

38. Juan J. Alonzo, *Badmen, Bandits, and Folk Heroes: The Ambivalence of Mexican American Identity in Literature and Film* (Tucson: University of Arizona Press, 2009), 32–45.

39. Walter Van Tilburg Clark, *The Ox-Bow Incident* (New York: Random House, 1940; reprint, New York: Signet, 1968); *The Ox-Bow Incident* (dir. William A. Wellman, 1943).

40. Niven Busch, *The Furies* (New York: Dial Press, 1948; reprint, New York: Criterion Collection, 2008); *The Furies* (dir. Anthony Mann, 1950).

41. Busch, *The Furies*, 34.

42. Vance and Juan marry in the novel but remain onetime lovers in the film.

43. Elmore Leonard, *The Law at Randado* (Boston: Houghton Mifflin, 1955 [c.1954]; reprint, New York: HarperTorch, 2002), quotation on p. 19. The movie version, mercifully out of print, is *Border Shootout* (dir. Chris McIntyre, 1990).

44. Ibid., 254.

45. Clark, *Ox-Bow Incident*, 98.

46. Busch, *The Furies*, 165.

47. Since the drama is not commercially available we draw this plot summary and our observation about the positive critical reaction from the *New York Times*, June 20, 1958.

48. Christopher Metress, "Submitted for Their Approval: Rod Serling, Television Censorship, and the Lynching of Emmett Till," *Mississippi Quarterly* 61 (Winter-Spring 2009): 141–70.

49. Lester H. Hunt, "'And Now, Rod Serling, Creator of *The Twilight Zone*': The Author as *Auteur*," in *Philosophy in the Twilight Zone*, ed. Noël Carroll and Lester Hunt (Malden, MA: Wiley-Blackwell, 2009), 19. It is also worth noting that the film adaptation of the *Ox-Bow Incident* is, like the *Twilight Zone* episode, an oblique attack on African American lynching that utlilizes non-black victims, including a Mexican. For an excellent analysis of the film's antilynching message and its limitations, see Wood, *Lynching and Spectacle*, 225–52.

50. F. Arturo Rosales, ¡Chicano! The History of the Mexican American Civil Rights Movement (Houston: Arte Público Press, 1996), 7.

51. The classic account of Gregorio Cortez's fight with and flight from Texas lawmen is Américo Paredes, "With His Pistol in His Hand": A Border Ballad and Its Hero (Austin: University of Texas Press, 1958). Our own reconstruction of the story owes much to Paredes as well as other sources identified in subsequent notes.

52. Richard J. Mertz, "The Gregorio Cortez Case" (MA diss., Texas A&I University, 1971), 19–20; Arnoldo De León, Mexican Americans in Texas: A Brief History (Wheeling, IL: Harlan Davidson, 1993), 50; Rosenbaum, Mexicano Resistance in the Southwest, 46–47.53 Victoria Advocate, June 24, 1901.

54. Paredes, "With His Pistol in His Hand," 94; Rosales, ¡Pobre Raza!, 93.

55. "Gregorio Cortez" in Américo Paredes, A Texas-Mexican Cancionero: Folksongs of the Lower Border (Austin: University of Texas Press, 1995), 64–67.

56. Julian Samora, Joe Bernal, and Albert Peña, Gunpowder Justice: A Reassessment of the Texas Rangers (Notre Dame, IN: University of Notre Dame Press, 1979), 58–60; Deseret News, June 20, 1901.

57. On the cultural impact of Holiday's song, see David Margolick, Strange Fruit: Billie Holiday, Cafe Society, and an Early Cry for Civil Rights (Philadelphia and London: Running Press, 2000).

58. José E. Limón, History and Influence in Mexican-American Social Poetry (Berkeley and Los Angeles: University of California Press, 1992), 65; The Ballad of Gregorio Cortez (dir. Robert M. Young, Embassy Pictures, 1982).

59. Ninfa Cuerza interview, South Texas Oral History and Folklore Collection.

60. For examples of Anglos exonerating the Rangers, see interviews with Robert T. Bluntzer, Andrew Champion, Zora Wright Fore, John Peavey, and C. W. Perkins, South Texas Oral History and Folklore Collection, Texas A&M University, Kingsville, Texas.

61. Celia Cuenca interview, South Texas Oral History and Folklore Collection. See also interview with Francisco Sandoval, Sr.

62. A useful introduction to contemporary vigilantism is the Anti-Defamation League report Border Disputes: Armed Vigilantes in Arizona, http://www.adl.org/extremism/arizona/arizonaborder.pdf.

63. The film appears to have been withdrawn from YouTube and this description is based on viewing notes in possession of the authors, October 18, 2009. For other examples of this stress on historical continuity, see Rodolfo Acuña, "Crocodile Tears: Lynching of Mexicans," HispanicVista.com, June 20, 2005, http://www.HispanicVista.com/HVC/Opinion/Guest_Columns/062005Acuna.htm, last accessed June 15, 2011; Andy Porras, "Mexicans can't forget their Texas legacy," El Reportero, May 25–June 3, 2011, http://www.elreporterosf.com/editions/?q=node/1225, last accessed June 15, 2011.

Index

killing of Sicilians in 1890s,
138–139
Ku Klux Klan killing in Mer Rouge,
150
Love, Harry, 107
Lozano, Torbio, 17–18, 61–63
Lucero, Cecilio, 95
Lucero, Cresensio, 263n107
LULAC. *See* League of United Latin
American Citizens
lynching, 14. *See also* burning alive as a
form of lynching; decapitation
as a form of lynching; hanging
as form of lynching; law officers,
role in lynchings; mob violence;
names of individual states;
shooting Mexicans as form of
lynching
blacks-on-black lynchings, 88, 89,
260n81
chronology of, 20–23
decline of mob violence, 128–158
last known lynching in 1928, 1, 4, 5,
160, 278n4
comparative analysis, 13–14, 239n4
provable number of deaths of
Mexicans, 5, 6
for crimes against Mexicans, 95–96,
264n113
culture of, 10
decline in after 1928, 165–167
difficulties of researching, 10–13
1890s as peak decade for, 163
executions, modes of, 80, 258n53,
258n57 (*see also* burning alive as
a form of lynching; decapitation
as a form of lynching; hanging
as form of lynching; shooting
Mexicans as form of lynching;
"spectacle" lynchings)
frequency of shooting Mexicans vs.
hanging, 79

Mexicans lynching Anglos, 95
Mexicans lynching Mexicans, 88–96
multiracial nature of, 13, 242n15
not considered a federal crime, 129,
163
efforts to make, 156–157
photographic records of lynching
victims, 1, 9–11, 241n11
prevention of lynchings. *see*
prevention of mob violence
"spectacle" lynchings, 80–83, 90, 95,
144, 155, 261n87
studies of black lynchings, xiv
use of term lynching
["linchamiento"], xi–xii,
239nn1–2
white-on-white lynchings, 88, 260n81
for crimes against Mexicans,
95–96

Madero, Francisco, 144, 145, 146
Magill, Samuel E., 142
Magón, Ricardo and Enrique, 120
Mancos Times-Tribune (newspaper), 161
Mann, Anthony, 170
Mariscal, Ignacio, 4
Maron, Anthony, 247n37
Marscal, Ignacio, 62, 63
Martinez, Juan (fictional character), 170
Martínez, Juan (Mexican constable), 55
Martínez, Merejildo (aka "Martinis"),
42, 249n62
Mata, Blas, 18
Mays, Louis, 151
McKinley, William, 134, 138, 139, 141
McMains, Oscar P., 101
McNelly, L. H., 168
McWilliams, Carey, 6, 168–169
Meastas, Edumenio, 162
media. *See* newspapers
Mendez, Santos, 62
Mesa, Cecilio, 246n25

Printed in the USA/Agawam, MA
July 19, 2022

795877.009